Hitotsubashi University IER Economic Research Series

Volume 46

The Economic Research Series is a publication outlet for high quality research by the Institute of Economic Research (IER), Hitotsubashi University. The aims of the series is to provide general public, professionals, and academic researchers with the original, latest, and most advanced research achievements by the staff of IER.

Founded in 1940 with the objective of conducting "comprehensive research on the Japanese and the world economy," IER has generated numerous outstanding research results. Notably, as one of the oldest and largest academic research institute in Japan, the IER has been playing a leading role in Japan through the development of outstanding databases on economics and society such as "Long-Term Economic Statistics Series" as well as advanced theoretical and empirical analyses and policy research directly connected to these data.

Since the first publication by Kazushi Ohkawa, The Growth Rate of the Japanese Economy, since 1878 in 1957, which has been praised as one of the most comprehensive analyses of Japanese economic growth, the Economic Research Series have published 44 volumes on various topics such as empirical analyses on Japanese economic growth, pensions in Asia, developments in India, and theoretical analyses on time series model.

Just before the beginning of the 21st century, IER added new missions, promoting original and cutting-edge research and establishing a joint research unit for members of the international research community, in addition to continuing its comprehensive economic research on Japan and the world. Every year, about 20 joint research projects are progressing in the joint research unit. The Economic Research Series will publish various research outputs of the joint research unit led by the staff of IER.

The Economic Research Series aims to meet a growing need for the comprehensive study of economic issues in Japan and the world economy. It will cover a wide variety of topics, from purely theoretical issues to current policy agenda, from the macro economies to individual behaviors, and from historical analysis to cross-country comparisons. As a series as a whole, it is expected to provide new insights into the understanding of the economy and economics as well as obtain effective policy implications to enhance social welfare.

More information about this series at http://www.springer.com/series/16117

Reiko Gotoh

The Ethics and Economics of the Capability Approach

Springer

Reiko Gotoh
Institute of Economic Research
Hitotsubashi University
Kunitachi, Tokyo, Japan

ISSN 0441-0025 ISSN 2524-5147 (electronic)
Hitotsubashi University IER Economic Research Series
ISBN 978-981-15-5139-0 ISBN 978-981-15-5140-6 (eBook)
https://doi.org/10.1007/978-981-15-5140-6

This Springer imprint is published by the registered company Springer Nature Singapore Pte Ltd.
The registered company address is: 152 Beach Road, #21-01/04 Gateway East, Singapore 189721, Singapore

Preface

The phenomenon of the coronavirus infection prevailing in 2020 as of this writing reminds us of essential problems for which different disciplines of the social sciences and humanities should cooperate and approach seriously. This is an extreme phenomenon that forces us to picture the whole earth in one color, say, with a social distancing strategy. It is certainly an exceptional emergency that requires medical triage as the first principle; yet, that is why we must recall the discussion between Rawls and Sen.

Rawls recommended a social system called "the property-owning democracy." His point was to respect the plurality of diverse societies, each of which should own the responsibility for its members and could form a consensus in its own way. Sen raised the questions, then, of how to overcome "closed impartiality" in each divided society and how to hold "open impartiality" among different societies. A key term proposed by Sen is "trans-positional assessments" by each individual, who actually belongs in various kinds of groups simultaneously and who can have a critical eye to compare diverse opinions based on different positions from inside. I believe that this book has been a trial for doing "trans-positional assessments" and a trial for acquiring "open impartiality" among different disciplines. The research interest is the following.

On September 2, 2016, Amartya Sen gave his keynote lecture "On Specifications and Measurement" at the Annual Conference for Human Development and Capability Association in Tokyo. When it comes to measurement, philosophers have had a long-standing problem of "non-commensurability." This is an inquiry into whether there is any objective way to compare, quantitatively, among different goods such as freedom and safety. Sen's lecture in Tokyo was a renewed attempt to scrutinize this problem from the point of view of normative economics.

Individual "utility function" is widely used in economics and supposed to be a magic wand that enables us to compare different goods. It is apparently possible for anyone, anytime, to compare her own marginal substitution rates. For example, how many more CCTVs can she accept in order to secure a little more safety? Or, how many more hours can she devote to her work in order to reduce her sadness a little more? Furthermore, neoclassical economics tends to make an assumption that individual preferences can compare all possible alternatives completely and consistently, including indifference relation. Under this assumption, one can choose from any kind of opportunity set the "optimal set," whose elements are at least as good as any other element available.

Having looked at these arguments, Sen focuses on an approach to measurement that neither forces comparison among intrinsically incomparable alternatives by using "utility functions" nor gives up on comparison altogether because no complete way of ordering is available. It tentatively classifies into the "maximal set" those alternatives that are judged "not better than, nor indifferent to, but at least not worse than the other alternatives." Alternatives in the maximal set are literally incomparable between each other, although clearly they are not worse than any alternative outside the maximal set. Any choice from this set has to be based on some external criterion.

The main point of his argument is as follows. On the one hand, philosophical arguments of non-commensurability tend to slip into indeterminacy and end up by endorsing the status quo. On the other hand, economic arguments of rational choice tend to presuppose transitive but complete preference orderings. The capability approach proposed by Sen distances itself from both traps. Its purpose is to help continue realistic improvements of policies and institutions, rather than to pursue a scholarly debate on non-commensurability nor to aim obsessively for "rational choice."

There were many issues in Sen's lecture on which one would like more clarification, of course. For example, in a society where the idea of rational choice has already prevailed, a choice from the "maximal set" of alternatives that are "not better than, nor indifferent to, nor worse than the other alternatives" can easily be misunderstood as the result of an optimal choice under a complete preference. Then, in order to avoid misunderstandings, one could decide to keep silent, decline to take up the opportunity to choose, and accept dying in the worst case. From such cases emerges the importance of external perspectives such as "ethical" concerns that can reflect and elucidate actual opportunities and circumstances of individual choices, which is nothing else than the perspective of the capability approach.

It has been almost 35 years since the capability approach was proposed, and now we can find various attempts to apply it in many disciplines and fields. Sen's lecture was extremely inspiring in making it clear that the central issue to be tackled is the problem of "specification and measurement," which economics takes pride in excelling at, and how to incorporate "ethical" concerns into economic analyses.

The theme of this book is considering the possibility of normative economic theory in general, examining the economics and ethics of "the capability approach" in particular. Our research interest is the following. The beauty of academic research is usually supposed to induce logically possible ideas of institutions from minimal assumptions. It is not all, however, academic research can accomplish. It can also provide theoretical constructions for ethically more desirable institutions by sufficient investigations into practical reason. The latter is the role of a "normative theory." It does not go beyond offering a theory that is yet to be empirically tested for its feasibility. However, whether a theory can really be feasible or not is expected to be open to the actions of people themselves, as Rawls pointed out with his beautiful term "realistic utopia" (Rawls 1999, 5–7). A normative theory can envisage and raise its feasibility only in the process where people themselves act on critical examination and public discussion on norms and institutions.

In this sense a normative theory cannot be self-contained, yet it is not a vacuum, because social norms do exist surrounding us as institutions, customs, and cultures do. Actually, some social norms strongly and explicitly affect us and others do not so much, while such an order might change as time goes by. People choose and refer to certain social norms, depending on their purposes and reasons. A normative theory remains part of the academic research and does not turn itself into a religion nor propaganda. Why? This is because it is based on a broad and extensive study of propositions, logics, and methodologies of past relevant theories, and it makes sure to be open to examination and criticism by people as well as to review and follow-up by professionals. The capability approach is characterized by critically examining actual institutions and norms and by incorporating ethical concerns including relational norms with other people and public judgments for the social world into economic analyses.

Before we begin our inquiry, it is worth explaining some terminology. According to Sen, "functionings" mean various individual "doings" and "beings" that are realized by using certain commodities (more precisely, by converting certain characteristics of commodities). For example, they can include "transporting" (moving), "relieving pain," or "relaxing." Then a functioning vector chosen (or merely realized) by an individual is defined as a combination of different kinds and amounts of functionings. And an individual's capability is defined as a set of functioning vectors with a set of commodities (goods and services), resources (income, time, assets, and so on), and a set of the individual's utilization abilities, given external conditions of social institutions, including market prices and other individuals' characteristics, and natural or historical circumstances.

Each functioning vector in a capability set is "real" in the sense that it exists as an available option, but not all vectors are simultaneously "actual." Whenever one functioning vector is chosen and becomes "actual," the other alternatives that are not chosen cannot be "actual." There is no guarantee either that the unchosen alternatives remain in one's capability set after one is chosen. This is because various factors and conditions can change, including market prices and other individuals' behaviors.

What remains "real" in the sense that one can deselect and select an alternative anew within a certain range is an individual's utilization abilities, which are inevitably influenced by her previously realized capabilities. Although there is a normative problem in directly specifying and measuring them (See Chap. 3), a certain functioning vector chosen from an individual capability set can affect her set of utilization abilities and further shape her capability set on another functioning space. If this is the case, what is really meant by individual freedom of choice? Its examination is one of the underlying themes of this book.

Lastly, let us summarize the implication of the capability approach in the configuration of representative modern economic thoughts. Marxist economics devotes itself to revealing and understanding the basic structure of human society, that is, material bases or institutional conditions, which deeply regulate individuals' existence and consciousness. "Old" welfare economics, represented by Alfred Marshall as well as J. M. Keynes's broad interests in aesthetics, ethics, and psychology, focused on the real values of human life realized by converting goods with individual abilities. In contrast, "new" welfare economics has somehow simplified economic analyses into a model of maximizing objective functions subject to resource constraints, all in one quadrant, by reducing the various kinds of social conditions to "income" and the wealth of life to "utility."

In this configuration of thoughts, the challenge of the capability approach is providing an inclusive framework to overview (a) environmental, social relational, and personal constraints in the third quadrant (the space of means), (b) individual value of life and freedom (represented by the capability set) and its evaluation in the first quadrant (the space of purposes), and (c) conversion abilities of individuals and of the social world itself (Rawls 1999), connecting (a) and (b), in the second and fourth quadrants (the space of transformations with personal, institutional, or natural contingent factors).

Actually, the capability approach is a challenge of economics that was born in the heart of the value theory in economics. It allows us to use the concepts, logic, and models of traditional economics by slightly changing their meanings and implications and by boldly broadening their research interests and perspectives. This strategy is expected to be effective, since a logically robust theory can be reexamined only by an original but controversial and similarly logically robust theory.

With this in mind, we might say that the capability approach is a theoretical device to reflect essential research interests and concerns of Marx, "old" welfare economics, and "new" welfare economics. Is it too exaggerated? I would like to leave the answer to the readers who kindly have this book in hand.

Tokyo, Japan Reiko Gotoh

Acknowledgements

I must express my indebtedness to people who have generously supported this book. This book is first dedicated to Amartya Sen, who has given us a "realistic utopia" to make ideals realistic by participating in cooperative activities, holding "open impartiality" to one another. Next, I would like to express my sincere gratitude to members of the Human Development and Capability Association (HDCA) for their intellectually and personally warm cooperation. Because of the focus of this book, I could not sufficiently mention Martha Nussbaum, yet I am hugely indebted to her excellent works and warm encouragement.

My interest in the theme was first crystallized into the book *Amartya Sen—Economics and Ethics* (with Kotaro Suzumura, 2001, in Japanese). This present book is also dedicated to Kotaro, who was a great scholar and thinker, and who pursued the progress of academics to the last minutes before he passed away.

I have hugely benefited from my colleagues, visitors, and students in the Institute of Economic Research (IER) and Hitotsubashi Institute for Advanced Study (HIAS) in Hitotsubashi University. Their intellectual comments and questions with firm knowledge and understandings of traditional economics make me reflect and confirm the importance of this project. Of them, I must acknowledge what I owe to Ryo Kambayashi, Chiaki Moriguchi, Koichi Tadenuma, Norio Takeoka, Takashi Ui, Daisuke Hirata, and Yuichi Yamamoto for their kind cooperation with this project.

In undertaking corrections, I have been immensely supported by Hiroyuki Kuribayashi, Kazuyo Tanimoto, Meiko Uesaka, Yoshiya Kamito, and Yoko Igarashi (an excellent team of the Research Center for Normative Economics, IER, Hitotsubashi University) and students in our seminars. They have suggested numerous improvements both on substance and style. Winston Priest checked my English with great carefulness and patience. The final version of the book reflects the impact of their comments. Some of the material in this book is based on my previous work published as follows.

A part of the Preface, Chaps. 2–8: *The Capability Approach—Ethics and Economics,* Iwanami-Shoten (in Japanese).
Chapter 8: Gotoh, R. (2017) "What political liberalism and the welfare state left behind: chance and gratitude," Hans-Uwe Otto, M. Walker and H. Ziegler (eds.), *Capability Promoting Policies: Enhancing Individual and Social Development,* Policy Press, pp. 23–41.
Chapter 9: Gotoh, R. (2019): Arrow and Sen—Forming of Social Choice Theory and Its Critical Extension. *Waseda Journal of Political Science and Economics*, 394, 30–40 (in Japanese).
Appendix 1: Gotoh, R. and N. Yoshihara (2003) A class of fair distribution rules à la Rawls and Sen. *Economic Theory*, 22, 63–88.
Appendix 2: Gotoh, R. and N. Yoshihara (2018) Securing basic well-being for all. *Review of Social Economy*, 76(4), 422–452.
Appendix 3: Gotoh, R. (2001) "The Capability Theory and Welfare Reform. *Pacific Economic Review*, 6(2), 211–222.

I thank the publishers, editors, and co-authors of three articles, for their kind permissions to use those articles in this book. Co-authors Naoki Yoshihara, Ryo Kambayashi, and Hideyuki Kobayashi make my ideals more realistic and tangible. Last but not least, I am grateful to my friends and family for their intangible and infinite support.

Contents

About the Author

Reiko Gotoh has been a Professor at the Institute of Economic Research, Hitotsubashi University, Tokyo, since 2013. She holds a Ph.D. from Hitotsubashi University. Her research fields are Philosophy in Economics, Normative Economics, and Reconstruction of the Welfare State. Her recent English publications are "Securing Basic Well-being for All," *Review of Social Economy*, 76, 4 (with N. Yoshihara), "What political liberalism and the welfare state left behind: chance and gratitude", H.-U. Otto et al. (eds.), *Capability Promoting Policies: Enhancing Individual and Social Development*, Policy Press. *Against Injustice: The New Economics of Amartya Sen*, Cambridge University Press, 2009 (co-edited). *Social Bonds as Freedom*, Berghahn Books (co-edited). In addition, she is the author of several Japanese books including *The Capability Approach*, Iwanami-shoten. *Economic Philosophy of Well-Being*, Minerva Shobo, *Economic Philosophy of Justice: Rawls and Sen*, Toyo-keizai Inc., 2002. *Amartya Sen: Economics & Ethics*, Jikkyo Shuppan, 2001 (co-authored).

Chapter 1
Introduction: Purpose and Summary

1.1 Purpose and Four Tasks

The purpose of this book is to explore how to formulate Amartya Sen's capability approach, which is central to his economics and ethics, and, based on its analyses, to investigate how to contemplate the value of freedom in the context of distributive justice in economic philosophy. Let me briefly describe my interests and challenges.

Modern economics could provide a perspective that would guide philosophy in the theory of *value* focusing on the concept of *utility*. Subjective utilities of what are considered "good" for people, i.e. commodities, wealth, or welfare, are aggregated and evaluated by the objective price system determined in society. The theory of *value* enables us, along with the "general equilibrium theory" based on it, to design a policy or institution without having (or positively excluding) any ethical point of view. The idea and analytical tools of the theory of *value* have had some considerable influence on various sciences.

The capability approach, originally developed by Amartya Sen, presents a novel idea and analytical tools to measure the value of freedom and evaluate its distribution. His new approach captures what is good for people in terms of capability and freedom. It also makes it possible to introduce ethical perspectives into economics again. In its background theory as well as in its methodological frameworks, the capability approach lies in renewing the theory of value.

Sen's concept of freedom is related to real potentialities ("capability") for what individuals can actually do or be by using their resources. The concept is also related to the reasons why they value those potentialities. The capability approach has attracted much attention in the practical fields of economic development, health care, social welfare, public transportation, and more, as it tries to measure individuals' objective states before they enjoy their subjective "utilities."

Many authors, however, have pointed out that the capability approach is quite difficult to formulate theoretically, despite its conceptual richness and practical versatility. The purpose of this book is to respond to these criticisms and clarify how to theoretically formulate the capability approach. In doing so, we try to identify the

R. Gotoh, *The Ethics and Economics of the Capability Approach*, Hitotsubashi University IER Economic Research Series 46, https://doi.org/10.1007/978-981-15-5140-6_1

significance of the capability approach in the history of economic theory, on the one hand, and improve the usability in its practical or clinical applications, on the other. This book has four specific tasks, which are summarized below.

1.1.1 Reflections on the Significance of the Capability Approach in the History of Economic Theory

The first task of this book is to reflect, in the light of the history of economic theory, on the significance of the capability approach in economic theory and have some preliminary historical outlook on how to formulate it. The motivation is as follows.

If a certain commodity is valuable only for a particular purpose, we can merely wish for their fortuitous encounter. However, when we have multiple and flexible purposes that can be realized by more than one commodity, there should be room for improving the overall effect (efficiency and equity/fairness) by a clever matching between commodities (instruments) and purposes. Let us suppose that our purposes here are individual "welfares" and commodities (instruments) are "labors for production." Now we face a central question in welfare economics. That is, in a common wealth, how can we combine "labors for productions" provided by individuals and "welfares" enjoyed by them, given its land, environment, population, technology, culture, and capital. The central concern of welfare economics, tackled and passed on by Adam Smith, J. S. Mill, Alfred Marshall, Arthur Pigou, and other followers, has been to examine and, if necessary, rearrange their actual and possible combinations between "productions" and "welfares" that are mediated by various communities, organizations, firms, media, and networks.

Neoclassical economics, established after the so-called marginal revolution in the late nineteenth century, proved in the framework of "general equilibrium theory" that (1) the perfectly free competitive market can realize a unique and stable equilibrium (in prices and in quantities of supply and demand) through voluntary choices and actions by mutually independent, autonomous, and rational individuals, and (2) the equilibrium satisfies the normative condition of the Pareto efficiency, which means that no one can be made better off without making someone else worse off. Since then, "new" welfare economics has concentrated very much on the refinement of the concept of "equilibrium" (for example, "Nash equilibrium" in game theory) and mathematical analyses of distribution rules that satisfy the Pareto efficiency criterion.

"New" welfare economics increasingly embraced this particular view of equilibrium as a situation where, as a result of constrained utility maximization by individuals, no one is willing to change his or her behavior, or neither agent has an incentive to deviate from it, given the action of the other agent (called "new" welfare economics). The concept of equilibrium was also supported by a normative point of view seeking individual autonomy, freedom, social stability, and order. We must note that, however, it can make us blind to real, serious problems such as starvation, deprivation, exclusion, or exploitation, which are happening in the very "equilibrium" state of the world. As Karl Mannheim said, the idea, as an ideology, cannot but affect people's perceptions in a way (Manheim 1936/2015).

Sen has been a critic of this trend of "new" welfare economics. Having inherited the tradition of "old" welfare economics, with its central concern for the wealth of societies and welfare of individuals, Sen developed his social choice theory and pursued a direction away from "new" welfare economics. He designed his capability approach by specifying and measuring the welfare of individuals by indexes of "capability" (welfare freedom) from the point of view of actual consequences (welfare) that individuals actually enjoy.

The challenge is to look at the distribution of individual "capabilities," which make it possible to critically evaluate existing economic systems, institutions, or policies, and design desirable alternatives. Chapter 2 describes this history in six phases including the genealogy of wealth and welfare (reconceptualization of national accounting), the genealogy of liberty and rights (development of social choice theory), the genealogy of rationality and reason (deconstruction of the revealed preference theory), and the genealogy of criticism of welfarism (integrated points of view of economy and ethics).

1.1.2 Theoretical and Mathematical Formulation of the Capability Approach

The second task of this book is to present an economic formulation of the capability approach, which allows us to carry out empirical studies and practical applications.

It is useful to capture the conceptual structure of the capability approach by formulating it with the help of set theory. The consumer theory is useful in clarifying the relation between the capability approach and the market, whereas the statistical method can be fruitfully applied to infer unobservable, unmeasurable conceptual facts from observable, measurable data. This book looks at these existing methods and points to a direction for critical development.

Sen defines individual freedom as "being able to choose her doings and beings which she has reason to choose." Then what he calls her "capability" is "the set of bundles of functionings which she can actually choose if she wishes." Here "functionings" refer to her doings and beings that she can realize by using her resources. They are basically assumed to be observable and measurable. In contrast, individual capability as the opportunity set of functioning bundles (alternatives) is not directly observable or measurable, but theoretically it can be captured by the set of resources available to her—what Ronald Dworkin (1981b) called external resources—and utilization abilities (internal resources) which she can actually realize. External resources are supposed to be observable and measurable while internal resources are not.

Note that, unlike an individual's desire or hope to choose a particular functioning bundle (of doings and beings), her "reason" for choosing it cannot be reduced to her subjective judgements. Whether she can choose a particular functioning bundle (i.e. whether it is included in her capability) and, if she cannot, why that is the case, concerns not only herself but also her society. In order to identify her "reason" for choosing it, one has to consider inter-subjective or more universal understandings among different individuals.

To be more specific, the "value of freedom" is taken to be social goals to be implementable by transferring resources (goods and services) in a society. For example, in Chap. 6 we discuss "securing basic freedoms for all." Or someone may recommend "increasing freedom in a nation–state" (increasing the total value of freedom). Setting various social goals like these and, given them, specifying, measuring, and, if necessary, improving individuals' capabilities can be one of the policy challenges. Indeed, the capability approach has been used in many fields and different regions in the world. In Japan, too, it has provided a guiding concept and been applied widely to studies in development assistance, gender inequality, planning for local public transportation, efficient and equitable distribution of health care resources, effective guarantee of opportunities for universal education and issues in environments, disaster, and social welfare.[1]

Capability constitutes a person's existence, however. Its development is closely related to her values and its perception deeply connected with her identity. Then, the evaluation of individual capability and reason for choosing a particular functioning bundle cannot be dissociated from her own intentions and behaviors. Here we find room for working with some ideas, developed by economics, such as rational choices made by individuals under fixed rules and constraints including the market price system where they are aggregated into a particular consequence. Working with these ideas, the capability approach can bring about some critical new attempts to reconstruct these ideas such as rational choice and opportunity drastically.

1.1.3 Exploration of the Methodological Framework for the Capability Approach

The third task of this book is to extract ethical characteristics of the capability approach, while looking at various tools in economics, on the one hand, and insights and findings on choice and opportunity in the other social sciences and humanities, on the other.

Freedom was discussed mostly in political philosophy previously, but the capability approach, by trying to measure the "value of freedom," has taken a big step toward describing, designing, and realizing "freedom" empirically in the manner of engineering. It has led to a major expansion of the traditional framework for

[1]This is only a small set of examples. The capability approach can be quite effective in interpreting the meaning of negative damages as well as positive achievements.

economic policies, which evaluates consequences of alternative institutions and policies based exclusively on individual subjective utilities (such as the satisfaction index). Theoretical and practical significance of this expansion has been in no doubt.

If, however, measurement of the "value of freedom" should end up in an exclusive pursuit of operational convenience, the process of deriving the value of freedom can become no different from that of reducing multi-dimensional measures (of utility or commodity) to one-dimensional value. This might, after all, reduce the value of freedom to a scalar value and the capability approach to the utility approach. For example, the fundamental theorem of welfare economics claims that voluntary choices made by individuals from given opportunity sets (with initial endowments and market prices, for example) lead to an equilibrium that is Pareto efficient (see Chap. 5, note 1). According to Sen, this theorem can be extended to weak efficiency about opportunity-freedom in the commodity space and, furthermore, this weak efficiency in the commodity space can be extended to weak efficiency about opportunity-freedom in the space of functioning and capability [Sen 1993c/2002a, 523(2002a)]. This proposition is critically examined in Chap. 5.

The utility approach allows describing an individual preference as well as an individual opportunity set always in terms of an integrated, single structure and a homogeneous type, however broadly we expand their domain. With this model, the consumption point chosen by her can be interpreted merely as revealing the result of her rational behavior to pursue the optimal (or the maximal) based on her interpersonally incomparable preference.

However, freedom should have different meanings from one which can be described by this model: an integrated preference, and the differences should have brought a new analytical perspective on the economic approach. The capability approach can pay attention to potentially unintegrated, multiple structure and heterogeneous types of preferences and opportunities, which can accommodate plural and potentially inconsistent purposes. This is because we can find room for ethical concerns other than efficiency concern in this approach. If a unique feature of the capability approach lies in this point, we need to create an appropriate methodological framework in measuring the value of freedom. This attempt is introduced in Chaps. 4 and 6.

1.1.4 Re-examination of Equality in Light of the Capability Approach

The fourth task of this book is to sketch out a new normative theory of equality based on the philosophy of the capability approach.

One might think of the general equilibrium theory for the free competitive market as a leading runner not only in economics but also in modern thought represented by liberalism in general. It might be true. Further, we add that the challenge of traditional economics implies the challenge of traditional liberalism. Both are critical of each other but essentially influenced by each other.

In contrast, we can say that the capability approach plays the role of accompanying various post-modern movements (such as feminism, multi-culturalism, minority movements) and accommodating them in academic fields. This book accesses the capability approach mainly from the economic side, while it accesses the domain of political philosophy.

Through criticizing mainstream economics, Sen has greatly contributed to expanding the scopes of core concepts in modern thought. The pillars are the following methodological characteristics. Sen made it clear that the efficient "equilibrium" state achieved by free, rational, and autonomous agents is neither a starting point nor an ultimate end of studies. He also showed that constructing a "general" model that holds for all variables and all parameters completely is not a prerequisite or a goal of theory. He has argued that the main challenge of academic studies is to provide approaches and theories that help avoid evident injustices and pursue more just policies, before we aim at selecting the optimal principle of justice under complete orderings of alternatives. These attempts were made in the name of criticism of *welfarism*, which we look at in Chap. 2.

Sen's works also contributed to reformulating some key concepts in political philosophy. These include, for example, the concept of "capability as freedom," beyond free competition or private ownership; "equality of basic capabilities," beyond fair equality of opportunity; "individual autonomy," beyond consumer sovereignty; "independence with support," beyond self-help; "positional objectivity," beyond the dichotomy of subjectivism and objectivism; "reason before identity," beyond embedded identity. These concepts in general prepare for a new concept of freedom and equality beyond liberalism (i.e. the diversity-adjusted equality of values of freedom). These will be discussed in Chap. 7.

In addition, Sen's capability approach raises an important subject of ethics of responsibility for others and obligation as the following sentences indicate. "If someone has the power to make a difference that he or she can see will reduce injustice in the world, then there is a strong and reasoned argument for doing just that (without having to dress all this up in terms of some imagined prudential advantage in a hypothetical exercise of cooperation)" (Sen 2009a, 271; parentheses in the original). In short, it is pointed out that you should do just what you are capable of doing.

Relatedly, Sen points out the need to distinguish between (a) the topic of rational choice under uncertainty, which allows applying the expected utility theory in inter-temporal and intra-personal redistribution and (b) the topic of just redistribution among different individuals (including inter-generations). Moreover, based on the concept of capability, he presents a logic that requires social assistance for those in need, respecting individual self-determination, and which provides a new insight dealing with the problem of incentives that, for example, the progressive tax system inevitably results in decrease of labor incentives.

Chapter 6 explores possibilities of the capability approach while extending frameworks of social choice theory and Rawls's idea of *original position*.[2]

After pursuing these four subjects, i.e. history, theory, method, and norm of the capability approach in Chaps. 2–8, the last two chapters draw a broad picture of what the capability approach is about and what characteristics and effectiveness it has. We also foresee its significance and possibilities in the academic field of economic philosophy. More detailed summaries of each chapter are as follows.

1.2 Summary of Each Chapter

The task of Chap. 2 is to trace the origin of the capability approach in the history of welfare economics. It confirms that Sen's main interest was to expose economic models to ethical considerations as an external or reflective point of view. In other words, it is to open up social values from closed relationships with privately hidden conceptions of individual utilities toward individual evaluations with public reasoning.

Chapter 3 reviews the conceptual and operational meaning of the capability approach in the context of specification and measurement. When we capture individual well-being not by commodities and utilities but by functionings and capabilities, what would be renewed definitions of familiar concepts such as difference, similarity, equality, opportunity, choice, power, rights, and freedom? This chapter explores this question by exploring several examples including an actual incident, a numerical device and recent research. The main issue is how to estimate unobservable capabilities based on observable functioning vectors, how to make intra- and interpersonal comparisons with multi-dimensional evaluations, and how to construct a list of functionings.

Based on these preliminary tasks, Chap. 4 formulates the capability approach in an economic framework. Technically speaking, the capability approach can be formulated as an extended maximization model in economics by extending its domain to include the functioning space. This extended framework, including both commodity spaces and functioning spaces, on the one hand, demonstrates the robustness of the general equilibrium model in economics, and on the other hand, clearly shows characteristics of the capability approach distinguished from the traditional utility approach.

In order to appreciate the individual capability we need to respect individual evaluations that cannot be reduced to market prices or monistic utility. This reflects Sen's interest in "income and wealth" that introduces a plural value index, named good, in measuring total wealth in a society as discussed in Chap. 2. Individuals

[2]The "veil of ignorance" covers up one's birth, attributes, social status, and personal preferences and characteristics. With this veil and besides, with a fact of human societies that there must be "the least disadvantaged" in "social primary goods," Rawls asks, what kind of principles can you derive concerning the distribution of "social primary goods"? See Rawls 1971a, 1993. See Chap. 6 of this book for details.

are defined by multiple objective positions and by multi-layered and incompletely integrated preference evaluations. It is thus suggested in Chap. 4 that the capability approach can compel us to carefully review basic concepts in traditional economic theory relying on the concept of equilibrium and individual rationality and criteria of optimality and efficiency.

This reexamination can not only give a useful perspective to applied or empirical research using the capability approach but can also affect related academic disciplines such as political philosophy. Based on this analysis, Chap. 5 tries to expand the campus of individual behavior by going beyond the dichotomy of the "subjective utility" versus "objective opportunity" and introduces two angles of "individuality" and "positionality" of different people to have a multi-faceted perspective on the dynamic relation between individual choice and opportunity set. Based on an individual identity, which can be derived from the combination of *individual* or *positional* and *subjective* or *objective*, we reformulate "equality of opportunity" with the concept of capability.

Chapter 6 reconstructs Rousseau–Rawls's social contract model by Sen's diversity-based social choice model, which is developed with a critical scrutiny of the universality-based Arrovian social choice model. Sen's model is characterized by the sequence of the pre-original position, the original position, post-original position, and actual society. The pre-original position is equivalent to Rousseau–Rawls's "original position," in which all individuals are symmetrically treated in choosing a social choice procedure. They are prepared to choose a social choice procedure, which can treat disadvantaged groups preferably in the outcome or in the process, with information that "diversity" is a fact of human society. The "group" here is a normative concept to understand the "positionality" of individuals and to measure their interpersonally comparable capabilities. However, the concept of "group" can be misleading in justifying what Sen called "closed impartiality" within a group. This chapter explores the possibility of "open impartiality" by introducing the idea of the "trans-positional assessments" mentioned in Chap. 5.

Chapter 7 discussed the problem of securing the substantive value of freedom, from the two angles of agency freedom and well-being freedom, by looking at a case that recently occurred in Japan. Agency freedom was analyzed by using the essence of Sen's social choice model, whereas well-being freedom was by adopting the extended model of the capability approach formulated in Chaps. 4 and 5. We sought a logic that enables us to respect individual autonomy and justify providing public assistance to a person who does not belong to any existing group such as a person with disability, a single mother, or an elderly person, who is regarded as deserving to receive public assistance.

Chapter 8 reflected on the basic concepts and framework of traditional economic theory in terms of "what has been left behind by political liberalism and the welfare state," for example, from the eyes of "the tiny bird" that is entirely different in nature from "ourselves." Rawls might recommend that we share the products of our cooperation with the little bird. Sen would propose that we find out "what the little bird has reason to value" through public discussion in which the little bird takes part as an agency, say, expert of the position he or she actually occupies. Martha

Nussbaum would suggest that we can "live with concern for and in relation to" the little bird and play with it after waiting for its recovery and rest.

Chapter 9 gives a rough sketch of similarities and differences between Arrow and Sen by focusing on "economics and ethics" and "theory and practice." A dialogue between Arrow and Sen, or their similarities and differences, can represent themes to be tackled by economics today. Arrow's research interest was in building a general theory by using a symbolic concept of utility devoid of substantive meanings. Sen sought to explicitly incorporate into his theoretical framework tensions between economy (welfare) and ethics, or between logic and reality (substance) as a subject of his original research.

Chapter 10 reexamines the capability approach in view of Sen's wide-ranging research of economic philosophy as a whole. Our tentative conclusion is that a distinguishing style of Sen's economics is its openness to collaboration with other academic disciplines and policy practices while also fostering public discussion, in contrast with mainstream economics that operates in a closed circle and tends to be possessed by its internal logic. We might say that the capability approach is a trial to describe this style of studying as a methodology of social science.

Appendix 1: "A class of fair distribution rules à la Rawls and Sen" (*Economic Theory* 22, 63–88; Gotoh and Yoshihara 2003) Challenges the traditional discussions on the Distributive Justice based on the Utility approach. They find that on the one hand, the equality of individual capabilities prohibits any individual from dominating any others in their capabilities, and on the other hand, it allows much diversity for individuals in their capabilities, sizes, or figures, defined over the multi-dimensional Functioning Space.

Appendix 2: "Securing basic well-being for all" (*Review of Social Economy*, 76:4, 422–452; Gotoh and Yoshihara 2018) Provides a Social Choice rule, which secures basic well-being for all, respecting both individual subjectivity and group-based (positional) objectivity, by using a certain well-being Index (such as functionings and capabilities) that makes it possible to identify the least advantaged in each group.

Appendix 3: "The Capability Theory and Welfare Reform" (*Pacific Economic Review* 6–2, 211–222, Gotoh 2001) Examines the foundation of welfare reform in the light of Sen's capability theory and the implications of his theory in the context of contemporary industrialized society. A method to capture the philosophical meaning of the *equality of capabilities* is explored from the point of view of a fair Distributive Justice; two concepts of Freedom, *Well-Being Freedom* and *Agency Freedom*; and the process of human life.

Chapter 2
Welfare Economics and the Capability Approach

2.1 Historical Inquiry into the Capability Approach

As Sen stated in his *Commodities and Capabilities*,

> The main purpose of this short book is to present a set of interrelated theses about the foundation of welfare economics and, in particular, about the assessment of personal well-being and advantage. I argue in favor of focusing on the capability to function, i.e. what a person can do or can be, and argue against the more standard concentration on opulence (as in "real income" estimates) or on utility (as in traditional "welfare economic" formulations). (Sen 1985a, "Preface")

2.1.1 Introduction: Origins of the Capability Approach

Historical roots of the capability approach have attracted much attention in welfare economics recently. The first appearance of the concept of "capability" can be traced back to Sen's 1979 Tanner Lectures on "Equality of What?" delivered at Stanford University, published later (Sen 1980a/1997a). More interesting issues, however, about his capability approach are these: What does it protest against in the methodological assumptions and reasoning styles that were previously taken for granted by welfare economics? In what direction does it try to change or expand them?

As we can see in the quotation above, Sen presented his capability approach as an alternative to the two traditional approaches in welfare economics, i.e. the resource (commodities) approach and the utility approach. His aim was to critically scrutinize advantages and disadvantages of the two traditional approaches and to develop an alternative approach based on them. That is, to confront those problems that are often missed or made invisible by economic theories, including the sufferings and the disadvantages faced by particular groups of people living in our society. To be more concrete, his challenges included critical examination of the reality and actuality of "equilibrium" or "agreement," which are expected to appear in ordinary human activities such as exchanges, contracts, voting, and other public actions.

R. Gotoh, *The Ethics and Economics of the Capability Approach*, Hitotsubashi University IER Economic Research Series 46, https://doi.org/10.1007/978-981-15-5140-6_2

Our task here is to clarify academic foundations of the capability approach and identify its contrasting relations with traditional welfare economics.[1] What was the capability approach after all and what can it be?

In considering these issues, this chapter highlights six lineages of Sen's economic philosophy, which together provided a fertile ground for creating the capability approach. The proposition and tentative conclusion of this book is that the capability approach is the confluence of these six lineages, which suggests unfinished business toward a possibility of economics and philosophy.

The first lineage is on "wealth and welfare." This includes his works on the concept and measurement of real national income and individual welfare, more broadly, those on the identification and the measurement of "values and prices" (Sen 1962, 1966b, 1967b, 1976c, 1979b/1984a, 1980b, 1981b, 1985a, among others). We can observe his interest in the problem of distribution in the early stage of this issue.

The second is about "poverty and inequality." This includes his studies on the theoretical and methodological framework of *Development as Freedom*)" (Sen 1999a), especially, on the relation between the principles of distribution according to needs and according to desert (work) or a descriptive proposition and a prescriptive proposition (Sen 1973/1997, 1976b, 1980b, 1981a, 1985a, 1987b, 1999a, among others). We can observe his interest in the diversity of individuals' characteristics including disability and an idea of diversity-based equality.

The third is on "freedom and rights." This includes his research on how to respect an individual's will, choice, and interest in forming collective choice and in realizing public interests. The protection of women's rights and the problem of domestic injustice are discussed in this context (Sen 1970a, b, 1976a, 1983, 1985a, b, 1990b, 1992b, 1993b, c, 1996b, 1999a, 2002a, 2009a, among others).

The fourth lineage is on "rationality and reason (or reasoning)." Broadly speaking, this is concerned with an individual's cognitive bases of forming ethical relationships and a cooperative society. The critical re-examination of Samuelson's revealed preference theory and Arrovian type of social choice theory are also in this category (Sen 1969, 1983, 1985c, 1995, 1997, 1999b, 2002a, 2009b, among others).

The fifth is about "criticism of welfarism." This is nothing else than Sen's long struggles to overcome the logic of monism, which cancels out all plurality and diversity. He tries to introduce, in forming collective choice, external (ethical) points of view, to critically examine plurality of and possible conflicts of individual plural preferences and evaluations (Sen 1970a, 1987a, 1993b, 1996b, 2009a, among others).

The sixth is on "normative economics." This contains his research on ethical issues with fact and norm, consequence and obligation, or well-being and justice, and integration of legal, economic, and ethical perspectives (Sen 1966a, 1967a, b, 1977b, 1985b, 1986, 1987a, 1993a, 1999b, 2000, 2002b, 2006b, 2009a, b, 2010; Sen and Williams 1982, among others).

Surely, these themes are closely connected with one another, and works cited here are just some examples. We need to examine each of these themes carefully in order to find the roots of the capability approach, but there are already excellent studies

[1] On this issue refer to Atkinson (1995, 1999). See also Basu et al. (1995).

on Sen's discussion on "poverty and inequality," and "liberty and rights."[2] Here we are going to focus on relatively less-explored themes of "wealth and welfare" and "criticism of welfarism" and "normative economics." See the final chapter for a more comprehensive picture of Amartya Sen's economics and philosophy including "rationality and reason (or reasoning)" in comparison with Kenneth Arrow's.

2.1.2 *Measurement of Real National Income*

Amartya Sen worked on the measurement of real national income in the latter half of the 1970s. Previous studies on this issue had tended to focus on comparing relative positions of different individuals in a group. In contrast, Sen was more interested in exploring how to reflect different meanings and effects of the same goods distributed among different individuals or groups on the comparison and evaluation of real national income. He was also trying to reexamine the ethical foundation (or legitimacy) of market prices as a basis for measuring real national income.

Real national income is typically calculated by using market prices of various goods. Market prices are certainly useful and practical, as they tend to be constant in taking values within a range, regardless of the levels of goods, and also anonymous in the sense of being independent of the distribution of various goods. However, in reality, relative and marginal values of goods are different for individuals or groups with different levels and distributions of goods or income. Real national income does not reflect this at all and can give a distorted, unrealistic picture of a society. Can we constitute a constant set of "prices" that reflect, to some extent, objective differences of individual or group situations?

This concern led Sen to explore an approach quite different in direction from new welfare economics at its height. His words quoted here clearly demonstrate that he himself was sure about it.

> … [T]hese comparisons differ from traditional welfare economics (e.g. the use of 'Pareto Optimality' or of 'Compensation Tests'), collective choice theory (e.g. the use of Arrovian 'social welfare functions'), and the standard theory of national planning (e.g. 'cost–benefit analysis' or 'optimal growth theory'), which are concerned with comparing *alternative* positions of the same group of people. (Sen 1976c/1982, 389; parentheses and emphasis as shown in the original)

Sen attempts to capture individual differences in relative or marginal values of various goods in three different ways. The first is by regarding the same goods distributed among different individuals as different goods. Here Sen uses the concept of "named good" suggested by Frank Hahn (1971). The second is by noting shapes of indifference curves (not utility levels) drawn based on individual utility functions. The third is by looking at objective information about individual shares of goods in the total amounts or income rankings of individuals.

---

[2] See Gotoh (2006b).

Is it possible at all to constitute a new set of "prices" that not only reflect these individual differences but also have some constant and anonymous features? Here we summarize Sen's attempts, based on two of his major articles on this topic.[3]

Sen begins by clarifying the precondition for market prices to be regarded as desirable indexes under more general assumptions about constant-weight valuation indexes such as Complete Ordering, Convex Preference and Strict Monotonicity. Complete Ordering requires that any pair of named goods vectors can be compared each other, stating, which is better or they are different. Convex Preference requires that for any two named vectors, their convex combinations are better than either. Strict Monotonicity requires that if vector x is dominant vector y, social preference prefers x to y. Let us give formal definitions.

First, we call the good j distributed to individual i the "named good" ij, with its quantity x_{ij}. Let us assume there are m goods and n individuals. Then denote by $i\ (x)$ the "individual basket" consumed by individual i, where x is an mn-vector, and the total amount of the m-vector **c** of goods consumed by all individuals is represented by:

$$c = \sum_i i(x) = \left(\sum_i x_{i1}, \cdots, \sum_i x_{im} \right)$$

Next, the set of named good vectors in X that are at least as good as x according to the weak binary relation of social preferences R (with P and I standing for its asymmetric and symmetric part) is called $R(x)$. That is, $R(x) = \{y \in X | yRx\}$. Then the following theorem can be established.

Theorem 1: The Basic Theorem of Constant-Weight Real Income Comparisons (Sen 1976b/1997a)

If individual preferences satisfy Complete Ordering, Convex Preference, Strict Monotonicity, then for any named good x, there exists a weight-vector that satisfies the following properties. That is, for any named good y, $px \gg py$ implies xPy.

By defining "real income ranking" as follows, Sen, further, obtains Theorem 2, described below.

Definition: Real Income Ranking

xP^*y if and only if there exists a hyperplane H through x bounding $R(x)$ such that for the normal p of H: $px > py$.

Theorem 2: Characterization of Real Income Ranking (Sen 1976b/1997a)

Given Axioms Complete Ordering, Convex Preference, Strict Monotonicity:

(i) P^* is a sub-relation of strict social preference P;
(ii) The relation of vector dominance on$X$ is a sub-relation of P^*;
(iii) P^* is asymmetric and acyclic, but not necessarily complete or transitive.

---

[3]See Sen (1976c/1982; 1979b/1984), among others.

After deriving this theorem, Sen points out that many previous studies on real income comparison effectively took the "individualist approach," since they defined social welfare as a function of individual welfares satisfying the Pareto principle. Here we make three more assumptions about this individualist approach.

(1) Individual welfare depends only on the individual's purchase. (2) All buyers are price-takers. (3) Buyers are rational in the following sense: their choice function is characterized by "binary relations," which represent their pair-wise rankings over alternatives.

The Pareto principle and these three assumptions enable us to justify the two axioms below. The m-price vector is denoted by q when x is already determined.

Axiom X: Efficient Exchange

Relative values of different goods for an individual i equal the ratio of their market prices, i.e. $p_{ij}/p_{ih} = q_j/q_h$.

Combined with the premise that marginal values of the same good are equal between any individual i and g, i.e. $p_{ij} = p_{gj}$, we can obtain Axiom D for "optimal distribution."

Axiom D: Optimal Distribution

Relative values of different goods for an individual equal the ratio of their market prices, i.e. $p_{ij}/p_{ih} = q_j/q_h$, and marginal values of the same good are equal among individuals, i.e. $p_{ij} = p_{gj}$.

With the two axioms above, we can establish the following theorem.

Theorem 3: (Sen 1976b/1997a)
Given axioms (such as) Complete Ordering, Convex Preference, Strict Monotonicity, Efficient Exchange, and Optimal Distribution, if $c(x)$ and $c(y)$ are two (anonymous) commodity vectors corresponding respectively to two named good vectors x and y, then $qc(x) > qc(y)$ implies that xPy.

This theorem shed light on the role of Axiom D, *Optimal Distribution* in justifying anonymous rankings of distributions made with market prices. Paul Samuelson interprets this theorem as describing a basis of an "economy of the good society" in the sense of "maintaining ethical values of marginal dollars equal among individuals" (Samuelson 1956, 22; Sen 1976b/1997, 394[1997]). In contrast, Sen rightly criticizes this theorem in the sense that Axiom D might hide inequalities among individuals other than the equality of marginal values in the distribution of goods.

Starting from this criticism, Sen turned to the question of how to construct "prices" that are different from market prices. Each individual has her specific absolute values for each good as well as relative values (substitution rates) among different goods. She also has her own conversion rates in her possibility frontiers of opportunity sets. When the possibility frontier is her budget line, the conversion rate coincides with the ratio of market prices. Typically, the conversion rate in her possibility frontier reflects her production skills as well as market prices of production factors, so it varies across individuals. Taking this as a fact, what conditions can enable all individuals to share the same relative prices among different goods and accept the market prices that give the same marginal values ("ethical dollars") to all? Can we plausibly claim that individuals are market price takers acting passively?

Sen designed some stationary methods to constitute "prices" that are more general than market prices. Below are two such examples.

First, he considered a method using distributions of each good to different individuals. It defines D_x as the set of distributions where individuals have the same percentage distribution of the total amount of each good. Then, for distributions of any named good in D_x, it seeks a sufficient condition for ranking a particular distribution x over another distribution y for any named good in D_x. This is shown in the following theorem.

Theorem 4 (Sen 1976b/1997a)
Let $c(x)$ and $c(y)$ describe two (anonymous) good vectors corresponding to the named goods x and$y$. Suppose preferences satisfy complete ordering, convexity, and strict monotonicity. Then there exists an m-vector commodity price u such that $uc(x) > uc(y)$ implies xPy.

The commodity price u is constituted by, for example, adding up individual i's marginal values p_{ij} weighted by her distribution d_{ij}, that is, $\sum_i p_{ij} d_{ij}$, for any individual i and for any good j.The second method uses income rankings of individuals, with the richest person ranking 1st and the poorest nth. Denoting by e_i an individual i's income, we define the following axiom E.

Axiom E: Ordinal Equity
For each x, the normal p of some hyperplane $H(x)$ through x bounding $R(x)$ and satisfying the condition specified in Axiom X, also satisfies for all i, g, and$j$:

$$e_i > e_g \text{ implies } p_{ij} < p_{gj}.$$

Axiom D, defined earlier, puts the same weight on marginal values for all individuals. In contrast, Axiom E put larger weights on poorer individuals. The following axiom shows a method to give weights to market prices directly.

Axiom R: Rank Order Weighting
For each x, an mn-vector of ranked goods for n persons and m commodities, the normal p of some hyperplane $H(x)$ through x bounding $R(x)$ satisfies for all i (the income rank of a person at q) and j; $p_{ij} = Aiq_j$, where A > 0 is some constant.

Axiom R satisfies Axiom E, Axiom X, and, interestingly, the following property $p_{ij}/p_{ih} = iq_j/gq_h$. Axiom X shows the ratio of marginal values of goods for an individual is equal to the ratio of market prices. This equation $p_{ij}/p_{ih} = iq_j/gq_h$, in contrast, shows that the ratio of marginal values of goods for any pair of individuals of different income rankings is equal to the weighted ratio of market prices.

Sen (1979b/1997b) further explores a method to measure "personal real income." One of the major issues here is to seek a way to critically examine the revealed-preference theory by focusing on individual convex preferences. The revealed-preference theory sees prices as representing "real opportunities for market transactions." The consumption point chosen is interpreted as "dominating" any other alternative available for the individual. This theory focuses on the "optimality" of realized individual choices. Then, what can be argued by the approach focusing on convex individual preferences in general? It only gives a conditional statement that it can identify a set of distributions inferior to x "if" the "price" used there reflects the relative weights (marginal substitution rates) among different goods and, moreover, "if" preferences are convex.

The contrast between the revealed-preference theory and the convexity approach becomes clear when, for example, the possibility frontier does not coincide with the budget constraint line but it is strictly convex.[4] Sen went on to relate the convexity approach to discussion of the "national income" above. Namely, he took the possibility set of distribution vectors of named goods as the domain and constituted a Bergson–Samuelson social welfare function for it. Then he supposed the "price" that reflects relative weights (marginal substitution rates) among different goods in an allocation x. This is the "price-supporting vector in allocation x" [Sen 1979b/1997b, 421 (1997b)] and it shows "locally relevant weights."[5]

The discussion so far can be summarized in the following two points. It is important, in measuring both personal and national incomes, to understand the significance of the fact that diverse individuals and groups own and consume various goods in a variety of ways. We have to bear in mind that first the "prices" to evaluate an allocation (through absolute or relative values of different goods) do not have to be market prices. We can design various conceptual "prices" that take into account diversity of individuals and groups who own those goods. Second, we have to recognize diversity of the ways we understand diversity of individuals and groups owning those goods. Sen turned to Frank Hahn's concept of "named good," which regards a good distributed to different individuals as different goods. In the two articles by Sen, individual differences about "named goods" are captured by distributions of goods or incomes. However, it should be noted that Sen indicates a possibility to interpret this concept in a wider context, as shown in the following quotation.

> In the framework used in the named goods approach, there is, of course, no ban on using non-utility information (e.g. judgements about the relative social worth of goods going to people with different conditions of material prosperity being based on their commodity holdings as opposed to suppositions about their utility levels). Nor is there a ban on using utility information in richer forms (e.g. making certain systematic suppositions about people's relative utility levels) (Sen 1979b/1997b, 422[1997b]).

Here Sen suggests that the concept of "named good" can be formulated as an objective constraint for individuals actually using the good or as a more systematic index for interpersonally comparable utility levels. From this we can see that the concept is not very far from those of functioning and capability that capture objective "doings" and "beings" realized by individuals using various goods.

---

[4] As an example, Chap. 3 defines and analyzes "relative values of functionings" for both cases where the capability set is linear and strictly convex.

[5] Note that one of the advantages of the convexity approach is its ability to produce a global partial order that specifies the set of inferior allocations based on these "locally relevant weights".

So far we have not yet seen any detailed explanation on why the frontier of the consumption opportunity set does not in general coincide with the budget line based on market prices. For example, we have to wait for the capability approach to provide an explanation that differences among individuals making use of goods are reflected in individual conversion rates of goods (or functionings, to be precise). There is no doubt, however, that Sen's doubt about acceptability of the unified market price brought an important perspective in the research field of measurement of real national income. Let us conclude this section by briefly considering this problem.

Suppose, for example, that prices for local public transportation and medicines are increased and those for food are decreased. Then a fit person's well-being can surely increase by buying and consuming more food. However, increased prices for medicines can suppress chronically sick people's "function to relieve pain" as they can buy less medicine now. Also they cannot increase purchase of food, whose price is cheaper now, because increased pain raises the cost of consuming and enjoying food. As a result, their functioning to obtain nutrition might also deteriorate. Similarly, increased costs for local public transportation can severely harm the functioning to move around for old or disabled people, who do not have any alternative means for transportation. Moreover, they might not be able to buy more food that is now relatively less expensive because their lack of transportation means less access to various foods. This can damage their functioning to obtain nutrition as well.

Even if a relatively small number of people are affected and changes in consumption of relevant goods and services are small, the overall loss of functionings for them can be quite large due to interdependence among different functionings. Then it might be reasonable to apply appropriate weights to diverse groups, depending on their differences, when measuring real national income. The capability approach can justify putting different weights according to differences, based on individual well-being, that is, on their functionings and capabilities.

The study of real national income was a forerunner of the capability approach. The birth of the approach then made it possible to extend the study of real national income by taking into account the differences among constituents of a society and provided a bridge between the study of consumption and that of social choice and welfare in general. It prepared for "criticism of welfarism" and "normative economics," which explicitly include ethical points of view in economics in particular, to be discussed in the following sub-sections.

2.1.3 Criticism of "Welfarism"

"*... [L]iberalism takes the individual as given,* and views the social problem as one of right relations between given individuals." (Knight 1921/1947, 69 [1947]; emphasis added by Arrow 1951/1963, 8 [1963].)

Following these remarks by Frank Knight, Kenneth Arrow declares that he adopts methodological individualism in his *Social Choiceand Individual Values.*

> [T]his is in fact what is found for the true orderings, knowledge for which is given by the individualistic assumptions. ... [T]he quasi-ordering of the social alternatives implied in the individualistic assumptions is different for different individuals, since each individual ranks the alternative involved according to what *he* gets out of them, ... (Arrow 1951/1963, 61–62 [1963])

In the context of economics, it is often assumed that value judgements about alternatives are ultimately reserved for the individual. This assumption is called "methodological individualism" (See Agassi 1975) and is supposed to be value-neutral. In contrast, Arrow's remarks above indicate that this assumption is not restricted to methodology but it has a normative meaning of respect for individual liberty and, further, contains an idea of individualism that regards the individual as the bearer of purposes and values.

As Friedrich Hayek points out, a typical example to satisfy the individualistic assumption is the competitive market mechanism and the general equilibrium theory that characterizes it. It is, however, just one example. Sen indicates that this property is satisfied not only by Arrovian social choice theory focusing on voting mechanisms and Bergson–Samuelson social welfare function as an extension of the Pareto condition. It is also satisfied by many theories of distribution, which base their value judgements ultimately on individual utilities and avoid making interpersonal comparison.

In traditional theory, social choice has been taken to be a function of individual preferences.... But the argument questioning the Pareto principle can be also used to establish the need to consider other information (e.g. the *motivation* behind those preferences). In this approach, judgements on social choices "would then no longer be a function of individual preferences only." (Sen 1970a/2017, p. 83[2017])

Sen saw a methodological problem underlying new welfare economics in its reduction of "individuality" to individual preferences. He called it "welfarism." In fact, what he called welfarism has a wide scope and different emphases depending on the context, but it has the following three features.

First, the domain for social welfare functions is restricted to individual preferences, which in turn have to be represented by interpersonally incomparable, ordinal binary relations (called "orderings") that satisfy reflexivity, transitivity, and completeness.

Second, social welfare functions (aggregation procedures) have to be neutral in the following sense. For any two social states, if any two individual preference valuation profiles rank the two states in the same way, their social ranking has to be the same. Note here that adding three conditions, i.e. Unrestricted Domain, the Pareto condition (for indifferent preference valuations, to be more precise), and the Independence of Irrelevant Alternatives make it equivalent to the condition of Neutrality.[6]

Third, individual preferences tend to be represented by utilities such as subjective pleasure and pain, satisfaction, and happiness.

---

[6]The basic idea of "neutrality" can be described as follows. "[I]f the individual preferences over (*x*, *y*) in one case are identical to the individual preferences over (*a*, *b*) in another case, then the social choice in the latter case would place *a* and *b* respectively where *x* and *y* figured in the former case." (Sen 2002a, 333).

The third criticism is part of the characterization of utilitarianism (consequentialism, sum ranking, and welfarism). (Sen and Williams 1982, 4) This criticism can be dealt with by switching its informational bases from utility to rights, well-being, and capabilities. However, the problem is more complex and this switching alone cannot properly answer the first and second criticisms, which are sometimes called "formal welfarism" (d'Aspremont and Gevers 2002).[7]

It should be noted that Arrow emphasizes that a person is "the agent of his own interests and decisions" on the one hand, and on the other he has "natural complementarity with others" in his contributions in works and contributions to society (Arrow 1974). Yet, unfortunately, the latter consideration is not explicitly formulated in his framework of social choice theory. Similarly, in *The Ethics of Competition*, Knight admits the significance of ethics, which can critically reflect the quality of competition, yet he assumes that "the standpoint of absolute ethics" exists fully outside the free and competitive market system (Knight 1931/1997, 46–47) . These ethical comments are, needless to say, important, but cannot be powerful enough to shake "welfarism" deeply rooted in economic theory, as long as it stays outside the scope of economic models.

After all, one has to extend economic models and their underlying thinking by introducing ethics as external and critical points of view, in order to overcome "welfarism." Social values cannot be determined solely in relation to individual values reflecting or representing subjective desires or self-satisfactions.

To do so, we should logically extend the domain of Arrovian social welfare function from the profile of individual values that are reduced to being ordinal and interpersonally incomparable, to the profile of individual values that can be qualitatively differentiated, that is, the domain of Sen's social welfare functionals.[8] Then, we should restrict the domain and the aggregation procedure from a normative point of view by introducing certain external points of view, such as ethics or morals, as axioms or normative conditions.

Suppose, for example, we aggregate rankings of two individuals about any two alternatives (different distribution methods, different policies). First we assume that we can observe relevant capabilities of individuals as the most basic information for social decision making. Then we loosen conditions of the unrestricted domain, binary independence, and Pareto principle for the aggregation procedure as follows.

First, we reconsider the foundations of or the motivation behind individual preferences. Do they reflect their situations objectively or represent their prudential interests faithfully, or do they show their appraisals of the objective situations of themselves? Then, we can ethically impose some conditions which request some help or intervention, if necessary, in the process of individual preference formation.

[7] Prasanta Pattanaik argues that "individual welfare judgements…incorporate individual values on institutional features of social states" (Pattanaik 2005, 377). See also Fleurbaey and Mongin (2005, 386).

[8] Refer to "A social welfare functional (SWFL) specifies exactly one social ordering R over the set X of social states for any given n-tuple $\{Ui(\cdot)\}$" of personal utility functions, each defined over X, one for each person i: $R = F(\{Ui\})$." (Sen 1970a/2017, 373[2017]).

Further, we examine the possibility of interpersonal comparison based on information about the foundation of individual preferences. If interpersonal comparison is possible, then we can put some priorities in the aggregation process for individual rankings, according to the ethically reasonable weights among individual rankings or the positions or names of alternatives.

The concept of capability is characterized by its openness to *the public*, beyond the individual's, in terms of the "reason" that a certain functioning vector should be included in her capability set. This means taking a balanced view of the multi-layered assessments of the individual, the society including people close to oneself, neighbors, and those belonging to various "positions" and *the public*.

Another key to go beyond "welfarism" lies in this process of forming "trans-positional assessments" across different position-specific assessments within an individual (as a virtual process) and across different groups (as an actual process). The concept of capability also provides a wider perspective for intra- and inter-personal comparability. We are going to examine this method in more detail in Chap. 5.

In practice, individual capabilities are specified as the set of utilization abilities for functionings by using the data related to individuals' positions, types, and groups. (See Chap. 3, Sect. 2.1). The definition of capability suggests that when different individuals have the same utilization abilities and have the same commodity vectors, different functionings achieved by them are a result of their choice of different points in the same opportunity set, based on their own preferences.

The concept of capability can also prepare for the normative definition of the group. That is, it helps identify a group of individuals who can be compared in terms of their capabilities focusing on certain sorts of functionings. We can compare the size and worth of capabilities across individuals in the same group but comparison is impossible across individuals in different groups.

Nevertheless, elaboration of assessments by incorporating external points of view, introduction of the ethical concept of the group, or logical expansion of the domain of social assessment procedures would surely force us to tackle many issues that have been avoided by academic research. In the following section we examine, in a wider context of sciences, implications for economics of introducing external or critical points of view.

2.1.4 Normative Economics: Ethics in Economics

In his classic work *The Representation of Nature in Contemporary Physics*, Werner Karl Heisenberg (Heisenberg 1958, 106) issued a warning against natural sciences as follows.

> The word "final" in connection with exact science evidently means that we will always find closed, mathematically describable systems of concepts and laws that fit certain areas of experience, are valid in them anywhere in the universe, and are incapable of modification or improvement. It cannot, however, be expected that these concepts and laws will later be suitable for the representation of new realms of experience. Only in this limited sense,

therefore, can the concepts and laws of quantum theory be designated as final, and only in this limited sense can it ever happen that scientific knowledge finds its final fixation in mathematical or any other language.

Heisenberg pointed out that the concepts and principles that are "universal" in limited empirical fields and "final" (in the sense that they allow no change or improvement) cannot be applied to another empirical field. This is worth noting in the methodology of social sciences as well.

The "general possibility theorem" presented by Arrow in 1951 was a logically robust result that allegedly showed the impossibility of democracy and hence shocked many people. It had several theoretical assumptions, however, and we have to be careful in its interpretation. A particularly important assumption is that social preferences have to count different individual preferences with the same weight, regardless of their nature, and reflect preference profiles for any two alternatives, whatever they are, in the same way (in the same ranking pattern). Sen's criticism against welfarism in the last section applied to this assumption of Arrow's model (called Arrovian Social Choice Model in this book).

The method for social decision making which puts equal weight on members' preferences (welfares) but captures them only in ordinal rankings can surely work well in some empirical fields as a way to respect all individuals. For example, they include a situation where international conventions and national constitutions are fully accepted and individuals can make well-informed, reasonable, and ethical judgements. We can probably argue that the economic model of global market competition is also close to the empirical field for the Arrovian model, because the supply and demand for an infinite number of individuals instantly ranks relative prices of all goods and that can lead to an equilibrium of the economy.

However, what about a situation where, for example, most people have little knowledge or experience about an issue while a small number of people concerned find it crucial? Here it might be reasonable in aggregation procedures to put more weight on preference judgements about certain alternatives made by the people concerned, rather than putting the same weight on preferences of all.

This method permits putting different weights on preferences of people concerned and the others. It does not require "neutrality," defined above, in the treatment of any two alternatives. Furthermore, it does not require "completeness" of individual preferences nor social preferences. Hence we can say it is a "consequentialist evaluation method." To use Heisenberg's phrases above, Sen's criticism of welfarism led to a broadening of the scope of the Arrovian model so that we could explore more appropriate methods for social decision making in terms of diverse "spheres of experiences" (issues).

We should bear in mind, however, that Sen's criticism of "welfarism" has significant implications beyond diversification of spheres of experiences. It also opened up the scope of the Arrovian model to a theory of "normative economics." Let us confirm this point by using the example we discussed above. Who is going to accept on what grounds this kind of aggregation method that puts greater weight on the people concerned than on the others on a particular issue?

Suppose that the answer is people in general, including those unconcerned. People concerned had indescribable experiences on this issue and had to think carefully about it from many different angles. Hence they accept this aggregation method as a responsible expert. Those unconcerned do not know much about the issue and therefore accept it as a responsible follower respecting the opinion of experts.

It is interesting to see that the form of the Arrovian model can make sense again if this assumption is valid. The model counts all individual preferences about aggregation methods equally and reflects preference profiles over any two alternatives onto social preferences in the same pattern. Note, however, the Arrovian model resumed here is not an empirical one but a normative one with sufficient information and external ethical points of view. The norm here includes not only the formal conditions for democracy embodied in international conventions and state constitutions but also a substantial condition explained below.

As explained earlier, people concerned accept a norm that they should play the role of experts on an issue, whereas people not concerned accept the norm that they should listen to people concerned. Based on the both ethical judgements and depending on the issue, the substantial condition we consider here requires that we should put priorities on the judgements made by people not concerned when making social decisions. Sen's criticism of welfarism introduced perspectives to scrutinize actual preferences held by real people in a critical, reflexive manner, and it also led to possibilities to characterize the Arrovian model as a normative theory beyond specific spheres of experience.

Finally, we can confirm the significance of "normative economics," highlighted by Sen's criticism of welfarism, by looking at the "observation problem" pointed out by Heisenberg (1958, 107).

> Science no longer is in the position of observer of nature, but rather recognizes itself as part of the interplay between man and nature. The scientific method of separating, explaining, and arranging becomes conscious of its limits, set by the fact that the employment of this procedure changes and transforms its object; the procedure can no longer keep its distance from the object. The world view of natural science thus ceases to be a view of "natural" science in its proper sense.

Here Heisenberg points out that the act of observation cannot be neutral towards the object of observation. This is because the act itself might change how the object is, that is, there are some possibilities that the light, reason, time, and space, for observation in themselves can change with the act. This "observation problem" was considered an inevitable serious problem whenever we try to analyze some phenomena, natural or human. Not only in the field of philosophy of sciences but also in social sciences, this "observation problem," along with the "value-free" problem posed by Max Weber, led to some reflection on the methodology about knowledge.

Surprisingly, however, this problem did not affect much of the development of economics. As far as the "value-free" problem was concerned, most economists were apparently able to avoid ethical problems of interpersonal comparison but concentrated on describing and explaining social phenomena. The economic theory for the pure free competitive market and its complementary system obtained the robustness as "closed, mathematically describable systems of concepts and laws that fit certain areas of experience, are valid in them anywhere in the universe, and are incapable of modification or improvement," according to Heisenberg (1958, 106). Positive economics to analyze real economic phenomena justified itself by relying on this economic theory and statistical theory. Economics has long been called a "positive science."

If, however, the "observation problem" raised in natural sciences questions the degree of certainty of scientific observation or measurement itself, then it would be difficult to defend economics in the name of "positive science." Furthermore, if economics should be concerned with the well-being (values or utility acquired through the production, distribution, and consumption of goods and wealth) of real people and the design of policies and institutions, it cannot remain a pure theory as "closed, mathematically describable systems of concepts and laws that fit certain areas of experience, are valid in them anywhere in the universe, and are incapable of modification or improvement."

2.1.5 Summary

People living their lives are "real," whereas no "system of concepts and laws" can be so, however beautiful and truthful it is. For example, Rawls's theory of justice uses the framework of "political constructivism" to organize or harmonize the "moral personality" and the "ordered society" by practical reason, rather than trying to deduce one based on the other. Neither concept is assumed to be "real" there. They are no more than the normative assumptions accepted by individuals who actually legislate principles of justice, together with some formal conditions for the idea of justice. It is their acts that make "real" an idea of just principles that might only be a utopia. (See on Rawls's "realistic utopia," in the Preface of this book.)

If we regard the "system of concepts and laws" itself as real, we could end up under the delusion that logical positivism suffered. We may be able to construct a closed, fictional world but this will take us away from the mission to reconstruct an open, real world of living. Unlike in natural sciences, however, one of the challenges of economics (or, more broadly, social sciences) is to discover how to identify, analyze, and solve various problems faced by actual individuals, groups, or a society. Scientific observation of the objects should be a means for this, rather than the end.

In fact, a key to solving the "observation problem" raised by Heisenberg lies in this feature of the challenge of economics and social sciences. We close this section by briefly describing the prospect.

First, it should be pointed out that there can be room for communication between the observer and the object of observation when the latter is an individual human being. Second, communication between the observer and the object is expected to lead to the benefit of the object if the purpose of observation is to solve difficulties faced by him or her. There is a possibility, of course, that the observer's words unexpectedly silence the object or the relation between the two should distort the nature of possible communication. If, nevertheless, the purpose of the observation is to solve the difficulties faced by the object, and discovery of the method is recognized as a common challenge, then there is a possibility to open up a channel of communication between the observer and the observed. To use a term in the field of social welfare, this act of observation is called "external intervention." It has been confirmed, however, that external intervention can sometimes help provide a positive value of respecting the agency (of the object), especially in the field of nursing or medical care, and effective approaches for this have been studied.

Scholars in economics should take seriously the "observation problem" raised by natural sciences, critically examine methodological foundations for economic theories and positive economics, and pursue a methodological framework to connect the two. This is not only crucial in order for economics to meet its inherent challenge but also useful in making clear its distinctive role. We can regard Sen's social choice theory and his capability approach as an attempt to meet this challenge.

Let us revisit the question we asked at the beginning of this chapter: Why did Sen decide to propose a new concept, different from commodity or utility? By capturing various capabilities of a person in the relevant issues, we can make interpersonal comparison of, and put different weights or priorities on, situations and values of different individuals. Different weight and priority require an external point of view, such as ethics, and their appropriateness should be open to public discussion. Sen's aim in proposing his capability approach may have been to correct the course of new welfare economics, which tended to concentrate on resources and utility.

However, his criticism of welfarism went beyond fine-tuning of new welfare economics. Through the economic theory of "values of freedom," Sen offered a prospect for the mechanism of the welfare state and public discussion that was different from the market or voting. This is the conclusion of the first section of this chapter. The following chapters will discuss how this approach can be placed in the development of modern theories of consumption assessment, human capital, household production, and Arrovian social choice. Before doing so, the next section reviews some basic ideas of the capability approach.

2.2 Philosophical Inquiry into the Capability Approach

2.2.1 Extended Welfare Space and Multi-Layered Preference Evaluations

2.2.1.1 The Idea of Multi-Spaces

When we recognize that someone is severely deprived of a certain value but it is not included in the space that the society can operate on, the deprivation cannot be dealt with by public policy nor measured for the purpose of economic policy. For example, as indicated by the Japanese word *seihin*, which roughly means "honorable poverty," there is no obvious link between an individual's subjective or ethical sense of "happiness" and her satisfaction of material or physical needs on the commodity space. To specify a certain function between these two might end up weakening special impacts of the word "happiness" (aesthetics or beliefs behind it).

A unique feature of the concept of capability is its power to clarify the relation between the commodity space and the functioning space. When people have the same level of utilization ability, there must be a non-decreasing relation between commodities and their capabilities. That is, an increase (decrease) of a commodity can increase (decrease) their function without causing a decrease (increase) in any of their functions. The commodity space is a space where society can operate through interpersonal distribution or transfer of endowment goods. To use a key term in Sen's *Povertyand Famines*, it is a space where individual entitlements, such as private ownership, are defined (Sen 1981a).

It is crucial in designing economic policies to scrutinize the effects on the functioning space of how we distribute commodities. If, for example, a local public railway network is to be downsized or abolished, it might greatly reduce the possibility of the "public transportation" function for someone unable, due to poor eyesight, to use any alternative means such as a car. In the commodity space, we can put those goods and resources that are useful for people's economic activities, beyond "commercial goods" distributed in the market. For example, there is so-called social capital, including a gift from others, an honorarium, or direct help. These can possibly expand people's opportunity sets or utilization abilities, without directly affecting their market prices. They can of course affect them by changing demands for the "commercial goods."

The capability approach, with its multi-space framework, can be quite effective in dealing with the problem of inequality that can be exacerbated in the processes of both production and consumption. For example, the capability approach can describe those mechanisms by which inequality in the commodity space is expanded into the functioning space because disadvantages in utilization abilities for goods can be added to disadvantages in purchasing power for goods.[9] Moreover, it can provide an analytical perspective different from the commodity market. For example, it can offer the following interesting analysis based on the theory of equity as no-envy (which requires that no one would prefer to be in another person's situation, according to her own preferences).

Suppose there are two individuals, A and B, and only B has limited vision. A has a higher wage rate and a stronger preference for leisure. B, lower in both, envies the situation of A. However, as we increase the amount of income transfer from A to B on the commodity space including income and leisure goods, there comes a point where A and B envy each other. If this income transfer goes further, there can be a situation where B stops envying A, whereas A envies B increasingly.

---

[9]In social epidemiology, for example, there are some studies analyzing mechanisms where certain socio-economic disadvantages are translated into health disadvantages via group categories such as race or gender (Marmot 2015). Group categories here are regarded as environmental factors beyond individual control.

Consider now the functioning space with two functionings "Commute by bicycle" and "Looking at paintings." As we make an income transfer from A to B, the latter may have more opportunities to use public transportation, including taxi, and enjoy live music performances, whereas A, with a smaller budget due to income transfer, may have fewer opportunities to buy a ticket for an exhibition at a museum. It would be quite difficult, without a great technological innovation, to expect a situation where A should envy the poorly sighted B riding a bicycle and looking at paintings in a museum.

If we restrict our discussion to within the commodity space, income transfer policies can threaten taxpayers with low income as they realize an "actual exchange of their positions" with recipients just below tax exemption rather than an "imaginary exchange" of points of views.[10] Income transfer policies can damage work incentives, as Rawls perceived, since actual exchange of positions through taxations might be against the sense of equality symbolized by the maxim "To each his own (*Suum cuique*)."

In contrast, the multi-space framework of the capability approach can shed light on individual differences in the public space and absolute disadvantages suffered by specific individuals while, at the same time, leaving some room for interpersonal incomparability in various functionings outside the public space.

There lies a vast, interpersonally incomparable world behind the interpersonally comparable space for public lives. Individual human lives themselves cover both spaces, and they resist any lazy interpersonal comparison. Even if they face the same *ex-ante* risks, unlucky individuals can go through immense suffering that is unimaginable for those more fortunate. Suffering, pain, and joy can be unique and fundamentally different for different individuals. They are different enough to break an illusion of "actual exchange of positions."

There is, nevertheless, a fundamental equality symbolized by the question: "Why you, not us?", which was raised by a Japanese psychiatrist who had devoted herself to caring for persons afflicted by leprosy (Hansen's disease) (Kamiya 1989). "By sheer chance, you suffered heavily and I survived. It could easily have been the reverse." This is the equality in existence,[11] to be discussed in Chap. 3.

The Sen's social choice model, to be formulated in Chap. 6, permits incompleteness because it reflects the insight about interpersonal comparability and incomparability in this multi-space world captured by the capability approach. This multi-space nature enables us to capture its rich, unintegrated "diversity." We examine this in the next section.

---

[10]Hobbes clearly points out that it is "equality" that leads to distrust, competition, and vanity (Hobbes 1641/1904), whereas "equality" here implies not "equality as a norm" that people may form through public reasoning but illusionary perception of "equality as a fact".

[11]We can find insights into this fundamental equality from the perspective of chance in many works by different authors including Rawls and Levinas.

2.2.1.2 Plurality of Preference Evaluation

A particular functioning vector is chosen in reference to an evaluation function defined over the functioning space, whereas the choice of a commodity vector is based on a utility function defined over the commodity space. If we could integrate these functions defined over different spaces, then it would be possible to maintain the basic framework of the traditional utility approach and extend it theoretically. For example, in Chap. 4 of this book, we attempt the following formulation on the "functioning space."

Each individual assesses relative or absolute values of various functionings according to a specific objective function. For example, she has an "evaluation function" that translates various alternative functionings into a certain level of well-being, or a "functionings production function" that combines certain achieved sub-functionings to produce main-functionings. When the assessment of relative values of different functionings changes smoothly according to the levels and composition of those functionings, we can draw well-defined indifference curves in economics[12] for functionings or production possibility frontiers on the functioning space.

A certain group of people or society might have collective assessments ("reputations" or "social norms"), beyond individual subjective ones, about relative values (marginal substitution rates) for various functionings. These collective assessments can be interpreted as quasi-market functioning prices that can hold in an equilibrium of the demand and supply of various functionings. Then we can say each individual chooses the best functioning vector according to her evaluation function, given these functioning prices.

Individual acts of exchange and rational recognition also provide an integrating logic that can cover both commodity and functioning spaces. Now, suppose we have a "meta-preference function" which integrates the utility function over the commodity space and the evaluation function over the functioning space. Then each individual chooses an optimal functioning vector, a commodity vector, and a utilization ability, according to her "meta-functioning function" given her own opportunity sets and market prices (relative values) defined over each space. Furthermore, these individual rational choices can lead to an equilibrium where prices and amounts to be traded in each space can be simultaneously determined. This can be described as a so-called extended general equilibrium model. If equilibrium points in each space satisfy the Pareto optimality according to this integrated "meta-preference function," then the fundamental theorems of welfare economics can hold in the multi-space as well. I will argue this point more in detail in Chap. 4.

If we focus on integrated rational behavior of individuals and their optimal choices in equilibria, the capability approach is, in its basic structure, very close to the human capital theory developed by Gary Becker, that is, the rational choice model

[12]Well-defined preference satisfies Continuity, (Strict) Monotonicity and Convexity. Continuity requires that if we prefer vector x to vector y, vectors very close to$x$ will also be preferred to y. Convex Preference requires that for any two named vectors, their convex combinations are better than either. (Strict) monotonicity requires that if vector x is dominant vector y, we prefer$x$ to y.

of traditional economics. In other words, the capability approach would also play the role of gyroscope to take the social order of market equilibrium as its ultimate goal and adjust individual demand and supply over multiple spaces to determine various prices.

This is no problem if individuals we study are no more than a *container* of their own preference functions that deal with trading various goods and services in the market. It means they are interested only in rational choices among their own capability sets. If, however, individuals we study are complex beings who exhibit a variety of doings and beings in various spaces, some of which can be inconsistent with one another and, moreover, if many of those different states of being can be discovered only as our own recognition and understanding develop, then the capability approach goes a step beyond the tool for automatic adjustment mechanism.

In reality, an individual's utility function and evaluation function, formed over different spaces, are not always consistent with each other. An optimal point specified by a utility function on the commodity space might not correspond to one by an evaluation function on the functioning space. Similarly, an equilibrium on the commodity space that satisfies the Pareto optimality might not do so on the functioning space. In this context, Sen's following remarks become important. "The fundamental issue really is whether individual preference orderings alone provide enough of a basis for a social judgement without going into the causation of and the motivation behind these preferences." (Sen 1976a/1997a, 302[1997a]).

When we take into account multiple spaces, it is quite natural to ask why we would give priority to one preference over the other as a whole, although each preference apparently appropriates in each space. It would be difficult to complete our discussion simply by assuming some super-rational, super-integrated "meta-preference function" and applying the extended general equilibrium theory.

The purpose of the capability approach to capture the functioning space was not merely to expand the scope of traditional economic theory but to enrich the analytical method of economic theory itself. It captures states of individuals not by a single index for utility values on the commodity space but by a multi-dimensional index for bundles of concrete doings and beings and further by opportunity sets of those bundles (sets of available functioning vectors). This makes the logic and ethics of the capability approach far more valid and acceptable for people. It enables us to interpret individual choices in normative terms. The capability approach had to be invented to capture this logic and ethics.

2.2.2 *Re-Examination of Freedom as an Opportunity Set*

2.2.2.1 Difficulty of Definition

The concept of capability is closely related to the concept of individual freedom because it makes sure that the individual is not prevented from choosing what she has reason to choose and it provides some means to realize what she has chosen. We have to be careful, however, in defining capability as an opportunity set of "what an individual can choose if she wants."

First, individual capability cannot be defined solely by factors related only to her, independently from the conditions including other people's preferences and market prices. If an individual is to switch from one functioning vector to another, the other individuals too would have to switch accordingly, but this might not be possible in general. Second, capability is a "substantial opportunity" when an individual makes a choice, not a substance owned by her. Clearly, she cannot choose two different functioning vectors at the same time from her capability set, nor can she switch from one to another anytime.

As an opportunity set, the budget set on the commodity space faces the same problem. Individual budget sets are not fixed before she makes a choice and they become unfixed afterwards as well. Even if the choices from opportunity sets can achieve an "equilibrium," individual opportunity sets themselves are fixed at the same time when the equilibrium point and prices are determined. Hence, there is no guarantee that the opportunity set should remain the same after choices are made, or that alternatives previously available but not chosen would be available again.

This problem was carefully studied by Tadenuma and Xu (2017). They extend the traditional Walrasian framework and define freedom based on the opportunity set as an individual's ability to realize at least one alternative among her own opportunity set. They argue that it is too demanding to identify such freedom as her ability to realize all the alternatives in her opportunity set.

Their proposition is very interesting in defining freedom by realizability of at least one alternative. They point out that this is the least we can require when considering interdependence with others and defining freedom of choice in general as achieved from the opportunity set. This minimum requirement for freedom of choice indicates the limitation of "general definition" itself.

In order to secure individual freedom with limited resources, people and society are prevented from interfering with other individuals and forced to help them sometimes. Analyzing freedom inevitably requires a perspective of interdependence of different individuals.

Suppose, for example, that individual 1′s choice of a certain act or situation in a room would require individual 2 to adjust his act or situation accordingly. If individual 1 sits quietly in the corner to read a book, individual 2 might have to leave the room without taking the book. We can use an Edgeworth box (a figure to illustrate exchanges between two persons for two goods, given their initial endowments and utility functions) to describe this situation as a distribution problem of two goods between two persons. Individual utility functions can take any form. Suppose, for example, individual 2 is not interested in being there nor reading the book but only in interfering with individual 1′s actions.[13] Even this case can be described and analyzed with an Edgeworth box by replacing the degree of involvement by individual 2's

[13]This case reminds us of an interesting issue of "involvement allocation" discussed by the sociologist Goffman (1963b). Note that Tadenuma and Xu (2017) give an axiomatic characterization of the equality of freedom based on the opportunity set by extending the no-envy theory.

preferences for goods (space and book). For example, we can say individual 1 has freedom to read one page of the book.

To judge the validity and limits of these descriptions and analyses, we need to develop our arguments in three directions. First, what is the right to freedom? Second, what does freedom as an opportunity set mean? Third, what is the equal guarantee? We can briefly look at these points below.

2.2.2.2 Right to Freedom: Capability is Not Workable?

It is one thing to ask what freedom is and quite another to ask what the right to freedom means. Freedom is, like security and love, an important value pursued by an individual or a society. It is a value to be created, maintained, cherished, and appreciated throughout one's life. Suppose there is a situation where the value of freedom has to be realized for some alternatives for a person, while considering interdependence with others. If there is a clear reason for one alternative to be chosen and realized by someone, depending only on her choices, then the others have corresponding duties to help realize it by adjusting their own acts, negatively or positively. The right to freedom requires this.

As Rawls suggested in his theory of justice, it would be nearly impossible to specify, measure, and distribute the total amount of value of freedom in a society. This seems to be the main reason why he considers that the concept of capability is not workable (Rawls 1999a, 13). However, it is also true that a society has to secure and protect the value of a certain freedom for some persons by imposing corresponding duties to others. It is in this context that the capability approach is quite effective. It can help specify the content and scope of the value of freedom to be protected and begin to measure what is missing there.

The "Condition of Liberalism," to be discussed in Chap. 7, requires that a person's preference over two specific social states (a pair of alternatives) should be reflected in their social ranking. This is a rather strong requirement in demanding that the right to decide (refuse, to be precise) is conferred on that individual. Taking this into account, it was explained that the relevant pairs of alternatives were limited to those social states that were different only in that specific person's situation and were the same for all the others. Mill called them "personal spheres."[14]

This explanation, however, immediately invites a difficult question of whether one can clearly identify those actions that do not affect others in the beginning. Apparently independent actions by individuals can possibly affect others when they are expressed clearly[15] and attract attention or interest from others. Or, individual isolated values might develop into a community value (trust, friendship, love, joy,

[14] "To individuality should belong the part of life in which it is chiefly the individual that is interested; to society, the part which chiefly interests society." (Mill 1859/1977, Chap. 4).

[15] According to Aristotle, what remains a subjective wish cannot be called a choice (Aristotle, 4th Century BC/1980).

and the fruit of collaboration) that is individually inseparable and provides some derivative value (externality) in a wider society.

If this is the case, we have to question the validity of the libertarian claim for respecting individual autonomous choices, assuming there are some personal spheres as a fact. Rather, we cannot ignore normative values or purposes when judging whether a society should allow or restrict individual actions or situations that can be realized, physically, by her own choice. And should a society seek to adjust boundaries of personal spheres in order to help realize individual actions or situations that cannot be realized physically by her own choice alone. Here we face the issue of specifying rights.

According to Ronald Dworkin, "the right is an individualized political purpose" and, like any other political purpose, it demands impartiality, generality, openness, non-reduction, and priority. The right has a unique feature in that its value belongs to individuals seeking "equal respect and concern" (their will or interest). That is, individual rights can "trample" restrictions made from a point of view of the "public welfare" (the common good), by virtue of individual actions or situations, even when it is just for one person.

In the context of domestic violence, for example, it has been pointed out and stressed that we need to protect the "individual sphere" of someone within her intimate zone. Violation of her "individual sphere" can include a wide range of physical and mental abuse, such as preventing her sleep, monitoring or interfering with her eating and bodily functions, or checking her mobile phone messages. Within her intimate zone, it would be more difficult to define the personal sphere clearly and completely separate from the others. Then, however, it becomes all the more important to establish the protection of "individual sphere" as a norm, institutionally, socially, and publicly.

Sen's "coherent goal-rights system" refers to a multi-dimensional system to regulate effectiveness of different individual rights in relation to various social goals (Sen 2002a). It allows varying degrees of weights and priorities of different rights, depending on people's specific conditions, private interests, and social environments. However, it requires that the variation should remain coherent and within a certain range (for details see also Gotoh 2016a). To specify individual basic capabilities is to answer the following question. How should we define "the right to well-being freedom" in this "coherent goal-rights system"?

Consider, for example, a pair of alternatives {x: stay well-nourished, y: go undernourished}. Suppose that a society ranks$x$ over$y$ whenever an individual ranks x over y. Then we can say her "right to well-being freedom" is recognized. In this case, the pair {x, y} becomes part of her basic capability and she can claim it from society if it is absent. In general, goals about her "right to well-being freedom" cannot always be realized, of course. We may not be able to satisfy her claim if, for example, an unpredictable natural disaster should destroy food supply chains completely in some areas.

What is important is, however, that society's obligation remains there as long as individuals have their "rights to well-being freedom." In the case above, for example, we can expand her opportunity sets by adding two extra alternatives {z: reduce under-nourishment a lot, *w*: reduce under-nourishment a little} and giving individuals decisive power over pairs of (z, w) and (w, y). In other words, we expand the individual "basic capability" into $\{x, z, w, y\}$ and require that more policies should be available. This can mean an economic policy of transferring social resources (from the rich to those who need it). Then an individual has an incomplete duty toward others' rights in the sense of "supporting them when she can." (Sen and Gotoh 2008)

2.2.2.3 Opportunity Set: Freedom as Substitutability

Now we turn to the next issue. An individual capability is not a substance owned by that individual but an "effective opportunity" that allows her choice when she decides to make one. Individual opportunity sets become clear when choices are made but they are not fixed beforehand and they become unfixed afterwards as well. This discussion includes an interesting topic that can be called the "non-identity problem" about capability.[16] This discussion, however, does not deny the significance and usefulness of the concept of individual capability and freedom as an opportunity set, for the following reasons.

First, if a person's capability consists of those alternatives that were available when she decided to choose for a reason, then the image of that capability can remain intact after choices are made and it can constitute an existential part of her individual identity. This image of capability can be a source of self-respect and self-valuation and it can lead to a sense of responsibility that is too strong sometimes.

Second, this image of individual capability can be an important factor in the design of public policy to realize the "right to well-being freedom." Even though we cannot predict changes in the opportunity set precisely, we can control their changes within certain limits and prepare multiple alternatives in advance so that choices can be redone afterwards within a restricted range. Suppose, for example, there is a person who escapes from domestic violence into a special facility, receives public assistance and care, and later leaves the facility by getting a job. We can claim that she should be entitled to receive a partial payment of public assistance to be off work while she is too ill to earn a living.

Third, a more fundamental reason lies in the meaning of "substitutability" attributed to the opportunity set. When someone loses, marginally, one unit of a good, how much of another good would she need to maintain the level of utility unchanged? The answer depends on the relative values she attaches to various goods (marginal rates of substitution among them, which can vary depending on their absolute levels). In an equilibrium, these rates should be equal to the relative market prices. This proposition, repeated often in this book, indicates that any good, however necessary and essential, can be substituted by another good. Some new, unexpected substitution might be possible, thanks to sheer chance, individual creativity, technological innovation, or product differentiation in the market. Can we say that "freedom as an

[16]Derek Parfit explains that different persons would be born in different results and hence it is difficult to judge different results from a point of view of the same person. (Parfit 1984).

opportunity set," explored in the literature on economics, means this substitutability in the beginning?

It is true that freedom as a substitutability may be possible only in a local, limited context. This is because individual choices are severely restricted by her social positions (school or workplace). A person cannot be free on the whole if her daily life is occupied by a series of trivial events, with restricted human relationships, goals, and tasks, and continues day in, day out, from today to tomorrow, alternating between joy and sorrow. It would be the same even if she occasionally dreams about a forgotten person and gets emotional or nostalgic, as long as the dream vanishes into air when she starts working in the morning as usual.

Let us suppose, however, this restricted freedom should give human lives some social and economic stability and, conversely, a local substitutability in this social and economic stability gives certain freedom to human lives. Then, what should a society care about? It should care about lack of the capabilities of people who cannot locate themselves anywhere in this largely free world, cannot survive with restricted freedom, or those who cannot exercise their freedom as substitutability while living in the market system full of differentiated goods and services, i.e. people who cannot improve their choice situations by themselves.

We can of course say that a person is perfectly free if she is not bothered by freedom as local substitutability but she can put herself outside the restricted free zone. We do not have to care about her but simply admire or respect her. Even so, we should care about her capability through an income transfer policy and other means if she still has some difficulties living in this world.

Chapter 3
Specification and Measurement in the Capability Approach

3.1 Similarities and Differences in Individual Capabilities

3.1.1 What Matters?

In July 2016, an awful crime happened in Japan in an institution for people with disabilities. Nineteen persons with the severest disabilities were killed by a man who had once worked there. Concerning the motive of the crime, the following words of the murderer were reported: "… because they are unhappy and they are useless."

This crime raised fundamental questions for people in society including the care-giving professions. One care-giver confessed that, "I have worked here to help people with disabilities, because they have special difficulties in their handicaps or impairments. Yet, I am worried that this "mindset to distinguish them from others might possibly turn into something negative, say, discrimination against them."

Without distinction and regarding all as fully equal, discrimination cannot happen, but then neither care nor assistance can be provided. If distinction is necessary for starting care or assistance, what should we do to prevent distinction turning into discrimination?

We can find two representative kinds of logic to respond to this difficult question. One is the logic that is argued by philosophers, which reminds us of a fact of continuity among persons as follows. "The fundamental facts of regarding disability: …all humans have capabilities that are defective in some regard, there being a continuum of disability" (Richardson 2006, 442). If persons with or without disabilities can be regarded as similar humans to one another, as the author points out, and be located on a continuous scale as exchangeable positions to one another, it is certain that discrimination against disabilities become factually impossible. This logic can be, moreover, expected to promote a universal acceptance of socially providing care as Nussbaum rightly points out:

> [I]f we recognize the continuity between the situation of people with lifelong impairments and phases of "normal" lives, we must also recognize that the problem of respecting and

R. Gotoh, *The Ethics and Economics of the Capability Approach*, Hitotsubashi University IER Economic Research Series 46, https://doi.org/10.1007/978-981-15-5140-6_3

> including people with impairments and the correlative problem of providing care…are vast, affecting virtually every family in every society (Nussbaum 2006, 101).

The logic of this kind has a considerable appeal and seems to be robust in its naturalistic foundation yet, I am afraid, it is fragile for two reasons. First, this logic grounds the norm of equality on our cognitive ability to recognize factual equalities among persons with or without disabilities. When we fail to recognize a factual equality for any two persons, this logic holds silent on the norm of equality or rather it justifies not applying the norm of equality to this case. Depending on the shortage of our cognitive abilities, such a case might occur in not a few probabilities, where someone might be legitimately discriminated against because of the lack of continuity with others.

Second, this logic treats differences only as a matter of degree and may give an illusion of exchangeability of individuals' situations (combinations of incomes, leisure, and abilities) depending on resource transfers. This illusion might cause people to fear endless competitions (See fear for "actual exchange of positions" argued in Sect. 2.2.1). Hobbes pointed that the "natural equality" brings about a situation, where "the weakest has strength enough to kill the strongest, either by secret machination, or by confederacy with others, that are in the same danger with himself" (Hobbes, *Leviathan*, XIII i).

Another representative form of logic is what is crystalized in the theoretical device of new welfare economics, that is, the assumption of interpersonal non-comparability, which makes it thoroughly difficult to say equal or non-equal for any two persons. For example, we can refer to the following words of Kenneth Arrow.

> If there is no empirical way of comparing two states (say, indifference curves of two different individuals), there can be no ethical way of distinguishing them. Value judgments may equate empirically distinguishable phenomena, but they cannot differentiate empirically indistinguishable states (Arrow 1963, 112).

Actually, this is a reason, explained by Arrow, that he adopts interpersonally non-comparable and ordinal individual preferences when he formulates social welfare functions that associate social preferences with individual values.

Note that logically these sentences include the following three statements. (a) We cannot differentiate empirical phenomena that can be regarded as neither equal nor unequal. (b) Without saying that, we cannot differentiate empirically equal phenomena.[1] (c) Furthermore, we can form a value judgement that equates empirically distinguishable phenomena, based on an ethical reason.

Let us make (a) the major premise of a syllogism, and make the hidden assumption of interpersonal non-comparability the minor premise of it. We can have a logical conclusion that we cannot differentiate persons with or without disabilities, because we cannot empirically distinguish them in their utilities.

---

[1](b) is pointed out by Sen (1986).

3.1.2 Liberal Equality Versus Diversity-Based Equality

This logical conclusion represents well the underlying idea of the new welfare economics, which requires fair participants in a general free competitive market system, as well as the political idea of *liberal equality* (Rawls 1971), which requires *non-discrimination* in public spheres including accesses to universal compulsive educations, fair employment, and other universal welfare benefits. It is certain that this logic provides a convincing reason for prohibiting discrimination based on differences, paying formally equal respect to individual diversity.

However, this logic does not help individuals to actively seek institutional compensation for their social or economic disadvantage, because it tends to close its eyes to diversities in society. For example, individual i would not have an obvious claim for resource transfer from individual j even when j is much wealthier than i. Any resource transfer from individual j to i can be criticized for net loss of total utility by transfer if the loss of individual j's utility is more than the gain of individual i's utility.

Rawls's theory of justice adopts an approach with ordinal and interpersonally comparable utilities and opens up a path to institutional compensation for social or economic disadvantages due to differences. Nevertheless, it is the differences in levels of social primary goods owned by various individuals that Rawls paid attention to. Difference in any other aspect is left out of the scope of his theory of justice. His words below prove this.

> I also suppose that everyone has physical needs and psychological capacities within the normal range, so that the problem of special health care and of how to treat the mentally defective do not arise. Besides prematurely introducing difficult questions that may take us beyond the theory of justice, the consideration of these hard cases can distract our moral perception by leading us to think of people distant from us whose fate arouses pity and anxiety. (Rawls 1975/1999b, 259 [1999b])

His remarks were heavily criticized by people who maintained discrimination against certain groups based on empirical distinctions, and also by people who wanted to claim social attention and assistance because, again, empirical distinction was possible. Sen was among the latter.

> ....[T]o take disabilities, or special health needs, or physical or mental defects, as morally irrelevant, or to leave them out for fear of making a mistake, may guarantee that the opposite mistake will be made. And the problem does not end with hard cases. The primary goods approach seems to take little note of the diversity of human beings (Sen 1980a/1997a, 366 [1997a]).

Social primary goods are supposed to be universally beneficial but distributive justice based on that concept tends to have a limited horizon looking only at already institutionalized rights. It might not be inclusive enough to deal with rare hard cases of severe disabilities or intractable diseases that are not yet fully institutionalized. In *Inequality Re-examined*, Sen justified unequal treatments favoring the disadvantaged.

> The powerful rhetoric of "equality of man" often tends to deflect attention from these differences. Even though such rhetoric (e.g., "all men are born equal") is typically taken to be part

> and parcel of egalitarianism, the effect of ignoring the interpersonal variations can, in fact, be deeply inegalitarian, in hiding the fact that equal consideration for all may demand very unequal treatment in favour of the disadvantaged (Sen 1992a, 1).

Chapter 6 will examine the scope of Sen's "equality of interpersonal variations (differences)" or "diversity-based equality." According to Sen, diversity includes "diversity of classification." In other words, existing categories are used to identify individual characteristics as well as social positions but they can be repeatedly challenged by and be often rearranged into new classifications. Note that personal activities of an individual to reintegrate her diverse identities in herself can lead to her trans-positional activities in public (Sen 1993b/2002a, 467 [2002a]).

3.1.3 Division Rules for the Equality of Differences

There are at least two ways to take individual differences into account. One way is to make sure that all individuals have "the same shortfall (absolute or proportionate) from their maximal attainment." Another way is to secure equal basic attainment for all, which actually demands "unequal treatment in favour of the disadvantaged." Sen calls the former *shortfall equality* and the latter *attainment equality*.

One strong argument against "attainment equality" is its alleged infeasibility. For example, Ronald Dworkin argues for equality of resources and against the capability approach because, according to him, the latter is not feasible or practical. Sen points out that "Ronald Dworkin argues against bringing in handicaps into the idea of equality of resources," because "[N]o amount of initial compensation could make someone born blind or mentally incompetent equal in physical or mental resources with someone taken to be normal in these ways" (Dworkin 1981b, 300; Sen 1997b, 321). Sen replied that if that is the case, we should try to maximize a disabled person's below-par functioning ability (Sen 1997b, 322). We can also refer to the following sentences.

> In the case of serious disabilities, attainment equality may be hard to achieve…but I would like to argue that it is not the case that the choice is made clear-cut simply by the non-feasibility of attainment equality. It can be argued that even when a disabled person cannot, in any way, be given the freedom to enjoy the same level of the functioning in question (e.g., the same ability to move about freely as others), there is nevertheless a good case—based on fairness—for trying to maximize his below-par functioning ability, rather than settling for the same shortfall (absolute or proportionate) as others have from their—much higher—maximal functioning (Sen 1992a, 91).

The distributive principle of "attainment equality" recognizes diversity among individuals, proposes (a list or levels of) basic values of freedom to be secured equally for anyone, and distributes more to disadvantaged people in order to realize those values.

3.1.4 Diversity as a Fact and Equality as a Norm

The utility approach in new welfare economics, as mentioned above and characterized by interpersonal non-comparability and complete orderings, gave logical support to the political idea of *liberal equality,* which calls for *non-discrimination* against "empirically indistinguishable" individuals.

In contrast, Rawlsian social welfare function (the difference principle), using complete interpersonal comparison of diverse situations of different individuals, brought about the political idea of *democratic equality,* which requires maximizing the expectation of the least advantaged (Rawls 1971a, 1999). This embodies ethics of full *exchangeability of positions* through social rearrangements of the distribution of "social primary goods."

It is certain that these theories have provided some normative foundation to support the market mechanism and universal welfare state policies that supplement it. Yet, these theories have often turned away from existing differences that are empirically distinguishable (claiming that it is possible to "treat them equally," that is, to ignore them after all).

In reality, the ethics of fully exchangeable social positions resulted in some perceptions of unfairness due to reverse discrimination and worsened incentive problems, and led to rolling back distribution policies according to differences.

In contrast, Sen's theory of capability-based diversity recognizes the plurality of spaces to understand human lives and make full use of the plurality of preferences and rankings, interpersonal comparability and non-comparability, incomplete orderings, and other factors, in order to help us to design distribution policies according to differences. Moreover, Sen's theory clearly shows that egalitarian policies according to differences are compatible with full recognition of the ultimate non-comparability of human existence, that is, the more fundamental equality norm.

Let us revisit the case introduced at the beginning. It seems to indicate that our society had the following structural problem with social evaluation that ultimately led to the tragic incident.

An interpersonal ranking of individual situations on a specific space within a particular range for a specific purpose tends to be transferred, without careful consideration, to any space for any range and further extended to a complete ranking of human values themselves. What is at stake is that this monistic structure (one-dimensional) of evaluation makes incomplete rankings on essentially different spaces internally consistent, which defines efficiency and measures social welfare including "real national income" accordingly. One of the social conditions that let the tragic case happen might be this monistic structure of evaluation itself.

In order to prevent "distinction" from turning into "discrimination," we need to recognize fundamental differences among individuals which lie behind interpersonal comparison and rankings and provide a basis for welfare policies. Moreover, we have to understand that interpersonal comparison of restrictions on various living functions should not, in any way, mean interpersonal comparability of human lives (human values) themselves and their potentials.

The statement that people with disabilities are unhappy can factually reflect disadvantages they are obliged to face in their functionings and capabilities, which society should pay attention to in choosing or reforming social policies, yet it cannot normally reflect any social evaluation (which is formed based on individual evaluations including the individuals with severest disabilities) that their lives are useless.

The capability approach allows us to make interpersonal comparisons based on distinctions for compensation policies. It urges us to be cautious about making judgements that can lead to discrimination. The capability approach shares the philosophy of freedom with political liberalism. Yet, we can say that it takes a great step from the "liberal equality" of Rawls and welfare economics to "equality of differences."

It is because, with the capability approach we can better understand concrete situations of individuals' difficulties in the space of basic well-being freedoms; moreover, we can rightly recognize the fundamental differences (non-exchangeability) and the fundamental equality (contingencies in our existences), starting from *diversity as a fact* and going toward *equality as a norm*. Let us move to the problem of specifying and measuring capability.

3.2 Preliminary Investigations for Modeling Individual Capability

3.2.1 Basic Formulation of the Capability Approach (Sen 1985a)

In *Commodities and Capabilities*, Sen begins Chap. 1with the following impressive words: "Much of economics is concerned with the relation between commodities and people. It investigates how people arrange to make commodities, how they establish command over ommodities, what they do with commodities and what they get out of commodities." However, "formal economics has not been very interested in the plurality of focus in judging a person's states and interests." Instead, economic analysis tries to "make do with one simple measure of a person's interest and its fulfilment. That measure is often called *utility*." (all the above quotations are from Sen 1985a, 1).

With this critical point of view in mind, Sen proposes an inclusive framework of economics, which can take into account "the plurality of focus in judging a person's states and interests" seriously. That is, namely, "the capability approach." The purpose of the following three chapters is to clarify the meaning of this statement by making the difference between the utility approach and the capability approach much clearer and is to examine the considerations of specifying and measuring capability, using simple economic modelling with some examples.

First, we confirm the skeleton of the capability approach formulated by Sen, which explicitly expresses important but usually hidden factors that intermediate commodities and utility. Let us denote the vector of commodities belonging to individual i by x_i, and the function to convert a commodity vector to a characteristic vector of commodities by $c(\cdot)$, and individual i's utilization function by f_i; then a vector of functionings b_i, which an individual achieves with his or her utilization function f_i and a vector of commodities x_i, is given by $b_i = f_i(c(x_i))$. In addition, the set of utilization functions and the set of commodities, from which individual i can choose a vector are denoted by F_i and X_i respectively. Then the individual's capability is defined as follows.

$$Q_i(X_i) = \{b_i | for\ some\ f(\cdot)_i \in \mathrm{F}_i\ and\ for\ some\ x_i \in X_i, b_i = f_i(c(x_i))\}.$$

$Q_i(X_i)$ is individual i's capability and reflects various combinations of functionings that she can achieve by changing choices of a commodity vector and a utilization vector. The value of the vector of functionings b_i is given by $v_i = v_i(f_i(c(x_i))$ with individual i's valuation function v_i. Interestingly, Sen distinguishes this valuation function v_i from the function $u_i = h_i(f_i(c(x_i))$, which tells us how *happy* the person is with the functioning vector.

Let us call the latter simply the happiness function. The difference between the happiness function and the traditional utility function $u_i = u_i(x_i)$ is obvious. The domain of the happiness function is functioning space, the same as the valuation function, while the domain of the traditional utility function is commodity space.

However, the difference between the value function and the happiness function is not obvious in their form. The difference is rather in philosophical meaning, which can give "the plurality of focus in judging a person's states and interests." Actually, Sen interprets the difference of philosophical meaning between the two functions as follows: "it [the happiness function] does not tell us how good that way of living is, or even how good a person himself thinks it is" (Sen 1985a, 8), yet the value function can. In other words, the valuation function is related to reflective activities, while the happiness function needs not be so (Sen 1985a, 19).

We will inquire into this point in more detail, focusing on the "positional objectivity" and "adaptive preferences" in Chap. 5. Here, let us introduce an example provided by Sen. That is, "a poor, undernourished person, brought up in penury, may have learned to come to terms with a half-empty stomach, seizing joy in small comforts and desiring no more than what seems *realistic*". Sen argues the following three points here.

- This mental attitude does not wipe out the fact of one's deprivation.
- It does not imply that the person would not value the removal of that deprivation.
- She may even see its value *ex ante* if the removal is seriously considered and examined as a possibility.

We should note that Sen proposes a framework that can explicitly formulate valuing activity as clearly distinguished from mental attitudes. The same person can have a mental attitude that seizes joy from deprivation and a valuation that desires the removal of that deprivation without contradiction, if the possibility of removal seems "realistic." With this consideration in mind, Sen warns that "*valuation neglect*, reinforcing *physical-condition neglect*, makes the utility-view of well-being fundamentally deficient," and asserts that "the functioning view has an easier run than the utility-view partly because it avoids premature fixity." (Sen 1985a, 20; italics in the original).

Note that avoiding "premature fixity" is an important attitude not only for researchers but also for people themselves. Sen points out thirdly that, for example, if one sees the value of "the removal of that deprivation" *ex ante*, she can express a value judgement that the situation experienced by her is nothing else than "deprivation," which should be removed in society. If this is the case, we can use an extended economic model, by expanding its framework so as to guarantee "the plurality of focus in judging a person's states and interests."

The above is the basic formulation of the capability approach presented by Sen. It has been developed in various forms of economic models such as production economy, consumption theory, social choice theory, and others. Most of these reformulations indicate that the capability approach can contribute to "the plurality of focus in judging a person's states and interests," which highly unified models in the traditional income and utility approaches cannot do. Among them, two articles are included in the Appendix.

3.2.2 Estimation of Unobservable Capability from Observable Functioning Vectors

Applying the capability approach requires us to consider the following problem. When can we observe a functioning vector of someone? How should we estimate her unobservable capability set based on her observed functionings? Moreover, how should we appraise the advantage or disadvantage of the functioning vector in comparison to her previous ones or those of other individuals?

For considering those questions, we simplify our analysis for a moment by assuming that preferences (or evaluations) behind individual choices are coherent in the commodity space and the functioning space. Then we can argue that an observed functioning vector should have been realized based on her maximization behavior to choose an optimal commodity vector and to convert it with her optimal combination of utilization ability. In this framework, we can have the following method to estimate individual capability.

The first is to directly measure the set of each individual's utilization abilities and the set of commodity vectors, and then theoretically estimate the set of her functioning vectors (i.e., capability) made available by her utilizing commodity vectors. To do so, we should assess the value of her resources such as income, time, personal assets, as well as national and local tax-benefit policies, and market prices of commodities, all of which restrict an individual's substantive opportunity set of commodities.

Moreover, we should observe the absolute and relative advantage of an individual's utilization abilities in producing plural kinds of functionings. Note that these advantages are here assumed to be comparable not only intra-personally but also inter-personally by using certain common scales.[2] Then we can estimate the maximum points of each functioning vector that she can really achieve by substituting different kinds of commodities and utilization abilities, which approximate the frontier of an individual's capability.

It would be difficult, however, to directly measure the set of each individual's utilization abilities for two reasons. One is a physical problem. A person's utilization ability is latent in itself, which can be recognized by herself and others only when she actually uses particular commodities or resources and converts them into certain functionings. The other reason is normative. Although utilization abilities are known to be changed depending on circumstances, they are essentially inherent characteristics of a person, which are taken as an individuality or personality. Therefore, a careless error or a slightest bias in their specifications and measurements might lead to an irreparable mistake that can harm her dignity.

We recall that one advantage of the capability approach is that it can leave aside the full, detailed picture of individuality or personality of individuals including innate characteristics, if any. Society is obliged to focus on a limited number of observable functionings that are relevant to each social context and are useful for making social policies. Taking this into account, we can think of two ways to constitute individual capabilities.

The first is to do interviews with different individuals and estimate their capabilities separately. We can regard their capabilities as a production possibility set with multi-dimensional functioning axes; then its frontier, the production possibility curve, can be directly estimated from marginal rates of transformation (MRT) among multi-dimensional functioning. MRT draws a trace of changing substitution rates of technologies in producing two kinds of functionings. It shows how many units' increase (or decrease) in function 2 would compensate for a marginal decrease (or increase) in function 1 with the same commodity vectors and utilization abilities.

If we consider a maximization problem that distributes two commodities to two abilities efficiently, given the production function of each ability, then we can draw a possibility frontier, each point of which represents an equilibrium between two abilities. The interviews are devised to capture functioning vectors that individuals could really achieve if they wished, rather than expected utilities under uncertainty.

The second way is a statistical method to approximate individual capabilities based on a data set related to achieved functionings of individuals who have a similar opportunity set of commodities and utilization abilities. Yet, individuals do various things by interacting with other individuals or environments, facing various social and natural contingencies. Some of their situations are similar to one another, and

[2]For example, the EQ-5D index is considered to objectively measure the following five items with the same scale: mobility, self-care, usual activities, pain/discomfort, and anxiety/depression. Mobility dimension asks about the person's walking ability while it introduces a sort of subjective evaluation into the weighing of these five items.

differences can be only a matter of quantitative degree, but the others are asymmetrically different depending on individuals' positions. For example, one might be seen as closely similar by another, while another be seen as totally different by oneself.

If this is the case, we should ask the following question again: how should we appraise its advantage or disadvantage in comparison with that achieved by others?

3.2.3 Inter-Personal Comparison

The clues of inter-personal comparison are, first, how to specify the *type* for which we can assume the similarity of the utilization abilities; and second, how to specify the *group* for which we can assume a common list of relevant functionings. Here the concepts of *type* and *group* are defined as follows (detailed characterization of *group* is in Chap. 6).

Type: A *type* is defined as a collection of people who have similar utilization abilities If any differences in achieved functioning vectors among individuals are regarded as reflecting only differences in their evaluation functions for substituting different kinds of functioning, they are classified as belonging to the same *type*.

Group: A *group* is defined as a collection of people who are different but are comparable in their types. More precisely, a group is defined as a maximal set of individuals, whose capabilities and utilization abilities can be compared as larger, smaller, or similar to one another. When all are interpersonally comparable, the group coincides with the universal set, and when all are not comparable, the group coincides with an individual.

Surely, in reality, there are some variations even among individuals of the same group or type, and they might possibly feel these variations within the same group or type more acutely than those across different ones. Moreover, an individual may belong to certain types of plural groups such as the heavily harmed type of atomic-bomb victims group or the lower-income type of single-mother group. Note that the group is an ethical concept, which can require compensation from society with fair reason.

For example, let us examine two functionings, "moving around" and "relaxing," of two hospitalized patients with the same illness. We can say each patient belongs to a different type in the same group if one has a high-utilization ability and another has a low one. Suppose they are offered the same nursing care services in quality and amount. Then, the different achievements of functionings among patients in the same type are socially neglected because it can be interpreted as being chosen from the same capability, while the different achievements of functionings among patients in the different type are compensated by differentiating the quality or amount of nursing care services regardless of individuals' subjective feelings.

We need to study how to classify individuals into groups and types in terms of both theoretical and statistical validities. In practice, we can make use of some social or natural attributes such as sex, age, disease, and disability, but their validity and significance must always be questioned. An extreme case can be when each type consists of just one individual. This means that individual utilization abilities are qualitatively different and interpersonally not comparable for the moment. What is important is, however, that if we can specify an individual as being qualitatively different from others in her utilization ability, we should classify that person as a member of a certain group, because someone may appear who has similar utilization abilities that at least can be comparable to that of another.

3.2.4 *Setting up the Functioning Space: Selecting a List of Functionings*

Practical application of the capability approach has the following additional challenges. (a) What functionings should constitute individual capability (selection problem)? (b) By what criteria should we weight different functionings (scale problem)?

Concerning the first question,Martha Nussbaum among others (Nussbaum 2000) has explored what kind of capability we should focus on and has tried to establish a universal list for functionings, based on Aristotelian philosophy,[3] whereas, in his article "Equality of What?", Sen asserts that, "Discussions in moral philosophy have offered us a wide menu in answer to the question: equality of what?" (Sen 1980a/1997, 353 [1997]). Sen's tentative answer in the article was not resources nor utilities, but basic capabilities should be our focus.

However, Sen himself has not changed his opinion that such a list cannot be determined theoretically or a priori but should be determined according to the particularities of issues and the context, and that the agenda and procedure should be open to public reasoning (Sen 2004). Combining both arguments, let us briefly note some considerations that we should take into account in examining a list of functionings.

There are two problems. First, functionings that are once selected into the list come to be socially recognized as definitely valuable and important in society, while those that are not selected into the list are due to be easily neglected and devalued. Second, the conceivable candidates of functioning lists tend to be consciously or subconsciously restricted to those that have already had corresponding social institutions (formal or informal).

The first problem is essentially serious, as laws and rules are always accompanied by an "invariant requirement" (Sen 1977a). This requirement demands, quite naturally, that two objects, x and y, should be treated in the same way, J, if they belong to the same information set I. The implication is rather strong, however. Let x and y be two individuals for example. They are going to be treated in the same way as long as they are regarded as the "same" in certain aspects, even if they are quite different in other aspects. Meanwhile, they are going to be treated in a different way if regarded

[3]On this issue, see, Kuklys 2005; Kim 2007; Coast et al. 2008; Coast et al. 2008a, b; Claassen and Rutger 2011; Comim and Nussbaum 2014.

as different in some focal aspects, even if they have many common features in the other aspects.

Behind this argument of Sen's there is the following idea. Equality in one sphere (information set) can lead to inequality in another. For example, equality in opportunity for education can lead to inequality in wage rates according to productivity. Equality in wage rates, in turn, might lead to inequality in satisfaction according to preferences. Then, what should we look at when discussing equality?

The second problem can be illustrated as follows. When a social inhibition says that public assistance should be spent only on consuming minimum necessities (e.g., minimum eating, clothing, housing), the "doing and being" deemed unnecessary (e.g., "taking part in a social activity" or "saving for the future") might be excluded from the selected list of functionings. Or, if the range of rehabilitation is restricted to standard activities shared among instructors, then "doing" such as "playing with birds and cats," or "participating in public reasoning" might not be selected into the list.

If this is partly due to lack of knowledge or information (on the part of instructors or the individual involved), then updating the current list of functionings based on further public discussion and reasoning has an implication of a fight against such a situation. Philosophical explorations of the universal list by Nussbaum and others can be interpreted to be a reference point for this fight.

In summary, specifying a functionings list not only clarifies the purpose of underlying social institutions but also visualizes the limit of their scopes and depths. It can also indicate that even rich lists of functionings are short of people's actual livings and capabilities. It is crucial to acknowledge these implications when making or improving a list of functionings. With this note in mind, let us examine more practical issues for applying the capability approach in the following section.

3.3 Towards Practical Application of the Capability Approach

3.3.1 What Matters Again

As has been explained so far, according to the capability approach, concepts of political philosophy such as individual freedom, rationality, efficiency, fairness, equality, equity, and justice can be redefined. And alternative social policies are evaluated in terms of their consequential influences (restrictions, expansions, and so on) on individuals' capabilities. In the following sections, we give a clearer perspective for practical applications of the capability approach and examine the methodological problems inherent in measuring individual capability, with several illustrative examples.

3.3.2 An Example

A functioning vector is a combination of plural functionings measured at different magnitudes of achieved levels. Suppose, for example, we focus on two actions, "write" and "move," and measure their achieved levels by units of hours. Someone spending long hours on commuting to work used to achieve 6 units of both "write" and "move." However, the figures subsequently became 10 for "write" and 1 for "move" after the individual suffered a severe lumbar spine injury. Later they changed to 7 for "write" and 2 for "move" after special transportation service became available. In this example, (6,6), (10,1), and (7,2) represent the functioning vectors achieved in three different situations, corresponding to, respectively, pre-injury, post-injury, and when special transportation service becomes available.

Note that we can think of many ways to measure various functionings. It is not necessary to make all different functionings comparable (by using the common unit of exchange) inter-personally nor intra-personally, nor to make each functioning cardinal (thereby making their differences and proportions meaningful). We can simply assume ordinal measurement (making only orders across alternatives meaningful), or we can assume incompleteness on neither inter-personal nor intra-personal comparability.

A functioning vector is "achievable" when (a) its realization is not prevented by external interference by others, i.e., the negative freedom is guaranteed, and (b) external and internal conditions and means necessary to realize it have positively been provided. Then the "capability" of someone at a certain point in time is the set of various functioning vectors achievable for an individual by changing the way she chooses resource allocation and a utilization ability at that time.

In the example above, she can achieve a maximum of 12 units of "writing" (and 0 units of "moving") if she devotes all her resources and utilization abilities to "writing." If she spent all of them on "moving," she could have achieved 10 units of "moving" (and 0 units of "writing"). After her injury, she could still achieve "writing" for 12 units (0 for "moving") but the maximum units for "moving" decreased to 1 unit (0 for "writing"). Now, it has increased to 2 units after a public care vehicle became available (0 for "writing") (Figs. 3.1, 3.2 and 3.3).

Consider that the functioning vectors achievable after her injury were also achievable before. Then we can describe her capabilities in the three situations as follows.

Pre-injury: { (12, 0), (10, 1), (7, 2), _(6, 6)*, (0, 10),_ (7, 1), (6, 1), (0, 2), (0, 1)}.

Post-injury: { (12, 0), (10, 1)**, (7, 1), (6, 1), (0, 1)}.

Public care vehicle: { (12, 0), (10, 1), [(7, 2) * **, (0, 2)], (7, 1), (6, 1), (0, 1)}.

Note: "{ }" indicates a set; *, **, and *** indicate they are achieved functioning vectors. The italicized pairs were achievable before her injury but not afterwards. Those in the box became unachievable after injury but achievable with a public care vehicle.

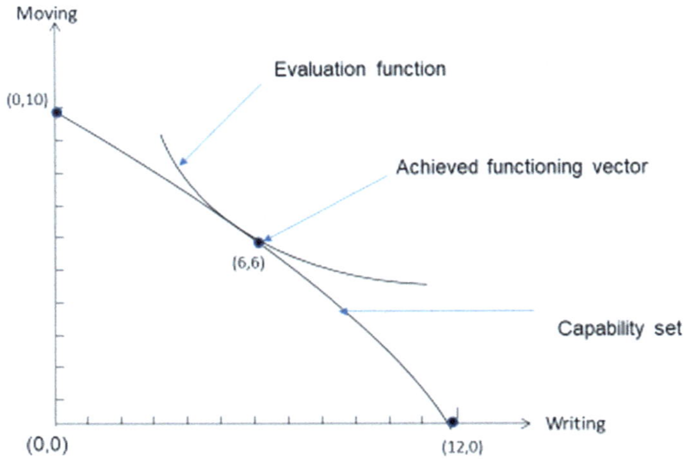

Fig. 3.1 Capability set, evaluation functions, achieved functionings before injury

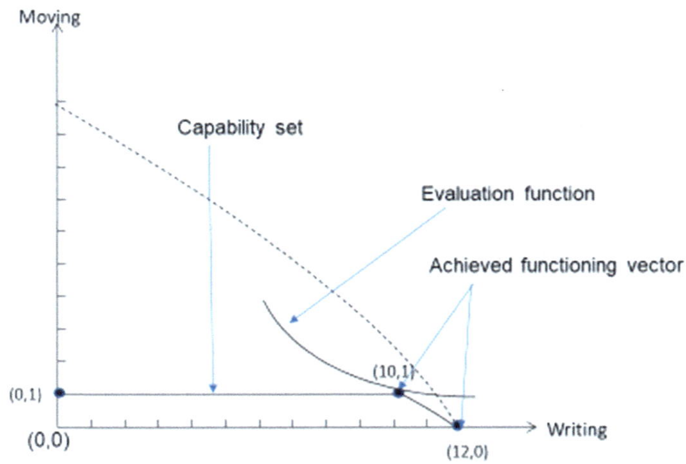

Fig. 3.2 Capability set, evaluation functions, achieved functionings after injury

Finally, "evaluation" is explained in relation to the following questions. The person in this example had achieved (6, 6) before being injured. Why did she increase "writing" and achieved (10, 1) after injury? Did her injury suddenly lower her evaluation of "moving" and increase the one for "writing"? If so, why did she cut down on "writing" and achieve (7, 2) after the service of a public care vehicle was provided by society?

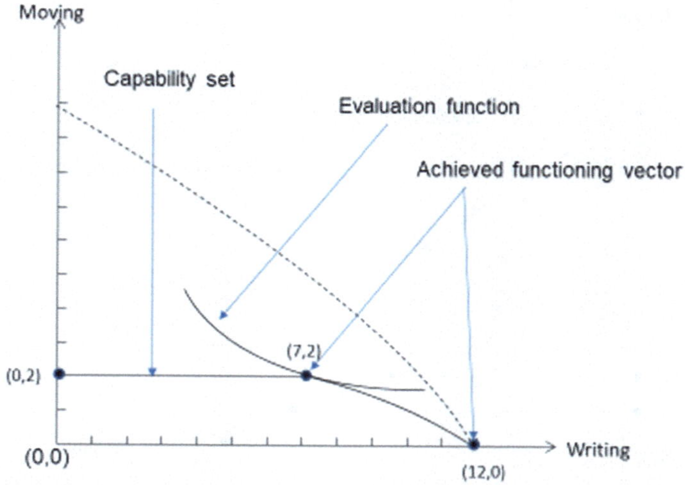

Fig. 3.3 Capability set, evaluation functions, achieved functionings with public care vehicle after injury

Suppose, in the example illustrated in the figures above, the person has the following evaluation function, which indicates a pattern of rankings for various functionings vectors. Note that V(*x*, *y*) is a numerical value of the vector (*x* amount of writing, *y* amount of moving) and " > " implies the left hand is higher in evaluation than the right hand.

$$V(6,6)* > V(7,\ 2)** > V(10,\ 1)*** > V(12,\ 0),$$
$$V(0,\ 10) > V(7,\ 1) > V(6,\ 1) > V(0,\ 2) > V(0,\ 1),$$
and V(12, 0) and V(0, 10) are not comparable.

We can see that her evaluation function suggests the maximum (optimal) values attainable from her corresponding capability sets under three situations (pre-injury, post-injury, and with a public care vehicle). With an evaluation function (a pattern of rankings), different choices were made under different situations, not because her evaluation function changed but because her "capability" itself was altered (see Fig. 3.4).

Figure 3.5, in contrast, shows a case where the individual evaluation function changes because of injury. In this case, with a newly formed evaluation function, the individual ranks her post-injury optimal functioning vector higher than her pre-injury one. Hence, we can say that she came to prefer much more writing and less moving. This interpretation, however, might overlook the problem of "adaptive preference formation" (discussed in more detail in Chap. 4). That is, there is a risk of resolving an internal conflict by adapting her evaluations (preferences) to the reduced capability after injury. If she says that she does not desire for her pre-injury optimal functioning

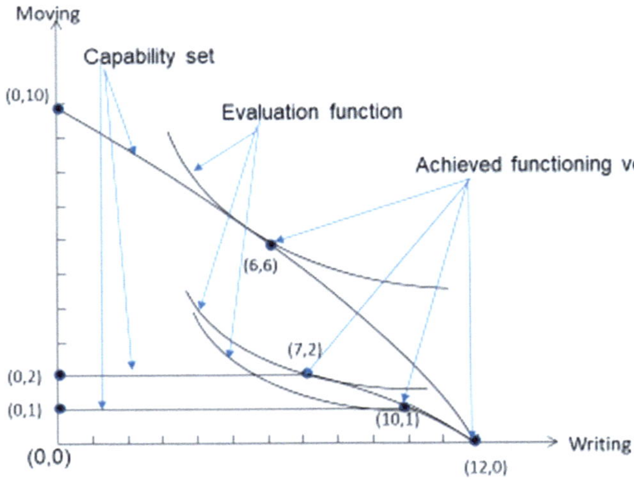

Fig. 3.4 Capability set, evaluation function, achieved functionings before injury, after injury, with public care vehicle

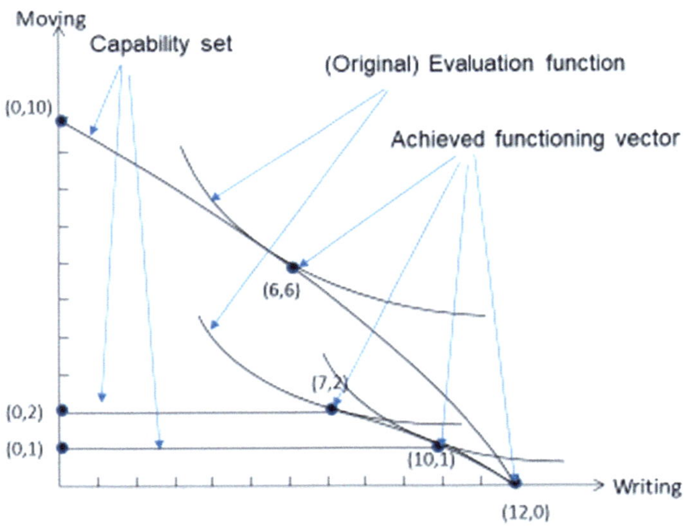

Fig. 3.5 Capability set, evaluation functions, achieved functionings before injury, after injury, with public care vehicle (evaluation function has changed between before and after)

vector anymore, we cannot conclude that society need not provide services such as a public care vehicle for increasing "going out/moving around."

Note that, first, these choices do not always have to be based on an individual's own evaluations. We can use evaluations reasonably formed by a reliable third party that fully take into account the individual's own interests. This is because, on the functioning space, the third party might be able to approach her objective interest better, although this has to be done carefully. The third party has to maintain good communication with her, in case there should be a gap between their evaluations and her own will. Second, previously we made some discrete sketches of someone's capability, focusing on the two functionings, "writing" and "moving." In the case of resources such as time or money, however, individual functionings and capability are assumed to change more continuously. The economic model of capability discussed in Chap. 4 is relevant to those cases.

3.3.3 Practical Meaning of the Concept of Capability

Now, what does the concept of capability, defined above, mean in practice? Here we briefly illustrate practical meanings of the concept, taking note of some of its features common to similar concepts such as power, right, obligation, control, and choice.[4]

A person's capability is a set of available functioning vectors, which represents her real freedom as opportunity to achieve functionings (doings and beings), realized by two means of resources and their utilization abilities. Sen points out that "freedom in general and agency freedom in particular are parts of an effective *power* that a person has" (Sen 2009, 271). What does it mean? We can explain the meaning, borrowing the concept of "decisive power" from social choice theory. This concept indicates that a part of social status, in which both "well-being freedom" and "agency freedom" are secured for an individual, would be changed depending only upon her will. (See Chap. 7).[5]

Her capability also reflects her *right* because it can impose some obligations on others and society so as not to interrupt her choices from her capability.[6] In addition, a person's capability represents also *obligation*. Sen notes that "it would be a mistake to see capability, linked with these ideas of freedom, only as a notion of human advantage, it is also a central concern in understanding our *obligation*." (Sen 2009a, 271, emphasis added by the author).

Meanwhile, the idea of freedom here does not necessarily imply her exclusive *control*. Instead, someone else can have reason to choose on her behalf by understanding her reason to choose. This means there is room for external intervention in the allocation of resources and the choice of utilization abilities available to her. It is

[4]Cohen 1993; Comim and Nussbaum 2014; Comim, Qizilbash and Alkire 2008; Deneulin 2002.

[5]This idea is closely related to the concept of *empowerment*. See UNICEF (1994), for example.

[6]For instance, it can be institutionalized as the "right to well-being freedom" or, simply, the "right to well-being." See Gotoh 2016a.

similar when the act of "choosing" itself can be regarded as a functioning. Suppose there is a person very happy "not to have to make a choice," but his or her achieved level of well-being might be higher by "choosing" him- or herself with assistance in choosing itself.

For example, here is someone who does not want to leave his room to take a bath in a nursing home. This would be his choice. One day, by chance, we find him somehow relieved when an assistant nurse helps him bathe. Apparently, he feels rather uneasy to be naked and alone. It is clear that his capability for "bathing" can be expanded with more services available to him. He might choose to "bathe" more often even though his relative evaluation for bathing remains the same.

Let me add that this case continues as follows. Now the person can bathe accompanied by an assistant whenever he wishes. Nevertheless, one day, he does not want to take a bath. He seems to be well, physically and mentally, with no sign of illness or injury. On that day, he seems more comfortable staying in his room in his favorite clothes instead of bathing and feeling clean. Tomorrow, he might make a different choice. He would need some resources including specific facilities, personal assistance, familiar furniture, the usual clothes, his own room, and so on, in order to achieve a certain level regarding bathing or resting. This example illustrates how we can observe changes in his "preference" or "evaluation" with some added resources (personal assistance), and see when intervention should happen. The concept of capability provides this perspective by shedding light on his potential functionings available to him behind those actually achieved by him at the moment.

3.3.4 Procedures to Form Social Evaluation

Now we look at some problems of intra- and interpersonal comparison of individual capabilities in a practical context. Suppose there are several alternative ways for assistance (positive or negative) and their advantages are to be assessed, and partially ranked, not by their effects on income, costs of assistance, or utility, but by the changes of their capabilities. It would then be necessary to weight individual capabilities of one person over time or across different persons. We explore this problem by looking at the design of regional public transportation service (RPTS).

Apparently, easy activities like shopping, going to a hospital, or visiting a friend can be quite difficult for some people. They might have a visual impairment, spinal damage, ineligibility for a driver's license, or no accompanying family member, and these factors can make them rather reluctant to go out at all. It is possible that some of them do not like shopping, do not need to go to a hospital, or have no friend to visit, and hence do not complain about being unable to go out. Actually, some people manage to use their private goods at hand to compensate for the lack of an RPTS. Yet, at the same time they might worry that it is not manageable by themselves in the near future. Or some people not only cannot manage it, but they suppress their desire to go out, and thus become a recluse.

The number of the latter group of withdrawn people might still be relatively small, but they should not be ignored or dismissed in a just society. In order to address these concerns, we advance our analysis by setting a goal of an RPTS policy as follows: Securing for all residents basic capability for going out/moving around, regardless of differences in their endowed private goods or utilization abilities.

3.3.5 Securing for All Residents Basic Capability for Going Out

As resources adequate to realize moving around, the following can be selected: income and wealth; human resources; time resources. In addition, we need to pay attention to the following point. Even if the levels and contents of an RPTS provision are common to all local residents, the accessibility of an RPTS can vary across individuals, depending on fares, locations of stops, frequencies and timetable, number of transfers, congestion, speed, and such factors. Especially, locations of stops, frequencies, and timetable may well make an RPTS an "indivisible" good with excludability and rivalry in its consumption.

This point indicates that differences in accessibility for individuals can cause discontinuous gaps in individual mobility capabilities. If individuals share the same burden (e.g., prices and taxes) to maintain an RPTS, this can cause a strong sense of unfairness among people. To begin with, individual differences in accessibility, if ad hoc, can cause a problem with "efficiency." For example, healthy regular commuters, on the one hand, can enjoy a high level of accessibility to RPTS while being worried about lack of exercise. On the other, sickly individuals with weak legs may have to keep struggling with a low level of accessibility. This situation can be improved for all, without making anyone worse off, by changing locations of stops or the timetable. This is a case of the Pareto improvement, that is, society is improved in terms of efficiency.

When there is no obvious room for the Pareto improvement as, for example, healthy commuters can become worse off by changed locations of stops, we would need a criterion of fairness for judging which of the two groups should be given priority. Actually, we have already stipulated the following law. "If requested by an elderly pedestrian, a pedestrian with a physical disability, or any other pedestrian with difficulty using the road who is crossing or attempting to cross the road, an officer or *any person who happens to be present at that location* must instruct, signal, or take other appropriate measures in an effort to ensure that the pedestrian is able to cross the road safely."[7] (emphasis added by the author).

Unfortunately, this law has not yet so much prevailed in society. What should we do for promoting people to take actions based on this law? This should be a theme for social choice based on individuals' public judgements and reasoning.

[7] Article 14: Protection of the Visually Impaired, Children Not Yet of School Age, the Elderly, and Others, "Road Traffic Act".

3.3.6 Substitution of Functionings with Resource Constraints and Individual Valuation

The idea behind capability measurement is that we should respect individual preferences, will, and freedom of choice about various combinations of functionings that are deemed reasonable for herself as well as for public reasoning in a society. Actually, it is noted that, although different functionings may have different and independent values, the level of achievement of different functionings can be replaced by one another in terms of individual evaluations of their values, given resource constraints (money, time, human assets, and so on). A decreased level of one functioning can be substituted for by an increased level of another, keeping unchanged the total amount of resources and of individual valuations.

Meanwhile, we must note that individual capabilities are characterized by various sorts of personal and social factors. Those factors partially depend on social institutions including informal social inhibitions and partially depend on her choices based on the individual's valuation functions. Therefore, in order to secure for all residents a minimum capability for going out or moving around, regardless of differences in their endowed private goods or utilization abilities, we should carefully examine whether or not an individual does have a capability from which she can actually choose.

For example, here is a person with a high achievement in the functioning "going to a hospital." This does not necessarily mean she has abundant resources available to her. Nor does it necessarily mean she has a biased preference for going to a hospital compared with enjoying shopping or meeting people. This can be rather explained by the following reason. She suffers from a chronic illness and needs regular treatment. Hence, her regular visits to a hospital with a public care vehicle can easily be approved by the public. However, unfortunately she cannot expect public understanding for enjoying shopping or meeting friends with a public care vehicle. Under this circumstance, if she chooses to go to a hospital more often than usual, that does not mean she is relatively rich in her resources or she evaluates going to a hospital relatively higher than other functionings.

Take another example. Suppose we find that someone goes out much less frequently than before and much less than others in society. Traditional economics would typically give the following interpretations to this observation. Her recent tendency for staying at home more often than going out reflects merely her change of preference, which is responsible for her to form. Alternatively, her recent tendency can be based on her rational choice to decrease the burden on her utilization ability by refraining from going out. These interpretations are partly correct, but also grounded on misunderstandings of her real situation.

For considering these problems, let us summarize this chapter by introducing a few results of our recent research (Kambayashi et al. 2020) which, by applying the capability approach, tentatively investigates the quality of "going out/moving around" (dis)enjoyed by elderly persons and persons with disabilities.

3.3.7 List of Utilization Abilities and Functionings for Going Out/Staying In

Based on the capability approach, we find the following conjectures.[8] First, one's diminished utilization ability of "going out" can lower the quality of "staying in" as well, which induces difficulties in environments, difficulties in social relations, and difficulties in individualities or personalities. Second, actually individuals tend to feel more difficulties in social relations when they are "staying in" than when they are "going out." Third, less activity of "going out" tends to bring about lower achievements in functionings such as realizing one's aims, promoting one's health, socializing with others, becoming excited or delighted, and so on. Thus we conclude that it is risky to take individual choice as given and trust her rational behavior entirely. In fact, finding a low frequency of someone's going out suggests that we pay closer attention to a potential lack of her capability itself, including the alternative of staying in too.

This problem cannot be separate from the kind of list of functionings we should be concerned about in considering social policies. In Kambayashi et al. (2020), in order to grasp individuals' utilization abilities, we used the following three medium-size categories as approaching individuals' actual experiences from the negative side (namely, more experiences imply fewer utilization abilities). That is,

- *how much difficulty in environments* (e.g., Managing level differences, Moving quickly in a risky situation) *did you experience*?
- *how much difficulty in social relations* (e.g., Striking up a casual conversation with others, dealing with other people's attitudes or remarks) *did you experience*? and
- *how much difficulty in individualities or personalities* (e.g., Withstanding sudden fatigue or a pain, Keeping your body and mind in a good condition) *did you experience*?

Moreover, in order to grasp individuals' capabilities, we used the following ten small-size categories which approach individuals' actual experiences from the positive side (namely, more experiences imply higher achievements). That is,

- I had a sense of security and relaxation on the whole;
- I had a sense of being myself and being comfortable;
- I did not incur too much burden including financial costs;
- I more or less realized what I wanted to;
- I felt good and healthy about my body and mind;
- I maintained a sense of control;
- I had some stimulating new experience or perspective;
- I had some unexpected encounter or discovery (person, view, streetscape, etc.);

---

[8]The following passages are based on Kambayashi et al. (2020).

- I was refreshed, enjoyed, or smiled;
- I talked and socialized with people.[9]

In summary, identifying a person's capability has an operational meaning of understanding the whole set of her achievable functioning vectors, under the restrictions of resources and utilization abilities available to her, by controlling the effects of her evaluations. There might be an opportunity set, from which an individual apparently seems to be able to choose, but actually it is very difficult for her to choose. This is the theme that we will discuss in the next two chapters.

[9]In analyzing, we combined these ten into several medium-size categories.

Chapter 4
An Economic Modeling of Individual Capability

4.1 Introduction: Fractal Structure of Individual Capability

As we discussed earlier, individual capability is defined as an opportunity set of the functioning vectors available to an individual under resources (commodities) and utilization functions (abilities) that she can actually choose. She can freely choose and realize what types of functionings to what extent, as long as they are in her capability set, from which an individual can actually choose to do or be. For example, she can choose how far to move safely by transportation or how long to relax and spend time in her room. However, it is not obvious how to formulate it in specific terms.

For example, the question arises: How should we judge whether she can actually choose, or, whether she could have really chosen some functioning vectors? What are the criteria to cut the responsibility of an individual's choice from her non-responsible capability, the shortage of which can legitimately form the basis of claims of compensation policies or social assistance from society? This is the question of the identification of capability as a substantive opportunity of the individual to choose.

To answer the question, this chapter first formulates an individual's capability based on the traditional economic model as a maximization problem. In this model, it is assumed that individuals try to choose optimal options to maximize their utilities, given systems of well-ordered free competitive markets with private ownership.

The general feature of the traditional economic model is in simultaneously capturing an individual's *subjective* evaluations and her *objective* constraints under the assumption of individual rationality. By extension from the commodity space to the functioning space, an individual's rationality can be in a parallel way re-defined as choosing optimal functionings subject to constraints according to her own evaluation function. If it is the case, the structure of the capability model remains essentially the same as the structure of the utility approach. Could we be satisfied with this result?

Here, we should recall that each functioning vector itself represents the life of an individual who "has reason to choose," and that the value of a functioning vector

R. Gotoh, *The Ethics and Economics of the Capability Approach*, Hitotsubashi University IER Economic Research Series 46, https://doi.org/10.1007/978-981-15-5140-6_4

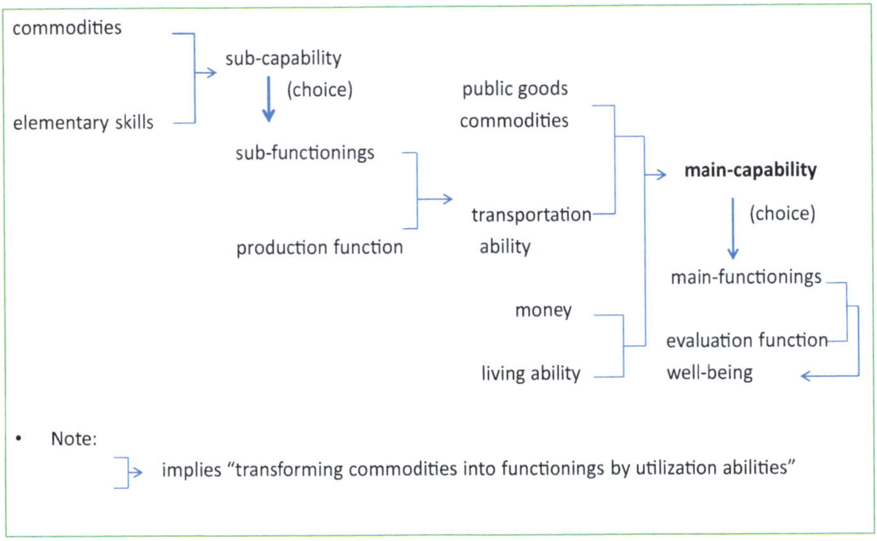

Fig. 4.1 Fractal structure of an individual's capability

can be an object of public concern and respect apart from her self-cognition. This is a characteristic of the capability approach, which is clearly distinguished from the utility approach.

Furthermore, our interest is in the problems of "adaptive preference" or "positional objectivity," regarding the inner relation between choice and opportunity, which might go beyond the dichotomy of *subjectivity* and *objectivity*, or *responsibility* and *non-responsibility*. Re-examination of these problems would help us to understand the methodological limit of the traditional economic model in measuring individual capabilities.

To re-examine the inner relation between choice and opportunity, this chapter focuses on, so to speak, the fractal structure of capability such that: an individual's capability in the main space of functionings is produced by transforming commodities with her *utilization ability*, while her *utilization ability* is produced by transforming *sub-functioning vectors* with her *production function*, while her *sub-functionings vector* is produced by transforming commodities by her general basic *skills*,[1] and so on. In sum, the level of an individual's capability is surely constrained by her total resources and skills as usually understood in economic models, yet there are various intermediate factors between capabilities and constraints.

This and the following section illustrate the structure by taking persons with limited vision as an example, and by focusing on their main functionings such as "moving by transportation" (T_i) and "decent living"(L_i). The following figure (Fig. 4.1) indicates the skeleton of the structure.

[1]In this chapter, the distinction of "functionings" and "sub-functionings" is only for analytical purposes. It does not mean that "sub-functionings" are in any way lower or less important than "functionings" in terms as examples of morality or aesthetics.

Before moving to the explanation of the structure of the model in the following two sections, let us note the relationship of my research to previous economic research in similar areas.

4.2 Relevance to Previous Economic Theories

4.2.1 "Compensation and Responsibility" or "Equality of Opportunity"

First, we must mention the relationship between the capability approach and the theory of "compensation and responsibility" (Dworkin 1981a/1981b, 2000; Fleurbaey 1994, 1995a/1995b; Maniquet 2004; Fleurbaey and Maniquet 2011). The latter (on compensation and responsibility) illustrates the reach of recent *fairness studies* in welfare economics and in analytical ethics (Arneson 1989). The main proposition of the theory is that society should only compensate "inequality of outcome" derived from factors for which agents are non-responsible, such as "circumstances," but it should not compensate for inequalities of outcome derived from factors for which agents are responsible, such as autonomous "choices." This theory is not sympathetic to "equality of welfare" but to "equality of opportunity for welfare," where "opportunity" in this context is defined as a fundamental opportunity, which does not include any influence of individual choices, which bring about arrays of opportunities to be realized later (Arneson 1989; Roemer 1998).

Indeed, if we can exclude from an individual's capability the influence of every choice and responsible factor, "equality of capability" can be defined in such a way that only the shortage of an individual's capability compared to "basic capability" deserves compensation, while the choice of functionings from her capability should be kept within her responsibility without any compensation, even if the results turn out to be highly restrictive of capabilities available later in her life.

In conclusion, we cannot formulate "equality of capability" as an Arneson type of "equality of opportunity" on the basis of which the criteria "compensation and responsibility" can straightforwardly be applied. This is mainly because, while the latter concentrates on a theoretical conceptualization of an ideal state that removes every influence of choice on the "opportunity set," the former aims at making incomplete comparisons between opportunities and choices at different stages.[2]

Yet, it is certain that we need some criteria if we try to measure the shortage of individuals' capabilities that can legitimately claim compensation policies for society, respecting differences of *individuality* in their abilities (including bodily or habitual propensities) and choices. In this context, this chapter adopts Sen's idea of "positional objectivity" (1993b/2002a), which indicates that an observation, claim, belief, or

[2]In a sense, the latter corresponds to "transcendental approach" in the dichotomy provided by Sen in *The Idea of Justice* (Sen 2009a), while the former corresponds to the "comparative approach".

action is regarded as "positionally objective" if it can be recognized through a bundle of parameters such as place, generation, race, gender, impairments, disabilities, and so on.

In this chapter, a *position* is defined operationally such that *difference of positionality* can allow institutional interventions, while *difference of individuality* requires refraining from institutional interventions. Practically, the two concepts are interrelated in that, once a factor of *individuality* is recognized as an object of a social support, it promotes the emergence of a new category of *position,* which allows institutional interventions.

4.2.2 The "Consumption as Production" Approach Proposed by Becker and Lancaster

Second, in modeling an individual's capability, paying attention to *subjectivity* and *objectivity*, we can refer to the "consumption as production" Approach (Lancaster 1966) represented by the *characteristic* theory *à la* Kelvin Lancaster (Lancaster 1966), Gary Becker's conception of "small factory" and "implicit market" (Becker 1965), and "household production approach" in general (Muellbauer 1974b; Pollak and Wachter 1975).

For example, (a) the scheme of iso-quant curves in a production factor space represents the *substitutability* (the marginal substitution rates) among factors for producing a certain good; (b) the frontier of an individual's opportunityset represents the *objective* level of the goods and resources and the *substitutability* (the marginal transformation rates) among goods, from which an individual can choose given his or her own skill and market prices; (c) the scheme of indifference curves over goods represents the *subjective* relative value among goods (the marginal substitution rates) and the *subjective* absolute level of each good. Note that the former two are interpersonally comparable, while the latter is usually interpersonally non-comparable.

Becker's concept of "small factory" represents household activity as "production functions" that produce "commodities" such as "seeing a play, which depends on the input of actors, script, theatre, and the playgoer's time," by combining time and market goods. Households choose the best combination of these commodities in the conventional way by maximizing a utility function subject to a budget constraint with an expenditure function and bounded resources. Moreover, interestingly, Becker explicitly tries to measure "psychic income (non-pecuniary income)," which brings about additional utility for a household through, for example, taking a pleasant job in preference to a better-paying unpleasant one or employing unproductive nephews. We can interpret "commodities" in Becker's approach as "functionings" in Sen's approach, to the extent that at least in their basic structure they are close to each other.

Yet, Sen and Becker part company in the evaluation of "commodities" and "functionings." Sen criticizes Becker (1976) in Sen (1985a), clarifying the difference between "commodities," which one can "produce" or "own," and "functionings," which are nothing but one's "state of existence." Actually, Becker assumes that "a unified treatment of all substitutions of nonpecuniary for pecuniary income" is possible, because "time can be converted into goods through money income" (Becker 1965/1995, 498). In Becker's scheme the values of "commodities" and their opportunities are fully decomposed and finally reduced to market prices and wages (called "full prices"), and their usefulness is instrumentally understood in terms of contributing to "work productivity" in the market as indicated by the concept of "human capital."

Whereas in Sen's scheme the values of "functionings and capabilities" can rarely be reduced to mono-layered indices such as market prices or wages, they are open to plural evaluating views and processes according to their meanings and usefulness in the actual lives of individuals. For example, the price of "moving by transportation" is different between persons with limited vision and persons without limited vision, if we include not only time and money but also safety or self-respect in the price. In this sense, the capability approach extends traditional consumer theories toward understanding diverse individuals' doings and beings with multiple criteria of evaluations.[3] In addition, the capability approach makes it possible to more carefully examine the relationship between an individual's evaluation (preference) to choose and his or her real opportunity (or restriction) to choose.

4.3 Basic Model

In analyzing capability of persons with limited vision in the context of modern Japanese society, we select, first, "moving by transportation" and "decent living" as the main functionings and focus on the structure of the former. Second, we assume that the *transportation ability* (called *trans-ability*) for "moving by transportation" is produced by the two sub-functionings of "accessing information technology (IT)" and "communicating in public," which embody more universal and abstract concepts of functionings such as "the sense of orientation" and "the cognition of distance."

The function (called "production function") that transforms sub-functionings into the *trans-ability* is different among individuals but can be assumed to be interpersonally comparable such that individuals who have a driving license and a car are advantaged relative to those who do not. Furthermore, we assume the same function to be shared by persons endowed with certain common characteristics such that persons with limited vision usually cannot drive a car or ride a bike; they need to use public transportation to move with the appropriate support of information.

With a certain production function the maximum level of the *trans-ability* is constrained by the opportunity set of sub-functioning vectors (called *sub-capability*).

[3] In reconsidering the foundation of the methodological framework of economics, Sen points out the fact that the motivation of individual activities can go beyond self-interest, self-welfare, or self-goals (Sen 1987a).

In the simplest case, an individual *sub-capability* is defined in the space of "accessing IT" (y axis) and "communicating in public" (x axis), whose upper bound is represented as a linear *iso-cost curve*. Let us describe it formally.

4.3.1 Definition of Sub-Capability

Suppose a society which consists of n-number of individuals (that is, $N = \{1, \ldots, n\} (n \geq 2)$, $where\, i \in N)$,then an individual *sub-capability* is articulated in this way[4]: denote two kinds of commodities by z_1, z_2; the skill to transform $z_1$into *sub-functionings* x_1, x_2 by a_1, b_1, the skill to transform $z_2$into *sub-functionings* x_1, x_2 by a_2, b_2; the market prices of commodities z_1, z_2 by p_1, p_2; the private resources (income, time, personal assets including family support) by y, and the public goods and social assistance by y_0, where a_j, b_j, z_j, p_j, y and $y_0 (j = 1, 2)$ are non-negative real number. Then, we have the following formulation, which represents *sub-capability*.

$$p_1 z_1 + p_2 z_2 \leq y + y_0, \text{ where } z_1 = a_1 x_1 + b_1 x_2,\, z_2 = a_2 x_1 + b_2 x_2$$
$$\text{That is, } (p_1 a_1 + p_2 a_2) x_1 + (p_1 b_1 + p_2 b_2) x_2 + y_0. \tag{4.1}$$

The equation part of this formulation expresses so to speak the *iso-cost curve*. It indicates the absolute ease or difficulty of an individual's realization of "accessing IT" or "communicating in public," given her command over commodities represented by the resource constraint and given her ability to use them. It also indicates her individuality, the relative ease or difficulty of an individual (the "marginal transformation rate" of two sub-functionings). Given this curve as an upper boundary, an individual can achieve various combinations of sub-functionings by changing the way of using commodities or her skills. For simplicity, in the following analysis we assume that $z_{i2} = a_i x_{i1}, z_{i2} = b_i x_{i2}$, then an individual i's *sub-functioning capability* is defined as: $p_Z(a_i x_{i1} + b_i x_{i2}) \leq y_i + y_0$. In Fig. 4.2, the *sub-functioning capabilities* of individual 1 (who is better than 2 in skill for accessing IT) and 2 (who is the opposite) are written.

4.3.2 Production Function of Transportation Ability and Optimal Point

Next, denote the amount of *transportation ability* by t_i and the production function by f, which produces *transportation ability* t_i using two sub-functionings x_{i1},x_{i2}. That is: $t_i = f(x_{i1}, x_{i2})$, where, the partial derivatives of t_i with respect to both x_1

[4]In defining Eq. (4.1), for simplicity, we omit the sign of an individual i.

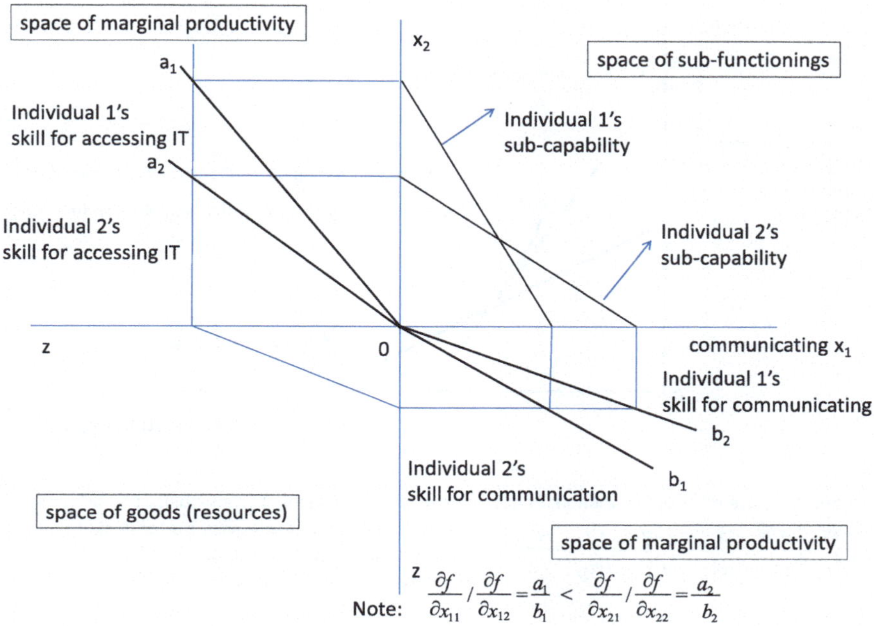

Fig. 4.2 The "fractal" structure of capability (spatial representation)

and x_2 are non-negative.[5] We assume the strict quasi-concavity of function f. Then, the problem to *choose the optimal sub-functionings for maximizing transportation ability* t_i under the constraint of resources and skills of an individual is formulated as:

$$\begin{aligned} &\text{Max.}\, t_i = f(x_{i1}, x_{i2}), \\ &\text{s.t. } p_Z(a_i x_{i1} + b_i x_{i2}) = y_{iz} + y_{0z}. \end{aligned} \tag{4.2}$$

To resolve this, let us construct a Lagrangian function with Lagrangian multiplier λ. That is, $\mathrm{L} = f(x_{i1}, x_{i2}) + \lambda\{y_{iz} + y_{0z} p_Z(a_i x_{i1} + b_i x_{i2})\}$. By differentiating this function partially with respect to x_{i1}, x_{i2} and λ, we obtain

$$\begin{aligned} &\frac{\partial f}{\partial x_{i1}} - \lambda p_Z a = 0, \\ &\frac{\partial f}{\partial x_{i2}} - \lambda p_Z b = 0 \\ &y_{iz} + y_{0z} = p_Z(a_i x_{i1} + b_i x_{i2}). \end{aligned} \tag{4.3}$$

[5]The marginal rate of technical substitution (RTS) can be deduced from a total differentiation of $t = f(x_{i1}, x_{i2})$ by assuming that $dt_i = \frac{\partial f}{\partial x_{i1}} dx_{i1} + \frac{\partial f}{\partial x_{i2}} dx_{i2} = 0$.

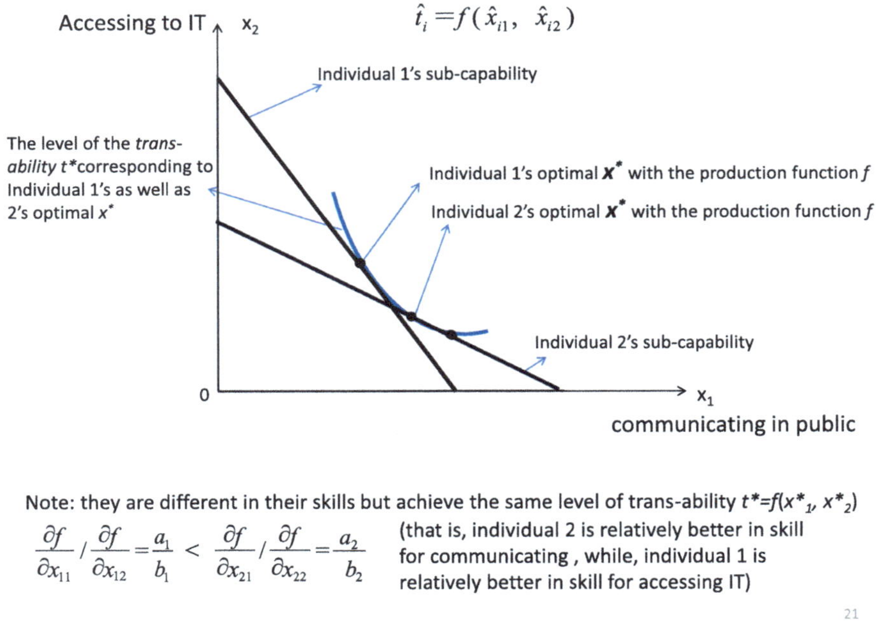

Fig. 4.3 Iso-quant curves, iso-cost curves, production function, and optimal points

Then, the first condition of maximization is such that $\frac{\partial f}{\partial x_{i1}} \Big/ \frac{\partial f}{\partial x_{i2}} = \frac{a_i}{b_i}$. For example, suppose that f is represented by a Cobb–Douglas function: $t = Ax_1^{\alpha}x_2^{1-\alpha}$, where A represents a coefficient of technology. Then the first condition of maximization is $\frac{\alpha x_1^{\alpha-1}x_2^{1-\alpha}}{(1-\alpha)x_2^{-\alpha}x_1^{\alpha}} = \frac{a_i}{b_i}$. Let us denote a sub-functioning vector that satisfies the first condition as x^* and denote the corresponding level of *transportation ability* by t^*, where $p_Z(a_i x_{i1}^* + b_i x_{i2}^*) = y_{iz} + y_{0z}$ and $t_i^* = f\left(x_{i1}^*, x_{i2}^*\right)$ holds.

In Fig. 4.3 iso-cost curves of two persons with limited vision, individual 1 and individual 2 such that $\frac{\partial f}{\partial x_{11}} \Big/ \frac{\partial f}{\partial x_{i2}} = \frac{a_1}{b_1} < \frac{\partial f}{\partial x_{21}} \Big/ \frac{\partial f}{\partial x_{22}} = \frac{a_2}{b_2}$ (that is, individual 2 is relatively more skilled in communicating, while individual 1 is relatively more skilled in IT) and the iso-quant curve that is common to them is written in the space of the "accessing IT" functioning and the "communicating in public" functioning. In addition, the maximal achievements of individual 1 and individual 2, which must be realized if they undertake these behaviors, are indicated.

4.4 Formulation of the Main Capability

We are ready to define the main capability, which consists of the main functionings of "moving by transportation" and "decent living". Actually, that capability has a structure similar to the structure of the aforementioned sub-capability.

Denote firstly "moving by transportation" of an individual i by T_i, the private commodities (for example, personal human supports) available for "moving by transportation" by r_i, public goods (for example, transportation systems) available for "moving by transportation" by r_0. Then, $T_i = t_i(r_i, r_0)$, where T_i, r_0 and r_i are non-negative and t_i is strict quasi-concave, that is, $\frac{\partial t_i}{\partial r_i} > 0$, $\frac{\partial t_i}{\partial r_0} > 0$, $\frac{d}{dr_i}\left(\frac{\partial t_i}{\partial r_i}\Big/\frac{\partial t_i}{\partial r_0}\right) < 0$. Secondly, let the "decent living" of an individual i by L_i, the private commodities for decent living be m_i, and the *utilization ability for decent living* (in brief, *living ability*) be l, which is assumed to be common among persons with limited vision. Then, $L_i = l(m_i)$, where L_i and m_i are non-negative, and the partial derivative of l with respect to m_i is positive and l is strict quasi-concave. Moreover, denote the total personal resources of an individual by $\overline{y}_i$ and total public resources available for her by $\overline{y}_0$, which are supposed to be fixed. As mentioned in the previous model, two skills a_i, b_i for transforming one commodity z into *sub-functionings* (x_{i1}, x_{i2}) and a production function f for transforming x_{i1}, x_{i2} into *transportation ability* t_i as well as the prices, p_z, p_r, p_0, p_m respective to z, r_i, r_0, m_i are fixed. Besides, we assume that an individual takes a maximization behavior in transforming *sub-functionings* into *trans-ability*, thus, x_{i1}, x_{i2}, and t_i are optimal (denoted by $x_{i1}{}^*, x_{i2}{}^*, t_i{}^*$) with regard to the production function f, given the amount of goods $\overline{z}_i$, then an individual i's main-capability is defined as a subset of the space of two-dimensional real numbers, $C \subset R_+^2$.

Definition (*Main functionings capability*) Given $x_{i1}^*, x_{i2}^*, t_i^*$ such that $t_i^* = f\left(x_{i1}^*, x_{i2}^*\right)$, $\overline{z_i} = a_i x_{i1}^* + b_i x_{i2}^*$ and given $p_z, p_r, p_0, p_m, \overline{y}_i, \overline{y}_0$and $\overline{z}_i$,[6]

$$C = \{(T_i, L_i)|T_i = t_i^*(r_0, r_i), L_i = l(m_i), p_z\overline{z}_i + p_r r_i + p_0 r_0 + p_m m_i \leq \overline{y}_i + \overline{y}_0\}. \tag{4.4}$$

Set C can be expressed as an *implicit function* $F_i\ (T_i, L_i; r_i, r_0, m_i) = 0$, which represents a kind of *joint production* that produces two kinds of production, T_i, L_i, by using production factors r_i, r_0, m_i. By the assumption that t_i and l are strictly quasi-concave, we can easily check that $F_i$is also strictly quasi-concave and set C is strictly concave for the origin.[7]

Moreover, denote the profit that an individual can obtain through her producing T_i, L_i as $\pi = Q_{Ti}T_i + Q_{Li}L_i - p_r r_i - p_r r_0 - p_m m_i$, where Q_{Ti}, Q_{Li} represent the

[6]We assume that set C satisfies the following conditions: (1) if resources or utilization abilities are zero, C is reduced to the origin (of the coordinate axes), (2) C is bounded and closed set, (3) C is comprehensive set.

[7]That is, $-\frac{dL_i}{dT_i} = \frac{\partial F_i}{\partial T_i}/\frac{\partial F_i}{\partial L_i} > 0$ and $-\frac{d^2L_i}{dT_i^2} = \frac{d}{dT_i}(\frac{\partial F_i}{\partial T_i}/\frac{\partial F_i}{\partial L_i}) < 0$.

shadow price of T_i, L_i, the meaning of which is explained later. With this model, let us assume that an individual performs a maximization behavior as a producer, that is, she chooses a main functionings vector, aiming at maximizing her profit. That is,

Definition (*Maximization problem as producer*) Given f, l, a_i, b_i and prices p_z, p_r, p_0, p_m, and $\overline{z}_i$, $\overline{y}_i$, $\overline{y}_0$.[8]

$$\begin{aligned} &\text{Max.}\,\pi = Q_{Ti}T_i + Q_{Li}L_i - p_r r_i - p_r r_0 - p_m m_i \\ &\text{s.t. } F_i(T_i, L_i; r_i, r_0, m_i) = 0. \end{aligned} \tag{4.5}$$

Then, we can construct a Lagrangian function with the Lagrangian multiplier λ as follows.

$$\begin{aligned} \mathrm{L} &= Q_{Ti}T_i + Q_{Li}L_i - p_r r_i - p_0 r_0 - p_m m_i + \lambda F_i(T_i, L_i; r_i, r_0, m_i). \\ &= Q_{Ti}\cdot(t_i^*(r_0, r_i)) + Q_{Li}\cdot(l(m_i)) \\ &\quad - p_r r_i - p_0 r_0 - p_m m_i + \lambda F_i(t_i^*(r_0, r_i), l(m_i); r_i, r_0, m_i). \end{aligned} \tag{4.6}$$

For simplicity, let us assume that $p_0 = 0$. Then, by differentiating this function partially with respect to r_i, m_i, T_i, L_i, and λ, we obtain,

$$\begin{aligned} &Q_{Ti}\left(\frac{\partial t_i}{\partial r_i}\right) - p_r + \lambda\left(\frac{\partial F_i}{\partial t_i}\Big/\frac{\partial t_i}{\partial r_i} + \frac{\partial F_i}{\partial r_i}\right) = 0 \\ &Q_{Li}\left(\frac{\partial l_i}{\partial m_i}\right) - p_m + \lambda\left(\frac{\partial F_i}{\partial rl}\Big/\frac{\partial l}{\partial m_i} + \frac{\partial F_i}{\partial m_i}\right) = 0 \\ &Q_{Ti} + \lambda\frac{\partial F_i}{\partial T_i} = 0 \\ &Q_{Li} + \lambda\frac{\partial F_i}{\partial L_i} = 0 \\ &F_i(t_i^*(r_i), l(m_i); r_i, m_i) = 0. \end{aligned} \tag{4.7}$$

Then the first-order conditions of the maximization of profit are as follows.

$$\begin{aligned} &\frac{\partial F_i}{\partial r_i}\Big/\frac{\partial F_i}{\partial m_i} = \frac{p_r - Q_{Ti}\left(\frac{\partial t_i}{\partial r_i}\right)}{p_m - Q_{Li}\left(\frac{\partial l}{\partial m_i}\right)}, \\ &\frac{\partial F_i}{\partial T_i}\Big/\frac{\partial F_i}{\partial L_i} = \frac{Q_{Ti}}{Q_{Li}}. \end{aligned} \tag{4.8}$$

The former condition means that the marginal rates of transformation of commodities r_i, m_i with regard to the function F_i are equal the ratio of their discounted prices of commodities, where the discount factors are (i) the marginal productivities of

[8]"s.t." = "subject to".

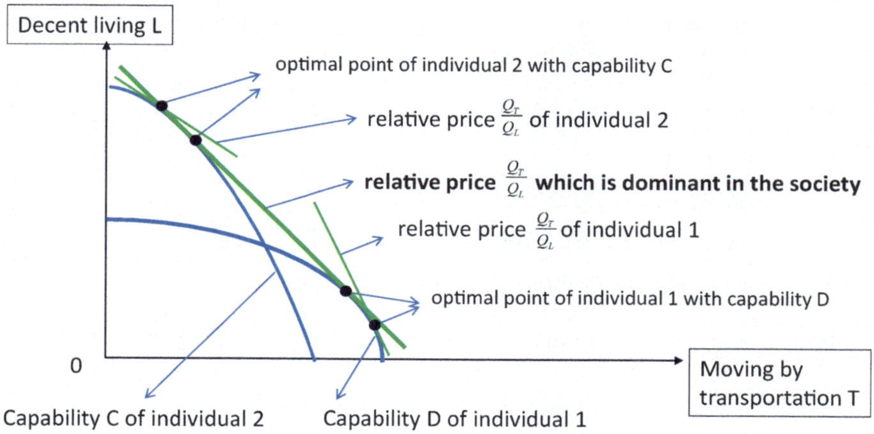

Fig. 4.4 Relative price (shadow price) between functionings

goods for *utilization abilities*, and (ii) the *shadow prices* of the functionings T_i, L_i. The latter condition implies that the marginal rate of transformation between two functionings T_i, L_i equals the ratio of the *shadow prices* of the functionings T_i, L_i.

Note that while the concept of "shadow price" often implies a hidden cost for converting certain things to other things,[9] here it represents more directly a *relative value* of functionings, which reflects a certain criterion based on an individual's personal goal or social norms. For example, in a society where "moving by transportation" is necessary for "working," and "working" is regarded as necessary for "independence", the relative price of "moving by transportation" for "decent living" $\left(\frac{Q_T}{Q_L}\right)$ shared by the majority becomes higher (See Fig. 4.4). It may induce some conflicts between the minority and the majority with regard to dominant social norms in a society. In the following section, let us introduce an individual's well-being evaluation function h_i, which captures an individual's goal that determines the relative value of main functionings.

4.5 Maximization Model with Capability Constraints

Let us define an individual's *well-being evaluation function* by h_i. Denote an individual's *well-being* by w_i, then h_i is expressed as $w_i = h_i(T_i,\ L_i)$, where w_i, T_i, L_i are non-negative and the partial derivative of h_i with respect to T_i, L_i are positive. Assume that an individual i maximizes her well-being evaluation function h_i subject to her capability constraint, given that an individual has chosen an optimal sub-functionings

[9]In the previous model, the marginal rate of technological substitution (RTS) of $t = f\ (x_{i1}, x_{i2})$ is interpreted to be a *shadow price* in this sense.

vector and achieved optimal utilization ability $(x_{i1}^*, x_{i2}^*, t_i^*)$ corresponding to it. Then the maximization problem can be expressed as follows.

Definition (*Maximization model with capability constraints*) Given $x_{i1}^*, x_{i2}^*, t_i^*$ such that $t_i^* = f\ (x_{i1}^*, x_{i2}^*)$, $\overline{z}_i = a_i x_{i1}^* + b_i x_{i2}^*$, and given $p_z, p_r, p_0, p_m, \overline{y}_i$ and $\overline{y}_0$,

$$
\begin{aligned}
&\text{Max. } w_i = h_i(T_i, L_i), \text{ where } T_i = t_i^*(r_0, r_i), L_i = l(m_i)\\
&\text{s.t. } F_i(T_i, L_i; r_i, r_0, m_i) = 0, \text{ where } p_z\overline{z}_i + p_r r_i\\
&\quad + p_0 r_0 + p_m m_i = \overline{y}_i + \overline{y}_0.
\end{aligned}
\tag{4.9}
$$

Then, we can construct a Lagrangian function with the Lagrangian multiplier λ.

$$
\text{L} = h_i(T_i, L_i) + \lambda F_i(T_i, L_i; r_i, r_0, m_i).
$$

By differentiating this function partially with respect to T_i, L_i, and λ, we obtain the first condition of maximization as follows.

$$
\frac{\partial h_i}{\partial T_i} \Big/ \frac{\partial h_i}{\partial L_i} = \frac{\partial F_i}{\partial T_i} \Big/ \frac{\partial F_i}{\partial L_i} \tag{4.10}
$$

This indicates that the marginal substitution rate of main functionings with respect to an individual's well-being evaluation function equals the marginal transformation rate of main functionings, which, by connecting with the above discussion, equals the rate of *shadow prices* of the functionings $\left(\frac{Q_{Ti}}{Q_{Li}}\right)$. Note that this equation can be re-written as $\text{L} = h_i\ (t_i^*\ (r_0, r_i), l(m_i)) + \lambda F_i\ (t_i^*(r_0, r_i), l(m_i); r_i, m_i)$. For simplicity, assume $r_0 = 0$. By differentiating this function partially with respect to r_i, m_i, and λ, we obtain

$$
\begin{aligned}
&\frac{\partial h_i}{\partial t_i}\cdot\frac{\partial t_i}{\partial r_i} + \lambda\left(\frac{\partial F}{\partial t_i}\cdot\frac{\partial t_i}{\partial r_i} + \frac{\partial F_i}{\partial r_i}\right) = 0\\
&\frac{\partial h_i}{\partial l_i}\cdot\frac{\partial l}{\partial m_i} + \lambda\left(\frac{\partial F}{\partial l}\cdot\frac{\partial l}{\partial m_i} + \frac{\partial F_i}{\partial m_i}\right) = 0\\
&F_i(t_i^*(r_i), l(m_i); r_i, m_i) = 0.
\end{aligned}
\tag{4.11}
$$

Thus, we obtain $\frac{\partial F_i}{\partial r_i} \Big/ \frac{\partial F_i}{\partial m_i} = \frac{\partial h_i}{\partial r_i} \Big/ \frac{\partial h_i}{\partial m_i}$ as the first condition of maximization. By combining this condition with the previous discussion, we have

$$
\frac{\partial h_i}{\partial r_i} \Big/ \frac{\partial h_i}{\partial m_i} = \frac{\partial F_i}{\partial r_i} \Big/ \frac{\partial F_i}{\partial m_i} = \frac{p_r - Q_{Ti}\left(\frac{\partial t_i}{\partial r_i}\right)}{p_m - Q_{Li}\left(\frac{\partial l}{\partial m_i}\right)}. \tag{4.12}
$$

This equation implies that the marginal rate of substitution between r_i, m_i, with regard to an individual's *well-being function* h_i equals the marginal rate of transformation between r_i, m_i with regard to her *joint production function* F_i, and both of which equal the ratio of the marginal productivities of the goods estimated by the *shadow prices* of main functionings. Let us denote goods that satisfy those conditions by $r^*{}_i$, $m^*{}_i$, then optimal main functionings and optimal *well-being* corresponding to them can be written as $T_i^* = t_i^*\left(r_0^*, r_i^*\right)$, $L_i^* = l(m_i^*)$ and $w_i^* = h_i(T_i^*, L_i^*)$.

In addition, if the hypothesis that an individual chooses optimal sub-functionings based on the *production function* is removed, the Lagrangian function is rewritten as $\mathrm{L} = h_i\ (f\ (x_{i1}, x_{i2})\ (r_0, r_i), l(m_i)) + \lambda\ F_i(f\ (x_{i1}, x_{i2})\ (r_0, r_i), l(m_i); r_i, m_i)$, then we obtain $\frac{\partial h_i}{\partial x_{i1}} \Big/ \frac{\partial h_i}{\partial x_{i2}} = \frac{\partial f}{\partial x_{i1}} \Big/ \frac{\partial f}{\partial x_{i2}} = \frac{\partial F_i}{\partial x_{i1}} \Big/ \frac{\partial F_i}{\partial x_{i2}}$ as the first condition of maximizing $w_i = h_i(T_i, L_i)$. If we combine this with $\frac{\partial f}{\partial x_{i1}} \Big/ \frac{\partial f}{\partial x_{i2}} = \frac{a_i}{b_i}$ (the first condition of maximizing $t_i = f(x_{i1}, x_{i2})$ based on an individual's production function f), we obtain $t_i = t_i^* = f\left(x_{i1}^*, x_{i2}^*\right)$. The cases where an individual does not choose optimal sub-functionings with the *production function* will be examined below.

4.6 Maximization Model with Resource Constraints

Next, let us formulate a more traditional model in which an individual maximizes her *well-being evaluation function* under resource constraints and determines the optimal sub-functionings and optimal (main) functionings simultaneously as a reference.

Definition (*Maximization problem with resource constraints*) Given f, l, a_i, b_i and prices $p_z, p_r, p_0, p_m, \overline{y}_i$ and $\overline{y}_0$,

$$\begin{aligned} \text{Max. } w_i &= h_i(T_i, L_i), \text{ where } T_i = t_i(r_0, r_i), \\ L_i &= l(m_i), t_i = f(x_{i1}, x_{i2}), z_i = a_i x_{i1} + b_i x_{i2} \\ \text{s.t. } & p_z z_i + p_r r_i + p_0 r_0 + p_m m_i = \overline{y}_i + \overline{y}_0. \end{aligned} \tag{4.13}$$

Note that, first, in this model an individual's well-being does not depend on main capability but on main functioning vectors; second, this model is indeed different from the traditional consumer model in the domain of an individual's well-being evaluation function, but is similar to the traditional model in that the constraints that the object function explicitly faces is resources-as-usual models. To solve this maximization problem, let us construct the following Lagrangian function with the Lagrangian multiplier λ.

$$\begin{aligned} \mathrm{L} &= h_i(T_i, L_i) + \lambda(\overline{y}_i + \overline{y}_0 p_z z_i - p_r r_i - p_0 r_0 - p_m m_i) \\ &= h_i(t(r_0, r_i), l(m_i)) + \lambda(\overline{y}_i + \overline{y}_0 p_z z - p_r r_i - p_0 r_0 - p_m m_i) \\ &= h_i(f(x_{i1}, x_{i2})(r_0, r_i), l(m_i)) \end{aligned}$$

$$+\lambda(\overline{y}_i + \overline{y}_0 p_z(a_i x_{i1} + b_i x_{i2}) - p_r r_i - p_0 r_0 - p_m m_i).$$

By differentiating this function partially with respect to x_{i1}, x_{i2}, r_i, $m_i$and λ, we have the following equations.

$$\begin{aligned}
&\frac{\partial h_i}{\partial f(x_{i1}, x_{i2})} \frac{\partial f(x_{i1}, x_{i2})}{\partial x_{i1}} - \lambda p_z a_i = 0\\
&\frac{\partial h_i}{\partial f(x_{i1}, x_{i2})} \frac{\partial f(x_{i1}, x_{i2})}{\partial x_{i2}} - \lambda p_z b_i = 0\\
&\frac{\partial h_i}{\partial t_i}\frac{\partial t_i}{\partial r_i} - \lambda p_r = 0\\
&\frac{\partial h_i}{\partial l}\frac{\partial l}{\partial m_i} - \lambda p_m = 0\\
&p_z \overline{z}_i - p_r r_i - p_0 r_0 - p_m m_i = \overline{y}_i + \overline{y}_0.
\end{aligned} \tag{4.14}$$

Then, we can have the following first conditions of maximization.

$$\begin{aligned}
&\frac{\partial h_i}{\partial x_{i1}} \Big/ \frac{\partial h_i}{\partial x_{i2}} = \frac{\partial f}{\partial x_{i1}} \Big/ \frac{\partial f}{\partial x_{i2}} = \frac{a_i}{b_i},\\
&\left(\frac{\partial h_i}{\partial t_i} \cdot \frac{\partial t_i}{\partial r_i}\right) \Big/ \left(\frac{\partial h_i}{\partial l} \cdot \frac{\partial l}{\partial m_i}\right)\\
&= \frac{p_r}{p_m}, \text{ that is, } \frac{\partial h_i}{\partial r_i} \Big/ \frac{\partial h_i}{\partial m_i} = \frac{p_r}{p_m}.
\end{aligned} \tag{4.15}$$

The former condition implies that the marginal substitution rate of sub-functionings with regard to h_i and the marginal rate of productivity of sub-functionings with regard to$f$ equals the ratio of the skills for sub-functionings.[10] The latter condition means that the ratio of the marginal substitution rates of commodities equals the ratio of their prices. By comparing this with the condition that is obtained by the model with capability, we have the following proposition. That is,

Proposition 1 Given that an individual shows a maximization behavior based on the well-being evaluation function defined on main-functioning vectors. Then, the difference between the "maximization model with capability constraints" and the traditional "maximization model with resource constraints" is recognized in the following two points.

(1) The "maximization model with resource constraints" brings about solutions that satisfy the Pareto efficiency with regard to resource allocation.

---

[10]More precisely, individual skills that are estimated by the prices of commodities.

(2) The "maximization model with capability constraints" does not bring about solutions that satisfy the Pareto efficiency with regard to resource allocation.

Proof

(1) The "maximization model with resource constraints" requires the ratio of the marginal substitution rates of goods to equal the ratio of their prices, that is,

$$\frac{\partial h_i}{\partial r_i} \Big/ \frac{\partial h_i}{\partial m_i} = \frac{p_r}{p_m},$$

(2) The "maximization model with capability constraints" requires $\frac{\partial F_i}{\partial r_i} \Big/ \frac{\partial F_i}{\partial m_i} = \frac{p_r - Q_{Ti}\left(\frac{\partial t_i}{\partial r_i}\right)}{p_m - Q_{Li}\left(\frac{\partial l}{\partial m_i}\right)}$, the marginal rates of transformation of goods r_i, m_i with regard to the function F_i to equal the ratio of their discounted prices of goods, where the discount factors are (i) the ratio of the marginal productivity of goods for *utilization abilities*, and (ii) the *relative value* (*shadow prices*) of the functionings T_i, L_i.

Proof The first point is obvious. And, we can easily confirm that if the *relative value* of functioning, or, the ratio of the marginal productivities of commodities for *utilization abilities* is neglected, both models coincide with each other in the second point.

4.7 Concluding Remarks

The analysis in this chapter can be summarized as follows. Suppose we use equations to derive functioning vectors from commodity vectors converted by individual utilization abilities and expand both opportunity sets of commodity vectors and individuals' utility functions whose domain is commodity vectors. Then we can obtain equations where individuals maximize their evaluation functions, whose domain is the functioning vector, with their opportunity sets of functioning vectors, i.e., capabilities. This equation at a glance seems to express a sort of super-rational model of individuals, who choose the optimal commodity vectors in order to maximize their functioning evaluation functions, constrained by three conditions imposed by the market with private ownership, that is, commodity prices, individual incomes, and utilization functions.

What this chapter makes clear is, first, that formulating the capability approach in this super-rational manner would not bring any structural change to the formula of the traditional utility maximization model. Not only that, it looks as if it contributes to enriching information for the domain and constraints of the utility approach and accordingly strengthens individual rationality. Then, some might conclude that there is no justification to intervene in those "equilibrium solutions" in the economy, at least in terms of efficiency. For example, if an individual has an integrated rational preference evaluation, some inhumane situations for her, such as domestic violence, overwork, isolation, and malnutrition, might be regarded as a result of her overall optimizing behavior over the course of her life.

However, an individual may well form an evaluation function over the functioning space, which is different from a mere extension of utility function defined over the commodity space. Her cognitive structure to perceive the functioning space can have different features from those for the commodity space. The optimal commodity vector actually chosen might not correspond well to the functioning vector judged as optimal based on an evaluation function over the functioning space. For example, a woman bears obstinate interventions from her husband, since she personally highly estimates a lawful married status and a traditional family model. Yet, suppose she acquires the critical concept of domestic violence and understands that any woman including herself should not accept it in terms of protecting basic capability which includes *the sense of security* and *the sense of self-respect* in addition to *decent living*. This knowledge might push her to form an evaluation function, which finally indicates an optimal commodity much different from before.

What this chapter also shows, second, is that the capability approach can actually go beyond the commodity space and provide a new perspective to review the wholeness of diverse spheres of human lives, the whole length of individual life-stages, and the overall picture of potentialities people have, in terms of what they can do and what they can be. The capability approach has a unique feature and cannot be reduced to the utility approach even from the point of view of efficiency.

Chapter 5
Philosophical Modification of the Economic Modeling of the Capability Approach: Adaptation, Positionality, and Identity

5.1 Introduction: Nested Relation Between Individual Choice and Opportunity

Chapter 4 raised a theoretical and practical question about how we can identify individual capability while paying attention to her choice. We also undertook a critical examination of the representation of individual capability described by the economic model of optimization (constrained utility maximization). This chapter inquires into a critical examination of traditional economic model and draws an extended campus, in which the capability approach can be more appropriately set up. Before that, let us confirm our research question once again.

Formulation of the capability approach based on the economic model of optimization led to an extension of the traditional utility approach, as the former explicitly considers information on individual utilization abilities and relative weights attached to different functionings. Under certain assumptions, it proved the robustness of the fundamental theorems of welfare economics,[1] on the one hand, but it also provided a perspective to examine their assumptions critically, on the other. It suggested that individual optimization behavior revealed on the commodity space is not always consistent with individual optimization behavior expected on the functioning space. The origin of inconsistency can be found in the plurality of individual preferences or evaluations. The task of this chapter is to re-formulate individual capability by focusing on this plurality and its implications and then to consider the significance of going beyond the standard economic model of optimization. In what ways can the plurality of individual preferences or evaluations clarify the background factors

[1] The first fundamental theorem of welfare economics states that any price equilibrium with transfers, and in particular any Walrasian equilibrium, is a Pareto optimum with a weak assumption of the local non-satiation of preferences. The second fundamental theorem of welfare economics tells us that under stronger assumptions, we can achieve any desired Pareto optimal allocation as a market-based equilibrium. (Arrow (1951b/1983); see for a simple introduction Mas-Colell, Whinston and Green, 1995, 549–551).

R. Gotoh, *The Ethics and Economics of the Capability Approach*, Hitotsubashi University IER Economic Research Series 46, https://doi.org/10.1007/978-981-15-5140-6_5

behind rational and autonomous individual "choice"? We elaborate our concern below.

According to the traditional utility approach, in the free and anonymous competitive market system, individual subjective preferences are the basis of optimizing behavior in the commodity space, and they are the central factor for attributing individual responsibility to oneself, as symbolized by the phrase "consumer sovereignty." In contrast, according to the capability approach, a "reason" for a person to realize particular functioning vectors might be different from "rationality" that instructs an individual to choose the best means for achieving a given purpose. Furthermore, "reason" can provide a connection between individual deliberation and public reasoning. It involves not only hers but also those of people around her. There may well be a public discussion on whether someone's opportunity set includes functionings that she has "reason" to choose, and, if not, on why that is the case.

The purpose of this chapter is to look at this normative implication of the capability approach, examine the nested relation between individual choice and her opportunity set, and especially investigate the multi-layered nature of individual optimizing behavior on the functioning space.

Here we refer to Sen's concept of "positional objectivity" (Sen 1985b, 1993a, 2002a) in order to go beyond the economic model of optimizing behavior and approach "reason" for individual choices. "Positional objectivity" is a concept to describe diverse "objectivities" of an observation, claim, belief, or action of an individual, depending on her social or natural "positions" (community, region, race, gender, physical or mental characteristics, and so on.) We use this idea in this chapter to introduce an analytical perspective of "individuality versus positionality" in addition to the standard one of "subjectivity versus objectivity."

Suppose, for example, there is a woman with limited vision who goes out only about once a month by using public transportation in a society equipped enough to reasonably accommodate people with visual impairments. When society provides some means for transportation but she is reluctant to use any, then, the traditional utility approach would judge that she just does not want to go out. Based on the "equality of opportunity for welfare," discussed earlier, society need not concern itself with her capability for moving about, which has been reduced due to her own preferences.

Imagine, however, that her preferences have been shaped very much by her position as a woman as well as a person with limited vision. Moreover, her latter position could have been hidden or dominated by the former. Then there can be a problem of "adaptive preference" (Elster 1982). If there is, then society should be able to help compensate for her lack of current capability for moving, even when she "chooses" not to use any social assistance and does not show any sign of complaint. For example, her society could provide a subsidized, assisted transportation scheme for registered residents with difficulties, which can drive them to a bus or railway station.

5.2 Formulating Generalized Main Capability

In the discussion so far, individual capability has been defined by a fractal, similar structure (between utilization abilities and capabilities), independently from her subjective preferences and evaluations. In other words, individual sub-capability has been captured by commodities available to her and her own utilization abilities (skills) to convert those commodities into functionings. Meanwhile, commodities have been defined as objective conditions detached from her subjective features, which can be extended to include public goods, social support, and informal assistance. Moreover, individual "production function" to convert sub-functionings into utilization abilities for main-functionings has an objective and technical feature, unlike her subjective preferences or evaluations. Thus, an individual capability formed independently of her subjective preference evaluations is called "production-function capability."

Given this "production-function capability," an individual's optimizing behavior can maximize her utilization ability for main-functionings. If that turns out to be insufficient, it can immediately be compensated for because she is not deemed responsible for that.

What we should have in mind, however, is the possibility that the value of a sub-functioning for a person is not merely an instrumental one to achieve a specific main-functioning, but also, for example, that for some other main-functionings, or it can have an intrinsic value in itself. If so, then she might choose a sub-functioning vector different from the optimal point suggested by the objective "production-function," while her evaluation function does not aim at maximizing her ability for moving but some other values. In fact, it would be an open question as to which evaluation function should be adopted to pursue which value here. Sen pointed this out in *On Economic Inequality* as follows, stating that

> … [T]he valuation be done not in terms of only one ("given") preference ordering (over functioning vectors), even if it is the one that the person opts for—possibly "on balance"—to determine what is maximal in the available set. Rather, the valuation can be done by using a set of plausible preference orderings (preferences a person *could have* quite reasonably had), and this would give importance to having other opportunities even when the maximal alternative (according to the "given preference ordering"), or the chosen option, is the same. (Sen 1973/1997, 202–203[1997])

Sen highly appreciated this plurality of preferences that "a person could have quite reasonably had" as an important feature of human beings.

Taking into account Sen's insight, we begin by extending the formulation of capability defined in the previous chapter. Then we introduce a more generalized evaluation function $v_i = \varphi_i\ (x_{i1}, x_{i2})$, where v_i, φ_i, x_{i1} and x_{i2} are non-negative, the partial derivative of φ_i with regard to x_{i1}, x_{i2} is positive. Assume that φ_i is strictly quasi-concave and an inverse function $\varphi_i{}^{-1}(v_i)$ exists, then the maximization problem to choose the intrinsic optimal sub-functioning vectors is written in the following way.

$$\text{Max. } v_i = \phi_i(x_{i1}, x_{i2}),$$

$$\text{s.t. } p_Z(a_i x_{i1} + b_i x_{i2}) = y_{iz} + y_{0z} \tag{5.1}$$

By forming a Lagrangian function with a multiplier λ and partially differentiating it with respect to x_{i1}, x_{i2} and λ, we obtain the first-order conditions for optimization: such that $\frac{\partial \phi_i}{\partial x_{i1}} / \frac{\partial \phi_i}{\partial x_{i2}} = \frac{a_i}{b_i}$. Denote the sub-functioning vector satisfying this condition, its evaluation value, and corresponding ability for moving by $\hat{x}_i = (\hat{x}_{i1}, \hat{x}_{i2})$, $\hat{v}_i, \hat{t}_i = f(\hat{x}_i)$ respectively. This sub-functioning evaluation function $v_i = \varphi_i(x_{i1}, x_{i2})$ makes it possible to realize individual i's "generalized main capability," which can be described as follows, given the available resources $\overline{y}_i, \overline{y}_0$, utilization abilities f, l, a_i, b_i, commodity prices p_z, p_r, p_0, p_m, the optimal sub-functioning vectors $\hat{x}_{i1}, \hat{x}_{i2}$, the optimal moving ability $\hat{t}$, and the optimal amount $\overline{z}_i$ for commodities used for sub-functionings.

Definition *Generalized Main Capability*:

$$C = \{(T_i, L_i) | T_i = \hat{t}(r_0, r_i), L_i = l(m_i), p_z\overline{z}_i + p_r r_i + p_0 r_0 + p_m m_i \leq \overline{y}_i + \overline{y}_0,$$

where

$$\hat{t} = f(\varphi_i^{-1}(v_i)), v_i = \varphi_i(\hat{x}_{i1}, \hat{x}_{i2}), \overline{z}_i = a_i \hat{x}_{i1} + b_i \hat{x}_{i2}\} \tag{5.2}$$

The equal part is represented by the implicit function $\hat{F}_i(T_i L_i; r_i, r_0, m_i) = 0$, which is strictly quasi-concave. Now we are going to see some analytical differences between this generalized main capability and the production function capability we introduced in Chap. 3. The maximal value of the "moving" function available with the former is denoted by $\hat{T}_i$, and that with the latter by T_i^*. Then we obtain the following proposition.

Proposition 2 *When the optimal sub-functioning vector realized with the generalized evaluation function is different from that with the moving ability production function, that is,* $(\hat{x}_{i1}, \hat{x}_{i2}) \neq (x_{i1}^*, x_{i2}^*)$, *then the following holds*:

(1) $\hat{t}_i = f(\hat{x}_{i1}, \hat{x}_{i2}) < t_i^* = f(x_{i1}^*, x_{i2}^*)$.
(2) *For any* r_0, r_i, $T_i = \hat{t}_i(r_0, r_i) < T_i = t_i^*(r_0, r_i)$.
(3) $\hat{T}_i = \hat{t}_i(r_0, (\overline{y}_i - p_z\overline{z}_i)/p_r) < T_i^* = t_i^*(r_0, (\overline{y}_i - p_z\overline{z}_i)/p_r)$.

In other words, the difference between the two can be stated as follows. First, the optimal moving ability with the generalized evaluation function is equal to or smaller than that with the moving ability production function. Second, for any commodity, the moving function realized under the generalized evaluation function is equal to or smaller than that realized under the production function. Third, the maximal value $\hat{T}_i$ attainable with the generalized evaluation function is equal to or smaller than T_i^* attainable with the production function. Figure 5.1 depicts both generalized main capability and production function capability.

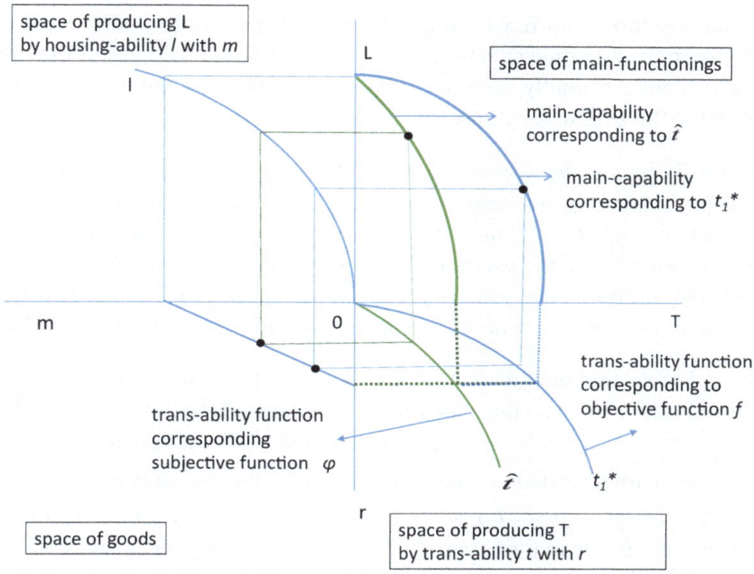

Fig. 5.1 Generalized main capability and production function capability

5.3 Extended Well-Being Evaluation Function

We turn to generalizing the well-being evaluation function too as an objective function for optimization behavior under resource constraints on the commodity space. It strikes a balance between the objective production function for main-functionings and the subjective evaluation of intrinsic values of sub-functionings. Let us examine formally how the structure of the maximization problem with resource-constraints will be influenced by this extension.

Definition *Generalized Constrained Optimization Mode*

Max. $W_i = \varphi_i(T_i, v_i, L_i)$, where $T_i = t_i(r_0, r_i)$, $L_i = l(m_i)$, $t_i = f(x_{i1}, x_{i2})$, $v_i = \varphi_i(x_{i1}, x_{i2})$, $z_i = a_i x_{i1} + b_i x_{i2}$.

$$\text{s.t. } p_z z_i + p_r r_i + p_0 r_0 + p_m m_i = \overline{y}_i + \overline{y}_0. \tag{5.3}$$

The conditions for optimization are as follows.

$$\frac{\partial \varphi_i}{\partial x_{i1}} / \frac{\partial \varphi_i}{\partial x_{i2}} = \frac{a_i}{b_i} \text{ and } \frac{\partial \varphi_i}{\partial r_i} / \frac{\partial \varphi_i}{\partial m_i} = \frac{p_r}{p_m} \tag{5.4}$$

The former condition implies the equivalence between the marginal substitution rate of sub-functionings for the *extended well-being function* and the ratio of the skills needed for those sub-functionings, and the latter condition implies the equivalence between the marginal substitution rates of goods and the ratio of their prices, both of which are essentially the same conditions as those in the original model as summarized in the following proposition.

Proposition 3 *Asume the maximization model with resource constraints. If the domain of the well-being evaluation function (the objective function) is expanded to include another kind of goal, the basic structure of the model does not change in that the first condition of the maximization requires decomposing the goals so as to reflect only the ratios of given market prices and an individual's skills. This result is robust if plural objectives are added to the original well-being evaluation function.*

Proof It is obvious that the first conditions take the same structure as in the original model. In addition, we can confirm the structure of the modeling in the following way. Denote $\frac{\partial \varphi_i}{\partial \phi_i(x_{i1}, x_{i2})} := \alpha$, $\frac{\partial \varphi_i}{\partial f(x_{i1}, x_{i2})} := \beta$, which represent the marginal utility (evaluation) of φ_i and f with regard to φ_i. Then, the left side of the former condition $\frac{\partial \varphi_i}{\partial x_{i1}} / \frac{\partial \varphi_i}{\partial x_{i2}}$ is decomposed to $(\alpha \frac{\partial \phi_i}{\partial x_{i1}} + \beta \frac{\partial f}{\partial x_{i1}}) / (\alpha \frac{\partial \phi_i}{\partial x_{i2}} + \beta \frac{\partial f}{\partial x_{i2}})$. The numerator (or the denominator) expresses the sum of the marginal productivity of x_{i1} (*or* x_{i2}) for φ_i and for f, which are estimated by the marginal utility of φ_i and of f. We can easily check that if $\alpha = 0$, that is, the marginal utility (evaluation) of φ_i is zero, this condition is reduced to $\frac{\partial f}{\partial x_{i1}} / \frac{\partial f}{\partial x_{i2}} = \frac{a_i}{b_i}$ and coincides with the "model without value function," while if $\beta = 0$, because the marginal utility (evaluation) of f is zero, this condition reduces to $\frac{\partial \phi_i}{\partial x_{i1}} / \frac{\partial \phi_i}{\partial x_{i2}} = \frac{a_i}{b_i}$ and coincides with the "model without production function."

Figure 5.2 illustrates the optimal points that individuals 1 and 2 obtain through maximization behavior under the assumption of the concavity of F_i and the quasi-concavity of h_i with an assumption of $w_i = h_i\ (T_i, L_i)$ for individual 1, while, both

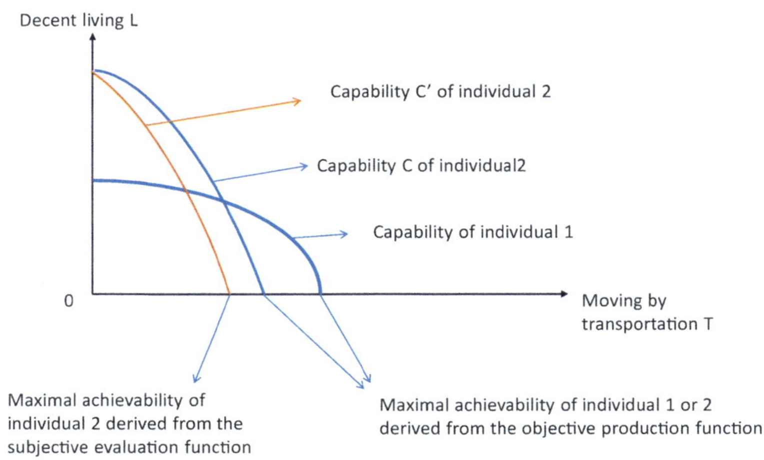

Fig. 5.2 Capabilities, evaluation functions, and achievements

$w_i = h_i\ (T_i, L_i)$ and $W_i = \varphi_i\ (T_i, v_i, L_i)$ for individual 2. That is, as for individual 2, two optimal points are written respective to two different capabilities derived from different evaluation functions.

5.4 The Problem of Adaptive Preference and Positional Objectivity

Let us come back to the specification problem of an individual's capability. Should we specify an opportunity set as an individual's capability, which she actually has, and from which she can actually choose, or should we specify the opportunity set as an individual's capability, which she could objectively have and from which she could objectively choose?

The discussion so far clarifies, on the one hand, that the results of the capability constraint model can be different from those of the resource constraints model, since the relative value of the functionings, which cannot be decomposed into market prices, is explicitly taken into account only in the former model. On the other hand, both models appear to be essentially similar to each other in that they allow us to interpret them as showing that an individual is *autonomous* in achieving the optimal with her *objective function*, whatever it is, subject to the constraints of the opportunity set.

As seen in the assumption of the idea of "equality of opportunity for welfare," the standard understanding in economics is that an individual's opportunity should include every alternative that an individual could choose, while it should exclude any trace of an individual's actual choices with her own responsibility. Then, the following criterion will be recommended as standard.

[Standard Specification of Capability as Opportunity] Suppose an individual chooses a maximization behavior based on her rationality. Then, her main-functionings capability should be identified so as to reflect the maximum achievability of main-functionings, which is logically deduced from her sub-functionings capability or resource constraints, apart from the maximum achievability that she actually realizes.

This condition would be plausible as standard, first, if we can assume that choice from opportunity is fully in one's hands or, in other words, if an individual's evaluation function is not automatically determined without her will but autonomously changeable by her will in accordance with her own responsibility. Yet, it would not be the case if the individual evaluation function is dubious as the "adaptive preference" in her circumstances. This would be the case, second, if "opportunity" can only reflect certain types of objectivity such as market prices, basic skills, and income, but it would not be the case if opportunity also reflected various types of "positional objectivity" (Sen 1993b/2002a, Chap.15). Let us first examine the problem of "positional objectivity".

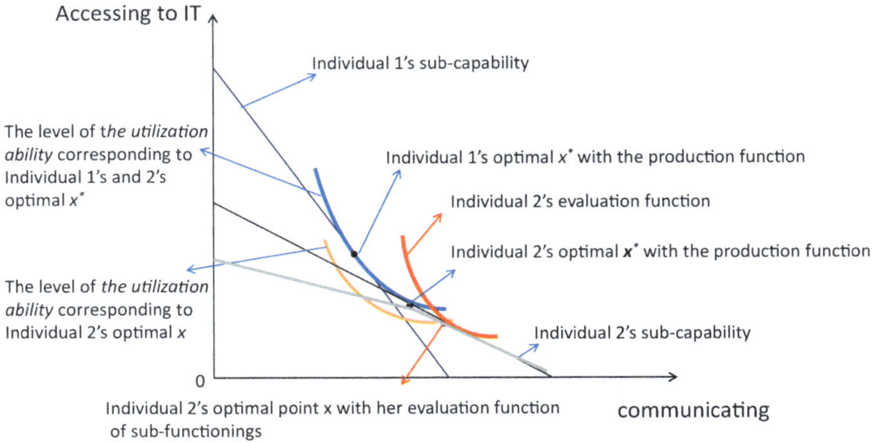

Fig. 5.3 Producing trans-ability by converting sub-functionings

Definition *Positional Objectivity (Sen 1993b/2002a)*

A "position" is formulated through a bundle of parameters, which represents historical, social, cultural, or personal characteristics of individuals. An observation, claim, belief, decision, or action is regarded as "positionally objective" if it applies to all persons who share similar characteristics and therefore can be defined without mentioning the proper name or pronoun for the individual concerned.

What is at stake is that a person may simultaneously belong to multiple positions such as social class, gender, citizenship, profession, disability, mental illness, and so on. In the above example, individual 2′s capability might be restricted in "moving by transportation", because of her family's excessive protection which she cannot resist for fear of losing her current "decent living," which she owes to her family. If this is so, we can admit the influence of *dual positionality* of *a person with limited vision* and *a woman* in individual 2, where the latter makes it infeasible to choose the optimal which is obvious in terms of the former.

The following Fig. 5.3 illustrates a case where individual 2′s real capability is restricted by dual-positionality such as a "woman" and a "person with limited vision."

In these cases, it seems reasonable to specify the individual's capability so as to reflect the restrictions derived from certain types of "positional objectivity." Let us next define "adaptive preference" more formally.

"Adaptive preference" is roughly defined as transformation of preference in response to oppressive circumstances, and which brings about choices that are satisfactorily rational but are not reasonable in terms of her true interest. The existence of the problem has often been pointed out by many authors, but its clear analysis is recognized to be difficult.[2] Here we classify two types of adaptive preference,

---

[2]Elster (1982), Nussbaum (2000), and Sen (1985a), among others, pointed out the problem of adaptive preference. See also d'Agata (2007).

the flexible (recoverable) and non-flexible (non-recoverable) types. The metaphor of "sour grapes" provided by John Elster is a representative example of the flexible type. Once an individual's utility function is transformed by her inability to obtain the grapes, if later she luckily finds a way to reach them, she will try to obtain them, since her preference itself has not changed. If an individual has transformed her preference itself, however, which is represented by the indifference curve so as not to prefer her previous situation to the current one, even if social support is now proposed to provide the formerly unattainable good, it might be difficult for her to change her behavior, as that would imply changing her preference.

Definition *Non-flexible Adaptive Preference*: Suppose there are three periods, characterized by the transformation of the individual's capability.

(i) if her capability in the second period (C′) is dominated by that in the first period (C), she does not envy the optimal point, which is achievable in the first period (O) in comparison with what is achievable in the second period (O′) (as well as the optimal point achieved by individual 1); moreover,
(ii) even though her capability in the third period (C″) becomes again what it was in the first period (that is, C″ = C), she chooses an optimal (O″) different from the optimal which was (and now again is) achievable in the first period (O),

then the individual is considered to have formed an adaptive preference to her situation in the second period(Fig. 5.4).

With concepts of "positional objectivity" and "adaptive preference," we have the following proposition.

Proposition 4 *Logically, an individual's capability represents an opportunity set, which precedes choice, and then the traces of an individual's choice should be removed in identifying an opportunity. Yet, if we cannot deny the possibility of "positional objective effects" and "adaptive preference," it is reasonable to specify an individual's main-capability, not by the maximum achievability logically deduced from her sub-functionings capability, but by the maximum achievability that she actually has.*

Reason:
We can identify the objective effects of an individual's position on her choices by comparing her capabilities before and after the change if her preferences are flexible type. We cannot do so if they are non-flexible type. In the latter case, economic policies to help recover her original capability can be considered wasteful. However, they could objectively increase her transportation functionings. Furthermore, her preference evaluations may possibly change in the future and according to her new capability in the third period, which is the same as capability in the first period. As long as there is this possibility, those economic policies can be effective to some extent.

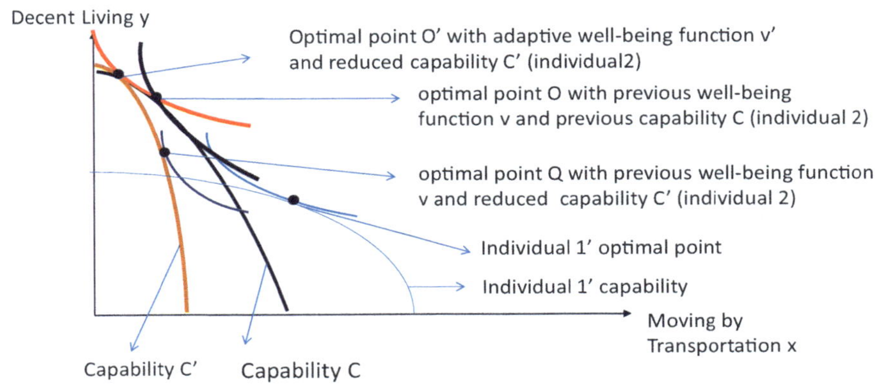

Suppose that the capability of individual 2 is reduced from C to C′ in the second period. According to her previous well-being function v, her optimal point should have moved to Q with reduced capability C′, where she should have felt "envy" for individual 1 and for her previous situation. In this case, if she chose a point different from Q as her optimal, we can doubt that she might have changed her well-being function to v′, with which she needs not feel "envy" for individual 1 and for her previous optimal point.

Fig. 5.4 A possible case of adaptive preference: an example of condition (i)

In addition, considering that the shortage of an individual's capability indicates the need and legitimacy for social support, and considering that the failure of supporting is far more serious than the failure of over-supporting, this proposition should be taken as plausible, insofar as there is a possibility of positional objective effects, however small they are.

5.5 Individuality, Positionality, Subjectivity, and Objectivity

In the previous section, we found that it is dangerous to try to remove any trace of an individual's choice in identifying her capability, because an individual's choice itself might possibly represent an objective restriction of her capability. Careful examination of the inner relationship between an individual's opportunity and choice is needed. Then, we should instead discern the influences of "positional objectivity" behind her evaluation and choice, part of which are transparent in public, but part of which are hidden inside.

Logically, four aspects of an individual identity can be derived from the combination of *individual* or *positional* and *subjective* or *objective* as Table 5.1 shows.

Table 5.1 Four aspects of an individual identity

	Subjective	*Objective*
Individual	i.e. individuality in satisfaction **does not count** as a constituent of an individual's capability	i.e. individuality in basic skill **counts** as a constituent of an individual's capability
Positional	i.e. adaptive preference **counts** as a constituent of an individual's capability	i.e. social inhibition (external intervention) **counts** as a constituent of an individual's capability

Inter-personally non-comparable

Inter-personally comparable

Except the case where an isndividual's choice is derived from the individual's *subjectivity and individuality*—for example, if an individual accepts extremely low achievability of "moving by transportation" in order to dedicate herself to finishing her life work—the influence of these factors should count as a constraint on her capability.

In summary, if we concentrate on analyzing an individual's *subjective and individual* values, a "maximization model with capability constraints" that an individual actually has is most appropriate; but if we are concerned with other values such as an individual's *subjective and positional, objective and individual,* or *objective and positional* values, we should go beyond the "maximization model with capability constraints" that an individual actually has and should directly try to capture the *shortage* of capability that an individual actually has, even though it includes the trace of her subjective choice.

5.6 Individual Identity and Capability

We should note two issues briefly before closing this chapter. First, so far we have focused on public policies and examined how to identify individual capability from an external point of view such as securing "basic capability" specified for a certain society and treat an individual only as an object of analysis. Yet, we should recall that an individual, who can simultaneously belong to multiple positions such as social class, gender, citizenship, or profession, is also a subject of analysis of her own situations. She can examine each position-situated evaluation and its result (the variation of capabilities corresponding to each position-situated evaluation) through the eyes of other position-situated evaluations. The capability approach can provide a framework to analyze such a "trans-positional assessment" (Sen 2002, 467), which consists of an individual's reflective activities on her plural position-situated evaluations within her identity, and which makes it possible to realize "open impartiality" in social choice procedures (see Chap. 6 for a more detailed discussion).

Second, so far we have assumed that an individual's preferences and concerns for functionings were basically projected on functioning vectors that she can achieve, whereas her capability was treated as a constraint on her optimizing behavior. However, she may well be interested in her capability itself rather than functioning vectors she can achieve. Furthermore, when she tries to picture her capability as part of her identity, she may be interested in the richest opportunity set that she could have had before or can have in the future if she has reason to value, rather than merely blaming positionally-objective factors that constrain her choices here and now.

It is reported, for example, that a prospective recipient of nursing-care services can sometimes behave quite unusually, in a certification examination of care needs, when asked by a care-service manager about what she can and cannot do. Similarly, when a hospital measures a patient's quality of life (QOL) in order to improve her nursing care, they occasionally assess her QOL higher by including the joy or benefit enjoyed by her family members, in addition to the activities and abilities available to the individual herself.

These instances show that to measure someone's capability is to evaluate her very existence, which, in turn, means forming her identity in a performative manner while involving other people's perceptions and reasoning. She might be able to leave aside the compensatory benefits she can earn by the measurement of her capability and consider other people's responses and situations in measuring her own capability. If no one can respect the possibility of individual capability ranging across multiple spaces, it might be difficult to make a realistic description of one's own capability defined on the interpersonally comparable functioning space (used for public policies) beyond the commodity space for anonymous market exchanges.

We should consider what can be called the reasonable identities, which individuals would have to formulate and critically re-formulate, looking at the above four aspects of an individual identity, that is, *individuality*, *positionality, subjectivity,* and *objectivity*. The capability approach can provide a framework to assist such individuals' reflections on their identities.

5.7 Concluding Remarks

Let us go back to the question we posed at the beginning. We saw that individual "utilization ability" to realize various functionings on each functioning space can vary, depending on her evaluations (or preferences) and autonomous choice on other functioning spaces or at different times. Taking this as a fact, should we judge a person's shortage of capability by looking at the existing opportunity set she actually has or the maximal one that she could have had through her previous sequence of choices? Our tentative answer to this question is that in the context of social policies we should focus on the existing one and compensate for it if necessary, as long as the "positional objectivity" and "adaptive preferences" can affect individual choices. We close this chapter by examining some expected criticism of this way of specifying capabilities.

As we discussed earlier, the theory of equality of opportunity, led by John Roemer among others, distinguishes between "responsible" (choice) factors and "non-responsible" (environmental) factors and justifies social compensation for unfavorable results only when they are caused by non-responsible factors. Many empirical applications of this theory have tried to identify non-responsible factors by enumerating categories such as race, gender, age, education (including one's parents' education), and income, in order to statistically examine their effects on various results, while all the other factors remain as responsible factors. This theory of "equality of opportunity" has been recently criticized by Ravi Kanbur and others who are seriously interested in realizing equality.[3]

Among others, Kanbur declared that we should not use the concept of "equality of opportunity" because in principle we cannot list all non-responsible factors. For example, important factors such as luck, genetic factors, and established tastes are difficult to measure and have been statistically treated as residuals or just ignored. Moreover, the fact that responsible factors for parents cannot be responsible factors for their children suggests that whether a factor is responsible or not can depend on the context, although this fact is often ignored.

Instead, Kanbur argues that the decision about whether to apply or not to apply a social compensation policy for some individual should be based not on the estimation of "opportunity set" she could have but on the "consequential" situation that she has actually realized. This argument can be directly applied to the formulation of the capability approach. He concludes that capability should be defined not as an opportunity set but as a realized functioning vector.

Let us respond to this argument put forward by Kanbur and others. First, they are right to point out that it is impossible in principle to enumerate all non-responsible factors, and then it is risky to adopt the dichotomy of the "responsible" and the "non-responsible." The concept of "positional objectivity," discussed above, can also be open to Kanbur's criticism, as it makes use of existing social categories when trying to capture external factors constraining people's choices in a society. However, we should bear in mind that the concept of "positional objectivity" provides a perspective to change and rearrange existing social categories, as it assumes that a certain characteristic recognized in one person here and now may well be found in other persons at other times elsewhere. Depending on how serious we take this possibility, we may or may not be able to better understand unpredictable difficulties that people might suffer, which are specific to only a few persons but essentially might be applied more generally to a population at large.

---

[3]See Kanbur (2016), Fleurbaey (2006, 2014), and Fleurbaey and Blanchet (2013), among others.

This possibility is, nevertheless, not going to overcome all the risk of the dichotomy of the responsible versus the non-responsible. Hence, Kanbur is also right to point out that it is possible to avoid this risk effectively by securing the "equality of outcome" and that might be an important theme for the capability approach. Here, we should also remember that the idea of securing the "equality of outcome" does not contradict the idea of securing "basic capability as an opportunity set." As we saw before, the concept of a person's capability might include "outcomes of her previous choices" and can work as "constraints on her future choices" at the same time. In pursuing the "equality of outcome" through compensation policies, consideration of this connection between an opportunity set and choice can shed new light on the concept of "capability as an opportunity set" as a key factor that is compatible with the "equality of outcome."

There is a more fundamental issue here. Suppose people are entitled to achieve a certain functioning vector. In an advanced market society, they can exercise their freedom to achieve another functioning vector, as long as they have agency freedom to some extent. For example, they can change the distribution of their own utilization abilities or do some informal exchanges with others outside the market. There must be some room at least for substitution among various functionings by individuals, even if the particular functioning vector they are entitled to can secure the minimum threshold for each functioning.

If our reasoning above is correct, securing the basic functioning vector does and should mean securing "capability as an opportunity set" as a fact and as a norm. Taking this into account, the concept of "capability as an opportunity set" should remain effective in securing the "equality of outcome."

Chapter 6
From Rawls's Social Contract to Sen's Social Choice

6.1 Introduction: Rousseau, Rawls, Arrow, and Sen

Rousseau once said, "[I]f the populace held its deliberations [on the basis of adequate information] without the citizens communicating with one another, what emerged from all the little particular wills would always be *the general will*, and the decision would always be good." He continued that "If the general will is to emerge clearly it is important that there should be no *partial society* within the state, and that each citizen should think only his own thoughts." (Rousseau 1762; 2017, 14, emphasis added by the author).

Partial society (for simplicity, hereinafter, "group") highlights the diversity of individuals who are prone to be neglected if alone. It brings about conflict of opinion based on differing interests. Rousseau feared that partial society might hinder the formation of general will.

The objective of this chapter is to examine a social choice model where the very group Rousseau tried to deny plays a significant role. The intention is not to oppose Rousseau's objective of forming "general will," but to strengthen this idea further by indicating the compatibility between "general will" and group will. The clue to strengthening is to explicitly take into account individuals' diversity for protecting the well-being of those who have the risk of being isolated from the public and thus being forgotten by the public. In such a case, it becomes all the more important to bring out respective groups' information in public and to promote forming respective groups' evaluations on the issues that are relevant to themselves.

With such an interest in mind, we try to extend Kenneth Arrow's traditional social choice model and John Rawls's theory of justice in this chapter. Arrow's social choice model considers individual preferences of all individuals as the only informational base (called "domain") to form social preferences by a certain procedure. This seems actually more in line with the concept raised by Rousseau above.

In contrast, this chapter envisages a social choice model whose objective is to "secure basic capability for all." Its characteristic is to consider both the evaluation by all individuals and the evaluation by groups as the domain to form social evaluation

R. Gotoh, *The Ethics and Economics of the Capability Approach*, Hitotsubashi University IER Economic Research Series 46, https://doi.org/10.1007/978-981-15-5140-6_6

under certain normative conditions. A capability index becomes the key to describing an individual state as well as forming the ethical concept of the group. Let us show the outline of the model.

Much as in an Arrovian (generality-based) social choice model, we compare policies pairwise and regard those that are nearer to securing basic capability for all to be "more just" and those that are the same in terms of basic capability to be "indifferent (equally just)". This is what Sen calls "comparative approach" in his book entitled *The Idea of Justice* (Sen 2009a), which advocates realizing a policy closest to securing basic capabilities according to society's feasibility conditions. The difference from the Arrovian social choice model is that this model does not require complete orderings of alternatives.

Next, similar to "the difference principle" proposed by John Rawls (Rawls 1971a), this model focuses on the least-advantaged individuals in constructing a reasonable distribution rule in society. If the least-advantaged individuals can be well identified, "securing basic capabilities for all" would logically require choosing a policy that brings capabilities of the least advantaged closer to basic capability, based on society's feasibility conditions. Rawls made the social primary goods, namely, rights and liberties, powers and opportunities, income and wealth, and social bases of self-respect, an index to identify the least advantaged. Among these items, he regarded income as an approximately unique index of the least advantaged. With an index of income, we could easily assume that the situations of the least-advantaged individuals in society can be fully compared with one another. Under an index that consists of two or more dimensions, if we assume full comparability among individuals in a society with respect to those chosen dimensions, we can generally define the least advantaged as those who are better off than no other individuals and *indifferent* to one another.

However, if we are to pay attention to the diversity of individual situations (disadvantage incurred), is it not too strong to assume that inter-personal comparisons can be generally made in order? Individuals who are dominating no other individuals (meaning that they are the least advantaged) are in actuality not *indifferent* to one another (that is, not at the same level in their disadvantage) but it may be only that it is impossible to make comparisons among themselves.

If they are *indifferent*, we could compensate the same amount of shortage from the common reference point (that is, basic capability). In contrast, if we may not be able to assume that the content of basic capabilities (list of functionings, level of respective functioning, substitution ability of functioning) is the same, it is impossible to make a comparison. Moreover, there is the issue of whether it is appropriate to simply label individuals as the least disadvantaged as a whole without having any concern and respect for their diverse difficulties to keep living.

For example, when people claim compensation as Hibakusha (atomic bomb survivors in Hiroshima and Nagasaki) or when patients with extremely rare intractable diseases speak out, they are requesting that particular issues inherent to their living situations be noted and that information about particular issues be made publicly accessible by others. This shows their hopes that their own reasons for requests should be found, shared, and referred to in identifying the content of basic capabilities (list of functionings, levels of respective functionings, substitution rates among functionings) that is used as a reference point.

In this respect, this chapter will weaken the prerequisites of Rawls's difference principle. Furthermore, we will expand the domain of definition for procedures to form social evaluation as follows.

- Individual-based appraisal of capabilities: Forms assessments of capabilities by individuals in an ordinal and inter-personally non-comparable index. Each appraisal is reflexive and transitive, but not necessarily complete.
- Group-based appraisal of capabilities: Constitutes various groups that fulfill the following necessary and sufficient conditions: the content of basic capabilities used as a reference point can be specified. An appraisal of capabilities is conducted among members for each group. It is inter-personally comparable in an ordinal index, reflexive, transitive but not necessarily complete. The least-advantaged individual(s) can be specified for each group.
- Group-based policy evaluation: Forms policy evaluation for each group under certain common criteria, focusing on the least-advantaged individuals. Such policy evaluation is also reflexive and transitive but not necessarily complete.

Moreover, the following condition is imposed on the process of forming social evaluation: for individual evaluation, "capability-based Pareto condition" and for group evaluation, "inter-group non-negative response."

By definition, members in the same group are assumed to have inter-personally comparable difference as regards capability, while members of different groups are assumed to have inter-personally non-comparable difference as regards capability. When all individuals are inter-personally comparable, the group coincides with the universal set, and when all are non-comparable, the group coincides with the individual.

This is the outline of the model thus far. This chapter presents the model as an example of a Sen-type (diversity-based) social choice model. The reasons are as follows: First, while building on the framework of social welfare functional, that is, a function of functions, advocated by Sen, the model uses not utility functional but capability functional as its informational base. Similarly, the model expands the domain of definition by partially introducing inter-personal comparability, and by imposing "securing basic capabilities for all," that is, a kind of "attainment equality" (see Chap. 3, Sect. 3.1.3) on social choice procedure. The model adopts "the comparative approach" in formulating social evaluation, and weakens the condition of "anonymity" when dealing with individuals (however, if in the same position of the same group, it is independent from a person's name), and also, the model does not require "neutrality" in dealing with alternatives. In addition, it does not request complete ordering but rather often recommends with some reasons *incompleteness*.

However, another feature of this model is that with some restrictions in its procedure, the model gives a decisive power to evaluations that satisfy the condition of *non-negative response* among various groups. This may expand the original framework of Sen's social welfare functional that only considers individuals' utilities as the basic unit in forming a social evaluation.

What we need to pay attention to is that, firstly, our interest here does not lie in making "once and final" social decisions (typically, a voting system). Rather, the social choice model introduced in this chapter is defined as a procedure for public reasoning and public deliberation to realize the objective of "securing basic capabilities for all." Secondly, the concept of "group" mentioned in this chapter is an ethical one, which is different from a physical, statistical, or narrowly defined political concept.

That is, taking the fact that in this society there exist people who suffer from severe disadvantages as a starting point, it is a concept structured around moral interests to clearly understand what sort of pains people are suffering, what institutional injustice is hidden behind such sufferings, and what society or we should do about them. Additionally, there is also a demand from the scientific front that making a group and clarifying the difference among individuals can facilitate analyses. However, the latter is placed under the control of ethical interest.[1]

The following is a relevant example. Having ratified it in 2014, Japan has drawn up legislation that takes into account the Convention on the Rights of Persons with Disabilities enacted at the United Nations in 2006. In discussing revision of the existing laws (Act for Supporting the Independence of Persons with Disabilities and Services and Support for Persons with Disabilities Act), many important discussions were raised such as how to assign a grade, level, and scope of disability pension, services offered for persons with disabilities, ratio of cost burden, implementation of self-determination with support, educational inclusion program in accordance with the disability level, and implementation of reasonable accommodation at work and school. These points could not have been raised without the presence of persons with disability themselves and their contributions.

Let me give a more concrete example. In identifying Complex Regional Pain Syndrome (CRPS), an intractable disease mentioned above, the determinant factor is not the "objective observations" by doctors and professional agencies but "subjective experiments" by the patients themselves.[2] The level of chronic pain, however, fluctuates substantially even during the day within the same person. Taking the first step in the morning may bring back a sense of a healthy state while it may at times result in severe and agonizing pain. When not in pain, the patient may forget how agonizing it had been and so, every time the pain surfaces, it comes with great surprise and brings deep anxiety.

[1]For example, refer to Hayek's words, "… [W]hat we perceive can never be unique properties of individual objects but always only properties which the objects have in common with other objects. Perception is thus always an interpretation, the placing of something into one or several classes of objects." (Hayek 1952/2018, 259 [2018])

[2]Note that "subjective experiments" is not on "psychological pain" or "grief" but on actual pain directly experienced by the patients." This is completely overlapping with the theme of the capability approach.

If this is the case, when we research patients one by one, it is likely that not so high a pain level is reported on average. In contrast, when compared among patients who experienced the similar fluctuation of the pain, we may understand the essential feature and influence of this intractable disease on a person's physical and mental state and capability. Furthermore, there is a possibility of finding solutions to mitigate pain through changing atmospheric pressure, light, sound, and smell. Public scrutiny and research with specialists and patient groups are extremely effective in categorizing, verbalizing, and generalizing the features of difficulties and sufferings as well as considering the policy in supporting their daily lives and opportunities of employment.

6.2 Social Choice Procedure for Securing Basic Capability for All

6.2.1 Individual Capability as Informational Basis of Social Choice

We refer to theories of justice in forming a group. Social and economic disadvantages that people suffer are classified roughly into the following three:

The first disadvantage derives from historical injustice such as war and crime that have been intentionally or unintentionally left untouched. The second disadvantage comes from natural and social contingencies such as gender, age, race, nationality, and other physical and mental features. The last disadvantage is the generic term for considerable difficulties that are actually being experienced by individuals in their living for reasons other than the previous two. Below, we will make a mathematical formulation of social choice procedure as public reasoning and deliberation concerning social support policies for individuals suffering from those three kinds of disadvantages.

Basic Model

First, let us assume a society N consisting of n number of individuals (n is more than two in finite numbers) ($N = \{1, 2, \ldots, n\}$). Consider that in this society, there are three groups with disadvantages. Group H has sufferers of historical injustice, group S has parties of attributive injustice, and group G has sufferers of non-categorical injustice.[3] An individual can belong to one of the groups or none of them with regard to her capability. Let us call a policy (bundle) x, the set of all conceivable policies X (more than three in finite numbers), and capability of an individual $i \in N$ realized

[3]For simplicity, we assume each group is independent but can be extended to a case where an individual participates in more than two groups' capability assessments and formations of local evaluation. They can enjoy benefit from policies tailored for each disadvantaged group. However, should such policies have a combined production effect, benefit to such individuals may be reduced at the time of provision.

under policy x to be $C_i(x)$. C_i can be interpreted as a "capability function" of an individual $i \in N$ that converts each alternative policy bundle (in actual case, a resource that becomes available under such policy) to a certain capability of an individual $i \in N$. A profile of capability function of individuals in society N is denoted $C = (C_i)_{i \in N}$.

Individual capabilities are appraised in the form of a binary relation that satisfies *reflexivity* and *transitivity* but does not necessarily satisfy *completeness*.[4] That is, we can say that "$C_i(x)$ is at least as good as $C_i(y)$," "$C_i(x)$ is better than $C_i(y)$," or "$C_i(x)$ is as good as $C_i(y)$" or "$C_i(x)$ cannot be compared with $C_i(y)$." We assume that each individual $i \in N$ forms an appraisal on C based on his or her own criteria (called individual i appraisal). Besides, we assume that each group t forms an appraisal on C (called group t appraisal). That is, each group t is assumed to share a common criterion for comparing the capabilities of their members, due to some understandings of their disadvantages. Denote the admissible set of the profiles of individuals' capability appraisals and group capability appraisals by A.

Given society N and a profile of capability appraisals, under a certain policy bundle, individuals with capabilities that do not dominate capabilities of any other individual in the same group is called "the least advantaged (under that certain policy bundle) within that group."

In appraising such "capability," this model has the following prerequisites.

- The minimum content and level of "basic capability" that society should guarantee the three disadvantaged groups are considered to be a given exogenous condition in the process of social evaluation.
- Within each disadvantaged group, it is assumed that each individual's capability can partially be compared with one another and the least advantaged can be identified under each policy bundle.
- Capability cannot be compared across different disadvantaged groups. Even more, comparisons cannot also be made between individuals independent of groups.[5]

These are conditions that are commonly imposed on capability appraisals of groups. Based on these definitions, let us move to the procedure to form social evaluations that realize the objective of "securing basic capability for all."

First, social evaluation is defined upon a set of possible alternative policy bundles $(X \times X)$ and expressed as binary relation R that fulfills reflexivity and transitivity but not necessarily completeness.[6] Specifically, judgements such as "x is at least as just as y" ($x R y$), "x is more just than y" ($x P y$: x R y and not $y R x$), "x is as just as y" ($x I y$: $x R y$ and $y R x$) are formed. Let us denote an evaluation of group $t \in (H,$

---

[4]*Reflexivity* requires that "for any $x \in X$, $C_i(x)$ is at least as good as $C_i(x)$." Transitivity requires that "for any $x,y,z \in X$, if $C_i(x)$ is at least as good as $C_i(y)$, and if $C_i(y)$ is at least as good as $C_i(z)$, then $C(x, i)$ is at least as good as $C_i(z)$." *Completeness* requires that for any $x, y \in X$, either "$C_i(x)$ is at least as good as $C_i(y)$" or "$C_i(y)$ is at least as good as $C_i(x)$ holds".

[5]Related to footnote 1, individuals who do not have any disadvantage can be included in the disadvantaged group G, if there is a possibility of inter-personal comparison with other members in G.

[6]Refer to footnote 2 for logical features of reflexivity, transitivity, and completeness.

S, G) with a profile of capability function of individuals $C = (C_i)_{i \in N}$ to be R^t_C, and a profile of evaluations of groups to be $(R^t_C)_{l \in \{H,S,G\}}$. Moreover, the set of possible evaluation profiles is denoted as D.

Next, procedures to form this social evaluation envisage roughly two types of informational bases. The first type is the profile of local evaluation formed by each disadvantaged group concerning conceivable policy bundles. We assume that an evaluation of each group is formed focusing on the capabilities of "the least advantaged" of each group. The second type comprises the capability appraisals formed by each and every individual in society. For simplicity, a profile of the capability function of individuals $(C_i)_{i \in N}$ in society N is supposed to be given. The procedure to form social evaluation (social relation function) F is defined as follows.

Definition: Social Relation Function (SRF)
Given a capability profile $(C_i)_{i \in N}$, function F gives a social evaluation R_C to a certain profile of individuals' capability appraisals and group capability appraisals in A and a group evaluation profile $(R^l_C)_{l \in \{H,S,G\}} \in D$. F is called a social relation function (SRF).

6.2.2 *Normative Conditions for Social Choice Procedure*

Be it Arrovian social welfare functional or Sen-type social welfare functional, a typical procedure to form social evaluation includes normative conditions such as securing of individual freedom and equal treatment for equals besides logical conditions such as consistency, completeness, existence, and uniqueness of solution. These are segmented down into the most primitive conditions called "axioms."

Social relation function defined earlier is a more common procedure that brings about social evaluation with reflexivity and transitivity. Below, we will impose normative conditions that embody the goal of "securing basic capabilities to all in a society which includes multiple types of disadvantaged groups." First, let us define conditions on local evaluation formed by each group.

Conditions on Local Evaluation-Forming Process
The informational base of each local evaluation is the group appraisal on individual capabilities in a group, which can be realized under each prospective policy bundle. The following three conditions are imposed based on this assumption.

- Basic capability condition (BCC): Evaluate social policy x as "more just" than social policy y whenever (1) capability of the least advantaged under x is at least as good as basic capability and that under y is worse than basic capability or non-comparable to basic capability,[7] or (2) capability of the least advantaged under

[7]Non-comparable cases include a case where there are multiple least-advantaged individuals within a disadvantaged group; and while one individual may have equal or more basic capabilities, because other individuals do not, it is non-comparable as a whole.

x is non-comparable to basic capability and as that under y is worse than basic capability.

- Restricted monotonicity condition (RM): each group evaluates a social policy x as being more just than another social policy y whenever the corresponding profile of the least advantaged members' well-being is better in x than y, given that all of their capabilities derived from both policies fall beneath their basic capability.
- Refrain condition (RC): when capabilities of the least advantaged realized under two social policies are both better than basic capability, expressing pairwise rankings of these two social policies should be refrained.

These three conditions are confirmed to form consistent group evaluation.[8] Next, the following two conditions are imposed in the procedure to form global social evaluation by aggregating an evaluation of each group.

- Non-negative Response (NR): If the evaluation of some disadvantaged group is "policy x is at least equally as just as policy y" and evaluations of all groups are "policy y is more just than policy x," then x should be judged more just than y.
- Weak Pareto (WP): If capabilities of individuals realized under policy x are all appraised better than those realized under another policy y, x should be judged more just than y.

NR requires giving priority to the evaluations of disadvantaged groups over the evaluations of non-disadvantaged individuals in the aggregation procedure, while there is no priority rule in the treatments of evaluations among the different disadvantaged groups. That is, even if the well-being contents of all non-disadvantaged individuals become worse in y than in x, the social evaluation must be that y is at least as just as x whenever a disadvantaged group t evaluates y as being at least as just as x and no other group evaluates x as more just than y. Such a requirement seems quite reasonable whenever persons with a particular disadvantage can be considered as "experts" on that disadvantage, and these persons are expected to provide a reasonable group evaluation. In this respect, NR together with the available class of group evaluations constrained by BCC, RM, and RC warrant the reasonableness of preferential treatments of specific types of groups in the aggregation procedure.

In contrast, WP requires no preferential treatment of any particular individuals' appraisals. It requests that assessment of individual capability of all individuals be treated symmetrically. That is, it uses the capability index instead of the usual preference index of the weak Pareto condition and looks equally at individual information and requests that policies that improve the capability of each individual should be considered more correct than the original policy. In terms of respecting the plurality of the conceptions of the good, WP also seems quite reasonable.

It is also worth mentioning that, although WP is a weaker condition of welfarism, the requirement of NR with the scheme of group evaluations makes SRFs non-welfaristic. To see this point, remember that the neutrality property of social choice rules is necessary for welfarism in the standard Arrovian framework. Yet, if SRFs

[8]Gotoh and Yoshihara (2018).

satisfies NR with the scheme of group evaluations satisfying BCC, RM, and RC, then it does not satisfy neutrality.

Is there actually a social procedure that satisfies both NR and WP? Gotoh and Yoshihara (2018) show that it is possible by adding two conditions as prerequisites.[9] Let us call the procedure that solely satisfies both NR and WP the "basic capability securing function."[10] This function does not guarantee the existence of "the most desirable" policy, which is at least as just as other feasible choices, because the identified social evaluation does not fulfill completeness. Depending on a set of feasible choices, it may not be possible to identify a most desirable policy. However, it is defined as follows in terms of any non-empty set S of a possible set of policy bundle X (in finite numbers) and it guarantees the existence of "maximal" policy proved by Sen.[11]

Definition: Maximal Set

An element y in S is a maximal element of S with respect to a binary relationR_C if and only if there are no other policy candidates x evaluated as "more just" than y. The set of maximal elements in S is called its *maximal set* and is denoted $M(S, R_c) = \{y | y \in S \& for\ no\, x \in S : xP(R_c)y\}$.[12]

Moreover, the "basic capability securing function" enables us to judge "patently unjust" those policies where capabilities of the least advantaged in a group are below the level of basic capability.[13] On the other hand, it enables us to judge a policy where capabilities of the least advantaged in a group are below the level of basic capability as "patently unjust but less unjust" if it brings about better capabilities than other unjust policies. Such evaluation allows us to choose a policy that can provide the "maximal" policies defined above.

6.3 Re-Defining Rousseau–Rawls's (Universality-Based) Social Contract

6.3.1 Political Constructivism and the Device of Original Position

Let us get back to the words of Rousseau at the beginning of this chapter. Rousseau was not insensitive to inter-personal difference. Rather, he regarded inter-personal

[9]Gotoh and Yoshihara (2018) proved this using a more general model.

[10]Refer to Gotoh and Yoshihara (2018) for a proof of the theorem that a procedure that fulfills both inter-group non-negative response and capability-based Pareto condition exists.

[11]If a social evaluation satisfies reflexivity and acyclicity (a weaker condition than transitivity), a maximal set always becomes non-empty. Refer to Sen (1995/2002a, 183 [2002a]).

[12]Sen (2017, 55).

[13]Refer to Sen (1999b, 287) for the phrase "patent injustice".

difference as the *raison d'être* of "politics as technology." He noted the following slightly ironical statement. "If individual interests did not differ from one another, the common interest would have nothing to bump up against, and so it would hardly be felt" (Rousseau 1762; 1954, 47). However, Rousseau's interest was, first of all, in forming "a general will" with a pre-theoretical hypothesis of "all the little particular wills," and not in respecting actual inter-personal differences themselves.

Based on Rousseau's idea on the social contract, Rawls reviewed more carefully the correspondence between the concept of a moral person and the first principles of justice. Then he exercised practical reason to examine, modify, and approve consistencies between them, rather than taking one for granted and founding the other based on it.[14] This method, called "political constructivism," is one of the methodologies in order to justify normative propositions or value judgements, along with foundationalism, intuitionalism, and naturalism.

For example, Rawls provides the following device of the original position. Imagine that parties with the "veil of ignorance" are going to choose the first principles of justice from a free and independent standpoint, where the "veil of ignorance" covers up one's birth, attributes, social states and personal preferences and characteristics. Suppose that they base their reasoning on the fact of human societies that there must be "the least disadvantaged" depending on the "social primary goods." Then, what kind of principles of justice would parties derive concerning the distribution of "social primary goods" among individuals? (See Rawls 1971a, 1993).

Rawls's idea of "original position" with the "veil of ignorance" can be interpreted to embody conditions of social choice procedure. Actually, it represents the following formal constraints on the concept of right: universality, generality, publicity, finality, and ordering (concerning the meaning and the implication of each concept, see Rawls 1971a; Gotoh 2014).

"Rousseau–Rawls type of original position" is a cognitive framework that precedes an ethical perspective, on which this chapter's model is based. It is a stage to judge the necessity of moral perspective or legitimacy of a decision-making process. If so, there is a possibility that the social choice model envisaged in this chapter may not be contrary to Rousseau's original idea, which relies not on groups' evaluations but on individuals' evaluations. The former can be rather an extended model that explicitly encompasses the "Rousseau–Rawls type of original position." This section will examine the philosophical implication of the social choice model envisaged in this chapter in connection to the "Rousseau–Rawls type of original position."

In Rawls's "original position," as is well-known, "the veil of ignorance" requests that any individual and personal information attributed to each individual's "name" should be concealed. This "veil of ignorance" signified the informational constraint on the decision maker (evaluator) of social rules, which is in other words, the impartiality condition. At the same time, it also represented informational constraint on the

[14]Refer to "I shall also assume that, if we grow up under a framework of reasonable and just political and social institutions, we shall affirm those institutions when we in our turn come of age, and they will endure over time" (Rawls 1999a, 7).

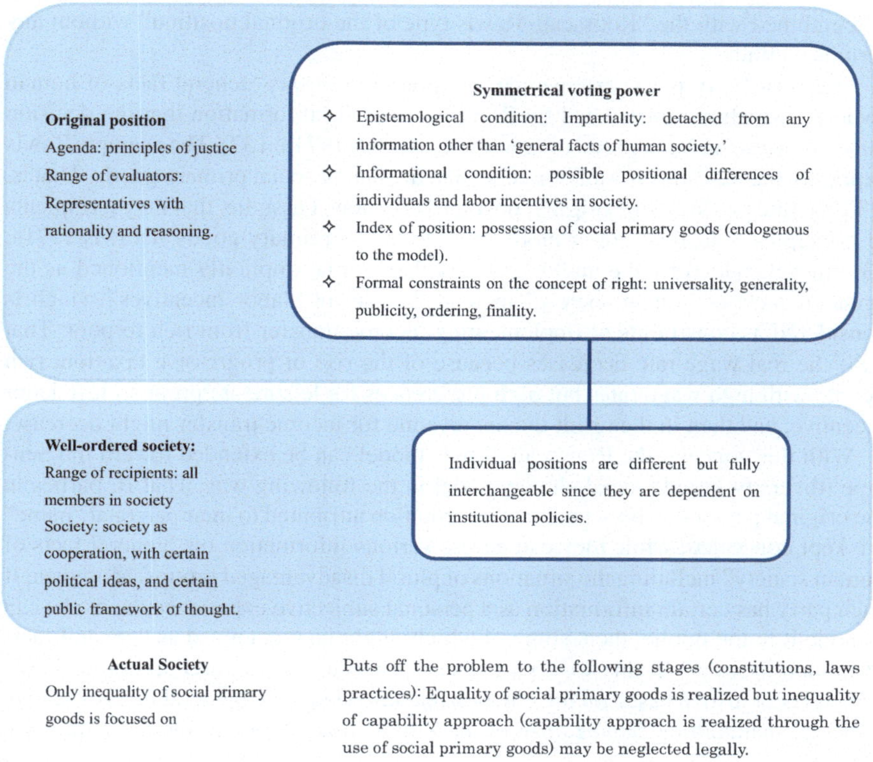

Fig. 6.1 Rawls's idea of "original position," well-ordered society and actual society

object of the social rule (receiver, people to whom the rule is applied) considering them to be the holder of social primary goods (see Fig. 6.1).

6.3.2 *The Sen-Type (Diversity-Based) Social Choice with the Capability Approach*

On the other handIn contrast, the Sen-type (diversity-based) social choice model with the capability approach does not allow a "veil of ignorance" to conceal information on various types of disadvantages—some of them cannot easily be wiped away by social rules—that individuals may suffer under different social rules. Rather, individuals with varying historical, social, and cultural backgrounds are experts on their own disadvantages that each experienced in their own particular and varying ways. Decision makers of social rules (evaluators) are expected to speak out as witnesses to the particular and diverse disadvantages that he or she experienced. Could this model be combined with the "Rousseau–Rawls type of the original position" without any serious conflict?

One possibility is the extensional interpretation of the "general facts of human society," which are introduced by Rawls as the only information that the decision makers can use under "the veil of ignorance" (Rawls 1971a, 137). The example Rawls explicitly mentions is information related to the fact of social primary goods. That is, "[T]hey [the parties in the original position] do know, I assume, that they [recipients of principles of justice] prefer more rather than less primary goods" (Rawls 1971a, 93, brackets added by the author). Others that can be implicitly mentioned as the "general facts of human society" include the fact of "labor incentives" which is considered as constraints of implementing income transfer from rich to poor. That is, if the real wage rate decreases because of the rise of progressive taxation, rich people with high wage rates but high preferences for leisure are prone to lose labor incentive, and then in the result the net revenue for income transfer might decrease.

With this concept, the Rousseau–Rawls model can be extended toward the Sen-type (diversity-based) social choice model in the following way. That is, parties in the original position, whose personal information attributed to their personal "name" are kept concealed, while they can access various information on "general facts of human society" including the situations of plural disadvantaged groups. Moreover, if each party has certain information as a personal subjective experience, he or she can provide it to the public, then, some of which might be recognized as "general facts of human society." In this way, parties can propose, choose, and accept desirable principles of justice based on information and knowledge of "general facts of human society," maintaining *impartiality* by detaching from their personal "name" (see Fig. 6.2).

Another more ambitious interest in "original position" concerns whether asymmetrical treatment among parties is acceptable—that is, whether it is acceptable to give priority to evaluations formed as groups when aggregating evaluation of individual decision makers. In the above extended model, decision makers with various disadvantages could provide their diverse personal information to the public, but in aggregating policy evaluation relevant to them, they did not receive any preferential treatment as a disadvantaged group. On the other hand, the proposed Sen-type social choice model in this chapter enables decision makers with diverse disadvantages to form groups and express group-based evaluations. And in forming social evaluation, they are to receive special (asymmetrical) treatment. Would it be possible to extend "Rousseau–Rawls's original position" to such direction (see Fig. 6.2)? An interim conclusion is that while such extension is possible, formal, epistemological conditions may remain. Let us explain below.

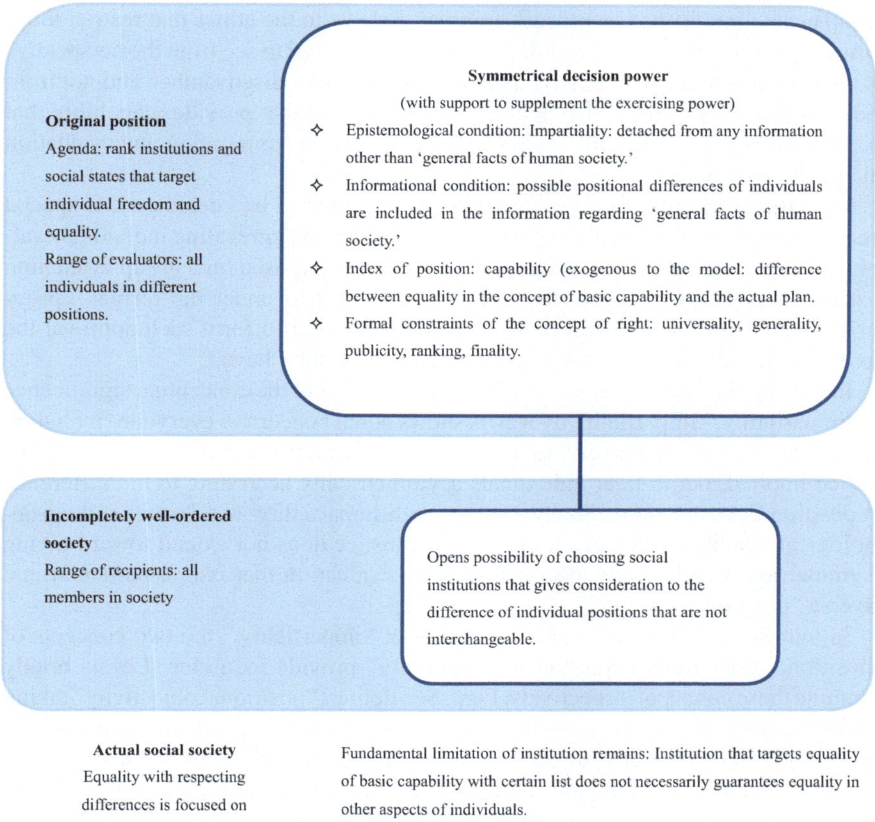

Fig. 6.2 Expansion of "original position": Rawls to Sen

6.3.3 Pre-Original Position: For Choosing Social Choice Procedure in Original Position

As previously discussed, individuals with particular and diverse disadvantages may find it difficult to note the details of their disadvantages and extract necessary discussion points for social evaluation if they are isolated and unknown in the overall society. Exchanging experiences with those in a similar situation who went through the same type of difficulties plays a decisive factor in understanding their own disadvantage. If that is the case, the process of forming a group evaluation is nothing other than an effective measure to create important information concerning "general facts about human society" that is relevant to the public.

Moreover, the essential point is that such formation of group evaluation is an ethical behavior that is similar to but totally different from strategic behaviors such as the expansion of vested interest in nature. The three conditions imposed on the group evaluation formation process are to give shape to the ethics that restrict those forming group evaluations. By doing so, they are required to see from the perspective of the least-advantaged among the members with similar disadvantage and not from their "named' positions." Also, with regard to a choice that provides capability that exceeds basic capabilities, they are requested to refrain from giving any evaluation such that "more is better."

With the above in mind, the following points need to be considered. If special treatment is given to evaluations of diverse groups when aggregating individual evaluations, and even more, if a certain level of ethics is imposed on a group evaluation process, these requests themselves need to be admitted under the formal, epistemological condition of "impartiality." We call the field to form such approval the "pre-original condition." What kinds of features should it have?

In considering this issue, it is beneficial to understand the conceptual significance of "impartiality." Impartiality by Rawls shows equal concern to everyone (including him- or herself) while also giving priority to the least advantaged. Rawls's theory of justice implied that to treat individuals asymmetrically according to the difference in position does not immediately conflict with impartiality as a formal and epistemological condition. However, his theory of justice does not extend toward giving asymmetrical weight to the decision maker's evaluation that is in a particular and diverse "position."

In interpreting Sen's idea on the concept of "impartiality," the two concepts of "positional objectivity" and "open impartiality" provide us a clue. Let us briefly examine these concepts respectively. First, Sen defines "positional objectivity" taking a hint from the phrase "a view from somewhere in society," which is an inverted version of Thomas Nagel's phrase "a view from nowhere." "Somewhere in society" or "position" mentioned in the phrase widely represents historical, social, cultural, and personal characteristics, and its qualitative differences are considered to attract social interests. When an observation, claim, belief, or action is recognized as a "position" through a bundle of parameters rather than through a unique identification with a proper name or pronoun, that is where we can recognize "positional objectivity" that surpasses personal subjectivity.

However, "positional objectivity" does not necessarily guarantee "truth." Individuals who share a given position have the possibility of sharing, without realizing it, "objective illusion." Or it might lead to an object of stigma (Goffman 1963a), inviting labelling and xenophobia as well. This was exactly what Marx pointed out in the epistemological condition of a person under social constraints. In this context, Sen provided the concept of "trans-positional assessment" mentioned in Chap. 5, which corresponds to such reflective activities as "drawing on but going beyond different positional observations" (Sen 1993b/2002a, 467). For example, a person who simultaneously belongs to multiple groups such as social class, gender, citizenship, or profession forms an evaluation from his or her group's perspective and also gains the opportunity to critically examine the evaluation through the eyes of other groups (Sen 1999a, 28).

The epistemic implication of "trans-positional assessments" becomes clearer in the light of the concept of "open impartiality," which is essentially based on the

Smithian notion of "the impartial spectator" (Smith, originally published in 1759). According to Sen, the device of the "original position" of Rawls remains at the level of "closed impartiality" in that "the institutionally constructive character of the Rawlsian system restricts the extent to which the perspectives of the "outsiders" can be accommodated within the exercise of impartial assessment" (Sen 2009a, 128). In other words, it does not require "forceful examination of local values that may, on further scrutiny, turn out to be preconceptions and biases that are common in a focal group" (Sen 2009a, 128). Here, "local values" implies values that tend to be unconsciously formed with a specific position such as a nation state.

In contrast, "open impartiality" requires one to be at a distance from any particular position, not only from one's own position within one's focal group, the group to which the evaluator belongs, but also from the position of the focal group itself. There is a similar structure to "trans-positional assessments" that broadly reflects different position-situated evaluations, but which is not reduced to a single impartial spectator. The latter is perfectly "neutral" (that is, disinterested in various differences) with regard to every position of all agencies, which is called "trans-positional invariance" and criticized by Sen.

With the concept of "open impartiality" as the base, there is a way to theorize the "pre-original position" stage, in which either a symmetrical model or an asymmetrical model is chosen from among symmetrical decision makers depending on the agenda. What is at stake is that an asymmetrical social choice procedure in original position can be selected as an appropriate procedure for a certain agenda from an impartial standpoint among the symmetrical decision makers in the "pre-original position" stage. Figure 6.3 illustrates two types of social choice procedures, (A) and (B).

In (A), individuals with disadvantages disclose their capability appraisals, with which the group is defined endogenously. And then, for respective policies, capabilities of the least advantaged within each group and concepts of basic capability of the group are directly considered as an informational base. It is a model where every individual forms a personal evaluation, which will be symmetrically weighed and aggregated to form a social evaluation. In contrast, in (B), individuals with disadvantages form groups, and form group-based evaluations based on the capability appraisals of the least advantaged within each group. The aggregation procedure to make a social evaluation gives priority to the group-based evaluations. In summary, "decision power" is symmetrical among all individuals in (A), while in (B) it becomes asymmetrical between individuals that belongs to a group and those that do not. "Post-original position," which will be explained later, is also noted in Fig. 6.3.

6.4 Background Philosophy for Consensus and Implementation

Finally, let us examine the following four criticisms expected to surface against the social choice model envisaged in this chapter.

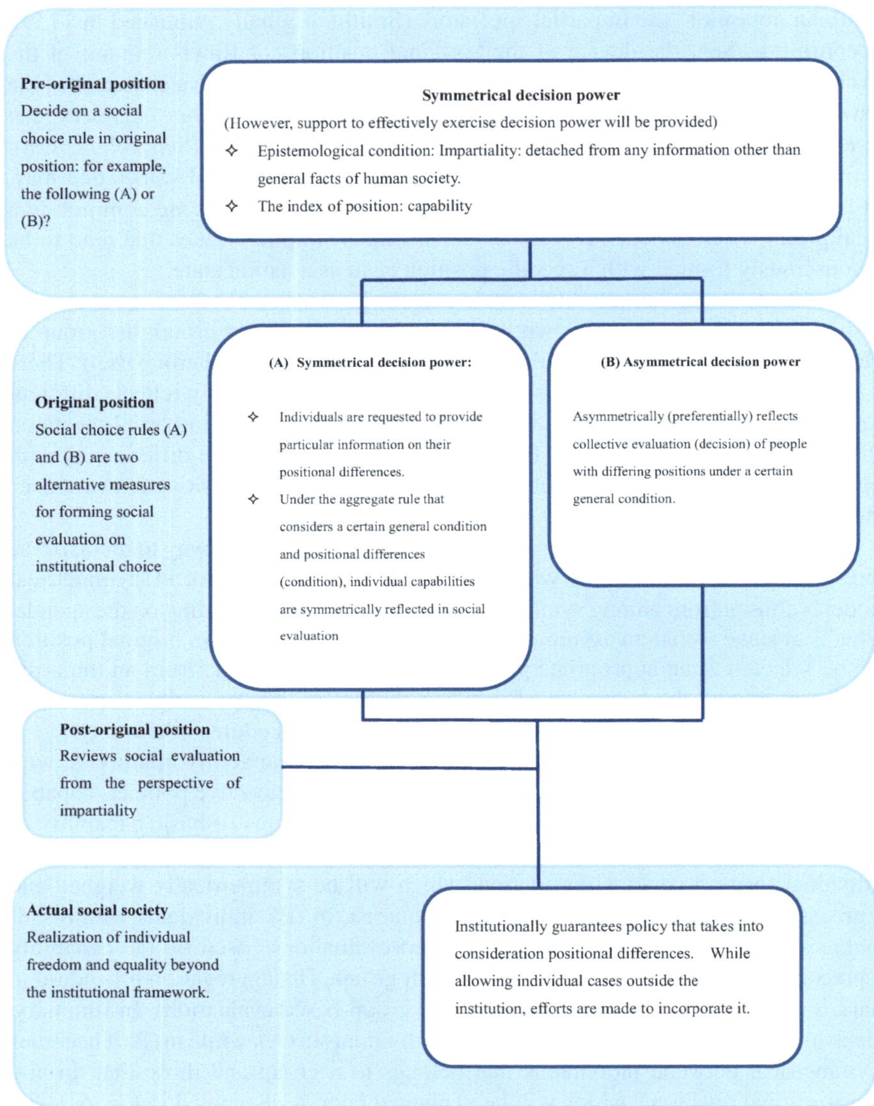

Fig. 6.3 Expansion of original position based on the capability approach: pre-original position, original position, postoriginal position and actual social society: In original position, parties choose social choice procedure with (A) symmetrical decision power or with (B) asymmetrical decision power

- Could financial resources to realize the socially chosen "just" policy bundle be constantly secured?
- How can the expected conflict of distribution among the groups of the least advantaged be solved?
- With regard to a policy that financially supports people suffering from disadvantage, could we reach social agreement including the general public?
- Can the content of "basic capability" that needs to be socially secured for each group be objectively defined?

Let us note the philosophy behind the social choice model while responding to these questions. With regard to the first question, we would like to first point out the following. The aggregation of financial resources changes depending on available natural resources or capital, technology, labor force, and individuals' preferences and evaluations. Therefore, if the concept of "basic capability" is defined exogenously, independent from these factors, apparently there is no guarantee in securing financial resources to realize it. For example, in the case of "the difference principle" proposed by Rawls, which requires "maximization of the expectations of the least advantaged," since the level of maximized expectations is defined endogenously, it can evade the problem of feasibility, whereas instead, this principle cannot secure whether such a level is at least the same as basic capability. There exists a serious trade-off between the guaranteeing of feasibility and the realizing of basic capability.[15]

To counter this difficult question, this chapter proposes that while defining the concept of "basic capability" exogenously, social evaluation that compares various alternative policies including those that may not be realized should be formed. The merit of this proposal is that by using "basic capability" as a reference point, we could clearly indicate what are "just" social states on the one hand, and on the other hand, we can pave the way to choose a "more just" policy among "unjust" but feasible policies.

As for securing financial resources, let us point out the following. Economic activities of individuals which are the source of tax are not unrelated to their normative judgements regarding policies. Rather, information that people refer to when judging policies, such as information on people suffering from various sorts of disadvantages, cannot but influence individuals' labor incentives, i.e., skill improvements and choices of working hours. It is difficult to sufficiently grasp this issue from the framework of neo-classical economics where each individual is supposed to choose his or her own work hours regarding utilities derived from leisure and income in terms of maximizing his or her self-interest under given economic environments.

Social evaluation in this chapter can also be interpreted as a normative evaluation of policies that an individual shapes. Social evaluation is derived from a social choice procedure that uses local evaluation formed by groups and capability as an informational base. While the procedure fulfills the refrain condition, it can be interpreted as a procedure for an individual to integrate its pluralistic identity. This may provide

[15]Refer to the last chapter of Sen and Gotoh (2008) for details.

a different perspective from that of neoclassical economics with regard to securing financial resources to realize public policies.

As for the second question, "How can we solve an expected conflict of distribution among the groups of the least advantaged?" we assume in this chapter that social evaluation of the overall society is formed giving priority to the local perspective (group-based evaluations) of the group that actually suffers from disadvantages. However, we first admit that there is no denying the possibility of conflict arising among the different disadvantaged groups. In considering this problem, it might be better to differentiate the following two types of conflicts.

One is a conflict based on each group's request to seek a guarantee of basic capability and the other is a conflict derived from a request for more support that exceeds basic capability. The former conflict is more serious in the sense that it is a conflict seeking "due proportion" (called "reasonable conflict") but can be evaded if the total financial resources in society are sufficient to cover everyone's basic capabilities. On the other hand, the latter conflict is a conflict requesting more than "due proportion" (called "unreasonable conflict"), which cannot be evaded even if financial resources are ample to cover everyone's basic capability. Social choice procedure in this chapter requests that each group refrain from creating conflicts for the latter.

This is exactly the reason that we limit the use of the monotonicity condition in this chapter. According to the consumer theory of neo-classical economics, monotonicity is defined as "For any two vectors x, y, if $x \geq y$ holds, x is preferred to y, if $x > y$, x is strongly preferred to y" and is understood as one of the efficient criteria without question.[16] The utility function defined in commodity space is usually assumed to fulfill monotonicity (strictly speaking, monotonicity is considered one of the prerequisites of preference for the continuous utility function to exist).[17] A Bergson–Samuelson social welfare function defined on utility space (as aforementioned, also Rawls's social primary goods) is assumed to fulfill monotonicity.

Nevertheless, in a case where local evaluations formed by specific groups are given priority when forming social evaluation, it is deemed acceptable to be cautious in applying this criterion. In this chapter, monotonicity is defined as a criterion, "a policy bundle that brings about more desirable capabilities is more just." And if two alternative policies both fall below basic capability, each group will be requested to adopt this criterion, but if they are equivalent to basic capability no request will be made. In the latter case, each group is expected to refrain from expressing the group's evaluation ("refrain condition") in public. The reason is that the object of public policy of "securing basic well-being for all" proposed in this chapter is to realize only basic capability and not more.

Moreover, as for the third question, that is, with regard to a policy that financially supports people suffering from disadvantage, "Could we reach social agreement

---

[16]Inequality of vectors is defined as follows. For all $x, y \in \mathbb{R}^k_+$, $x \geq y \Leftrightarrow (x-y) \in \mathbb{R}^k_+$; $x > y \Leftrightarrow [x \neq y$ and $x \geq y]$; $x \gg y \Leftrightarrow (x\text{-}y) \in \mathbb{R}^k_{++}$.

[17]Continuous utility function exists when preferences have completeness, reflexivity, and transitivity as well as continuous and strong monotonicity.

including the general public?", we assumed in this chapter that the individuals will agree to give priority to the local perspective (group-based evaluation) of the disadvantaged groups when forming social evaluation. But there are various ways of giving consent. For example, we can assume that an individual forms his or her own public judgement, respecting information of various group-based evaluations (Fig. 6.3A).

In an actual case, individuals may internalize a group's local evaluation as if it might be their own evaluation through actually supporting this group. Or, they may form their own public judgements through struggling to balance the local evaluation of a different disadvantaged group and their own interests, and lastly, by reproducing a social choice procedure that integrates such conflicts. Moreover, they may announce that they will not refrain from expressing any personal evaluation and rather entrust evaluations of other constituents with more information.[18] These cases are both regarded as measures to indicate recognition of local evaluations formed by various disadvantaged groups.

Personal public judgements influence one another in forming a social public judgement. However, personal public judgements are not necessarily formed prior to social public judgement but at times they may be formed almost simultaneously, or it may be that personal social judgements are determined only when social evaluation can be taken into consideration. Social choice procedure in this chapter is nothing other than an explicit expression of conditions that need to be accepted by personal public judgements in order to secure basic capabilities to everyone. To explicitly state this point, the post-original position is included in Fig. 6.3. Here, discussion to reflect on the appropriateness of the conditions is held. The "impartiality" condition is requested here as well.

Finally, the fourth question—namely, "Can the content of basic capability that needs to be socially guaranteed to each group be objectively defined?" The concept of "basic capability" is considered to be a reference point for each group to judge whether a certain policy is just. Its content is allowed to be different for each disadvantaged group while leaving open the possibility of being the same across all groups. In practice, it is possible to inductively finalize the conceptual meaning and specific content of basic capability through judging whether each alternative policy is sufficient to secure basic welfare to the least advantaged in the group. However, we need to make an assumption theoretically for the following point. The concept of basic capability for each group needs to have "positional objectivity," which allows people from outside the group to scrutinize and recognize it. That is, basic capability of each group reflects accurately the actual state of the group members and at the same time it is important to be able to explain the reason and rationale of social assistances to people outside the group.

---

[18] Attention to social evaluation by individuals is related to Sen's following words. "But it is important to distinguish between a person's preferences as they actually are and what he thinks he would accept as a basis of public policy given the preferences of others and given his values on collective choice procedures." (Sen 1970a, 66)

6.5 Concluding Remarks

In the standard social choice theory, a set of social constituents is directly equivalent to a set of decision makers, and their preferences are counted with the same weight when aggregating. On the other hand, while all social constituents are considered decision makers and their opinions are equally taken into consideration (independent from their names), the theory considered in this chapter assumes that a procedure where submitted opinions (reflecting various positions) are weighed differently qualitatively will take place. However, to weigh them differently, a basis for criteria needs to be open and publicly announced. In practice, such weighting should be done at a public discussion on a stage where an interested party, affected party, and fair evaluator are assembled together.

Such a social choice model as a measure for public discussion proposed by Sen significantly extended the range of Rawls's justice principle regarding formation of an individual's public judgement. When each individual belongs to different types of groups simultaneously and has to commit to multiple opposing requests, conflict among the groups may surface in the form of each individual's internal conflict and crisis of identity. In the face of such a situation, how would an individual try to pursue integration? One possible way is the "integrated meta preference function" discussed in Chap. 5, which pursues integration based on the person's private interest and comprehensive belief. In this case, a particular request of each group will be weighed using the existing private interest and comprehensive belief as a fixed point and thus, is highly likely to return to the impossibility theorem. However, it may not be realistic that an individual committed to multiple groups continues to unconsciously hold just one private interest and comprehensive belief. The reason is as follows:

An individual belonging to multiple groups internally commits to individual requests from each group and at the same time has an opportunity to observe externally. And he or she reevaluates the group's individual request through the eyes of another group's concern which will also be implemented for his or her own internal identities. Simultaneously, individuals will be blessed with an opportunity to gain a more public perspective that allows him or her to measure impartially the universal and human significance of each group's particular request. Sen's idea of "reason before identity" (1999b) was to grasp this process. In that way, it may open up possibilities to form, to a certain extent, common judgement on how to weigh each act of justice (a resource allocation measure for fair implementation) among individuals that gained public perspective. And even if multiple differing judgements are left on the table, they would be considered by what Rawls called "public reasoning" or "overlapping consensus".

Nevertheless, it is not easy for individuals to transcend their own private perspectives and egos to understand the necessity of basic capability and the meaning of securing it for all.

An individual in a certain position does not necessarily recognize the meaning of his or her necessity of basic capability before public reasoning or debate. There are cases where individuals refrain from making a request for society, considering that his or her necessity is peculiar or selfish. Vice versa, criteria of monotonicity may be limitlessly applied, which is justified under the pretext of great cause. That is precisely the reason why, as Sen noted, the process of social choice procedure becomes all important as a forum for public debate, where people with loosely multi-tiered identities—at times the direct negotiator or indirectly affected person or unbiased evaluator—may gather together to interpret and identify the universal and human meaning of various individual requests.

Chapter 7
Freedom and Death: Why Did She Not Apply for Public Assistance?

7.1 Introduction: A Case of Starvation

In January 2012, two sisters were found dead due to starvation in Shiroishi, Sapporo City, Japan. The elder sister had been unemployed, fighting a chronic disease, and looking for a job, while taking care of her younger sister with mental disabilities at the same time. She had consulted the Shiroishi ward office three times before. Their only income was the monthly disability payment of 66,008 yen for the younger sister. Their rents were unpaid and the sisters were not covered by the (supposedly universal) national health insurance. According to the Public Assistance Act, the minimum cost of living for the sisters' household amounted to 184,720 yen per month.

Why were the sisters unable to receive public assistance? The ward office's answer to this question was quite simple. "Because they didn't show the will to do so." This answer simply refuses to provide any more discussion, given the "principle of application" being taken for granted by the current public assistance system.[1] It is rather difficult to argue against the claim that the sisters' rights were not unfairly violated.

The Japanese Constitution guarantees the right to well-being (a minimum standard of living). It is argued, however, that it is preceded by the right to pursuing happiness and the right to personality.[2] John Rawls's theory of justice stipulates the "difference principle" that supports the right to live, but the principle of "equal freedoms and fair opportunities" has a clear priority over it. In an advanced market economy, receiving no public assistance tends to be regarded as a result of an individual's

[1]The "principle of application" is legislated in Article 7.1 of the Public Assistance Act: "Public assistance has to be provided only after an application is made by someone in need of protection, his or her supporter, or his or her family member living with him or her. However, it *can be* provided without application when he or she is in a critical and urgent situation" (emphasis added by the author).

[2]Japanese Constitution, Articles 12 and 13.

R. Gotoh, *The Ethics and Economics of the Capability Approach*, Hitotsubashi University IER Economic Research Series 46, https://doi.org/10.1007/978-981-15-5140-6_7

own choice in her private sphere, which in turn is considered to reveal her (bounded rational) preferences under given constraints. Can laws, institutions, and academics say nothing about this?

To shed light on this problem, this chapter will apply two different approaches, used in welfare economics, to analyze "the right to freedom."[3] One is AmartyaSen's social choice approach and the other is also Sen's capability approach. Below I briefly explain why I adopt these two approaches. The reason I emphasize "Sen's social choice approach" in particular is that, to be described in Chap. 9, we recognize a shift of direction from Arrow's social choice theory to Sen's. Driving the shift is "the right to freedom" for individuals, which is the subject of this and the next chapter.

As seen so far, Sen has been exploring the concept of freedom in economics with wide-ranging perspectives. In *Collective Choice and Social Welfare* (Sen 1970a/2017), he reinterprets Kenneth Arrow's general possibility theorem (Arrow 1951a/1963) by focusing on the conflict between the Pareto Principle and the Condition of Liberalism. Arrow's general possibility theorem shows that there is no social welfare function that satisfies all four conditions (Unrestricted Domain, Pareto Principle, Independence of irrelevant alternatives, and Non-dictatorship) simultaneously, where a social welfare function refers to a procedure to derive a social preference from individual preferences held by members of society.[4]

Sen replaced the conditions of Independence of irrelevant alternatives and Non-dictatorship in Arrow's theorem with the condition of Minimum Liberty, holding conditions of Unrestricted domain and the Pareto principle, and proved an impossibility in a similar way. As we discuss later, Minimum Liberty connotes an individual's "decision power" to disturb certain social states from being realized as outcomes depending only on her preference whatever it is. It represents a kind of strong "right to freedom" in the sense that individual values (either arbitral preferences or delivered evaluations, or either false interests or true interests) can regulate a part of social states.

Furthermore, his *Development as Freedom* (Sen 1999a) proposes a framework for economic development as a process for people to realize "comprehensive freedom to lead the kinds of lives they have reason to value," by utilizing various "instrumental freedoms" (such as political freedom, economic advantage, social opportunity, transparent guarantee, and protective security). In order to capture this concept of comprehensive freedom, Sen also proposed two concepts of agency freedom and well-being freedom.

Agency freedom is concerned with an individual's purposes and acts. It looks at whether her will and choices are respected. Well-being freedom is about consequential states (well-being) for the person (called "capability"). It looks at whether

[3]See Gotoh (2016a) for details.

[4]Unrestricted Domain implies that the rule must work for every logically possible profiles of individual preferences. The Pareto Principle implies that if everyone prefers x to y, society must also prefer x to y. Independence of irrelevant alternatives implies that social choice over a set of alternatives must depend on the rankings of the individuals only over the set of alternatives. Non-dictatorship implies that there should be no individual such that whenever he prefers x to y, society must prefer x to y, irrespective of the preference of everyone else (Sen 1970a/2017).

her interests (i.e., values available to her) are directly respected as they are (without necessarily being so by her own will or choice). Agency freedom is usually captured by subjective measures such as utility or satisfaction. Well-being freedom is also captured by objective measures such as positional evaluation by those in the same circumstance as she is.

What is at stake in the following? On the one hand, Sen's social choice theory focuses mainly on agency freedom in helping us analyze what is meant by the statement "She didn't show her will to apply," whereas the latter looks at the issue in terms of well-being freedom represented by her capability for "decent living" and "self-respect." On the other hand, as we indicate in the following sections, these two research methods are closely interrelated and complement each other.

This incident has already produced some excellent reports and analyses. There are also many research articles on welfare policies including Japan's public assistance system. Referring to these works, however, this chapter adopts economic angles to study the subject for the following reasons.[5]

First, economics assumes that individuals make rational choices based on their preferences and evaluations under given constraints. Then it provides analytical perspectives to examine circumstances for and external constraints on rational choices made by individuals. It reflects the essence of liberalism, i.e., respect for individuals, and a functional view of individuality and agency. These two approaches, first elaborated by Sen, which this chapter adopts, basically follow the analytical framework of economics but radically criticize some core conventional assumptions and premises in order to approach a truer look at human conditions. This incident happened in the midst of the spread of liberal thought and the development of social security systems after the end of the Second World War. The analysis of this incident by the aforementioned two approaches sheds light on a blind spot and suggests some points to consider.

Second, as will be clear later, analyses of this incident based on Sen's two approaches do not go beyond the academic framework. There are some limitations and inefficiencies in staying within a constrained, stylized academic framework. However, academic studies can sometimes break the wall of silence for individuals who are sacrificed by natural contingencies or historical injustice, and it is certain that academic studies affect not only the administration and practice of actual legal systems and institutions but also the social norms formed and transformed by people on a daily basis. Besides, it will be worthwhile contributing to the community of economics, rather than the global market for economics, by adopting an academic style and words.

In the following I am going to analyze Sen's Social Choice Approach. Let me begin the next section by examining its cornerstone: "The Impossibility of a Paretian Liberal."

---

[5] As for the normative characteristics of Japan's public assistance system, see Gotoh (2009, 2016b).

7.2 The Impossibility of a Paretian Liberal (Sen 1970a/2017, 1970b)

7.2.1 Summary of the Theorem

"The Impossibility of a Paretian Liberal" (or so-called Liberal Paradox) means the following. When equal freedom for individual preferences (the assumption of unrestricted domain) is guaranteed, we cannot logically deny the possibility of a conflict between the Pareto Principle (of socially respecting unanimous preferences over a pair of social alternatives) and the Condition of Liberalism (for an individual's decisive power over a pair of social alternatives).

Let us begin by explaining the meaning of "freedom" in the Liberal Paradox. For the present context, two concepts of freedom are incorporated. The first is implied by the "unrestricted domain" and forbids any social intervention against individual will and preference revelations.'[6,7] However, it says nothing about whether revealed wills or preferences of individuals are actually realized in the process of social decisions.

The second concept is what Sen calls the "Condition of Liberalism" (Sen 1970b/1997a, 287[1997a]), which directly means "decisiveness" that an individual has in forming social decisions. That is, if an individual prefers one alternative to the other in a pair of alternatives (social states), the latter (less preferred alternative) should not be chosen by society. Note that this does not guarantee the social choice of the alternative preferred by her; hence this is a "rejection decisiveness" (Sen 1970a/2017, 330[2017]) to be precise, but we call this an "individual decisive power" to avoid confusion.[8]

The Pareto Principle means a kind of "collective decision power," in the sense that anyone can exercise her decisive power when everyone agrees to her opinion. It represents a condition for democracy in the sense that it gives every member an equal weight in preventing the exercise of "collective decision power," while it gives non-members of society no weight in preventing the exercise of that power. Note that social choice theory's underlying assumption of counting every individual with an equal weight in social decisions also represents a condition for democracy.

Suppose it is reasonable to expect that at least two individuals in a society have an "individual decisive power" over at least one pair of alternatives, respectively.

---

[6]This is closer to the concept of "freedom to choose one's own strategies," formulated in game form in Gaertner et al. (1992), for example, as the result of choice is not yet socially realized. However, if an individual chooses a particular strategy and its consequence constitutes part of the corresponding social state as it is, her strategy set itself can be regarded as something over which she has the "individual right".

[7]In Arrow's framework, the condition of Unrestricted Domain is supposed to capture, above all, the universal nature of the decision rule, i.e., social decision procedures must be defined over all logically possible preference profiles. In addition, Arrow also assumes a requirement of universality that they have to bring a non-empty set of social alternatives from any subset of the set of all logically possible alternatives. For details, see Chap. 9.

[8]More precisely, it implies "an individual right to rejection decisiveness".

If this is not possible, it would be because of the Pareto Principle as a condition for democracy and also due to the unrestricted domain as a condition for freedom. We can understand "the Impossibility of a Paretian Liberal" as condensation or crystallization of the hidden conflict between liberalism and democracy, which has long been pointed out by many political philosophers such as Schmitt (1923/1988).

7.2.2 Logical Solutions

Sen began criticizing the Pareto Principle immediately after proposing the theorem, on the basis that we cannot take for granted the ethical nature of the Pareto Principle. Sen divides individual preferences into those meant to be social preferences ("public judgements") and the others. He then suggests applying the Pareto Principle only to public judgements of the latter and not the former. Furthermore, he considers an individual who accepts the "Liberal condition" as a norm. Such an individual makes only her public judgements that are consistent with this condition. Sen proves a theorem whereby this paradox can be solved if just one such individual should exist (Sen 1976a; Suzumura 1978, 1979; See the Short Appendix at the end of this chapter for details).

It has been pointed out by other economists that the Pareto Principle is not sufficient as a criterion for resource allocation. However, few authors claim that neither is it necessary. Sen is unique not only for questioning the ethical status of the Pareto Principle in a political context but also for looking at it in terms of publicness as individuals' moral features. This approach led to discussion of public reasoning and deliberation later in his work.

7.2.3 The Scope of the Impossibility of a Paretian Liberal

Sen went further to criticize, so to speak, the idea of "positional independence." That is, under any preference profiles, when people's preference rankings over a certain pair of alternatives remain the same, the social ranking of the two alternatives should remain the same, independent of their positional relations with the other alternatives.[9]

Sen emphasized that the Independence of irrelevant alternatives condition is not used to derive the "Impossibility of a Paretian Liberal." At the same time he points out that the "Pareto condition" incorporates this feature, as it requires that under any preference profile, if social rankings over any pair of alternatives are the same across

[9]It is known that Unrestricted domain, Pareto Indifference condition, and Independence of Irrelevant Alternatives are equivalent to the Neutrality condition. Sen criticized this Neutrality condition in the name of Welfarism (Sen 1979a/1997a). Note that Independence of Irrelevant Alternatives as well as Anonymity has some affinity with a political or philosophical idea called the Neutrality of the Good. The naming of "positional independence" here owes to the concept of "positional objectivity" (Sen 1993a/2002a).

all individuals, the social ranking of the two alternatives should remain the same, independent of their positional relations with the other alternatives.

It should be noted that the "individual decisive power" also incorporates this requirement, as it demands that under any preference profiles, for at least one pair of alternatives, if a particular individual ranks them in the same way, their social rankings should remain the same.[10]

As we already explained, the "unrestricted domain" condition requires the expression of "under any preference profiles" in the previous paragraph to be "any logically possible preference profiles." Earlier we found in this condition liberalism in a narrow sense that wills and preferences revealed by individuals should not be interfered with. We have to note that the broader the scope of logically possible preference profiles (freedom for individuals) becomes, the stronger the force of legal systems and institutions that control their freedom appears, i.e., the system of order becomes tougher *vis-à-vis* free actions of individuals. The "unrestricted domain" condition indeed requires a high level of generality and universality for the initial states and requires a high level of transparency for the legal or ethical systems that restricts the level of generality and universality in the initial states.

Subsequently, Sen went on to criticize the situation whereby people merely discuss general, complete, and highly abstract rules that can be applied to any set of feasible alternatives for any logically possible preference profiles, under the narrow definition of liberalism. He also argued against concluding the discussion only by proving some logical impossibility or possibility.[11] This was because, in practice, on the one hand concrete interpretations and handlings of many hard cases are left to legal and administrative discretions while on the other hand their results, whatever their contents are, can often be justified by the name of those general, complete, and highly abstract rules.[12]

7.2.4 Challenges for the Paretian Liberal Approach

Discussion on the compatibility of a Paretian Liberal Condition also presupposes the existence of a system of rights where individual spheres for rights are consistent with each other (see the Short Appendix of this chapter). However, a serious problem can arise regarding inconsistencies among various rights. It is not only about conflict between rights of different individuals (when individual preferences are given). It is also about conflict between different rights held by a particular individual or inconsistency between specific rights and the access to decision procedures. For

[10]Sen proved his own Impossibility of a Paretian Liberal by using the universality of the domain to show the existence of a preference profile where individual rights and the Pareto principle are not compatible.

[11]See Sen (1966a, 1967a) for his skepticism about rational universalizability of morality.

[12]Majority rules are a good example of the universal rule. Note Sen's following remark, for example. "Majority rules have a political limitation of being unable to adjust different freedoms." (Maskin and Sen 2014, 40).

example, it would not be obvious how to weight different rights such as freedom of action, freedom to work, and freedom to live, or how to relate specific rights and the right to weigh them. Some real incidents suggest that in certain situations society should present certain kinds of rights of a certain range of individuals prior to presenting other kinds of rights, sometimes even before their decisions are made.

In order to examine these problems we have to go beyond the framework for formal aggregation of individual (ordinal and interpersonally incomparable) preference and step into the situation of social choice. Sen's widening concern with individual freedom and rights has led to an extension and deepening of Arrovian social choice theory. In the following section we look at its characteristics by analyzing the case we introduced in the beginning.

7.3 Analysis of Agency Freedom with Sen's Social Choice Theory

7.3.1 The Basic Model

Suppose there is a society with a certain number of members. Individuals declare their reflexive and acyclical preferences over a nonempty set of alternatives.[13] We call a "social choice function" a procedure specifying a nonempty subset (or a "choice set") from a set of alternatives based on the profile of their declared preferences.[14] We assume that a "social choice function" satisfies the following two conditions.

Pareto Principle: For any pair of alternatives x and y, y must not be chosen from a set of alternatives including x if all individuals prefer x to y (as long as x is available).

Individual Decisive Power: For a pair of alternatives x and y, y must not be chosen from a set of alternatives including x if a certain individual prefers x toy (as long as x is available). Similarly, x must not be chosen from a set of alternatives including y if she prefers y to x (as long as y is available).

Moreover, we assume that in general, social choice functions satisfy the condition of "unrestricted domain," that is, individuals can have any preference over their set of alternatives.

---

[13]Individual preferences do not satisfy completeness and transitivity but they satisfy acyclicity, which guarantees that no choice set is empty (Sen 1970a/2017, 1970b).

[14]"Social choice function" defined here is a version of "the functional collective choice rule (FCCR)" as its domain is a set of individual preference profiles and its range is a set of subsets of the universal set. However, it is different from a standard FCCR because it does not require completeness of corresponding individual preferences nor consistency among alternative sets (Sen 1970a, 2002a, Chap. 3).

7.3.2 Social Choice Relation Between Client and Officer

Suppose that the elder sister (individual 1) has been offered by a welfare officer (individual 2) the following four options [Seek (a job), Not Seek, Apply, Not Apply].[15] Furthermore, individual 1 has been told that she has a decisive power over the following pair of options.

Individual 1's decisive power: (Apply, Not Apply)

Let us remember that individual 1 and individual 2 can have any preference over the four options. Then suppose they have the following preferences (in descending order). We assume the other members of society all have the preference held by individual 2.

Individual 1's preference: Seek > Apply > Not Apply > Not Seek

Individual 2's preference: Not Apply > Seek > Not Seek > Apply

This shows that individual 1 prefers Apply to Not Apply, while she shares a preference for Seek over Apply with individual 2. Note also that individual 2 and the rest of society want individual 1 to choose Not Apply more than anything. With these assumptions, let us examine which alternative will be socially chosen by a social choice function that satisfies the Pareto principle and the principle of "individual decisive power."

We can see that all individuals prefer Seek to Apply and prefer Not Apply to Not Seek. Thus, the Pareto principle excludes Apply and Not Seek from the choice set. Also, individual 1's "decisive power" means Not Apply cannot be socially chosen. This leaves us with Seek as the only result of our social choice. Accepting this result, individual 1 does not apply for public assistance and goes home to start seeking a job.

7.3.3 Three Modifications: What Does Officer's Evaluation Represent?

Three remarks follow the previous discussion. First, we described alternatives regarding individual 1's action alone. Now we can describe extended alternatives by including individual 2's (and the other members') situation. Individual 1's application (and receiving of public assistance) would increase a financial burden on individual 2, while individual 1's use of "the job seeker's assistance system" would decrease individual 2's financial burden.[16] When individual 1 chooses neither Apply

[15] We assume that Apply and Seek are different, independent alternatives. For example, the former can use public assistance and the latter can use the "Job seeker's support system," which we discuss later.

[16] "The job seeker's assistance system" is a system under which people who are not qualified to receive employment insurance aim to find a job earlier by improving their skills through job training.

nor Seek, individual 2's financial burden will remain the same. In this case, the alternative set will be extended as follows.

{(Seek, Less Burden), (Apply, More Burden), (Not Apply, Same Burden), (Not Seek, Same Burden)}

Let us suppose that individual 1's decisive power is re-defined over the pair [(Apply, More Burden), (Not Apply, Same Burden)] and individual 2 now has newly an "individual decisive power" over two social states [(Seek, Less Burden), (Not Seek, Same Burden)].[17] Based on these suppositions, if individual 1 and 2 express the following preferences, we can easily confirm that the choice set becomes empty. This example is nothing else than what Sen calls the Liberal Paradox.

Individual 1's preference: (Not Seek, Same Burden) > (Apply, More Burden) > (Not Apply, Same Burden) > (Seek, Less Burden)

Individual 2's preference: (Not Apply, Same Burden) > (Seek, Less Burden) > (Not Seek, Same burden) > (Apply, More Burden)

Second, here let us assume that concerning the following two options, (Apply, More Burden) or (Not Apply, Same Burden)], individual 2 now has the same preference as individual 1. Thus we see the following individual preferences.

Individual 1's preference: (Seek, Less Burden) > (Apply, More Burden) > (Not Apply, Same Burden) > (Not Seek, Same Burden)

Individual 2's preference: (Seek, Less Burden) > (Not Seek, Same burden) > (Apply, More Burden) > (Not Apply, Same Burden)

When we apply the procedure we used before, there is only (Seek, Less Burden) left in the choice set. Hence we have the same conclusion as before that individual 1 does not apply for public assistance.

Third, we go back to the original set of alternatives and consider the case where individual 1 regards Apply as the most preferable option for him or her, while individual 2′s preference holds as previously. Then, individual preferences change as follows.

Individual 1's preference: Apply > Seek > Not Apply > Not Seek

Individual 2's preference: Not Apply > Seek > Not Seek > Apply

---

Such people may receive "training in support of job seekers" or "public job training" for free in principle. "Hello Work" will support such people in a positive manner during the training period and after the end of the training period. To people who meet certain requirements of income and assets, etc., "benefits for receiving job training" are provided during the training period. See "Law on support of employment of specified job seekers through implementation of job training, etc." (Ministry of Health, Welfare and Labor 2011, no. 93).

[17]In the standard interpretation, individual rights are confined to individual private spheres, i.e., where one's action does not affect the others. This chapter does not adopt the "private sphere" interpretation as we focus on conflicts among individual decisive powers. Rather, we assume there are some social norms that determine individual "private sphere," on which an individual can have a decisive power.

In this situation, the Pareto Principle and the condition for Individual Decisive Power leave two alternatives, Apply and Seek, in the choice set. We need a third criterion to select just one alternative. Suppose we adopt the "Reservation of social decision" as the third criterion. Then individual 1 ends up going home without applying for public assistance after all. We are going to discuss how to solve the problem by changing sets of alternatives themselves below after the next section.

7.3.4 Note: Validity of the Social Choice Model

The above model describes the elder sister's circumstance not as a game played by two symmetric players but as a social choice situation that symbolizes Japanese society. Is this description appropriate in the beginning?

This social choice model will not be appropriate if the welfare officer behaves as an actor with his or her own interests and purposes or if the client (the elder sister) expects such behavior and merely acts accordingly.

However, there may be a positive reason to adopt the social choice model if we can make the following assumptions. First, the welfare officer (individual 2) might behave not as an individual but as a "professional," who is expected to follow social norms or popular opinions in making social decisions. Second, the welfare officer might stand as a representative of the social conscience (what Kant calls *gemainshaftlicher Sinn*) rather than merely as an advisor for the client (individual 1).[18] Third, it might be difficult for an individual to reject any result which, she knows, is reached through a procedure that satisfies certain reasonable criteria.[19]

Let us elaborate on the last point. According to Thomas Scanlon, what people can reasonably reject depends not only on their important purposes and the conditions of their lives but also on the society they live in. In this particular case, the elder sister faced options (Apply, Not) and (Seek, Not) but might not have been able to reasonably reject the social conscience that prefers Seek to Apply. Moreover, even when the result was against her interest, she might have given up arguing against it because it was the "consensus" reached via a due process. The social choice approach is appropriate in analyzing these conflicting situations with a small number of individuals, as it makes it possible to describe situations with a small number as a condensed situation of a whole society.

---

[18] According to Kant, "communal senses (*sensus communis*)" implies the idea of social conscience (*gemainshaftlicher Sinn*), i.e., "to reflect on and care about (a priori) how all other people are represented within oneself." It occurs by "cross-checking human reason in general and one's own judgements." Its purpose is "to avoid illusions that might poorly influence one's judgements based on some individual subjective conditions that can easily be regarded as objective." (Kant 1999, 180–181).

[19] See Scanlon (1982).

7.3.5 *Can She Access the Decision Process of the Alternative Set?*

Now let us go back to our original question. Can we say that agency freedom of individual 1 was respected in this social decision process? Individual 1 was guaranteed a decisive power over (Apply, Not). She could exercise that power and reveal any preference (the unrestricted domain). Her decisive power was not overturned by any social choice procedure that satisfied the Pareto Principle. If individual 1 had accepted the result of social choice (by all members of the society including the two individuals) and decided not to apply, then we might be obliged to say that her agency freedom was respected.

There is another issue we have to consider, however. As Sen points out, individual choices can vary, depending on the set of alternatives (and as the external reference standard changes). Was she able to have a say in setting her set of alternatives in the first place? If she were, would she have chosen to act differently? We would imagine that the answer to the latter question is affirmative and the former negative. To see this, we add a hypothetical analysis next.

Suppose that individual 1 now has four extended alternatives as follows: (Seek and Apply, Seek and Not Apply, Not Seek and Apply, Not Seek and Not Apply). As we change descriptions of the alternatives, individual 1's decisive power is also changed so that it is over the pair (Seek and Apply, Seek and Not Apply).[20] Suppose that preferences of individuals 1 and 2 (the others) are also changed as follows.

Individual 1: Seek and Apply > Not Seek and Apply > Seek and Not Apply > Not Seek and Not Apply

Individual 2 and others: Seek and Not Apply > Seek and Apply > Not Seek and Not Apply > Not Seek and Apply

Applying the social choice function described above, we can exclude, by the Pareto principle, Not Seek and Apply and Not Seek and Not Apply. By individual decisive power, we can also exclude Seek and Not Apply, which leaves us only with Seek and Apply. If individual 1 accepts this result, she applies for public assistance on that day and goes home to prepare for job hunting.[21]

This hypothetical reasoning indicates a possibility that individual 1's preference was constrained by the set of alternatives offered to her. Moreover, it shows that she was unable to participate in the process of deciding on her set of alternatives with

[20]This is based on a judgement that individuals are free to apply or not, as long as they do job hunting. Adding another pair (Not Seek and Apply, Not Seek and Not Apply) to her individual decisive power will not change the result.

[21]Note that the Japanese public assistance system established the "Independence Support Program" in 2005 and the "Independence Support System for the Needy" in 2013, both of which aim at promoting labor supply, but the former is for current recipients to exit the public assistance system, while the latter is for current non-recipients not to enter the public assistance system. Actually, there is no scheme that promotes getting a job with an income support.

enough information available to her. If these were the case, we can hardly claim that her agency freedom was guaranteed.

We can now finish our analysis using Paretian Liberal perspectives. We are going to discuss its implications in the concluding section. Now we will analyze well-being freedom, which focuses on situations of individuals as a consequence of individual choices. If an expected situation as a result of her choice had possibly made her hesitate to Apply, can we really say it was her own choice?

7.4 Analysis of Well-Being Freedom with the Capability Approach

The Capability Approach aims to capture individual well-being, i.e., what one can actually do or be at the moment by using various resources available for him or her. With an economic framework introduced in Chaps. 4 and 5, let us formulate and operationalize this approach.

7.4.1 The Basic Model

An individual's capability is defined as the set of "functionings" (various doings and beings) that she can achieve with resources (commodities) available to her and her ability to utilize them. The same amount of her resources and abilities can result in different vectors of (achieved levels of various) functionings, depending on how they are used by the individual. Her capability shows the limit on her achievability of various functionings.

An individual's opportunity set is, first, represented for example by the set of consumption points available to her on the commodity space. The size of her opportunity set represents her resource constraints and the shape of its frontier shows relative prices of different commodities. Individual preferences (utility function) are defined over infinite number of consumption points with several assumptions, therefore "optimal points" are specified from the opportunity set, that maximizes her utility.

Moreover, an individual's capability is represented by the set of functioning vectors she can choose on the functioning space, which is itself a subset of the real value space. The size of her capability represents her resource constraints and the shape of its frontier conversion rates of various functionings. Individual preferences are defined over various functioning vectors on the functioning space. The optimal point is one in her capability set that is preferred most by the individual.

Further, in order to analyze the effect of changes in resource constraints on the capability set, we construct our basic model consisting of the following three spaces:

(i) Functioning space, on which capability sets and evaluation functions are defined.
(ii) Resource (commodity)-functioning space, on which utilization abilities (functions) are defined.
(iii) Resource (commodity) space, on which commodity (opportunity) sets, market prices, budget constraints, and utility are defined.

(i) and (iii) are connected by (ii) (see Fig. 7.2 for example).

We suppose actual lists of functionings, resources, and utilization abilities depend on the theme and context. "Capability" (set), commodity, utilization abilities (functions), and preference and evaluation (function), defined in each space, are usually assumed to satisfy, respectively, convexity (capability set, commodity set and utilization abilities), and quasi-strong concavity (evaluation, utility), but these are relaxed, depending on the theme and context.[22]

7.4.2 *Specifying the Functioning Space*

We take two functionings, "Retaining self-respect" and "Living a decent life," as the x and y axes of the functioning space. We assume that achieved levels of each functioning are, at least ordinarily, measurable by an intra- and interpersonally comparable unit.[23] We simplify our arguments by assuming that individual preferences defined over functioning vectors satisfy some of the standard assumptions of rationality in economics (reflexivity, transitivity, completeness, monotonicity, and others).

We assume also that individual 1′s (the elder sister's) current levels in both functionings (in point b^*) are higher than if she receives public assistance (in point b'). If she receives public assistance (in point b'), her self-respect would diminish but her living standard would be higher.[24]

In order to understand the elder sister's decision not to apply for public assistance, we can explain why we capture her capability in the space of two functionings, "living" and "self-respect," and describe her three situations as above.

As explained earlier, the Japanese public assistance system requires any applicant and recipient to "use up" all his or her assets (life insurance, flat or condominium, any other "expensive things," gifts, and so on) by selling them. However, assets are associated with credit, trust, reputation, prestige, or whatever Rawls called the "social basis of self-respect."

---

[22] These assumptions are sufficient conditions for the existence and uniqueness of the optimal point.

[23] This means that they do not have to be cardinally comparable.

[24] Here we exclude an uncertain possibility of Apply but Do Not Receive. However, we can examine the case of Apply but Do Not Receive as resulting in point c which is dominated by point b in both "self-respect" and "decent living".

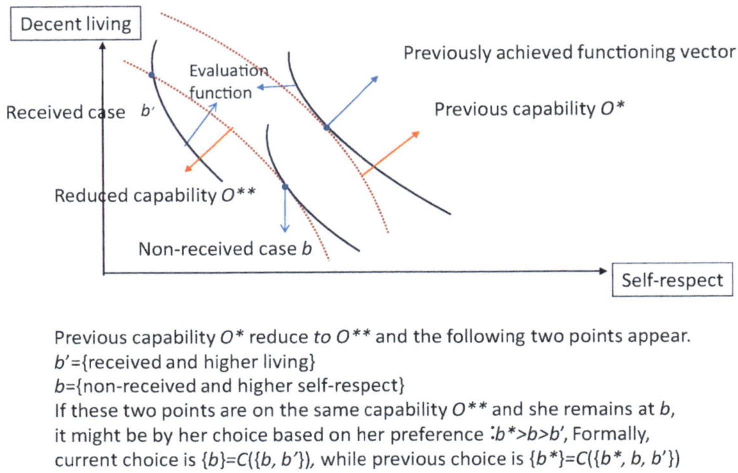

Fig. 7.1 Receiving public assistance or not, on the same capability frontier

What we call "self-respect" here has to be distinguished from "self-esteem," since self-respect is defined regarding her own situation, not regarding differences (by comparison) with others. It also derives from her reflection rather than from evaluations by others.[25] It would be difficult for her to maintain self-esteem independently of differences with others or evaluations by others in society today. For example, if one's own assets turn out to have very low prices, her self-esteem would be very much damaged and her self-respect might be threatened. Even then, she may be able to keep her self-respect if she can recognize the historical significance and intrinsic values of those assets in her life.

This chapter focused on a specific functioning of self-respect (and of "living" because the social basis of self-respect has never been regarded as something to be socially secured, despite growing social acceptance of liberal thoughts and recognition of the importance of self-respect in individual lives. One of the purposes of this chapter was to reflect on the meaning of this situation in relation to the rational behavior of individuals.

7.4.3 A Hard Choice from the Reduced Capability Set

We begin by studying a case where two statuses of receiving and not receiving public assistance are on the same capability frontier (Fig. 7.1).

By definition, an individual can choose any point on her capability frontier, depending (only) on her preferences. In this case, she can move from point b (not receiving public assistance) to point b' (receiving public assistance with a higher

[25] See Rawls (1971a), Kant (1785 = 1972, 243n).

living standard) by, for example, selling her assets and giving up on a certain amount of her self-respect. Or she can also move back from point b' (with public assistance) to point b by buying some assets and giving up on a certain amount of living standard.

We can say that it would be her own choice based on her preferences if she decides to remain on point b without public assistance. She could have chosen either point if she liked. If she recognized that she could have chosen the point she did not after all and decided not to receive public assistance, then it was nothing other than her own autonomous choice. We can say that preferences rationalizing such a choice tend to favor self-respect rather than living as depicted in Fig. 7.1.

In reality, however, receiving public assistance not only diminishes her self-respect in exchange for a higher standard of living. It might have transformed her capability. That is, receiving public assistance might have changed her capability from one with a higher achievability of self-respect to another with a lower self-respect. If she had to make a decision in such a situation, the meaning of her choice would be rather different. We can examine this in the next section.

7.5 Could She Have Reasonable Prospects for Exercising Agency Freedom?

7.5.1 Capability for "Decent Living" and "Self-Respect"

Let us take income and assets, two mutually independent factors in the resource space, instead of the functioning space we examined above. Their initial endowments and their relative price determine the commodity set.[26] In general, a change in the amount of income or assets diminishes the commodity set. A change in the relative price alters the shape of the commodity set. We assume that the income level for the sisters and the relative price of assets are lower when they decide whether to receive public assistance. This means that their commodity set has changed to one with a much lower level of achievable income for them.

Next we constitute the "income–living space" that converts income into a "living" functioning via an individual "income usability" (including selecting, shopping, or saving abilities). We can also constitute the "asset–self-respect" space that converts assets into her self-respect" via her "asset usability" (including enjoying, appreciating abilities). In general, her "income usability" can shift upward or downward, depending on her health and other factors, whereas her "asset usability" depends on her own views and interpretations. Remember that the elder sister had some trouble with a chronic disease. We therefore assume that her income usability decreases while her ability to maintain her self-respect (asset usability) does not change.

Within this framework, we infer her capabilities, on the functioning space, when she receives public assistance and when she does not. First, with no public assistance,

[26]Here the relative price of income and assets is the price to exchange them in the universal market. A decrease of the asset value due to depreciation is regarded as a decrease of the amount of the assets.

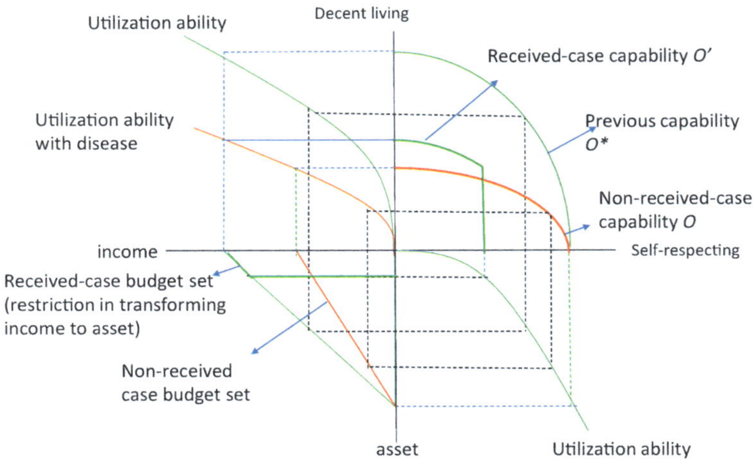

Fig. 7.2 Transformation of one's capability by transformed income-asset levels and resource usability

her lower income means a diminished set for income and assets on the commodity (income–asset) space. Coupled with her decreased income usability, this greatly reduces her achievable level of "living." Her achievable level of self-respect remains the same, however.

When she receives public assistance, her achievable level of "living" decreases less. However, the marginal transformation rate between two functionings, i.e., living and self-respect, decreases significantly at a certain point. After this point, it is difficult to make a choice between two functionings such as accepting a lower standard of living and improving on one's self-respect (see Fig. 7.2).

7.5.2 *Possible Dilemma: Constrained Maximization Problem*

For each of these capabilities, we examine an optimal point that gives the highest evaluation based on the elder sister's evaluation for functioning vectors.[27] In Fig. 7.3, point *b* (consumption point with no public assistance) shows the optimal point for the elder sister's capability when receiving no public assistance, while point *b*′ does the optimal point when she receives public assistance. With her preference assumed in Fig. 7.1, she evaluates point *b* higher than point *b*′. In this situation, if she seeks

---

[27] In the analysis below we assume that receiving no public assistance results in the older sister's lower income and decreased relative price of assets over income (due to the effects of selling off assets) whereas receiving public assistance will not change the relative price because the effects of selling off assets are offset by decreased demand for assets.

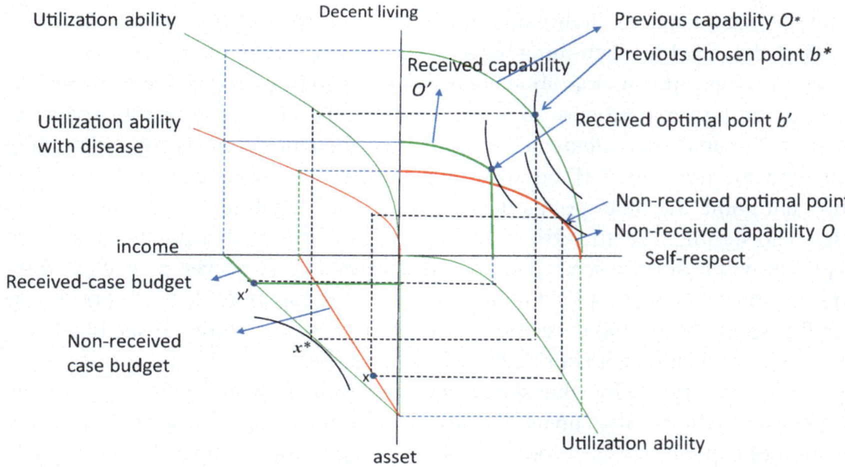

Fig. 7.3 A choice problem faced by an individual: optimizing behavior under transformed capability

constrained maximization with her preference regarding functioning vectors, she decides not to receive public assistance.

Now, Fig. 7.4 shows that individual 1's preference has adapted to one that favors living much more than self-respect. Her new preference gives point *b*′ (consumption point with public assistance) a higher evaluation than point *b* (consumption point

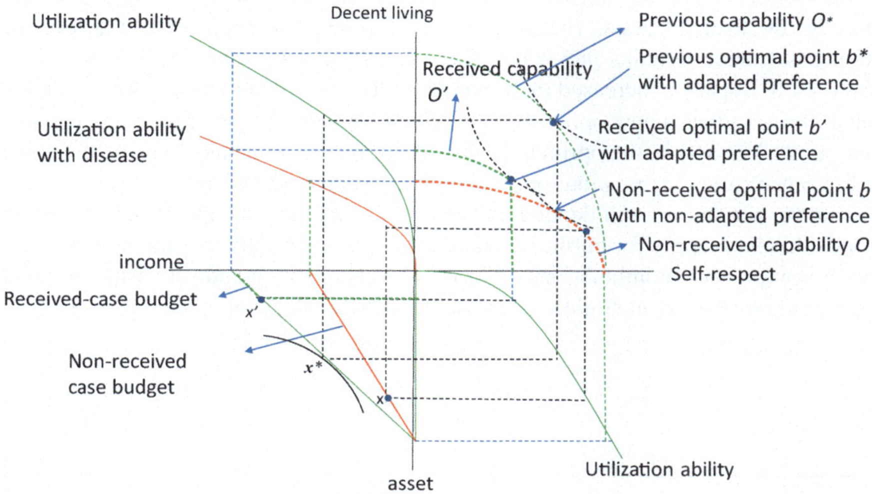

Fig. 7.4 The optimal point after adapted preference for "received capability"

with no public assistance). In this situation, if she aims for constrained maximization with her preference for functioning vectors, she chooses receiving public assistance.

In either case, information about individual capabilities recedes into the background, as in the standard case of budget constraints on the commodity space, as long as we assume individuals act to maximize their preferences for functioning vectors under constraints.[28] If the role of a capability set is reduced to helping select the optimal point, the other points that are within her capability set but not chosen will have no significance after all. In an extreme case, those other points, apart from the optimal point, did not need to exist in the beginning. However, as is clear from our discussion so far, we cannot completely reduce her capability to the "opportunity set" in this sense. She could have chosen any point in her capability, if she liked, and each such point would characterize her life as a person.

For example, it is possible that she changes her evaluation and evaluates receiving public assistance higher than no public assistance, while at the same time keeping her evaluation of capabilities as before. That is, she may evaluate capability C (capable of having a higher self-respect in exchange for a lower living) higher than capability C' (incapable of doing so). In this situation, she faces a cruel dilemma between her evaluation of functioning vectors and evaluation of capabilities.

7.5.3 Appearance of the Third Capability and Changes in Choice Behavior

We consider the following imaginary case in order to examine individual evaluations of capabilities. Suppose that Article 4 of the Public Assistance Act is modified to increase the limit of assets that a recipient is allowed to keep while the level of public assistance remains the same. This means the achievable level of the elder sister's self-respect is increased in exchange for the level of her living. This expanded capability set gives a new optimal point, which we call b^{**} (see Fig. 7.5). Suppose that points b^{**} and b (the optimal point without public assistance) are on the same indifference curve. In this situation, if we ask her whether she wishes to receive public assistance, her answer will depend on her own evaluations of capabilities. Then she is most likely to apply for public assistance if receiving public assistance makes her capability (possible combinations of various levels of living and self-respect) much larger, although it might slightly decrease her achievable level of self-respect.

---

[28] In the analysis below we assume that receiving no public assistance results in her lower income and decreased relative price of assets over income (due to effects of selling off assets) whereas receiving public assistance will not change the relative price because effects of selling off assets are offset by decreased demand for assets.

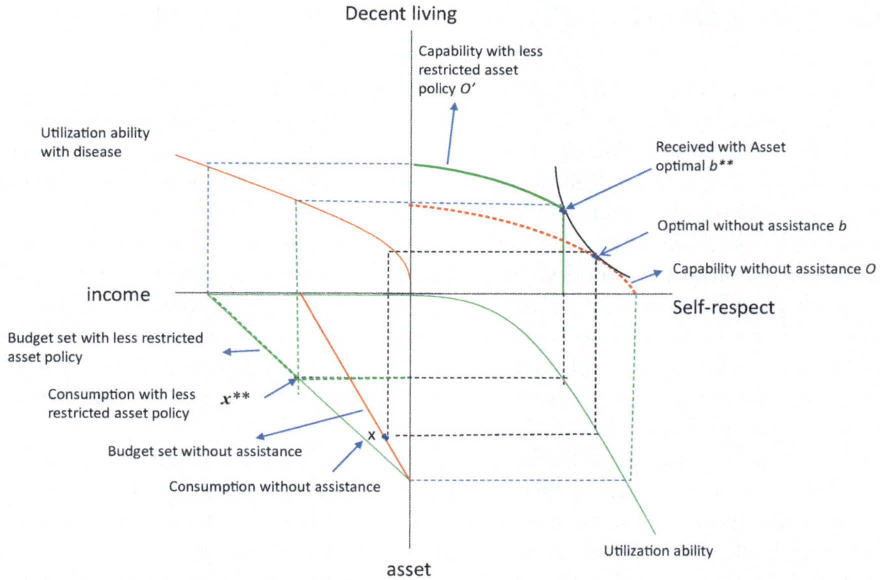

Fig. 7.5 Imaginary choice situation: improved capability by an increased asset limit

7.5.4 Trade-Off? Capability with More Decent Living or More Self-Respect

We examined possible consequences of receiving public assistance by using the capability approach. Let us note the following points. The goals of the current public assistance system are, first, to improve living standards of the recipients and, second, to promote their ultimate exit from the system (called "independence"). Leaving aside the issue of incentives, these goals are considered to be in a complementary relation with each other.

In contrast, maintaining recipients' self-respect is not explicitly mentioned as an objective of the public assistance system. Rather, the current system provides a rationale for putting "decent living" and "self-respect" in a trade-off relation. That is, the current system can require a recipient to give up on her self-respect as a price for the benefit of her improved living. When this rationale or requirement is explicitly pursued in practice, her capability including self-respect is severely distorted.

7.6 Concluding Remarks: What Does Choosing Imply?

The elder sister had visited the welfare office three times. The reason she nevertheless did not receive public assistance was, according to the record, "because she didn't show her will to do so." If that was true, what was the real problem here? The purpose of this chapter was to analyze this problem by shedding light on the "non-choice elements" that deeply affect individual rational choices.

Analyses in this chapter referred to the basic framework of economics. This was because economics has traditionally paid attention to individual (economic agent) choice behaviors under given constraints and provided a useful theoretical framework to describe the relation between individual and collective choices. However, traditional economics has not paid enough attention to background circumstances for individual choices, since it was convenient to regard any economic phenomena as "their own rational choice."

This chapter also assumed throughout that the elder sister would behave rationally. Note that "rationality" here is broader than (and does not contradict) the definition of rationality used in standard economics, because it admits that individuals not only form their preferences autonomously but also try to understand the social conscience (sense of community) and accept social decisions. Also, individuals here are allowed to have preferences not only over consequences of choices (achieved functionings) but also over opportunities (capabilities). This chapter adopted Sen's social choice approach and the capability approach in order to better capture individual choice circumstances and the agency and individuality of choosing individuals. Results of our analysis can be summarized as follows.

Our analysis using Sen's social choice approach shed light on the possibility of someone dying even when social choice procedures involving her can ostensibly satisfy all conditions of free expression of individual preferences, the Pareto Principle (collective decision power), and respect for the individual decisive power. This also led to the following reflection. The elder sister could certainly express her own preferences freely. She could also reject "Not Apply" by her "individual decisive power." However, she was unable to take part in the process to decide and understand what the important information to protect her own and her sister's interests would be and what alternatives would be available or not in her choice (action) set. Therefore, we can hardly say the elder sister's agency freedom was guaranteed.

Our analysis using the capability approach has made clear the following. We have to look not only at achieved functionings of individuals but also at capabilities open to them, in order to guarantee their well-being freedom. In modern society it is essential for individuals to have reasonable prospects for living and self-respect. However, she had a very limited and miserable prospect for the future assignment of capability. By applying for public assistance, her capability would shrink in self-respect in exchange for a better prospect for decent living, while by rejecting public assistance, her capability would shrink in decent living in exchange for a better prospect for self-respect. If a person does not want to limit her capability by her own will and action, that is, if she is going to resist abandoning her well-being freedom, she is likely to face an ultimate choice, which is too heavy to be made by one individual. Actually, abandoning well-being freedom by oneself is similar to suicide and she had not committed suicide at the last moment.

These are the (tentative) conclusions of this chapter from analyzing the starvation case using Sen's social choice approach and the capability approach. Here are some remaining issues to be tackled in the future.

Aristotle says that "choice will be the deliberate desire of things in our own power" (Aristotle 1980, III.3). According to him, "[D]eliberation is concerned with things that happen in a certain way for the most part, but in which the outcome is *obscure*, and with things in which it is *indeterminate*," therefore, "we call in others to aid us in deliberation on important questions, distrusting ourselves as not being equal to deciding" (Aristotle, 1980, III.3, emphasized by the author).

The elder sister visited the welfare office seeking to find an advisor with whom to deliberate on important questions. However, the officer she met there was no advisor to deliberate with but an embodiment of the social conscience. She had to make a judgement while the outcome was still obscure and indeterminate. She did make a decision but it might not have been what Aristotle would have called a "choice."

If she did not know what alternative actions she could choose, did not have any reasonable prospect for her living and self-respect, and did not have any advisor to consult, then could the fact that she "didn't show her will to apply" for public assistance justify anything at all?

Let us say again that this incident happened in the middle of the widespread support for liberal thoughts and social security systems in post-World War II Japan. The main issue of this incident, the principle of application, is supposed to be the leading guardian of individual "freedom of choice." Nevertheless, as we have seen in this chapter, it would be dangerous to assume that individual choices ("not to apply," for example) automatically would have satisfied her own interests if actually she had cared about the social conscience when forming her preference and if actually she had made a choice by accepting a social decision procedure.

We can probably say that the Principle of Application is a blind spot of the welfare state. If this is the case, what alternatives do we have? In general, the gap between an individual's will and her interests can be recognized only after she makes a choice and suffers a clear disadvantage. It is thus quite difficult to prevent this in advance, but our analyses can offer some suggestions in this context. For example, we can provide caseworkers as advisors, create some variants of the current options, select a set of indispensable functionings, and choose a set of resources as means, for living a decent life in Japan today. These are nothing new and are surely available within the framework of the modern Japanese welfare state.

A more essential problem is to consider the implementation of relevant policies. Even though there are cases where an individual's choice depends on factors that she cannot control, which may cause irrecoverable loss for her, their number can be rather small and they can be left simply as the residual. Then they will not affect economic theories nor people's minds, let alone any institutions. It is estimated that

45 people (31 men and 14 women) starved to death in total in 2011 and almost 2000 people if we include death due to malnutrition.[29] In Tachikawa City, Tokyo, roughly 40 people died alone in 2012.[30]

Should we leave them as the residual or do anything to help them? If we indeed do something, what would be a rational measure? Is action justified because anyone can be one of them, or because we have to tighten the governing mechanism of the state and social order, or because it will be beneficial to them, whoever they are? The question to be tackled in the future is: How can we form the will and logic to keep reforming the existing welfare state for disadvantaged individuals' own benefits, however small their number is?

7.7 Short Appendix: Outline for the Solution of a Paretian Liberal Paradox

(i) Construct a system of rights in which all individuals' rights (a non-empty set of pairwise relations that directly associate individual rankings with social evaluations) are mutually consistent.
(ii) Form individuals' "public judgements (partial orderings)" by extracting those parts that they themselves want to be respected publicly from their preference orderings. Redefine the Pareto Principle based on these preference profiles that incorporate their individual public judgements (see Sen 1976a).

7.8 Variations of an Individual's "Public Judgement"

(Example 1) It "reflects all individual rankings in a system of rights" and "refrains from expressing those individual rankings that might be inconsistent with the other individuals' rights." (Sen 1976a)
(Example 2) It "reflects all individual rankings in a system of rights" and has preferences that do not depend on other individuals (and focuses only on the individuals' own situations). (Suzumura 1978).
(Example 3) It remains indifferent as long as other individuals' rights are concerned. (Hammond 1995).

[29] From *Vital Statistics 2011*, Ministry of Health, Labour and Welfare in Japan.
[30] Tachikawa City's "List of incidents of solitary death reported to the city," September 2012, Special Accounts Committee.

7.9 Variations of the Theorem

If there is at least one individual who forms her "individual public judgement" that respects a system of rights, then the Pareto principle and the condition for minimal liberty are compatible (see Sen 1976a; Suzumura 1978; Hammond 1992) and we can construct a complete Paretian extension rule respecting individual rights. When we design a game form with such a rights-respecting Paretian extension rule, individuals can always act lawfully, whatever actions they take in such a game (Suzumura and Gotoh 2001).

Chapter 8
What Political Liberalism and the Welfare State Left Behind: Chance and Gratitude

8.1 Introduction: The Visit of a Wounded Bird

Four men stand in four different corners of a room, each holding a gun. They all set their sights on each other and none of them can put down his gun. They are at a deadlock in a four-way standoff.

Then, suddenly, a wounded little bird flies down and falls right in the middle of the four men. Strangely, its faint breath travels across their guns and is perceived clearly on their hands.

At this moment, the four men all lower their guns, deeply appreciating the fact that they have escaped the worst situation at the last minute.

Can we call what was perceived by the four men beauty, truth, goodness, or love? What does it mean to "be perceived on their hands"? We are not going to discuss whether it is a bodily sense, empathetic feeling, intellectual interpretation, or rational reasoning. Nor do we have to specify what is symbolized by the wounded little bird. After all, it does not matter what went through the minds of the four men; this could have been different for each one. What matters is the fact that the four men put down their guns, the fact that something other than bullets struck the four men, who then lost whatever reasons they had to continue holding their guns, and the fact that the unexpected presence of the small bird suddenly changed the critical situation faced by these individuals and in turn totally changed their behavior.

Let us continue with the tale. The four men abandon their guns and take up hoes instead. They cooperate in cultivating the soil, resulting in a rich harvest in autumn. Now many lively birds visit the field and their songs can be heard. Wealth and peace are finally achieved, and they live happily ever after.

However, here is one question we have forgotten to ask: What then happened to the wounded little bird?

This chapter was originally published as "What political liberalism and the welfare state left behind: chance and gratitude," Reiko Gotoh, in Hans-Uwe Otto, M. Walter and H. Ziegler (eds.), *Capability Promoting Policies: Enhancing Individual and Social Development*, Policy Press.

R. Gotoh, *The Ethics and Economics of the Capability Approach*, Hitotsubashi University IER Economic Research Series 46, https://doi.org/10.1007/978-981-15-5140-6_8

The wounded little bird was left behind and ascended quietly to heaven. No one noticed it. When autumn came the leaves covered it, and snow covered it in winter. There was no sign at all of the injured bird by early summer when the four men began fighting with each other again, this time with hoes: "To whom do these crops belong?".

This fight continued, again, until another wounded little bird fell down from heaven. The unexpected appearance of the injured bird brought the four men to their senses, and they put down their hoes.

How many times on earth must people repeat the same mistake, as summarized in Fig. 8.1?

Cooperation among "ourselves" is not only unjust but also unstable if we forget and neglect the visitor from outside, who triggered our cooperation, and if we delude ourselves that cooperation was achieved by "ourselves" only, pushing the visitor's existence into a category essentially similar to our own, based on (as explained later) a scientific cognition of continuity.

However, how can we understand the tiny bird that is entirely different in nature from "ourselves" without losing equality as a norm? Is there any risk that the asymmetric being is going to be treated as a means for symmetric beings to achieve their cooperation? Before talking about this, let us briefly reflect on the reach and limit of the welfare state, looking at the constitutionally guaranteed welfare system of postwar Japan as an example in order to elaborate upon our theme.

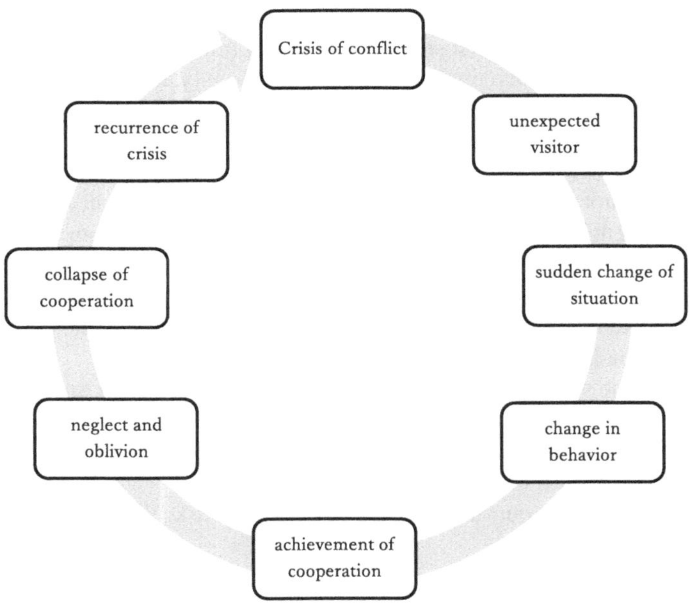

Fig. 8.1 A visit of chance and recurrence of crisis

8.2 The Modern Welfare State and Democratic Equality

After the Second World War, Japan adopted a pacifist constitution and developed a respectable system to secure basic well-being for all. To use Rawls's words, which are mentioned in the previous section, the constitutional idea of Japan's social security and welfare system can be summarized not only as embodying the concept of "liberal equality" but also as stepping in the realm of "democratic equality" (Rawls 1971a, 65 fn.).[1] Let me begin by explaining these concepts.

According to Rawls, "liberal equality" means equal treatment of equal beings, that is, all individuals should formally be treated equally as legal subjects. It is represented, for example, by the equal guarantee of "rights to civic liberty," which says that no one should have his or her body, mind, or conscience violated without a legitimate reason. The idea also means securing rights to political liberty, that is, equal access to various social decision procedures, especially to those crucial to oneself. In contrast, what Rawls calls "democratic equality" refers to the effective or "real" equal treatment of unequal or substantially different beings. For example, it is represented by securing "rights to well-being," which demand compensation of income or wealth for individuals below a certain threshold level of well-being.

The Japanese constitution declares that realization of individual rights may be restricted, under general conditions of circumstances, only by similar rights of other individuals or similar effects of other kinds of rights, not by values of the state or society beyond its constituent individuals. It also declares that anyone is entitled to pursue his or her own interest, express his or her own will, and change various social decision procedures by exercising various rights he or she holds, as long as one follows a due procedure (equal rights to civic liberty and political liberty). In addition, everyone should have equal access to education, work, and public services; moreover, anyone in a difficult situation is entitled to receive public assistance in order to maintain a minimum standard of wholesome and cultured living (equal rights to well-being freedom).

The concept of rights is indeed a "trump" political value (Dworkin 1977). According to Rawls, "[T]he only reason for circumscribing the rights defining liberty" is that "these equal rights as institutionally defined would interfere with one another." (Rawls 1971a, 64) It reminds us of the intrinsic value of persons that stands against the logic of number, holistic values, and power.[2] Such a micro as well as universal perspective of a right certainly describes the political ideal of *equality* in its highly abstract form. However, discussions focused on the endowment of rights may have caused, paradoxically, concerns about individual well-being to recede into the

[1] For details of the relationship between Rawls's political liberalism and Japan's welfare state system, see Gotoh (2001, 2015b).

[2] Here "trump" means "priority," that is, not to be outweighed without any justification. The essential characteristic of a right is that it is ultimately attributed to an individual (to his or her will or interest). To use Dworkin's words, an individual can claim "equal concern and respect" from society. See Dworkin (1977).

background. Why? We can find some of the reasons for this by looking at theoretical premises and the common-sense thinking supporting individual rights.

The statement "anyone is entitled to some rights" has a passive connotation. It does not mean that these rights are actually exercised or that goals of the individuals exercising them are actually achieved. In order to exercise their rights, individuals have to visit a particular place, follow a particular procedure, fill out an application, and so on. Furthermore, after exercising their rights in this way, they have to prove by themselves that they satisfy the first condition. Many factors exist that can prevent or interfere with one fulfilling this process.

Suppose, for example, a woman is reduced to poverty. There can be innumerable conditions that have to be met before she learns of the existence of public assistance that would allow her to achieve basic well-being, decides to receive it, and finally completes the necessary application. Once completed, this application may turn out to lack some of the required conditions, or the woman may face certain obstacles in meeting its demand.[3]

Even if this process discourages her from securing her rights to well-being and only ends up making her even more tired and hungry, her individual rights are not regarded as violated or threatened, unless and until events or acts that prevent the exercising of her rights are clearly recognized. When there is an implicit assumption that anyone can exercise his or her own rights, individuals who have not done so are regarded as having chosen not to do so. In other words, the non-exercising of their rights could be justified as a consequence of respecting their will and a subjective evaluation of their own interests.

In this context, we must recall that Rawls clearly distinguishes between guaranteeing liberty and securing the worth of liberty. He explains that the latter could be a social goal only in political liberty (for example, voting) and a kind of social and economic liberty that is stipulated by "the difference principle" under "the fair equality of opportunities."[4] When it comes to liberties of speech or the pursuit of happiness, Rawls (1971a, 204) noted that "the worth of liberty to persons and groups is proportional to their capacity to advance their ends within the framework the system defines."[5]

Concerning the worth of social and economic liberty, Rawls admits that social intervention should be carefully checked when it may discourage people's will and efforts, and the purpose and scope of compensation policies are to be restricted to the effects of factors that cannot be chosen or controlled by individuals.[6] This implies that when someone wants to realize his or her rights and ask for compensation because

[3]Refer to Chap. 7, which relates the case of two sisters in their forties who starved to death. One of them had visited a welfare office three times prior to this but did not apply for public assistance.

[4]The "fair equality of opportunities" and "the difference principle" is contained in the second part of "the two principles of justice" proposed by Rawls (1971a).

[5]In contrast, the capability approach proposed by Sen focuses on the worth of liberties. See Gotoh (2015a).

[6]Note that, as will be mentioned later, Rawls is more interested in securing basic well-being for all rather than making a clear selection of factors, as he recognized that a real problem is that we cannot clearly distinguish between responsible factors and non-responsible factors.

of the shortage of basic well-being, that individual has to prove that the result was not due to his or her choice but to bad luck or an unfavorable environment.

Who, however, could clearly prove this to someone else in words? And can that person do so while maintaining his or her will and continuing to act to realize his or her rights against overwhelmingly depressive prospects? Usually, as Sen has pointed out, it is difficult for an individual to choose his or her possible actions, unless he or she can take part in the process of setting possible actions with the help of an informed adviser, because individuals' choices are strongly framed by the set of alternatives available to them, or by the decision-making procedure itself (Sen 2002a; See also Chaps. 4 and 5).

In addition, we can observe the following problem. When someone claims that individual choices can affect the result, even in an extremely unlucky situation, this claim is praised as evidence of the triumph of human beings' free will. On the other hand, when someone else states that luck can change the outcome of even the wisest choices, this statement emphasizes the fundamental boundaries of reason and rationality as well as of legal fictions. Either proposition tends to invite negative views on designing policies for compensating the worth of liberty.[7]

Finally, as clearly explained in the following sentence, which was introduced in Sen's criticism (Sen 1980a/1997a, 365–366[1997a], including note 28), Rawls's theory of justice was first developed for symmetric relations among rational and reasonable individuals, leaving aside "hard cases."

> I also suppose that everyone has physical needs and psychological capacities within the normal range, so that the problems of special health care and of how to treat the mentally defective do not arise...prematurely introducing difficult questions that may take us beyond the theory of justice, the consideration of these *hard cases* can distract our moral perception by leading us to think of people distant from us. (Rawls, 1999b, 259, emphasis added by the author)

Consequently, it turned out that very serious problems were left to individuals to solve in the welfare system. Family became a social fortress containing individuals in situations of destitution, hardship, or abuse. Changes in family structures and household types meant that only stem family members shared a destiny with individuals in need (husbands, children, grandchildren, sisters, and brothers), in isolation from other distant relatives, based on the natural (but, in reality, socially and historically constructed) sense of responsibility. As the welfare state gradually established a universal social security system (pensions, health care and nursing care) covering common risks, it lost sight of individuals who had met with bad luck and received no help other than from close family members.

These "incidents" are usually considered an "exception" or "residual," carefully separated from and sidelined by the main legal system. They may deeply disturb

---

[7] This is because the former claim leads to an argument for respecting the free will of human beings, and the latter statement leads to the psychological justification of neglecting sufferers because of bounded rationality.

people's ordinary lives for a short while through images on the TV screen but they are soon overwritten by another new "exception" or "residual" and easily forgotten.[8]

Can we recover these exceptions and residuals or what has been forgotten by the welfare state? In the following sections, we consider this problem by examining academic studies of the theories of justice and, more broadly, political liberalism in general. Institutions and policies occasionally change the normative consciousness held by people drastically, while institutionalized academic studies influence institutions and policies to some extent.

8.3 Theorizing Conceptions of Political Liberalism: Tolerance and Non-Discrimination

To begin with, we sketch an outline of political liberalism by drawing on works by Rawls. A conception of political liberalism is characterized by the fact that its content is prescribed by the reciprocal acceptance of "real" people who are situated in some ideally *fair* conditions. Here, reciprocal acceptance means an acceptance that is presumed and expected by anyone situated in a similar condition.[9]

It has been postulated that people seeking freedom and independence avoid committing themselves to any comprehensive doctrine on the conception of the good, including libertarianism which attaches the supremum value to freedom. The most important virtue for political liberalism is to take an equal distance from any particular religion, moral doctrine, or belief, as well as to be equally tolerant of them.

It is natural for political liberalism to renounce any unequal or discriminatory treatment, based on particular factors such as origin of birth, profession, gender, disability and ill health, or income and wealth. These factors are called by Rawls "social or natural contingencies," or "morally arbitrary" matters.[10] When we apply the device of a "veil of ignorance" to our daily life, shutting out all kinds of individualized information not only about ourselves but also about other people, it becomes effectively impossible to discriminate against anybody based on these particular factors.[11]

---

[8]This is the main criticism of Rawls's theory of justice by Sen; see Sen (2009a).

[9]Rawls drew on Kant's moral theory and looked at the conclusions reached by reasoning using a political constructive procedure with the idea of the "veil of ignorance," which covers up one's birth, attributes, social states, and personal preferences and characteristics, while they base their reasoning on the fact of human society that there must be "the least disadvantaged." Who actually becomes "the least disadvantaged" might change depending on the distribution of "social primary goods." (See Rawls 1971a, 1993 and see Chap. 7 of this book).

[10]It is not permissible to prevent someone from exercising his or her rights, damage his or her self-respect and dignity, or restrict his or her access to education, work, or public services, based on differences in these factors.

[11]The "veil of ignorance" is in *Political Liberalism* (Rawls 1993) developed to represent the core idea of political liberalism, which requires detaching oneself from all individualized information.

The analytical framework of the welfare economics on distributive justice has contributed considerably to supporting the idea of non-discrimination in political liberalism. Take the Lorenz curve as an example, which captures the extent of income inequalities by referring to the straight, 45° line that represents perfect income equality and gives a strong visual impression of continuity among individuals (Lorenz 1905). Qualitative distinctions in all other aspects disappear into the background and only quantitative and continuous differences in income remain. This implies that a categorical distinction such as poor and non-poor vanishes and only relative positions such as lower or higher remain.

A similar logic leads us to neglect categorical distinctions between those with and without disabilities, if we can order persons with physical or mental disabilities from slightest to severest in a real number scale, for example. If we imagine the sequence of points converging to zero with a large number of people, only quantitative and continuous differences would remain, while the rationale of discrimination for those with disabilities disappear.

What happens if we adopt the framework of multidimensional indices as a composite (vector) of different dimensions showing different continuous quantities? It would then be difficult to regard someone as being more or less disadvantaged, even if he or she is at the lowest level in almost all dimensions but one. This is because, first, considering the limitations of human cognitive ability, we cannot deny any possibility of the crossover of rankings in a yet-to-be recognized dimension that may overwhelmingly dominate the other dimensions in its importance. More generally, we have no objective criterion to weight and substitute different dimensions for one another across different individuals.[12]

As mentioned in Chap. 3, Arrow points out by drawing on Leibniz's principle of the identity of indiscernible "value judgments may equate empirically distinguishable phenomena, but they cannot differentiate empirically indistinguishable states" (Arrow 1951a/1963, p. 112[1951]); therefore, welfare economics has denied the logical possibility of discrimination. This is apparently the academic contribution to non-discrimination in political liberalism.[13]

We must note, however, that the logic that denies differences across individuals as a fact has led to a cautious approach to the acceptance of any principle of redistribution that accommodates essentially asymmetric relationships among individuals. When individual characteristics are quantitatively continuous, it becomes arbitrary to identify those who should receive resource transfers.[14]

---

[12]For example, the internal organs of someone with a severe mental disability are not themselves necessarily severely damaged.

[13]In reality, people discriminate against certain individuals based on prejudice and their gut feelings. This occurs by picking one disadvantage in just one dimension as something that dominates the other dimensions and attributing it to a particular individual. On the contrary, the "science" of political liberalism denies as fact the very existence of differences as a decisive disadvantage dominating other dimensions, considering the limitations of human cognitive ability.

[14]People can perform at the highest level even if their income is in the lowest quantile. Even today in Japan, there are many cases where someone's poverty is retrospectively recognized only after he or she "starves" to death.

This is indeed why people are too cautious about Rawls's difference principle. As is well known, it has attracted a wide variety of people concerned about the distribution of income and wealth, partly because its expression is modest and restrictive in claiming that "social and economic inequalities are permitted only when they contribute to maximizing expectations of the worst-off people" (Rawls 1971a) instead of claiming to eradicate social and economic inequalities completely. It suits the intuition that there must be a limit to reducing inequalities even though equality is important.

Welfare economics confirms this intuition by pointing out the effects of Rawls's difference principle on individuals' work incentives. In other words, giving greater weight to the least advantaged might result in a miserable outcome for themselves or/and for society as a whole because it may invite the reduction of capable individuals' work incentives. For example, they argue, productive people must lose their willingness to work as the income tax rate progressively increases. This logic has led to many research contributions about the extent to which redistribution will maximize the share of the worst-off people, when taking into account labor supply responses to such a redistribution system.[15]

The argument is developed not only for individuals' rational behavior in choosing the optimal combination of income and leisure but also for the following feelings of unfairness brought about by the difference principle.[16] Why should we privilege a specific position by calling for the "maximization" of the "worst-off" position despite the fact that, if individual differences are only quantitatively continuous, then the non-worst-off positions are also interchangeable by resource transfer?[17] This logic might give policy makers a good excuse for adopting a lower weight of transfer, either for avoiding negative effects on the least advantaged or for promoting gross national income in a whole society. In summary, the analytical framework of welfare economics, which does not provide an argument for going beyond agnosticism about qualitative differences among individuals, cannot provide a sufficient reason to support inter-personal transfer.[18] The problem of distributive justice, therefore, tends to be reduced to intra-personal distribution under uncertainty or inter-temporal distribution across different life-stages of an individual.[19] We need to find a new theory.

---

[15]It provided an inspiration for the development of important research fields in economics such as the optimal taxation theory or incentive theory (endogenous theory of optimal redistribution). See, for example, Mirrlees (1971).

[16]In neoclassical economics, this is explained by a decrease in the price of leisure (real wage). See Varian (1980) on optimal tax rates under uncertainty about the ability to work. See Gotoh (2014) for criticisms against the work incentive argument based merely on neoclassical economic models.

[17]Rawls recognized these arguments but he realized that a real problem is in the fact that we cannot make a clear distinction between responsible factors and non-responsible factors. People can perform at the highest level even if their income is in the lowest quantile.

[18]Refer to, for example, Sen's criticism of the new welfare economics, condensed into "welfarism." See, for example, Sen (1977b/1997 1997a). See also Gotoh (2001).

[19]For example, insurance systems equalize the expectations of persons who suffer dangers and those of persons who escape dangers, by transferring money from the latter to the former.

8.4 Expanded Social Cooperation or "Patronal Treatment" Scheme?

Let us go back to the tale we discussed earlier. What was symbolized by the wounded little bird's story? It can be articulated as follows.

Among essentially unsettled symmetric beings,
Unexpectedly appears an asymmetric being,
Who can shake the relation among them,
Hence, can provide a chance for cooperation.

Symmetric beings owe their cooperation to an asymmetric being. Supposing this is true, we can infer a reasonable axiom of reciprocity that says we should respect and thank the asymmetric being who brings about cooperation. This could be substantiated as a resource transfer scheme from symmetric to asymmetric beings, when "asymmetric beings" are people whose positions are not interchangeable with others' positions merely by transferring resources, or they are people whose hardships or sufferings cannot be adequately compensated for with resources in the first place.

This is an attempt to reformulate Rawls's theory of justice by incorporating those hard cases (such as severe physical or mental disability) excluded by Rawls himself. It is at the same time an attempt to restructure the scope of his conception of the "system of social cooperation" by accommodating people who are not yet recognized and included in "social cooperation." (see Fig. 8.2).

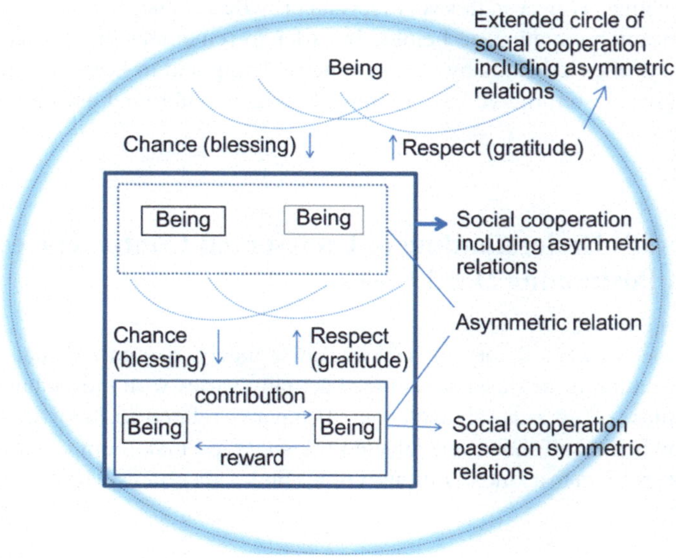

Fig. 8.2 Social cooperation including symmetric and asymmetric relations

However, we must bear in mind the following serious problem when expanding the system this way. Is there any risk that asymmetric beings are going to be treated as a *means* for symmetric beings to achieve cooperation? Is the expanded system of social cooperation any different from an imperialist state that expands by swallowing its peripheries into its territory?[20]

It is true that welfare governance can sometimes go hand in hand with power. The benevolence (by means of benefits) and protection for specific minorities provided by power is often loudly advertised and quietly accepted by people, as it could make up for the oppression or violence forced on other minorities by the same power. An attempt to develop the system to include those outside the system has the possibility of overturning the trend from treatment to contract, a possible setback from a contract between free and equal agencies to a patronal treatment by the governor for the governed. Or, it might produce a gigantic governance power like a hydra with "contract relationships" at its center and "benevolence and protection" at its periphery, leaving asymmetric beings rarely treated as an end itself.

How can we possibly follow Kant's moral principle to "Treat any individual as an end, not merely as a means to an end" (Kant 1785/1970)?

Let me briefly state my conclusion in advance. Key to answering this serious question is to seek a normative conception that prescribes a resource transfer scheme from symmetric to asymmetric beings, going beyond the concept of "fairness," which prescribes conditions of contracts among symmetric relations based on equality as a fact. For example, equal treatment for equal cases, the same wage for the same work, or the same reward (benefit) for the same contribution (cost).

The wounded little bird cannot do the same work nor bear the same cost as symmetric beings. However, this very fact can provide a chance to bring and maintain cooperation among symmetric beings. In order to remember the chance (benefit) brought to symmetric beings by the asymmetric being and to keep the respect (and gratitude) given in return, we have to move to a less conditional normative concept than fairness.

8.5 Rawls's Understanding of Undeserved Contingencies and Postponing Hard Cases

Let us re-visit Rawls's theory of justice. Rawls indeed recognized that the maximized expectation of the least advantaged actually varies with individuals' choices of work times, or, in general, with their behaviors related to labor incentives in society. Rawls himself, however, rejected the so-called maximum criterion, which reduces the problem to a kind of rational choice under uncertainty (Rawls 1974/1999, 247[1999b]).

---

[20] According to Gunther Teubner, this is exactly the kind of *aporia* faced by Luhmann's system theory based on the concept of "autopoiesis" as well as Derrida's "justiciance" (Teubner 2008).

Moreover, Rawls acknowledged the gravity of the effects of various natural or social contingencies. Consider, for example, Rawls's words in explaining that the philosophical background of the difference principle contains a deep insight into the effects of social or natural contingencies. "[N]o one should benefit from certain undeserved contingencies with deep and long-lasting effects, such as class origin and natural abilities, except in ways that also help others" (Rawls 1974/1999b, 246[1999b]).

Here, Rawls questions the legitimacy of the "principle of distribution according to merits." What is usually taken for granted and attributed to individual merits can in fact be based on "collective merits." Alternatively, an individual owes his or her "merit" at least partially to the fact that he or she can escape some natural or social contingencies that strike his or her neighbor but not him or her. In this case, it is not obvious to what extent those merits can be attributed to "the person him- or herself."

In addition, the following notes made by Rawls in the context of how to identify the least advantaged in society suggest a possibility that goes beyond the concept of fairness that is essentially based on symmetrical relations.

> If, for example, there are unequal basic rights founded on fixed natural characteristics, these inequalities will single out relevant positions. Since these characteristics cannot be changed, the positions they define count as starting places in the basic structure. Distributions based on sex are of this type, and so are those depending upon race and culture. (Rawls 1971a, 99)

In order to achieve substantively equal basic rights, some asymmetrical treatments according to fixed characteristics are needed. The philosophical background of Rawls's theory of justice provides a perspective that makes it possible to interpret "social cooperation" as accommodating not only those who can work but also those who cannot work and are in need of resource transfers. If society recognizes that there remain some individuals who suffer severe disadvantages in the exercising of basic rights, they are to be treated with a necessary concern in implementing Rawls's difference principle.

However, unfortunately, Rawls did not fully develop this core thought of his theory. Rather, as clearly explained in his reply to Sen's criticism, Rawls left aside "hard cases" (those of disability, hardship, or destitution) after all, hoping these would be dealt with at the legal stage in a real society (see Sen 1980a/1997a; Rawls, 1982). Below, I outline two ways in which to restructure Rawls's theory of justice to include this core thought.[21]

[21] In Gotoh (2014), I have indicated that the framework of Rawls's "justice as fairness" is inevitably restructured if the concept of "capability" is introduced into his theory of justice, although Rawls himself considered that the concept of "capability" could be smoothly introduced in the legislative stage without changing his basic framework.

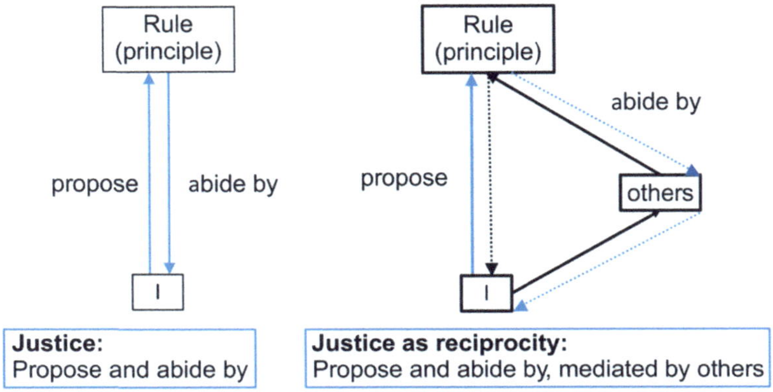

Fig. 8.3 Normal concept of Justice and the concept of Justice as reciprocity

8.6 Justice as Reciprocity: Cooperation Among Asymmetric and Symmetric Beings

First, in conceptualizing the relationship between asymmetric and symmetric beings, sketched earlier by the metaphorical tale of the wounded bird, let us examine the concept of reciprocity that Rawls focused on, namely, "justice as reciprocity," along with "justice as fairness."[22] It is similar to retributive justice but also different from it in the following way: that is, typically, in a way that can be illustrated by the following quotation.

> [T]hey are ready to propose principles and standards as fair terms of cooperation and to abide by them willingly, given the assurance that others will likewise do so. (Rawls 1993, 49)

This quotation expresses the idea of "justice as reciprocity," which is realized by being intermediated by rules, while the choice and implementation of rules are intermediated by reciprocal relationship among individuals.[23] "Justice as reciprocity" is observed in practices of explanation to others and of acceptance from others based on a bilateral relationship (see Fig. 8.3). The phrase "given the assurance that others will likewise do so" is interpreted as indicating something that alleviates "the strains of commitment to justice."[24]

---

[22]"[T]hey [the concepts of justice and fairness] share a fundamental element in common, which I shall call the concept of reciprocity …. It is this aspect of justice for which utilitarianism, …, is unable to account; but this aspect is expressed, and allowed for, even if in a misleading way, by the idea of the social contract" (Rawls 1971b, 190–192).

[23]For a detailed view of this conception of reciprocity in the context of Rawls, see Gutmann and Thompson (1996) and Gotoh (2009).

[24]"[T]he strains of commitment to justice" is explained by saying that "the parties must weigh with care whether they will be able to stick by their commitment in all circumstances" (Rawls 1971a, 176).

In Gotoh (2009) I developed an idea of public reciprocity based on Rawls's idea of "justice as reciprocity." Public reciprocity is similar to but different from the concept of mutual advantage that motivates private contracts or cooperative games, in that public reciprocity does not require symmetry or proportionality in its contributions and rewards relationship; moreover, it does not rule out cases where only one side will gain without a corresponding burden.[25] It is similar to but different from the concept of "gift," which is realized in the context of direct or personal relationships followed by a counter-gift at some time in the remote future, whereas public reciprocity does not presume that relationship. Instead, it is realized through certain rules, which are adopted through political reciprocity, and which in themselves represent bilateral correspondences in society as a whole.[26]

The following rule is taken as an example: if you can work and afford to provide, do so; if you are in need, receive help and be well. With this rule, we can rely on the fact that a neighbor with similar abilities to ours would also work and provide, and that a neighbor with similar difficulties to ours would also receive, although the amount provided or received may be quite different for the neighbor than for us. Moreover, we can rely on the fact that someone who provides nothing and only receives would also provide if he or she had the ability to work, as long as he or she could accept the same rule we follow. This kind of reasoning invites the idea of public reciprocity. (See Fig. 8.4).

Second, we should try to describe and understand the situation of the wounded little bird as accurately as possible in order to provide better social assistance, without leaving the bird as an exception or a residual. Whether or not we can conceive of such a situation as something that could possibly be experienced by ourselves, we can admit the fact that it has happened to someone somewhere, and can then find a way to help the person in this situation as a social responsibility, respecting him or her as an equal being in society.

The capability approach proposed by Sen can be quite effective in describing and understanding individuals' concrete situations in detail (for example Sen 1985a, 1999a). This approach makes a partially interpersonal comparison in multidimensional indices, by evaluating various contributions, burdens, meanings, and benefits in specific historical, cultural, and social contexts from the point of view, or "position," of those individuals. To capture a person's capability is essentially to understand his or her predicament from his or her own position. Sen suggests further that multiple positions actually occupied by an agency himself or herself should provide a basis

---

[25]On this point, Lawrence Becker, the author of *Reciprocity*, seems to take a similar position, since his concept of "proportionality" goes beyond the literal meaning of the term: "…when we seem unable to do anything that equals either the benefits we have received or the sum total of the sacrifices that have gone into producing those benefits. Here it is important to remember that such benefits typically come to us by way of people's participation in on-going social institutions …. What is fitting is reciprocal participation in those institutions" (Becker 1986, 113–114).

[26]This definition of gift is different from the classical one, and closer to what Marcel Henaff calls a "ceremonial gift," which is a form of reciprocity and not a unilateral transfer. See Henaff (2009). See also Gotoh (2009, 2013).

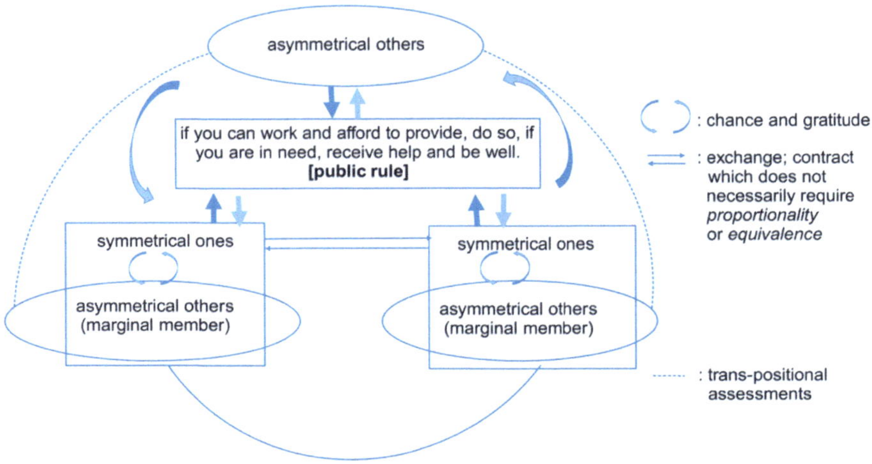

Fig. 8.4 Social cooperation with public (rule-based) reciprocity

for "trans-positional assessments" and for "open impartiality" in his or her cognition as well as in the construction of public judgements (see Chap. 6 and also Gotoh 2014, 150–151).[27]

8.7 Conclusion

Connecting the core thought of Rawls's theory of justice with Sen's capability approach makes it possible to expand the concept of fairness conceived almost exclusively for symmetric beings to the concept of public reciprocity, which includes reciprocal relations between symmetric and asymmetric beings. Underlying this process should be "equality as a norm," which requires *equal concern and respect for all*, accepting "differences as a fact."

Equality as a norm here cannot be accommodated by a criterion of distributive justice such as formally uniform distribution.[28] It is an independent political value in its own right and does not need to be based on or supported by any other political, moral, or economic value. In other words, when someone asks, for example, "Why equality?" we can answer simply and finally "Because equality is a paramount social value," instead of excusing ourselves by saying "Because it leads to social stability and, hence, our own benefits in the end." Note that having equality as a norm is compatible with having Rawls's veil of ignorance, as well as public reciprocity.

---

[27]Related to this point, an interesting issue is argued in Frazer (2014).

[28]The concept of "Equality as a norm" is similar to but different from the concept of "equality as a moral ideal" provided by Frankfurt (1987).

Confirming these points, let us go back to the original question. How should we understand the little bird, which might be completely different from "ourselves"?

Adam Smith would suggest putting ourselves in the position of the little bird through "imaginary exchange of positions" (Smith 1759/1969).[29] Immanuel Kant could tell us just to be kind to the little bird, and we do not have to understand it.[30] Rawls might recommend that we share the products of our cooperation with the little bird regardless of whether he or she can work. What would Sen suggest?

Sen would propose that we find out what the little bird has reason to value through public discussion in which the little bird takes part as an agency, say, expert of the position he or she actually occupies. Once that is clear, we can start producing goods and services that we all value. If I may add here that perhaps Martha Nussbaum would suggest that we can play with the little bird after waiting for its recovery and rest. It is because she includes "being able to live with concern for and in relation to" other species, and "being able to laugh, to play, to enjoy recreational activities" in the list of "central human functional capabilities," a certain threshold of which should be secured for all. (See Nussbaum 2000, 78–80).

---

[29]Smith (1759/1969). The "imaginary exchange of positions" is a refined method, if we do not end up jumping on the stereotype of "suffering" in general, or unconsciously imposing "my" own aesthetic idea or moral codes, or making judgements based on "our" own customs and common sense, and if we can obtain the point of view of an "impartial spectator".

[30]Even if one is not moved by the suffering of others, he or she can perform "an act of kindness" for others as his or her moral duty from his or her own good will, which Kant considered sufficient.

Chapter 9
The Birth and Growth of Modern Social Choice Theory: From Arrow to Sen

9.1 Introduction

At the beginning of the twenty-first century, two intellectual giants visited an academic hall in Tokyo one after the other. They were Kenneth Arrow and AmartyaSen. Their images, in one of the intellectual halls of fame in Japan, reminded us of Plato and Aristotle depicted in Rafael's painting *Scuola di Atene* (The School of Athens). It looks as if Arrow, pointing to the heavens (like Plato), is explaining the joy of constructing a rigorous logical world, whereas Sen, pointing horizontally to the world (like Aristotle), is persuading us of the pleasure of applying logic to realities.

The two are surrounded by many people engaged in their own favorite works, in their own styles and positions. Some are trying to see the real world better, while others try to shed light on their own standpoints from which to see the world. We can find the bright face of Tony Atkinson or the warm smile of John Rawls there.

This is of course an illusion created in the author's mind. As I will argue later, Arrow declares his departure from Platonic realism! Neoclassical economics does not go well with "heroes," in the first place. The free, competitive market with countless participants will not approve of the intellectual monopoly by any individual. It is the wisdom of modern sciences to avoid establishing any particular authority or power without challenging it. This wisdom seems to have worked quite effectively for neoclassical economics.

Occasionally, however, some distinguished names have been engraved on particular periods by their epoch-making contributions. That was the case with Arrow and Sen. Arrow has taught six Nobel Laureates and Sen can attract tens of thousands of researchers, practitioners, and citizens from all over the world. A dialogue between Arrow and Sen, or their similarities and differences, can represent themes to be

---

This chapter is an English translation of a paper originally published in Japanese as "Arrow to Sen, Shakaitekisentakuriron no seiritsu to sono hihantekitenkai" Reiko Gotoh, in Waseda Journal of Political Science and Economics, Vol. 394, 2019.

R. Gotoh, *The Ethics and Economics of the Capability Approach*, Hitotsubashi University IER Economic Research Series 46, https://doi.org/10.1007/978-981-15-5140-6_9

tackled by economics today. The purpose of this chapter is to draw a rough sketch of similarities and differences between Arrow and Sen by focusing on "economics and ethics" on the one hand, and on "theory and practice" on the other. The major concern of the chapter is as follows.

Immanuel Kant argued that it would be fine enough for a person to respect basic moral rules and behave accordingly, even if she cannot be genuinely kind to others. Kantian ethics has something in common with economics in focusing on "the constitutional" rather than "the natural." Kantian ethics and morals are interested in a tuple of individual revealed good wills or rational actions, which is largely what economics is interested in. While, of course, Kant is much different from economics in the conceptions of value and reason.

Underlying the focus of economics on a social institution or system is the following view of human beings. However egoistic, sadistic, or cynical a person might be, she would not go beyond the framework of, or go against the purpose of, the social system—for example, a progressive tax system that transfers resources in society, caring about various disadvantaged individuals—if she can recognize such a system in her public judgement.

Let me add that there is no assumption of pure, absolute evil that is associated with a particular characteristic of an individual. Rather, it is pointed out that anyone is busy consuming a decent amount of goods and services for surviving and she cannot be committed to the completion of evils. For example, we can refer to the following view on social progress. "No doubt men, even now, are capable of much more unselfish service than they generally render: and the supreme aim of the economist is to discover how this latent social asset can be developed most quickly, and turned to account most wisely" (Marshall 1920/2013, 13[2013]).

AmartyaSen is surely an economist and he understands this ultimate concern of economics and shares it with great figures like Adam Smith, Alfred Marshall, Léon Walras, Vilfredo Pareto, Arthur Pigou, Karl Marx, Maynard Keynes, and Joseph Schumpeter. He shares this concern also with Kenneth Arrow and Paul Samuelson, whom he deeply admired but kept challenging intellectually. They would all agree that the primary theme of welfare economics is to investigate how a society can fully respect individual initiatives and interdependent relationships. What, then, can distinguish Sen from the others?

It is widely known that Samuelson regarded economists as skilled artisans (Suzumura and Gotoh 2001/2002; Samuelson 1947/1983). They examined logical performances of social welfare functions but took social values represented by them as exogenously given. Arrow, who wrote *Social Choice and Individual Values* (1951/1963), also did not venture into discussing contents of social values themselves but focused on logically analyzing relations between social choices and individual values. His research themes were largely to illuminate various paradoxes and dilemmas behind the surface of modern legal, political, and economic systems that were developed in universal terms.

The most skilled artisans usually have a decent philosophy (aesthetics, motto, understanding of human nature, view of the world, and so on), and Samuelson was a fine writer with excellent style and expressions. Arrow, as described in the next section, was a man of outstanding philosophical knowledge and sophistication. However, few artisans make conscious efforts to objectify their own philosophies and critically scrutinize them, as that is beyond their professional works. For Samuelson and Arrow, philosophical statements often took the form of sporadic expressions of their intuitions and experiences, which had the look of a part-time business done in their free time.

Sen was different. Certainly, he recognized the need for skilled economic theorists and statisticians, and he aimed at, and succeeded in, becoming one himself, but he did not try to restrict the role of economics. Rather, he fundamentally questioned various assumptions underlying standard economic theories and statistics and clarified their achievements and limitations. Furthermore, he sought to found an area of research to design a new set of analytical tools to develop an alternative theory or approach in economics, and he himself made some fundamental contributions. The area can be called "'economic philosophy."[1]

It was in the 1970s, long before his winning a Nobel Prize in economics in 1998, that Sen started challenging standard economics by fully employing his internal sense of artisanship and philosophical concerns. This was roughly when Arrow received a Nobel Prize in economics (in 1972), and Sen was trying to expand the scope of economic theory. At the same time, it was becoming clear that the big social experiment, or the complementary story behind it, was failing, only to leave irrecoverable damages and despair to those who had recovered from the disasters of the Second World War and tried to revive their states or nations. It became increasingly clear to many people that it would be almost impossible to unite the world with just one value or principle.

9.2 The Philosophical Scope of Social Choice Theory

This section goes back to the birth of modern social choice theory given by Arrow and reviews where the theory itself stands, the basic framework of which is shared by Arrow and Sen. There are three issues to be considered here.

First, what role did social choice theory play for welfare economics, which was in transition from the "old" one to the "new" one?

Second, what perspectives did social choice theory have that were different from those of the emerging game theory and the decision theory under uncertainty?

Third, what philosophical scope did social choice theory provide anew?

These are all big questions that should be examined independently but, unfortunately, there is not much historical information on each. We can only give a rough, combined sketch of the problems. We begin with the third issue.

---

[1] Actually, this is the title of Joan Robinson's famous book (Robinson 1962). Sen himself does not use this term. He rather uses the words "economics and ethics." We use this term based on the tradition of Japanese economists, as mentioned in Chap. 10.

Arrow's *Social Choice and Individual Values* (1951a/1963), mentioned above, is not only a seminal work in mathematical economics but also one in economic philosophy full of philosophical ideas and insights. Unexpectedly, first he makes a conscious effort to place his own theory in the methodology of philosophy of sciences; second he attempts to place the social context of his own theory in the theory of the state; and third, he tries to place in the academic paradigm the perspective to be explored by his own theory.

These are only briefly mentioned in his work, and we have to interpret their meanings helped by some supplementary documents and our imagination. For that, we go back to Arrow's student days.

By the time the Second World War broke out, the United States had already developed some original philosophies, including pragmatism, neorealism, and critical realism, but the war brought in various new theories and ideas with refugee intellectuals escaping the Nazi regime. For example, the Austrian School, who had developed the subjective utility theory, moved to the United States with Ludwig von Mises and Friedrich von Hayek. Logical positivism, championed by the Vienna Circle including Karl Menger (son of the economist Carl Menger), also crossed the ocean to the United States, directly with Rudolf Carnap or through Bertrand Russell, who had developed analytic philosophy in Cambridge, England, with Wittgenstein. Interestingly, these trends were joined by the economics of Thorstein Veblen, Frank Knight, Ronald Fisher, et. al. and fostered both neoclassical economics and its rival theories (See Coser 1988, among others). It was around this time that major economic theories were born, including theories of uncertainty, statistics and probability, and game theory, which provided foundations for modern economics. We can put the birth of social choice theory in this larger picture.

Note that logical positivism sought after a style of philosophy, based on mathematics and natural sciences, which was different from idealism or metaphysics. Knowledge can be divided into two types, formal logic and empirical knowledge. Mathematical models and scientific tests were adopted as a method for philosophy. However, logical positivists were not unanimous in their attitudes toward the controversy between traditional realism versus nominalism. They focused on what was observable and rejected idealism, but their views were different on how much those mathematical models or empirical sciences can approach the reality and how real the derived scientific knowledge or philosophical statements are. These are remaining conundrums and a driving force to create a new academic form.

The birth of modern social choice theory was partly helped by a historical chance. At that time, even in the United States, where academic freedom and freedom of speech were highly regarded, some prominent scholars had their university appointments rejected for having made inappropriate or immoral remarks. For example, Russell did not get a chair in logic at City University of New York for his "immoral position about sex and marriage." This led to Arrow, then a student at CUNY and admirer of Russell, taking lectures on logic from Alfred Tarski, who replaced Russell. Tarski, a mathematical logician, had escaped Poland threatened by Nazis and moved to the United States, where he was developing a unique theory of "semantic theory of truth" (Tarski 1944) while having close contact with Rudolf Carnap. It was this Tarski who taught Arrow basics of "binary relation" ("ordering" satisfying reflexivity, transitivity, and completeness), which later became a major tool for social choice theory (Arrow 1950).

This "binary relation" and the set theory taught by Tarski, and the standard axiomatic approach to mathematical logic (common to Rawls's political constructivism), became the central method in modern social choice theory invented by Arrow. Around that time, the "new" welfare economics was moving away from realism to nominalism, as far as its scientific method was concerned, but its themes were still in the realm of realism. Arrow pushed this move further in the direction of nominalism. This is the answer to the first question posed earlier. Let me explain briefly.

In his *Social Choice and Individual Values*, Arrow clearly says: "To the nominalist temperament of the modern period, the assumption of the existence of the social ideal in some Platonic realm of being was meaningless" (Arrow 1951a/1963, 22[1963]). He concludes that utilitarianism and hedonic psychology as well have turned from realism to nominalism because they sought to "ground the social good only on the good of individuals." Furthermore, as mentioned in previous chapters, he accepted Leibniz's "principle of observability" such that value judgements cannot differentiate empirically indistinguishable states, which led him to adopt the concept of ordinal and interpersonally non-comparable preferences (Arrow 1951a/1963, 112[1963]).

As Sen summarizes nicely, the concept of "utility," a crucial tool for economic analysis today, originally had a rich set of meanings including (dis)pleasure, desire, or happiness obtained by consuming goods. One of the promotors of the Marginal Revolution, Carl Menger (father), and others have shifted their attention from absolute levels of utility to its marginal changes but it still had some substantive meanings (Menger 1871/1976). Taking over William Jevons's interests, Alfred Marshall developed his welfare economics in Cambridge, England. His focus was on "the part of individual or social actions by human beings that is most closely connected with acquisition and use of material conditions of welfare."

However, the economic analysis of existence, stability and uniqueness of "general equilibrium," which attracted Arrow's interest then, only required subjective and relative valuations of the substitutability of various goods, not utility levels reflecting individual conditions. In fact, Arrow recalls that the main tool of economic theory after the Second World War was a collection of consumption indifference curves (represented by the Edgeworth Box). Individual utility functions are, functionally speaking, merely representing preference relations (binary relations) satisfying continuity and convexity. The structure of Bergson–Samuelson social welfare function is the same. Arrow saw that what was "new" about Samuelson's "New" Welfare Economics was simply a reduction of utility to preference (and further to choice). After that, Arrow decided to abandon the economic theory "merely to translate established results into another language."

9.3 Voting Theory and Philosophical Perspectives

Arrow needed another perspective of the "voting theory," dating back to Condorcet and others in the eighteenth century, in order to make a departure from the standard economic theory and cultivate a new field. The perspective exhibits a sharp contrast with game theory developed concurrently by von Neumann and Morgenstern. At that time, based on individual subjective risk preferences, von Neumann and others were designing the concept of cardinal and interpersonally non-comparable utility as an analytical tool for cooperative and non-cooperative games. Why did Arrow not adopt it? Why did he try to describe the situation to be analyzed not as a game theoretic bargaining among interested agents but as a problem of "social choice" aggregating individual evaluations formed by different individuals? This is the second issue mentioned above.

We can refer to a famous episode again to consider this conundrum. As is well known, Arrow's interest in the problem of social choice, which eventually led to his Impossibility Theorem, had been triggered by a question of what on earth it means for a certain society to have one unified utility function. It was asked by his then boss at the RAND Corporation, Olaf Helmer, in the context of bargaining among nations for disarmament. If Helmer had reduced the problem to one of a bargaining among agents with different interests at that time, it would have been analyzed by game theory immediately and hence would not have led to the birth of social choice theory.

Consideration of the formation of a utility function within a community led Arrow to thinking about the Bergson–Samuelson "social welfare function" but later he noticed that this theme had the same structure as that of voting theory dealing with the Condorcet Paradox. In other words, he realized that to explore the possibility of constituting a "social welfare function" was to seek, like voting rules, the possibility of realizing a consistent "social choice." Voting theories were based on "binary relations," which exclusively depend on individual preferences that are ordinal and interpersonally non-comparable in levels, and which need not deal with direct bargaining among agents, unlike in game theory.

These two contexts provided a background for the birth of modern social choice theory, which studies procedures to aggregate individual preference orderings and constitute social preference orderings. It is worth restating the theory's main features in sum. First, it abstracts away from substantial meanings and contents of the concept of utility and relies exclusively on individual (ordinarily interpersonally non-comparable) preference orderings that are only to be aggregated. Second, it clarifies certain (logically or normatively) desirable characteristics, puts them into explicit axioms, and explores, within a certain formal logic, logical consistencies among them. Note that ordinarily interpersonally non-comparable preference orderings (binary relations) that were also continuous and convex later played a key role in his proof, with Gerald Debreu, of the existence of a general equilibrium in the free competitive market (Arrow and Debreu 1954). Common analytical equipment for aggregation helped produce two famous theorems.

Arrow called the theorem in social choice theory, rooted in voting theory, a theory of democracy. In contrast, the latter was called a theory of the market, dating back to Walras's general equilibrium theory. These two theorems derived from the common analytical equipment helped give birth to the rhetoric that democracy and the market were twins with the same structure (beyond differences in the ethics of individual preferences and conditions in aggregation). For Arrow, however, this meant more than rhetoric, because his intuition behind these theorems was led by his belief in political philosophy that democracy and the market are similar in the sense of being informationally based solely on ordinarily non-comparable individual preference orderings. We revisit Arrow's philosophical scope to confirm this point below.

What Arrow calls nominalism, that is, the method to "ground the social good only on the good of individuals," is somewhat common to "methodological individualism" in sociology and economics (Weber 1920; Agassi 1975; Hodgson 2007)[2] and "political constructivism" in political philosophy (Rawls, 1993; see Chap. 6 of this book). It is characterized by inserting in the social objective function no external good (e.g., the national or communal good) that exists outside the individual and might dominate and suppress the good of individuals.

Arrow was aware from early years that the development of nominalist scientific methodology was deeply related to the spread of "capitalist democracy" such as that of Great Britain, France, and Scandinavia, as they appeared to be relying on the force of democracy to push back the pressure from suppressive totalitarianism (Arrow 1951a/1963, 1). Also, he correctly foresaw that his "interpersonally non-comparable ordinalism" would refuse social intervention into individual preferences and promote a "political democracy and laissez-faire economies or at least an economic system involving free choice of goods by consumers and of occupation by workers" (Arrow 1951a/1963, 23).

It is not clear whether Arrow supported the system of "capitalist democracy" after all, whether he believed in nominalism by completely rejecting realism, and whether he agreed with "interpersonally non-comparable ordinalism." We can infer from his words that he himself did not have an individualistic view of the world but rather he was fully aware of the inseparability and the communal nature of people, as a fact as well as a norm. For example, stating great sympathy with Rawls's idea of the "pooling of talent" [3]for redistributing the fruits of labor (Rawls 1971), he complained: "It is difficult to persuade students who take for granted the allocation according to contribution." (Arrow 1973, 99).

We can conclude that Arrow was waiting for a persuasive critic to convince or convert him but he did not start the process by himself. Someone had to take up the task. The main reason for his silence might have been his integrity as a

[2]Agassi (1975) provides the term "institutional individualism" as a replacement, which implies that institutional structures do affect individual choices, while only individuals have aims and responsibilities in choosing.

[3]This is also Rawls's term used in explaining the philosophical background of the difference principle (see Chap. 8). If talents are considered as "undeserved contingencies," the fruits of talent can be pooled in society for redistribution. This term invites a strong critique in negating "individuality.".

scientist who disliked logical leaps. We can find his integrity in the following essay (Arrow 1977, 225).

> [R]educing an individual to a specified list of qualities is denying his individuality in a deep sense. In a way that I cannot articulate well and I am none too sure about defending, the autonomy of individuals, an element of mutual incommensurability among people seems denied by the possibility of interpersonal comparisons. No doubt it is some such feeling as this that has made me so reluctant to shift from pure ordinalism, despite my desire to seek a basis for a theory of justice. (Arrow 1977, 222–223)

What would be the logical consequence of carrying through nominalism while tentatively accepting criticism against realism? If there are any limits, Arrow restricted his work as an economist to shedding some light on them. As mentioned earlier, Arrow was already at the center of the paradigm of economics. Whatever his personal view was, his scientific methodology as a researcher had to limit the scope of economics. It was this growing gap between academic fields that AmartyaSen tried to bridge in the 1970s.

9.4 Public Judgement and Information About Individuals Concerned

Sen published *Collective Choice and Social Welfare* in 1970, about 20 years after Arrow established modern social choice theory. During this period, Sen completed his Ph.D. at Cambridge, where Joan Robinson and Morris Dobb were active in research, and he made significant contributions to economic growth, resource allocation, and income distribution (Sen 1962, 1966b).

For example, he was interested in balancing two distribution principles, the "according to work" principle and "according to needs" principle, and searched for the clue to resolving the problem of the labor incentive.[4] Subsequently, he continued his research and lectures at the University of Delhi in India on social choice theory and on the foundation of ethical statements. The above book was its culmination. Let us see the latter first. Based on the debate with some philosophers including Richard Hare, well known for his study on the moral language (Hare 1952/1963), Sen presented his following unique views in some philosophy journals.

The first is about a conundrum known at least since David Hume discussed it. That is, if we cannot deduce "ought" from "is," then we cannot justify a norm based on facts. For Sen it would be a mistake to justify a norm by facts, as it would reduce the former to the latter. Rather, he argued, norms have to be justified for different reasons. The second is Hare's "universal prescriptivism," which requests moral languages to have "universalizability" in their applications.[5] On the contrary, Sen argued, morals or ethics often take the form of "non-basic statement" that can be revised if its factual

[4]Sen stresses that our incentives to work cannot be reduced to economic rewards or self-interest motivations. (See Sen, 1973/1997 Chap. 8).

[5]Hare (1951/1963).

assumptions are considered to be revised, or they take a form of "non-compulsive judgments" that there should be enough reason to follow, but at the same time, not inconsistently, it is possible for us not to follow on some other reasons. Most of them are a "non-basic statement" or "non-compulsive judgments" and therefore there may be different balances between different statements, depending on the context and issue (Sen 1966a, 1967a).

In these arguments, Sen clearly had a perspective that was different either from logical positivism, which bases knowledge only on logic and experience, or from Arrovian nominalism, which focuses on individual preferences only as signals and which disregards their substantive contents or ethical natures. For Sen, norms exist not purely as human cognitive constructions but have their own substances and are connected with individual beings through their bodies, minds, and social relations. However, norms are not completely beyond human cognition. With no public recognition, in general, it must be difficult to continue claiming any norm should exist. Yet, public recognition is not sufficient. It might be collectively against individual rights.

Based on these considerations, Sen focused on the divergence between choices and preferences in general and on the divergence between choices with socially conscious preferences (that is, behaving as if their preferences were socially conscious preferences) and true preferences in particular (Sen 1973/1997). This idea is rephrased in the following framework.

According to Sen, individuals can make *public judgements* when deciding on social matters, which are quite separate from their preferences on personal matters (Sen1979a/1997a). The distinctive feature of public judgements is in their domains, which include information on situations or utilities of other people. Considering public matters, individuals are supposed to examine plural criteria of morality and justice and to balance them properly, exercising their public judgements.

Behind this idea there is an assumption that individuals already follow certain norms, including one for maximizing their self-interest, and they are prepared to reselect and reweight appropriate norms for social matters. When such individuals actually select specific norms and weight them, the process will ultimately be through public discussion. This is because public decisions on social matters must care primarily about individuals who are affected by the decision, and the appropriate balance of norms to be selected would most depend on information on those concerned. Therefore, a key to reaching the truth on social matters lies with provisions of information by those concerned, and with public acknowledgement for their provisions of information.

It is important to recognize that economic theories factually affect the formation of public judgements by constructing systems or rules, or more directly, by its assumptions. If the mainstream economic theory makes an assumption of the rational "economic man," whose sole objective is to "maximize his self-interest," and tries to conceive corresponding economic systems, then the mainstream economic theory can affect actual individuals. This is related to the debate, going on since Max Weber, on whether or not sciences can be value-free (Weber 1917/2011). Sen tackled this debate and formed a clear view that sciences cannot be free only from socially dominant values but, rather, sciences inevitably affect those values (Sen 1977b/1997a).[6]

These, together with keen interests in poverty and development in his native India, provided Sen with his original perspective to critically examine the basic framework of modern social choice theory founded by Arrow. His interest helped substantiate the concept of utility in social choice theory, which had been made rather abstract by Arrow. It also led to the birth of a new theory, i.e., the capability approach. We look at the former in details in the next section.

9.5 Sen's Critical Development on Arrovian Social Choice Theory

Sen's critical development on social choice theory established by Arrow can be summarized as follows. Sen effectively broadened the domain of individual preferences by (1) allowing those that satisfy cardinality and interpersonal comparability and (2) distinguishing between private (personal) preferences about personal matters and public judgements to be counted in social choice.

Even with a broader domain of individual preferences, we cannot escape from the impossibility result, as long as we maintain, as an aggregation procedure, those axiomatic conditions that pay attention only to transitivity, completeness, and ordinal forms of individual preferences. We might be criticized for adding some conditions unnecessary to prove the impossibility result. Furthermore, if we assume that individuals have meta-rankings that can integrate multi-layered individual preferences and that those meta-rankings are ordinal and interpersonally non-comparable, then we might well remain in Arrow's framework, at least formally. What was original about Sen in social choice theory after all?

First, we can point out that Sen developed a broader framework to reexamine various aggregation procedures, such as the Libertarian principle, the no-envy principle, utilitarianism, and Rawls's difference principle. He did this by introducing new axioms with interpersonally comparable preferences or multi-layered preferences or by modifying existing assumptions or hidden conditions. A notable example among the modified axiomatic conditions is the Pareto principle. It is regarded as a key to the solution to the impossibility of a Paretian liberal, which Sen himself had proved.

The Pareto principle says that a society should prefer x to y if all its members prefer x to y. This condition is often justified in terms of citizen sovereignty (self-determination by citizens) and vigilance against totalitarianism that can suppress individual autonomy. When the Pareto principle is violated, that is, when a unanimous preference of a society is not reflected in its social preference, an outside force may have interfered in the process. Sen acknowledges this justification of the Pareto principle but poses a question: Is it necessary to introduce an outside force when we talk about rejecting a unanimous preference?

[6] See also Putnam and Walsh (2012).

His answer to this question is negative, of course, and he presents an alternative solution (see, the Short Appendix of Chap. 7). That is to distinguish between individual *i*'s private preference, for example, x to y, and individual *i*'s public judgement on whether or not she should provide her private preferences for deciding social matters. The public jusgement shows a reflective version of the private preference, which is screened in terms of what kind of personal preferences should count in social choice. As a result of screening, individuals might refrain from ranking x to y not to disturb some other person's more essential reason to rank y to x. Sen argues that the Pareto condition must be defined on those reflective meta-preferences, not on unscreened preferences.

The second important point regarding Sen's originality in social choice theory is that Sen takes as the default setting a domain more expansive than Arrow's original setting (a greater "unrestricted domain"), which allows for cardinal and interpersonally comparable preferences or multi-layered preferences. This expanded domain requests researchers or planners to clarify the reasons why they use such restricted domains that exclude cardinal preferences or interpersonally non-comparable preferences.

This broader framework fits well with the very idea of the rule of law, as it provides all the rules in advance, including exceptional or conditional arrangements, for every kind of conceivable social state in the world. Remember that we can find the idea of the rule of law in the axiomatic approach provided by Arrow in the context of social choice, which allows all conceivable preferences as informational bases of social choice.

Besides expanding the domain, Sen's originality is that his framework of social choice does not require completeness from the rule of law but positively embraces incompleteness from a normative point of view. In other words, he accepts having the limit of the scope of each law's applicability and, rather, setting exceptions in difficult cases. It retains some room for intra- and interpersonal non-comparability and still aims to consider inclusive social choice mechanisms for all.

Third, Sen's originality is that he respects individual ethical attitudes by having a framework, as mentioned above, to distinguish between private preferences and public judgements in individual preferences. People may have some particular tastes about their own private matters while trying to make a balanced judgement on social matters by considering appropriate social norms. A simple model to describe individuals by their private preferences only can risk ignoring their ethical attitudes and private preferences as well. Its essence can be illustrated by the following example given by Sen (1977a/1997a) and modified by the author.

There are two brothers with one toy. They keep quiet and do not move. Their silence is broken by the older brother, who extends his arm and takes the toy. Now the younger says, "You cheated!" The older one replies, "Cheat? What would you have done?" The younger says, "I would have given it to you." The older one is now triumphant: "Well, perfect! That's exactly what you wanted!" And the younger brother replies: "Exactly what I wanted?" He is at a loss for words.

They seem to be talking at cross-purposes. Where does this divergence come from? The older brother acted purely in his self-interest and desire while the younger did not. To be more precise, the younger had some reservation about what he should do. However, the older one interpreted the younger's act exactly as his own, i.e., purely in terms of self-interest and desire. The older brother ignored the younger's intention to give the toy to others, paying attention only to the form or expression "wanted." In other words, the older brother recognized no plurality in the points of view of their judgements. Here was the cause of the divergence.

Different acts and choices can have different points of view and motivations behind them. A particular act chosen in a certain context can have different reasons for its justification. However, the older brother used the logic of unification, which would refuse discussing them or even acknowledging their existence. It can totally ignore plurality and diversity of different individual preferences. No wonder the younger brother was at a loss for words.

Sen finds that the logic of unification, symbolized by this example and its problem, is in fact common to the utility approach as a tool for mainstream economics. He once tried to describe it by the word "welfarism" (See Sen1979a/1997a). Sen and Williams (1982), in their introduction, called it "monism" as a broader concept and examined its problems carefully.

9.6 Concluding Remarks

This chapter has drawn a rough sketch of some essential features of Arrow's founding of modern social choice theory and Sen's economics in the 1970s. We conclude by briefly summarizing similarities and differences between Arrow and Sen.

Arrow's research interest was in building a general theory by using a symbolic concept of utility devoid of substantive meanings. He then only implicitly, if at all, wished that actual people would autonomously choose and accept some ethics of, say, the common good or reciprocity, so that good social choices would be made. Similarly, Sen saw a possibility of good social choices in people's autonomous acceptance of those ethics. Unlike Arrow, however, Sen sought to explicitly incorporate into his theoretical framework tensions between economy (welfare) and ethics, or between logic and reality (substance) as a subject of his original research. The 1970s saw a quiet disagreement between Arrow and Sen on this point.

It has been more than 20 years since Sen won a Nobel prize in economics in 1998. It might be more accurate to say almost half a century anniversary, because the essence of Sen's economics, including his social choice theory, welfare economics, and economic philosophy, flourished in the 1970s. In reality, however, many of the conundrums pointed out then remain unresolved today.

Chapter 10
Final Remarks: Economic Philosophy of Amartya Sen

10.1 Philosophy as a Subject of Economic Theory

> In the democratic context, values are given a foundation through their relation to informed judgements by the people involved. [What is at stake is] the need to make sure that the weights—or range of weights—used remain open to criticism and chastisement, and nevertheless enjoy reasonable public acceptance. Openness to critical scrutiny, combined with—explicit or tacit—public consent, is a central requirement of non-arbitrariness of valuation in a democratic society. (Sen 1997, 207)

A distinguishing style of Sen's economics is its openness to collaboration with other academic disciplines and policy practices while also fostering public discussion, in contrast with mainstream economics that operates in a closed circle and tends to be possessed by its internal logic. We might say that the capability approach is a trial to describe this style of studying as a methodology of social science.

We call the discipline (approach) developed by Sen "economic philosophy" for the following reasons. While social norms and ethical values can implicitly provide a reference for every social science, economic philosophy takes them as a subject of academic inquiry. It does not "outsource" analyses of social norms and ethical values to other disciplines or practices, nor deal with them only implicitly by appealing to researchers' intuitions or jargons.

The tools Sen used were logic and expression. The logic was provided by an axiomatic approach with mathematics, and the expression was a combination of ethical approaches employing symbolic examples and literary approaches using poetry, fables, metaphors, and rhetoric.

Ethics and freedom are closely related to each other in Sen's arguments, and in this respect Sen inherits Kant's moral theory. Ethics matters only when there is room for an individual to choose his or her own acts based on free will without being forced by legal norms or political powers, nor induced by economic incentives.

The assumption of a rational *Homo economicus* maximizing his or her self-interest is criticized not only because it fails to consider the other human incentives of various sorts described by Adam Smith and others. It is criticized because the assumption

R. Gotoh, *The Ethics and Economics of the Capability Approach*, Hitotsubashi University IER Economic Research Series 46, https://doi.org/10.1007/978-981-15-5140-6_10

of *Homo economicus* does not allow regarding a person as a free being. If his or her acts are always induced by interests, there is nothing else than rational calculation of interests and no individual freedom exists beyond that (called a "rational fool" by Sen1977b).

Poverty is a big problem not only because severe constraints on income or wealth make people easily controlled by market fluctuations but also because they leave little room for people to choose their own acts based on motivations other than economic interests. The capability approach has an advantage of capturing the real freedom enjoyed by a person, not as a "rational fool." He or she can have not only a motivation for self-interest maximization but also have a freedom to choose not to follow a motivation for self-interest maximization. He or she has a freedom to act, for example, ethically considering their relations with others or politically reflecting public interests and concerns, given his or her capabilities to choose various kinds of actions including non-ethical or non-political ones.

Sen pursued a possibility for individuals to make public judgements in a way different from psychological dispositions. Making public judgements should be based on fine balances among plural non-basic or non-compulsive principles, each of which can be reasonable in themselves to some extent (Sen 1969, 1970a; see Chap. 8 of this book). With this plurality in mind, Sen mention argued, utilitarianism can be criticized for working as a basic and compulsive principle, i.e., being regarded as applicable to the universal domain and as the unique legitimate criterion (called "monism," Sen and Williams 1982, 3).[1]

Furthermore, Sen went on to criticize even John Rawls's political liberalism, because it allows a universalistic interpretation in constructing ideal institutions, although it factually attacks the uni-dimensionality of utilitarianism and incorporates multi-dimensional features. As a result, Sen looked to a method to go beyond New Welfare Economics, Arrovian social choice theory, and Rawlsian political liberalism.

At its core were the capability approach to care about diverse individual situations equally in constructing more just distribution systems and Sen's social choice model to respect diverse individual evaluations equally in forming better social choices as well as better social decision procedures.

It is very difficult to prove, both empirically and logically, the validity of theories in social sciences, let alone to falsify them (as Popper noted). When their purpose is to improve individuals' well-being, the process of their judgements inevitably depends on individual evaluations of their well-being. If respect of people's free will imposes restrictions on the social decision procedures, the result inevitably varies according to individual choices. The capability approach and Sen's social choice model are obliged to face the fact of indeterminacy and incompleteness, while aiming to provide people with guidance for practice. What kinds of consequences a theory can actually bring about depend on many individuals' present and future activities, which themselves are influenced by these theories.

[1]On "monism" see also Anderson (1993).

Table 10.1 Contrast between neoclassical economics and new methodology of economics

	Neo-Classical Theory	New Methodology of Economics
Interpretation (Epistemology) Being (Ontology) Evaluation (Value theory) (Non-differentiate)	maximization based on his/her own preferences subject to constraints, such as his/her own private property, market prices and others' preferences in equilibrium	(differentiate) How should we make right judgements? How can human beings live well? What kinds of values should we pursue, why?

10.2 Ternary Perspectives: Ontology, Value Theory, and Epistemology

On a final note, let me share my view in placing Sen's economics in terms of "economic philosophy." Another economic philosopher, Yuichi Shionoya, reexamined the methodological frameworks of social sciences from the following ternary perspectives: beings and doings (ontology), values and evaluations (value theory), and interpretations and recognitions (epistemology) when searching for a new methodological framework for economics (Shionoya 2009). His ternary perspectives can help clarify that neoclassical economics provides a logic to give an undifferentiated explanation for all three perspectives without clearly distinguishing them. That is, according to neoclassical economics, an individual's situation is nothing else than a direct consequence of her own act of maximizing self-interest based on her own preferences (however they were formed) under certain constraints (whatever they are) and given market prices. Table 10.1 shows the contrast between neoclassical economics and the new methodology of economics.

In reality, however, there is no guarantee of consistency among existence, values, and perception. More often than not, there are some gaps among individual objective circumstances, the values they pursue, and their interpretations and recognitions of the world. As we have discussed so far, the capability approach can shed light on the gaps among ternary perspectives, that is, beings and doings (ontology), values and evaluations (value theory), and interpretations and recognitions (epistemology). Sen's economic philosophy enables us to make critical and comprehensive examinations of relationships between individuals and institutions.

We can borrow Shionoya's framework to classify Sen's wide-ranging contributions and obtain the following bird's-eye-view of his economic philosophy in the following chart. The rows represent six themes in economic philosophy derived inductively from Sen's works and his methodological research ("science and literature") underlying them. The columns have ternary perspectives of economic philosophy. An asterisk (*) shows which theme has been studied from which perspective(s).

Table 10.2 The universe of Amartya Sen's economic philosophy

Philosophical Angles / Themes of papers	**Interpretation (Epistemology)**	**Being (Ontology)**	**Evaluation (Value Theory)**
Wealth and Income	*	**	***
Poverty and Inequality	***	**	*
Rationality and Reasoning	***	**	*
Freedom and Rights	**	***	*
Market and Democracy	**	*	***
Ethics, Law and Philosophy	*	*	*
Science and Literature (mathematics, logics, poems, fables)			

The more asterisks one has, the stronger Sen's commitment is to the theme and perspective. (A Borda scoring method is used here) (Table 10.2).

We do not attempt to classify Sen's countless works into these cells now, but let me just point out the following: Each cell signifies an academic discipline with an independent theme and perspective. Hence there can be eighteen areas of study (six themes and ternary perspectives). To each we can add its applied, practical, or empirical field, and Sen's economic philosophy can be a loose association of at least thirty-six areas of inquiry. Finally, the methodology ("science and literature") supporting these areas may possibly include different methodological issues to be studied.

Only three themes among these, i.e., "Wealth and income," "Poverty and inequality," and "Rationality and reasoning," belong to narrowly defined welfare economics. However, a person's life, well-being, and freedom cannot be reduced to these elements only. It is inevitably related to rights, ethics, laws, institutions, and customs. Sen's economic philosophy has shown abundant possibilities of economic study, whose goal has required open collaboration with many different disciplines and people in practice.

Such a broad scope of his economics mirrors his personality and interests very well. At the same time, however, we have to bear in mind that this reflects considerations and experiences of countless social scientists and practitioners in the historical past and in the present that people today want to hand over to the future.

Let us close our inquiry by briefly discussing some of the research topics to be pursued in the future. First, we can pursue some comparative studies of similar but different normative concepts. The concept of "human rights" has been developed mainly in legal studies, and that of "human security" in politics.[2] For example, the capability approach may resonate with UNESCO's "right to learn," which was advocated as the right to "read one's own world and write history" and then, "the right to develop individual and collective skills."[3]

Second, we can compare the capability approach with the neighboring fields such as the human capital approach, equivalent income approach, and hedonic approach. These approaches treat qualitative differences (Graham and Green 1984; Heckman and Corbin 2016), by weighting or integrating multi-dimensional indexes with a kind of "shadow prices".[4] Besides, there is a large literature on distribution rules with multi-dimensional indexes, including ranking opportunity sets.[5]

How about practical implications of the capability approach? It has turned out to be far more versatile than expected (we may call them "the capability studies"). It is also applicable to firms and organizations for capturing equilibrium dynamics, as the theory of human capital does. However, if we try to remain loyal to Sen's and Nussbaum's motivations, it seems natural to understand the concept of capability as opposed to that of adversity.[6]

Take an example of atomic bomb sufferers (see Chap. 6), who have argued most strongly for compensation for the dead and the abolition of nuclear weapons. It is difficult to understand the survivor with a sense of guilt or shame toward the dead who were next to her by a uni-dimensional measure such as her utility. So it is, even with the concepts like "social primary goods." Each case forces us to scrutinize institutional constraints imposed on her and moral conditions that restrict her.

Searching for the list of functionings and capability to overcome adversity is not only beneficial for the people involved in catastrophic situations. As Chap. 8 indicates, knowing their adversities can help facilitate cooperation among ordinary people. This is another thesis of ours, in the theory of capability, to be proposed and defended in this project.

---

[2]Comparison with the political philosophy of Rawls and others remains an intriguing theme (Brooks and Nussbaum, 2015; Gotoh 2015).

[3]Fourth International Conference on Adult Education (1985) Paris, France, 19–29 March, 1985; Ireland and Spezia (2014).

[4]It would also be interesting to examine the relationship of the capability approach with the income approach, including arguments for basic income (Cohen 1993; Pogge 2010; van Parijs 1995), theories of basic needs (Yamamori 2016; Doyal and Gough 1991), disadvantage (Wolff and De-Shalit 2007), and multidimensional well-being (Brandolini 2009).

[5]There is a large literature on distribution rules, including ranking opportunity sets. See, among others, Klemisch-Ahlert (1993), Bossert et al. (1994), Puppe (1995), Farina et al. (1996); Farrina et al. (2004), Kolm (2010), Miyagishima (2010, 2012), Pattanaik and Xu (1990, 2000, 2014), Suzumura and Xu (2003), Xu (2002, 2003, 2004), Alkire and Foster (2011), Alkire (2016). See also Basu and Kanbur (2009).

[6]For example, we can find a certain similarity between Emmanuel Levinas and Sen in the following sentences. "Nourishment, as means of invigoration, is the transmutation of the other into the same, which is in the essence of enjoyment. ... All enjoyments are in this sense alimentation" (Levinas 1961, 111[1979]).

In summary, the capability approach contains many issues to be explored in theoretical research and in empirical research as well as in practical applications.[7] It can be a core subject, in and outside research institutes, of life-long learning for people with disabilities, the elderly, sufferers from daily abuse or catastrophic incidents, their family and supporters, and anyone who wants to "read one's own world and write history."

[7]In Robeyns (2017), Ingrid Robeyns persuasively summarizes the reach and possibility of the capability approach inheriting a lot of precious previous contributions. See also papers and collections including Qizilbash 1996, 2006, 2007, 2011; Gasper 1997; Garnham 1999; Robeyns 2003, 2006, 2009a, b; Deneulin et al. 2006; Bruni et al. 2008; Comim et al. 2008; Putnam 2008; Chiappero-Martinetti ed. 2009; Brighouse and Robeyns eds. 2010; Alkire, Foster et al. 2015.

Epilogue

Finally, let us close this small book with some additional remarks. Our attempt to formulate the capability approach using the framework of traditional economic theory made us realize the need for examining the assumptions of the framework (as a matter of course). This was our first discovery. If this is the case, we should bring back into economics the insights we have obtained here.

This methodological concern might be shared by researchers in applied economics, including labor economics, development economics, behavioral economics, and public economics. Suppose we are going to design a labor policy that can support the goal of "repeated fresh starts freely" (for working or learning) for every person in society. Then, an economist may ask: how is it essentially different from the principle of "free entry and exit" in a fully competitive market? Another may say: "free entry and exit" is easily justified by individual rationality and efficiency in a property-owning society, whereas "repeated fresh starts freely" has to face many challenges, since it must secure the capability of persons for repeating fresh starts freely. How can we manage financial feasibility or deal with the incentive problem? Notwithstanding their similarities in appearance, realizing "repeated fresh starts freely" looks far more difficult than "free entry and exit."

Needless to say, however, human lives, well-being, freedom, and equality are of paramount importance in the research in social sciences and humanities. If these values are behind the question of what labor policy can support "repeated fresh starts freely," they should not be easily compromised.

Here we can find a final answer to the original question: What is the capability approach proposed by Sen? It is an approach for explicit analyses of the values and norms that have so far been implicitly assumed in economic theory as normal. The capability approach aims for improvements of welfare economics, by accessing difficulties that people face in the midst of industry, the workplace, the public sphere, home, and social interactions. I would be most grateful if this book is a small step for repositioning economics in broad cooperation with the humanities and social sciences.

March 2020
Reiko Gotoh

R. Gotoh, *The Ethics and Economics of the Capability Approach*, Hitotsubashi University IER Economic Research Series 46, https://doi.org/10.1007/978-981-15-5140-6

Appendix A
The Capability Theory and Welfare Reform

Reiko Gotoh

A.1 Introduction

Faced with structural changes in population and the economy such as increasingly higher rates of aging and unemployment, the industrialized countries have commonly undertaken welfare reform. The primary emphasis of this reform has been to turn the recipients "from welfare to work" in order to break the cycle of dependence on welfare over generations and promote independent living. Such reform is not new. For example, the theme of the new conservatism espoused by Margaret Thatcher and Ronald Reagan was to make a huge reduction in the cost of welfare that would leave welfare recipients self-supporting. But present-day welfare reform is more complicated and more difficult to achieve than ever before. This is not only because the situation is becoming more serious but also because proponents are keenly aware that to promote independent living, reform must provide appropriate guidelines and concrete programs for advancing individual well-being and for balancing social responsibility with personal responsibility.

In this regard, we can learn much from the capability theory introduced by Amartya Sen (1980a, 1985a; 1985b, 1987a, 1992a). It is useful to examine the foundation of welfare reform in the light of his theory and to its implications for contemporary society.

This Appendix was originally published as "The Capability Theory and Welfare Reform" Reiko Gotoh, in *Pacific Economic Review*, Volume 6, Issue 2, pages 211–222, (John Wiley & Sons, 2002)
The author belonged to the National Institute of Population and Social Security Research, Japan when this article was first published. She is grateful to Professors Kotaro Suzumura, Yuichi Shionoya, Ko Hasegawa, Naoki Yoshihara, for their helpful comments and discussions on these issues. She also appreciates the suggestions of an anonymous referee.

R. Gotoh, *The Ethics and Economics of the Capability Approach*, Hitotsubashi University IER Economic Research Series 46, https://doi.org/10.1007/978-981-15-5140-6

Previously, John Rawls (1971a, 1993) proposed the two principles of justice based on the concept of *social primary goods*. Social primary goods represent the citizen's needs to identify and develop two moral powers: namely, the capacity for a conception of the good and the capacity for a sense of justice (Rawls 1993, pp. 188–189, 189n.). The former is the capacity to form, to revise, and rationally to pursue one's own conception of the good, and the latter is the capacity to understand, to apply, and to act reasonably from the public conception of justice (Rawls 1993, p. 19). Both of these moral powers are indispensable to the substantial support of political liberty and democracy. The task of justice is to construct fair relationships among citizens by establishing the first principles that precede all laws and underlie the basic structure of the various systems of a society.[1]

On the other hand, the concept of *functionings* proposed by Sen contains the basic components of human well-being to ensure a decent, independent life and for which the society should be held responsible. The object of the capability theory is to secure a "real" opportunity for every individual to achieve *functionings*[2] by formulating a rule for the fair distribution of resources in the stage of legislation or social policies. In that stage, individual variations in personal characteristics can be identified and adequately considered in determining the means of resource distribution.[3]

To clarify the foundation for welfare reform, we must inquire more specifically into the nature of human well-being, which such reform should implicitly aim to promote in every society. Simultaneously, we must start not from a political conception of the individual–the citizen–but from actual individuals who have multiple goals and diverse physical and intellectual characteristics. On these two viewpoints, the capability theory is more appropriate for our purpose because it provides a theoretical framework for addressing the nature of human well-being and the diversity of individuals by endogenously analyzing the interrelationship among resources, personal characteristics, and human well-being through the medium of *functionings*.

In getting an idea of the well-being of the person, we clearly have to move on to 'functionings', to wit, what the person succeeds in *doing* with the commodities and characteristics at his or her command. For example, we must take note that a disabled person may not be able to do many things an able-bodied individual can, with the same bundle of commodities (Sen 1985a, p. 10).

To examine welfare reform in the light of the capability theory, however, we must undertake two tasks. One task is to formulate the capability theory in terms of a fair distributive justice that can be applied generally to the industrialized countries as

---

[1] "The initial focus, then, of a political conception of justice is the framework of basic institutions and the principles, standards, and precepts that apply to it," (Rawls 1993 p. 11).

[2] A "real" opportunity is distinguished from "formal" opportunity which means equal applicability (or equal non-applicability) of specific barriers or constraints. See Sen 1992a, p. 7.

[3] This interpretation of the capability theory is consistent with the framework of Rawls. "[T]he variations that put some citizens below the line as a result of illness and accident (once we allow for these) can be dealt with, I believe, at the legislative stage when the prevalence and kinds of these misfortunes are known and the costs of treating them can be ascertained and balanced along with total government expenditure."(Rawls 1993, p.184) See also Sen 1992, p.83n. and Sugden 1993, p. 1955f.

well as the developing countries. The other task is to define the essential problems and alternative solutions that the capability theory seeks to address by clarifying the conceptions and methods of the theory from a philosophical viewpoint.

These two tasks are not easy to perform. The purpose of this essay is to create a vision for their accomplishment. Let us sketch our planning briefly. First, the point of formulating the capability theory is to explore an appropriate measure of resource distribution in terms of fair assignment of capabilities among the constituents of a society. Second, the point of clarifying the philosophical meaning of the *functionings* and the *capability* is to reinterpret them in terms of freedom and a process of human life, focusing on Sen's two concepts of freedom, *well-being freedom* and*agency freedom*.

The structure of this paper is as follows. After providing a framework for considering distribution problems in Sect. A.2, we will deal with the first point in Sect. A.3. A method to formulate the "equality of capabilities" and its philosophical meaning in the process of human life are explored here. Then, Sen's two concepts of freedom—their conceptual differences and complementary relationship in the context of welfare policy—are examined in Sect. A.4. Individual evaluation of capabilities, as it relates to agency freedom, is inquired in Sect. A.5. In conclusion, Sect. A.6 reviews problems that seem particularly relevant to welfare reform in the industrialized countries and suggests future subjects for the application of Sen's capability theory to actual welfare policies.

A.2 Distribution Problems

Let us consider the following distribution problem *in principle*. Suppose a simple cooperative production economy, where one input, labor, is used to produce one output. How should we assign two kinds of resources: the product and the leisure time for members–each of whom has a different preference, a different skill, and a different consumption ability–who cooperate in generating a product by contributing their labor and utilizing a common production technology? To consider *in principle* means not to accept the historically contingent facts as given but, in appraising the essential problems, to reflect on the premises of our reasonable intuitions and daily convictions in the light of relevant fundamental arguments and theories.

It may be assumed that individual situations will vary. If one contributes more labor hours to production, needless to say, she will have less leisure time and require more resources as compensation. A higher-skilled worker can make a greater contribution to production in the same amount of time and may claim more resources as a reward. If one has a difficulty in her legs, she may not be able to make enough contribution, but she will need more resources to move.

A person with a high skill level nevertheless may contribute less to production in order to pursue her extreme favor to leisure. On the other hand, a person who has had no opportunity to work because she is less skilled may have developed an inclination to be lazy during the long period of her unemployment. Moreover, some people who have been barred from the opportunity of receiving a basic education because of their social class at birth never develop their potential skills and abilities. All of these cases illustrate the fundamental human diversities that are derived partly from personal subjective preferences and partly from personal objective characteristics, most of which have been regarded as a given in economic analysis.

What factors should we pay attention to in determining a fair distribution of resources? In the history of distributive justice, the principle of natural reward,[4] which requires a positive relationship between the contributions of individuals and the distribution of resources, has been broadly accepted. Traditionally, based on the private property right, the equilibrium allocations spontaneously reached through voluntary exchanges by private agencies are conceived to be just in themselves. Furthermore, several concepts of equity, such as *fairness-as-no-envy* (Foley 1967; Kolm 1972; Varian 1974) and *egalitarian equivalence,* (Pazner and Schmeidler 1978) which aim to compare individual advantages exclusively in terms of individual ordinal preferences, have been proposed.

In contrast with those theories, Professor Sen has proposed the "equality of capabilities". This concept calls for the equalization of individual advantages that reflect interpersonal variations in transforming resources into capabilities to pursue one's own ends. "[A] more adequate way of considering 'real' equality of opportunities must be through equality of capabilities (or through the elimination of unambiguous inequalities in capabilities, since capability comparisons are typically incomplete)" (Sen 1985a, p. 7). And he has proposed to construct an index that makes it possible to assess an individual's advantages with enough accuracy to design welfare policies.[5] This approach focuses, not on the difference in resources to which individuals are entitled or the difference in personal subjective preferences for resources, but rather on the difference in personal objective characteristics. Furthermore, it tries to capture as the informational basis of the fair resource distribution, not the objective characteristics themselves, but something produced by resources and personal objective characteristics.

A.3 Equality of Capabilities

As for equilibrium based on individual voluntary exchange, a distribution that compensates for a difference in the outcome arising from personal objective characteristics (production skill and ability to utilize resources) usually cannot be expected. And the precept of distribution according to contribution is not concerned with the difference in opportunities for making contributions, which is based on individual

[4]Originally introduced in Aristotle's *Nicomachean Ethics*.

[5]Note that Sen does not intend to rank the capability sets completely: "The capability comparison may be aimed just at determining which of two particular persons is the more advantaged...There is no compulsion to rank the capability sets completely, nor to have a partial order extensive enough for a 'best' capability set to be identified (and chosen)." Sen 1985a, p. 66.

skill and the total hours available for production. Furthermore, under this precept, the difference in individual abilities to utilize resources has no basis for influencing the means of distribution unless it influences their skills and their choice of work hours.

On the contrary, the "equality of capabilities" requires the equalization of *a kind of* consequence, namely, individuals' capabilities. *A kind of* consequence means a result of the process of resource distribution, yet it is distinguished from the usual meanings of consequence, such as utility–pleasure, happiness, or desire-fulfilment–which a person finally obtains by utilizing resources.[6]

An individual capability represents the various combinations of functionings that a person can really achieve given his own limitations, that is, the resources assigned to him and his personal objective characteristics to utilize them (Sen 1981, app. A and B. Sen 1985a, pp. 13, 40). Moreover, a combination of functionings represents a person's achievement: what he or she manages to do or to be—for instance, moving, communicating, ingesting nutritious food, being free from serious sickness, constructing ideas, and presenting her opinions.[7] "A functioning is thus different both from (1) having goods (and the corresponding characteristics), to which it is posterior, and (2) having utility (in the form of happiness resulting from that functioning), to which it is, in an important way, prior." (Sen 1985a, pp. 10–11)

It is significant that even if given limitations are the same, a person can still achieve, within a certain range, a diverse vector of functionings, namely, a different combination of doings and beings by changing the way one uses resources and her own ability to utilize them. The "equality of capabilities" pays attention not to the difference in the achieved functionings but to the difference in the capability to achieve functionings, that is, the extent to which a person can choose freely.

It is important to distinguish between choice and non-choice factors in the determination of capabilities Q_i. …Resource allocation and policy making will have to address the question, among others, of expanding the limits of choice reflected in X_i [the feasible set of commodities: 'entitlements'] and F_i [the feasible set of utilization functions] (Sen 1985a, p. 27. The brackets [ ] indicate that these are my additions).

It is possible, however, to define the traditional concept of utility not over a dimension of resources but over an extended dimension as consisting of resources and the ability to consume them (Fleurbaey 1994, 1995; Roemer 1996). Moreover, it is possible to define the utility space consists of several kinds of utility (e.g., comfortable, delightful, refreshing, cheerful) that can be defined independently of one another (if possible); in this case, the formulation of a set of utilities will have the same mathematical structure as the formulation of the capabilities described above.

---

[6]Regarding this point, Sen's capability theory is distinguished from welfarist-consequentialism. See Suzumura K. and R. Gotoh, 1999. There are several trials to pay attentions to the consequences of resource distribution in broad terms. See, e.g., "social primary goods" (Rawls 1971), "resources" (Dworkin 1981), "opportunity for welfare" (Arneson 1989), and "equal access to advantage" (Cohen 1989).

[7]Sen provides many examples of the kinds of functionings– e.g., being in good health, avoiding escapable morbidity or premature mortality, being happy, having self-respect, and taking part in the life of the community. (Sen 1992, p. 39).

The distinctive feature of the concept of capability thus seems to be not its operational meaning but its philosophical meaning. The vector of functionings that an individual achieves by consuming resources does comprise her objective abilities that are indispensable to the further pursuit of her own goals, independently of her subjective recognition of that fact. Though both functionings and the ability to utilize resources are individual abilities, the former becomes the goal of resource utilization and the latter becomes the means to achieve that goal. Of course, this relationship between the two concepts is only relative. Achieved functionings become the means to achieve other goals as utilization abilities increase.

Such a sequence generally makes it possible for an individual to live independently and realize her own life plan by herself. Therefore, although achieved functionings are a consequence in that they result from the utilization of resources that follows the process of resource distribution, we can reasonably interpret them, from the philosophical point of view, as a process of the realization of individual human life.[8]

Thus to formulate capabilities more substantively by identifying the lists of the functionings and corresponding commodities, one must understand the process of mutual development among the different kinds of functioning as a whole. This is a theme of the theory of the good,[9] and it may be difficult to find the universal answer–e.g., what kinds of functioning are most necessary for human well-being?[10] One approach to this issue is to accumulate the answers that can be specifically acquired in the context of each society and consider them in relation to one another and to related theories of good to draw a more comprehensive, synthesized picture (Griffin 1986; Nussbaum 1990; Doyal and Gough 1991; Nussbaum 1993).

A.4 Well-Being Freedom and Agency Freedom

The acquisition of the new option of functionings means the expansion of freedom in that it leads to a broader range of the activities that a person can perform independently. Professor Sen calls such freedom *well-being freedom*.[11] Another kind of freedom is the freedom not to be interfered with by anybody in achieving one's goal,

---

[8]This interpretation may be regarded as Aristotelian "in the sense of referring to a person's *potential* capabilities that could be developed, whether or not they are actually realized." Sen 1992, p. 45n.

[9]"The philosophical basis of this approach can be traced to Aristotle's writings, which include a penetrating investigation of 'the good of man' in terms of 'life in the sense of activity'." Ibid., p. 39.

[10]This kind of difficulty does not reflect a flaw in the capability approach; rather, it is derived from the nature of human well-being. "[T]he functionings approach is intrinsically information-pluralist. Although some consensus of valuations and the usability of various objective criteria may take us a great distance in establishing an extensive partial ordering in the comparison of well-being, it would be quite wrong to expect anything like the kind of complete ordering that utilitarians have made us prone to demand." Ibid., p. 200.

[11]"[T] he latter [well-being freedom)]is one's freedom to achieve those things that are constitutive of one's well-being." Sen 1992, p. 57.

whatever it is. Sen terms this *agency freedom*.[12] In what way should we make these two concepts of freedom being accommodated with each other? This is the second task in our examination of the capability theory. Two prominent features of both concepts can be explained as follows:

We can see the person, in terms of *agency*, recognizing and respecting his or her ability to form goals, commitments, values, etc., and we can also see the person in terms of *well-being*, which too calls for attention (Sen 1987, p. 41).

The well-being aspect is especially important in such matters as social security, poverty alleviation, removal of gross economic inequality, and in general in the pursuit of social justice. That case is not conditional on the person himself attaching overwhelming priority to his own well-being in his agency objectives (Sen 1992, p. 71).

An illustration may point out the distinction a little more clearly. Let us assume that there is a policy providing a device that permits a person to vote even though her hand is seriously handicapped. The provision of some supporting instrument secures her action of voting, which means the equalization of the well-being freedom because her willingness to vote can be actually realized despite her handicap. But suppose that in the next election she decides after the careful consideration not to vote; through this decision, she intends to protest that the election procedures are not fair. In this situation, if her will to withdraw is interfered with, i. e., if she is forced to vote, one can say that her agency freedom has been violated.

Presumably agency freedom and well-being freedom are generally incompatible. The most extreme case is when an individual has a goal that logically contradicts the well-being freedom.[13] Thus it becomes important in the legislative stage to adjust these freedoms by considering the following two questions: what kinds of agency freedom should we equally guarantee to every individual? and what kinds of well-being should we secure in social responsibility? Taken together, two questions indicate that we must determine the content and the level of capability to be secured in social responsibility to promote a person's well-being, giving priority to the kinds of agency freedom that are equally guaranteed to support a person's activity to achieve a goal, whatever that goal might be. In this regard, Sen suggests:

Society might accept some responsibility for a person's well-being, especially when that is in some danger of being particularly low. But this does not imply that society must take an equal interest in the promotion of that person's other agency objectives as well (Sen 1992, p. 70).

There is a particular sphere in which such an agency role may be especially important, and that is the person's own life. Various concepts of "autonomy," and

---

[12]"Agency freedom is freedom to achieve whatever the person, as a responsible agent, decides he or she should achieve." Sen 1985b, p. 204. Note that Sen use the term "agent" not as it is employed in the literature of economics, but in the sense of "someone who acts and brings about change, and whose achievement can be judged in terms of her own values and objectives, whether or not we assess them in terms of some external criteria as well". Sen 1999, p. 19.

[13]For example, increased opportunities to perform actions involving self-sacrifice imply enhanced agency freedom but reduced well-being freedom.

"personal liberty," relate to this special role of agency in personal life, going well beyond considerations of well-being (Sen 1985b, p. 186).

From the preceding discussions, we can extract three kinds of inner connection between freedom and capability. First, as we saw in Sect. A.3, functioning is intrinsically related to freedom in that it constitutes one's ability to do or to be independently in the process of his life. Second, a person can actually achieve any option of his capability, as long as he intends to do so. This means that society is required to positively make some assignment of transferable resources. Third, a person has immunity from the interference of others (including the society) with regard to choosing any option within his capability. The agent who chooses one's functionings from his capability is the person himself.[14]

We must recall that the "equality of capabilities" does not directly indicate a combination of functionings that one should actually achieve. The goal of this precept is to equalize the real opportunities that an individual may choose on her own free will.[15] The final achievement of functionings is left to individual autonomy. So far as there exists some factor that is beyond the person's control and restricts her sets of functionings, the objective of resource distribution is to compensate for the deficiency in her options. We will examine this point more closely in the next section.

A.5 The Value of Agency Freedom

Even if individuals have the same consumption abilities and the same resources, and end up having the same capabilities, say, the same set of vectors of functionings, the well-being they actually achieve may not be the same. This is because a person's evaluation of the functionings gets in the way of her capability and the functionings she actually achieves. n individual forms a pattern of the evaluation, based on her conception of the good. An individual evaluation of the functionings indicates us how good the individual herself thinks some kind of living (doings and beings) is. It is distinguished from her utility, which represents how happy she *is* with the living (Sen 1985a, p. 12). Given the conditions surrounding her—e.g., objective characteristics of herself, social systems (rules, norms, and institutions), and exterior environment (natural resources, productive technology, characteristics and behaviors of others),

[14]In the capability space it is difficult to distinguish the second and third type of freedom, see Sen (1992, p. 87). Gotoh and Yoshihara (1999) tries to formulate the capability approach, distinguishing between them. According to Berlin's terminology, the second may be called the positive freedom and the third the negative freedom. However (Sen, 1988) has proposed another interpretation of Berlin's two concepts of freedom. This very important but complicated discussion is beyond the scope of this essay.

[15]"Capability is, thus, a set of vectors of functionings, reflecting the person's freedom to lead one type of life or another." Sen 1992, p. 40.

she will choose the optimal functionings for her goals and life plan, based on her own pattern of evaluation pattern.[16]

An individual evaluation pattern concerning the relationship of the functionings may be described by the difference curve in the space of infinite real numbers. And even if it is a reliable measure of the relative values of each functioning, it may be ambiguous for the level of achievement of each functioning such that the higher is the better.[17] Furthermore, it cannot completely compare every pair of vectors. On some particular comparisons, she may be compelled to be silent. Yet each individual ends up discovering the most optimal vector of functionings, after assuring her intention to achieve her goal, in relation to the limitations she must accept, at least for the time being.

Incidentally, the optimal combination of resources (income and leisure time) that corresponds to optimal functionings does not always lead to optimal utility. This is because individual mental responses are multilayered, and there is no assurance that one of the subjective responses—say, desire-fulfilment or happiness—correctly corresponds to one's goal or life plan that has been rationally and reasonably formed. Moreover, Professor Sen points out, the mental responses are apt to be distinct from one's valuing activity, because "Valuing is not the same thing as desiring, and the strength of desire is influenced by considerations of realism in one's circumstances. In contrast, valuing is not" invariably reflected by the amount of pain if the valued object is not obtained" (1985a, p. 21).

The utility-based approach has avoided "any direct reference to the person's own valuational exercise—the mental activity of valuing one kind of life rather than another" (1985a, pp. 20–21). Apparently the reason why Sen calls the judgment of functionings not "preference" but "evaluation" lies in the individual's substantive endeavor to formulate a more considered judgment after reflecting her multilayered inner responses to commodities (1985a, p. 12). It is the subjective judgment of the individual herself, but it is a reflective one. Thus it can reflect the value of functionings more objectively and more meaningfully.[18]

The process of discovering optimal functionings by oneself does not usually occur on a single track. It offers the possibility of many mistakes and much waste. Nevertheless, the reason for respecting such a trial process and for leaving it to individual autonomy lies in the value of agency freedom.

[16] '[T]he maximum element' in terms of the evaluation of the functionings will not necessarily be chosen, since maximizing one's own well-being may not be the only motive for choice. See Sen 1985a, p. 14.

[17] It seems that usually the ranking is incomplete. See 1985a, p. 12.

[18] "[M]ore objectively" does not indicate that everyone must have the same valuation of the different functionings." See, Ibid., p. 57. But is expected that "the differences [based on valuation] are, by their nature, more limited". Ibid., p. 56.

A.6 Poverty in Abundance

From the discussion thus far, a vision to adapt the capability theory of Sen to the social security of the industrialized countries has been made clear. The first task is to identify the list of functionings that are most relevant to each society for promoting the independent activities of individuals and to identify the commodities and services that are indispensable to the realization of those functionings, considering the interrelated and developing structure of the different kinds of functioning.

The second task is to design a total social system, one that comprises not only a fair distribution system that will secure the basic capability for all, but also a fair process of realizing individual well-being in which each person can rationally and reasonably form, pursue, and revise her own life plan and autonomously choose the optimal functionings on her responsibility.

This is a general vision in that it is applicable to both industrialized and developing countries. But in applying this vision a specific problem in the industrialized countries must be taken into account.

Apparently, industrialized and developing countries differ in the kinds of functioning that are most urgently needed and the kinds of commodities that are indispensable to their realization. However, the distinguishing feature of the industrialized countries is that the objective deficiency of the commodities available or in individual abilities to utilize is not the central issue addressed by welfare policies.

Usually, the addition of a new commodity, if it is connected with the characteristics of the commodities that the person already has, will enable him to achieve new vectors of functionings. And the acquisition of new vectors of functionings should promote one's prospect to achieve his life plan based on his conception of the good. In turn, the next step to promote that person's life plan awakens in him the need for additional commodities. A person may fully appreciate the value of commodities through the recognition of the mutual interdependency between one commodity and another and between commodities and functionings in the process of pursuing his life plan based on his conception of the good.

It seems, however, that individual recognition of these mutual interdependencies between them is becoming increasingly vaguer. Why is this so? One reason is that somewhere the sequence of individual actions, starting with the formation of a life plan and proceeding to the selection of optimal vectors of functionings with an appreciation of the value of commodities, has been suspended. For example, if a person desires a particular commodity not because he finds it will enhance his functionings, but because it is merely novel or popular, he would not go ahead to perceive its connection with the characteristics of the commodities already in his possession. And in this way, if various commodities purchased one after the other are seen only in fragments, their mutual interdependency is difficult to observe.

This phenomenon is relevant to the tendency such that the essential characteristic of each commodity tends to be isolated from the existent social systems and the environmental conditions within the individual's perception.[19] It is difficult to have a perspective of existent social systems and the environmental conditions that restrict the process of producing commodities, and in turn are restricted by it, if one can only perceive the various commodities in fragments. It is also difficult to form a meaningful, realistic life plan unless the individual can fully understand the tensions that exist between her goals and the given social systems and environmental conditions.

On the one hand, since various natural and social contingencies may undermine one's objective abilities to live an independent life, industrialized countries must continue to frame policies that secure individual capabilities. On the other hand, the abundance of commodities and the complexity of procedures to supply them in the recent past seem to make it more difficult for people to pursue their own goals rationally and reasonably. Furthermore, such difficulties tend to weaken the individual will and the capacities for rational and reasonable action.

This severely dissociates the theoretical assumption of Rawls as discussed in Sect. A.1 of this essay. Given such a phenomenon, it is feared that any policy for securing an independent life for the individual members of society may have an adverse effect. Furthermore, any policy for guaranteeing agency freedom may be nullified. Because if their basic will or their capacity to pursue their own goals and to achieve their life plan are weak, they may rely totally on the given social policies and abandon their agency freedom.[20]

Herein lies the difficulty of welfare reform in the industrialized countries. We are thus compelled to reexamine the methods of applying Sen's capability theory to actual welfare policies in the light of this reality of contemporary society.

A.7 References

Arneson, R. (1989). Equality and equal opportunity for welfare. *Philosophical Studies, 56*, 77–93.

Basu, K. (1987). Achievement, capabilities and the concept of well-being: A review of commodities and capabilities by Amartya Sen. *Social Choice and Welfare, 4*, 69–76.

Cohen, G. A. (1989). On the currency of Egalitarian justice. *Ethics, 99*, 906–44.

Doyal, L., & Gough, I. (1991). *A theory of human need*. London: Macmillan.

Dworkin, R. (1981). What is equality? Part 2: Equality of resources. *Philosophy & Public Affairs, 10*, 283–345.

Fleurbaey, M. (1994). On fair compensation. *Theory and Decision, 36*, 277–307.

Fleurbaey, M. (1995). Three solutions to the compensation problem. *Journal of Economic Theory, 65*, 505–521.

Foley, D. (1967). Resource allocation and the public sector. *Yale Economic Essays, 7*, 45–98.

---

[19] Sen introduces the "characteristic approach" à la Gorman and Lancaster in that he defines the function converting a commodity vector into a vector of characteristics of those commodities.

[20] Sen suggests that increased freedom might be disadvantageous to us and the expansion of choices might decrease our ability to choose. "The expansion of choices to be made is both an opportunity (the choices can be made by oneself) and a burden(the choices have to be made by oneself)…the expansion of some types of choices can reduce our ability to choose life-styles that we might treasure." Sen, 1992, pp. 63–64.

Gotoh, R., & Yoshihara, N. (1999). A game form approach to theories of distributive justice-formalizing needs principle. In H. de Swart (Ed.), *Logic, Game theory and social choice, Proceedings of the International Conference, LGS '99, May 13–16, 1999*. Tilburg, Netherlands: Tilburg University Press.
Griffin, J. (1986). *Well-being: Its meaning, measurement and moral importance*. Oxford: Clarendon Press.
Hayek, F. A. (1988). *The fatal conceit: The errors of socialism*. London: Routledge.
Kolm, S.-C. (1972). *Justice et Equite*. Paris: Editions du Centre National de la Recherche Scientifique (H. F. See, Trans., Justice and Eqity). Cambridge, MA: MIT Press, 1997.
Nussbaum, M. (1990). Aristotelian social democracy. In R. B. Douglas et al. (eds.), *Liberalism and the good* (pp. 203–52). London: Routledge.
Nussbaum, M. (1993). Non-relative virtues: An aristotelian approach. In M. Nussbaum & A. Sen (Eds.), *The quality of life* (pp. 242–269). Oxford: Clarendon Press.
Pazner, E., & Schmeidler, D. (1978). Egalitarian equivalent allocations: A new concept of economic equity. *Quarterly Journal of Economics, 92*, 671–687.
Rawls, J. (1971). *A theory of justice*. Cambridge, MA: Harvard University Press.
Rawls. J. (1993). *Political liberalism*. New York: Columbia University Press.
Roemer, J. E. (1996). *Theories of distributive justice*. Cambridge, MA: Harvard University Press.
Sen, A. K. (1980). "Equality of what?" The Tanner lectures on human values (Vol. I). Salt Lake City: University of Utah Press.
Sen, A. K. (1981). *Poverty and famines: An essay on entitlement and deprivation*. Oxford: Clarendon Press.
Sen, A. K. (1985a). *Commodities and capabilities*. Amsterdam: North-Holland.
Sen, A. K. (1985b). Well-being, agency and freedom. *The Journal of Philosophy, 82*, 169–221.
Sen, A. K. (1987). *On ethics and economics*. Oxford: Blackwell.
Sen, A. K. (1988). Freedom of choice: Concept and content. *European Economic Review, 32*.
Sen, A. K. (1992). *Inequality reexamined*. Oxford: Clarendon Press.
Sen, A. K. (1999). *Development as freedom*. New York: Alfred A. Knopf.
Sugden, R. (1993). Welfare, resources, and capabilities: A review of Inequality reexamined by Amartya Sen. *Journal of Economic Literature, 31*, 1947–1962.
Suzumura, K., & Gotoh, R. (1999). *Freedom, well-being and the welfare state*. Paper Presented at the Twelfth World Congress of the International Economic Association, Buenos Aires, August 23–27.
Varian, H. R. (1974). Equity, envy and efficiency. *Journal of Economic Theory, 9*, 63–91.

Appendix B
A Class of Fair Distribution Rules à la Rawls and Sen

Reiko Gotoh and Naoki Yoshihara

Abstract. This[21, 22] paper discusses and develops "non-welfaristic" arguments on distributive justice à la J. Rawls and A. K. Sen, and formalizes, in cooperative production economies, "non-welfaristic" distribution rules as game form types of resource allocation schemes. First, it conceptualizes the Needs Principle which the distribution rule taking individuals' needs into account should satisfy. Second, one class of distribution rules which satisfy the Needs Principle, a class of **J**-based Capability Maximin Rules, is proposed. Third, axiomatic characterizations of the class of **J**-based Capability Maximin Rules is provided.

JEL Classification Numbers: D 63, D 71, I 31

[21] This appendix was published in *Economic Theory* 22, 63–88 (2003).
[22]† We are grateful to an anonymous referee of this journal, Professors Marc Fleurbaey, Nicolas Gravel, Ryo-ichi Nagahisa, Prasanta Pattanaik, Kotaro Suzumura, Koichi Tadenuma, and Yongsheng Xu for their fruitful comments. An earlier version of this paper was published with the title name, "A Game Form Approach to Theories of Distributive Justice: Formalizing Needs Principle" as the Discussion Paper No. 407 of the Institute of Social and Economic Research, Osaka University, and in the proceedings of the International Conference on Logic, Game, and Social Choice held at Oisterwijk in May 1999. That version was also presented at the 3rd Decentralization Conference in Japan held at Hitotsubashi University in September 1997, at the annual meeting of the Japan Association of Economics and Econometrics held at Waseda University in September 1997, and the 4th International Conference of Social Choice and Welfare held at University of British Colombia in July 1998. This research was partially supported by the Japanese Ministry of Education and the Ministry of Health and Welfare.

R. Gotoh, *The Ethics and Economics of the Capability Approach*, Hitotsubashi University IER Economic Research Series 46, https://doi.org/10.1007/978-981-15-5140-6

B.1 Introduction

In this paper, we discuss fair allocations in cooperative production economies, mainly basing our arguments upon those of Rawls and Sen.

There have been two representative criteria on distributive justice, one of which is "*distribution with regard to individual contributions*", and the other being "*distribution with regard to individual needs* ". While the former criterion justifies resource allocations through competitive mechanisms, the latter criterion may play an important role in judging what redistribution policies are justifiable to achieve social security. In discussing fair allocations based upon the latter criterion, it is important to give a precise concept of *individual needs* as an objective one, as done by Rawls (1971, 1993) and Sen (1980, 1983). While Rawls (1993) argued upon the *citizens' needs* as indexed by primary goods, Sen (1980, 1983) understood the needs in terms of his *capability* approach. Sen's *capability* is interpreted as the set of an individual's various states of well-being possibly attainable by her through various ways of utilization of her share of resources. Based upon Sen's arguments (1980, 1983), the needs of individuals should accordingly be conceptualized as a lack of a reference level of capability, which is given for a given social context, but which may vary among various social contexts. Our object in this paper is just to propose an allocation scheme which meets the latter criterion discussed above, called the **J**-*based capability maximin rule* which is based upon Sen's capability.[23]

While most literature on fair allocation problems discussed allocation schemes of social choice correspondence types, we, in this paper, are particularly interested in *game form* types, which we call *distribution rules*. These are similar to *cost sharing rules* discussed in Moulin and Schenker (1994). A distribution rule is a function from the set of profiles of all individuals' labor time to the set of profiles of all individuals' shares of output. One reason for our approach is to clarify the aspect of interaction among individuals in assigning capabilities through the application of the allocation schemes.[24] Note that Sen's argument (1980) on equality of basic capability leaves out this aspect of interaction. In contrast, we can explicitly capture this aspect in our model by adopting the game form approach of allocation schemes, so that the determination of each individual's capability is influenced not only by his own strategy (choice of his labor time), but also by that of any other individual under a given distribution rule.

Another reason for our approach is related to the Rawlsian first principle of justice [Rawls (1971)], which seems to require allocation schemes to guarantee every individual an equal right to choose her own labor time freely. Such a procedural aspect of

---

[23]Herrero (1996) also discussed recently designing allocation schemes of social choice correspondence types in pure exchange economies by using Sen's capability index.

[24]This aspect is also pointed out by Atkinson (1995), where it is argued that the activity of monopolistic commodity supplier is influential in each individual's capability level determined by her share of commodity.

allocation schemes can be formally specified in the game form types,[25] while social choice correspondences specify no procedural aspect of decision making.

In this paper, we discuss the fairness of resource allocations by arguing the fairness of capability assignments given through the determination of resource allocations. Although recent literature on ranking of equal opportunity sets like Kranich (1996, 1997), etc.,[26] may give us various criteria for evaluating the fairness of capability assignments, in this paper, we are not interested in what criteria the ranking on "fair" capability assignments should satisfy. Instead, we focus upon the problem of how social agreements on the ranking of "fair" capability assignments would be arrived at, so that we simply suppose that in the society, there exists a social procedure for determining "fair" capability assignments. In particular, we are interested in the types of social decision procedures which evaluate the fairness of capability assignments through the evaluation of what is the desirable *common capability*, and call them *social welfare functions*. The common capability is given by the intersection of all individuals' capabilities under the profile of individual handicaps and feasible allocations. The **J**-based capability maximin rule is just defined as being rationally chosen through a *Paretian* social welfare function whenever this function always generates a social ordering over common capabilities, which contains the set-inclusion relation as its subrelation. In other words, the **J**-based capability maximin rule is defined to guarantee every individual a maximal common capability with respect to set-inclusion. So, we first discuss under what conditions there exists a Paretian social welfare function which always generates a social ordering containing the set-inclusion relation, so that it always rationally chooses the **J**-based capability maximin rule.

Next, we axiomatically characterize the social ordering on capability assignments which rationalizes the **J**-based capability maximin rule. A characterization result of this ordering is obtained by adopting the axioms of *Pareto inclusion on capability assignments* and *anonymity*, and an *equity* axiom based upon a particular *inequality measure* of capability assignments. Note that Herrero, Iturbe-Ormaetxe, and Nieto (1998) and Bossert, Fleurbaey, and Van de Gaer (1999) discussed the axiomatic characterizations of ranking opportunity set profiles on the basis of *common opportunity sets*. As discussed below, these characterization results cannot be directly applied to our discussion of ranking capability assignments based upon common capabilities, because of the different mathematical structure in economic models assumed in this study. So, our results are independent of the above literature.

Third, discussing several axioms on fairness of distribution rules, we analyze desirable properties which the class of **J**-based capability maximin rules satisfies. Our first characterization result on the class of **J**-based capability maximin rules is that it is the unique class of rules which meets the *Needs Principle* defined below and satisfies

---

[25]Right structures of freedom of choice can be best captured by game form approach. See Gaertner et al. (1992).

[26]The literature of equal opportunity on basis of ranking opportunity profiles also includes Herrero (1997), Kranich and Ok (1998), Herrero, Iturbe-Ormaetxe, and Nieto (1998), Bossert, Fleurbaey, and Van de Gaer (1999), and Arlegi and Nieto (1999).

two axioms of *solidarity* concerning changes in individual supplies of labor time and individual handicap levels respectively. Our second characterization result shows that a subclass of capability maximin rules meets both axioms of *responsibility* and *compensation*. Although previous literature on responsibility and compensation by Fleurbaey (1994, 1995a; 1995b), etc.,[27] was mainly based upon evaluating individual welfares or incomes, we evaluate the state of individuals by using the capability.

For the rest of this paper, Sect. B.2 defines a basic model; Sect. B.3 discusses axioms on distribution rules; Sect. B.4 proposes the capability maximin rules and analyzes their characteristics.

B.2 The Basic Model

There are two goods in the economy, one of which is labor time, $x \in \mathbb{R}_+$, to be used to produce the other good, $y \in \mathbb{R}_+$, where $\mathbb{R}_+$ denotes the set of non-negative real numbers. The population in the economy is given by the set $N = \{1, \cdots, n\}$, where $2 \leq n < +\infty$. Individual i's consumption vector is denoted by $z_i = (l_i, y_i)$, where $l_i = \overline{x} - x_i$ denotes his/her leisure time, and y_i denotes his/her assigned share of output, and $\overline{x}$, $0 < \overline{x} < +\infty$, denotes the upper bound of labor time. It is assumed that all individuals have the same consumption set $[0, \overline{x}] \times \mathbb{R}_+$. Individual i is characterized by *utilization ability of resources*, a_i, and *production skill*, s_i, both of which are assumed to be representable by real numbers. The universal set of utilization abilities, which is common for all individuals, is denoted by $A \subseteq \mathbb{R}$.[28] The universal set of production skills for all individuals is denoted by $S \subseteq \mathbb{R}_{++}$, where $\mathbb{R}_{++}$ denotes the set of positive real numbers. Thus, individual i's characteristics are denoted by $(a_i, s_i) \in A \times S$.[29]

A production process is described by a production function $f : \mathbb{R}_+ \to \mathbb{R}_+$ which is assumed to be continuous, increasing, and $f(0) \geq 0$. The set of such functions is denoted by F.

Let there be m types of relevant *functionings* for each individual, which are common for all individuals and are attainable by means of his/her leisure time and share of output. Let us assume that we can measure these functionings by means of adequate non-negative real indices. Thus, an achievement of functioning k by individual

[27]The recent literature on the issue of *responsibility* and *compensation* initiated by Dworkin (1981) and followed by Arneson (1989) and Cohen (1989, 1993), includes Bossert (1995), Bossert and Fleurbaey (1996), Fleurbaey (1998), Fleurbaey and Maniquet (1994, 1996), Iturbe (1997), Iturbe and Nieto (1996), Maniquet (1996), and Roemer (1993, 1996).

[28]For any two sets X and Y, $X \subseteq Y$ whenever any $x \in X$ also belongs to Y, and $X \subsetneq Y$ if and only if $X \subseteq Y$ and *not* $(Y \subseteq X)$.

[29]There may exist a functional relationship between production skill and utilization ability such as $s_i = s(a_i)$ and s_i is strictly monotonic with respect to a_i. All the main results in this paper are valid, *mutatis mutandis*, even when such a relationship holds between s_i and a_i.

i is denoted by $b_{ik} \in \mathbb{R}_+$. Individual i's achievement of relevant functionings is given by listing b_{ik}: $\mathbf{b}_i = (b_{i1}, \cdots, b_{im}) \in \mathbb{R}^m_+$.[30]

Individual i's utilization ability, leisure time, and share of output determine the vector of functionings he/she can achieve. It is assumed that there is a functional relationship which relates a triple of ability, leisure time, and share of output to a set of m-dimensional functioning vectors viz. $C : A \times [0, \overline{x}] \times \mathbb{R}_+ \twoheadrightarrow \mathbb{R}^m_+$ such that $C(a_i, l, y) \subseteq \mathbb{R}^m_+$ for all $i \in N$. We call C a *capability correspondence*. The intended interpretation is that individual i with a_i is able to attain the vector of relevant functionings $\mathbf{b}_i \in C(a_i, l, y)$ by utilizing the consumption vector (l, y). For simplicity, we assume that each admissible capability correspondence has the following properties:

(α) For all $(a, l) \in A \times [0, \overline{x}]$, $C(a, l, 0) = \{\mathbf{0}\}$.
(β) If $(a, z) \leq (a', z')$ (resp. $(a, z) < (a', z')$), then $C(a, z) \subseteq C(a', z')$ (resp. $C(a, z) \subsetneq int\ C(a', z')$, where $int\ C(a', z')$ is the *interior* of $C(a', z')$ in $\mathbb{R}^m_+$).[31]
(γ) For all $(a, z) \in A \times [0, \overline{x}] \times \mathbb{R}_+$, $C(a, z)$ is compact and comprehensive in $\mathbb{R}^m_+$.
(δ) Given $a \in A$, $C : \{a\} \times [0, \overline{x}] \times \mathbb{R}_+ \twoheadrightarrow \mathbb{R}^m_+$ is continuous.

Let $\mathcal{C}$ be the class of capability correspondences satisfying these properties.[32] The condition (α) implies that no one can survive without consumption of output (income). The condition (β) implies the (strict) monotonicity property of capability correspondences with respect to utilization ability a and resource z. The conditions (γ) and (δ) are technical requirements for analytical simplicity.

The *objective characteristics of the economy* is defined by a list $\mathbf{e} = (\mathbf{a}, \mathbf{s}, C, f) = ((a_i)_{i \in N}, (s_i)_{i \in N}, C, f) \in E \equiv A^n \times S^n \times \mathcal{C} \times F$, where A^n and S^n stand, respectively, for the n-fold Cartesian product of A and that of S. *A feasible allocation for* $\mathbf{e}$ is a vector $\mathbf{z} = (z_i)_{i \in N} \in ([0, \overline{x}] \times \mathbb{R}_+)^n$ such that $f(\sum s_i x_i) \geq \sum y_i$. We denote by $Z(\mathbf{e})$ the set of feasible allocations for $\mathbf{e} \in E$. Given the objective characteristics of the economy $\mathbf{e} = (\mathbf{a}, \mathbf{s}, C, f) \in E$, the *feasible assignment of capabilities under* $\mathbf{e}$ is a list $(C(a_i, z_i))_{i \in N}$ satisfying $(z_i)_{i \in N} \in Z(\mathbf{e})$.

A distribution rule is a function $h : E \times [0, \overline{x}]^n \to \mathbb{R}^n_+$ satisfying the following property: for any $\mathbf{e} = (\mathbf{a}, \mathbf{s}, C, f) \in E$ and any $\mathbf{x} = (x_i)_{i \in N} \in [0, \overline{x}]^n$, $h(\mathbf{e}, \mathbf{x}) = \mathbf{y} = (y_i)_{i \in N}$ such that $(\overline{x} - x_i, y_i)_{i \in N} \in Z(\mathbf{e})$. Notice that given $\mathbf{e} \in E$ and $\mathbf{x} \in [0, \overline{x}]^n$, the distribution rule h specifies a feasible assignment of capabilities for $\mathbf{e}$. In this formula, the strategy space of every individual is represented by $[0, \overline{x}]$, and each

[30] For any two vectors $\mathbf{a} = (a_1, \ldots, a_p)$ and $\mathbf{b} = (b_1, \ldots, b_p)$, $\mathbf{a} \geq \mathbf{b}$ if and only if $a_i \geq b_i$ $(i = 1, \ldots, p)$, $\mathbf{a} > \mathbf{b}$ if and only if $\mathbf{a} \geq \mathbf{b}$ and *not* $(\mathbf{b} \geq \mathbf{a})$, and $\mathbf{a} \gg \mathbf{b}$ if and only if $a_i > b_i$ $(i = 1, \ldots, p)$.

[31] Incidentally, $\partial C(a', z')$ appearing below is the *boundary* of $C(a', z')$ in $\mathbb{R}^m_+$.

[32] Following Sen (1985), we may define a value function $v_i : \mathbb{R}^m_+ \to \mathbb{R}$ for each individual $i \in N$, and define his utility function $\overline{u}_i$ by:

$$\overline{u}_i(z) \equiv v_i(\mathbf{b}(z, C(a_i, z), v_i)), \text{ where } \mathbf{b}(z, C(a_i, z), v_i) \equiv \arg \max_{\mathbf{b}_i \in C(a_i, z)} v_i(\mathbf{b}_i), \text{ for all } z \in [0, \overline{x}] \times \mathbb{R}_+.$$

If $C(a_i, \cdot, \cdot)$ is convex-valued, and v_i is continuous, strictly monotonic, and quasi-concave on $\mathbb{R}^m_+$, then $\overline{u}_i$ is continuous, strictly monotonic, and quasi-concave on $[0, \overline{x}] \times \mathbb{R}_+$.

individual can be guaranteed equal freedom in choosing her own labor time, and the rule remunerates her with leisure as she sees fit.

B.3 Two Fundamental Principles of Distributive Justice

In this section, we consider two fundamental principles of distributive justice, the *Contribution Principle* and the *Needs Principle* , which the society should consult in determining distribution rules while it guarantees every individual equal freedom of choice of labor time.

First, we define the *Contribution Principle*:

Contribution Principle (CP) : *For all* $\mathbf{e} = (\mathbf{a}, \mathbf{s}, C, f) \in E$*, all* $\mathbf{x} \in [0, \overline{x}]^n$*, and all* $i, j \in N$*,* $[s_i x_i < s_j x_j \Rightarrow h_i(\mathbf{e}, \mathbf{x}) < h_j(\mathbf{e}, \mathbf{x})$ and $s_i x_i = s_j x_j \Rightarrow h_i(\mathbf{e}, \mathbf{x}) = h_j(\mathbf{e}, \mathbf{x})]$.

The class of distribution rules which satisfy the Contribution Principle is defined by $CR \equiv \{h | h$ satisfies **CP** $\}$. There are many rules which satisfy the Contribution Principle. Moulin and Schenker (1994) discussed the axiomatic characterizations of this type of distribution rule. An example of such a rule is the *proportional sharing rule* PR, which distributes outputs in proportion to each individual's labor contribution: for all $i \in N$, $h_i^{PR}(e, \mathbf{x}) = \frac{s_i x_i}{\sum s_j x_j} f(\sum s_j x_j)$.

The next principle we discuss is the *Needs Principle.* This should define a reference level of the *real opportunity of well-being* for each social context, a lack of which should be taken into account as *one's needs* and being a subject for compensation. Note that, in this paper, the real opportunity of well-being is Sen's *capability*. Then, the Needs Principle is defined as follows: given $\mathbf{e} = (\mathbf{a}, \mathbf{s}, C, f) \in E$ and $\mathbf{x} \in [0, \overline{x}]^n$ such that for all $i, j \in N$, $x_i = x_j$, let $\mathbf{y}^H(\mathbf{e}, \mathbf{x}) = (\frac{f(\sum s_i x_i)}{n}, \cdots, \frac{f(\sum s_i x_i)}{n}) \in \mathbb{R}^n_+$ be a *hypothetical distribution.*[33] Then, a capability profile under $(\mathbf{e}, \mathbf{x}, \mathbf{y}^H(\mathbf{e}, \mathbf{x}))$ is determined as: $(C(a_i, \overline{x} - x_i, y^H(\mathbf{e}, \mathbf{x})))_{i \in N}$. Notice that by definition of the capability correspondence C, in this case, there is one individual $i^* \in N$ such that for any other $j \neq i^*$, $C(a_j, \overline{x} - x_j, y^H(\mathbf{e}, \mathbf{x})) \supseteq C(a_{i^*}, \overline{x} - x_{i^*}, y^H(\mathbf{e}, \mathbf{x}))$. Then, let $C^H(\mathbf{e}, \mathbf{x}) \equiv C(a_{i^*}, \overline{x} - x_{i^*}, y^H(\mathbf{e}, \mathbf{x}))$, and call it a *reference capability under* $(\mathbf{e}, \mathbf{x})$.

Needs Principle (NP) : *For all* $\mathbf{e} = (\mathbf{a}, \mathbf{s}, C, f) \in E$ *and all* $\mathbf{x} \in [0, \overline{x}]^n$ *such that for all* $i, j \in N$*,* $x_i = x_j$*, there is no* $i \in N$ *such that* $C^H(\mathbf{e}, \mathbf{x}) \supsetneq C(a_i, \overline{x} - x_i, h_i(\mathbf{e}, \mathbf{x}))$.

The class of distribution rules which satisfy the Needs Principle is denoted by $NR \equiv \{h \mid h$ satisfies **NP** $\}$.

The above definition of the Needs Principle is explained as follows: if for some $j \neq i^*$, $C(a_j, \overline{x} - x_j, y^H(\mathbf{e}, \mathbf{x})) \supsetneq C(a_{i^*}, \overline{x} - x_{i^*}, y^H(\mathbf{e}, \mathbf{x})) = C^H(\mathbf{e}, \mathbf{x})$, this difference in capabilities between j and i^* under the hypothetical situation $(\mathbf{x}, \mathbf{y}^H(\mathbf{e}, \mathbf{x}))$ is based only upon the difference in their utilization abilities, because, under the hypothetical

[33] This hypothetical distribution can be regarded as the derivation from the *equal-division-for-equal-work* (*EDEW*) proposed by Kranich (1994). Note that the Needs principle defined below does not necessarily require distribution rules to satisfy the *EDEW*.

situation, every individual enjoys the same resource vector. Thus, individual i^*'s least favorable situation in capability under the hypothetical distribution is attributed to her least favorable position in utilization ability. Consequently, if individual i^*'s situation after the application of the distribution rule is even worse than her situation under the hypothetical distribution, it would be presumably reasonable to recognize such a rule as failing to meet her *needs*. Thus, the Needs Principle requires the society to reject such a distribution rule.

It is easy to show that the Contribution Principle and the Needs Principle are incompatible. This incompatibility is obtained, irrelevant to whether the value of production skill is strictly monotonic with respect to the value of utilization ability or not.

B.4 A Distribution Rule according to Needs

In this section, we propose a class of desirable distribution rules which are relevant to the Needs Principle discussed in the last section.

B.4.1 Common Capabilities and Formulation of Social Ordering over Distribution Rules

Given $\mathbf{e} = (\mathbf{a}, \mathbf{s}, C, f) \in E$ and $\mathbf{x} \in [0, \overline{x}]^n$, let $Y(\mathbf{e}, \mathbf{x}) \equiv \{\mathbf{y} = (y_i)_{i \in N} \in \mathbb{R}^n_+ \mid f(\sum s_i x_i) \geq \sum y_i\}$ be a set of feasible distributions of produced goods for $(\mathbf{e}, \mathbf{x})$. To move from the space of goods to the space of capabilities, let

(2) $\mathcal{FC}(\mathbf{e}, \mathbf{x}) \equiv \{(C(a_i, \overline{x} - x_i, y_i))_{i \in N} \mid \mathbf{y} = (y_i)_{i \in N} \in Y(\mathbf{e}, \mathbf{x})\}$

be a set of feasible assignments of capabilities under $(\mathbf{e}, \mathbf{x})$. Let

(3) $\mathcal{FC}(\mathbf{e}) \equiv \bigcup_{\mathbf{x} \in [0, \overline{x}]^n} \mathcal{FC}(\mathbf{e}, \mathbf{x})$ and $\mathcal{FC} \equiv \bigcup_{\mathbf{e} \in E} \mathcal{FC}(\mathbf{e})$.

For each $(C(a_i, \overline{x} - x_i, y_i))_{i \in N} \in \mathcal{FC}(\mathbf{e}, \mathbf{x})$, let

(4) $CC(\mathbf{e}, \mathbf{x}, \mathbf{y}) \equiv \bigcap_{i \in N} C(a_i, \overline{x} - x_i, y_i)$,

which is to be called the *common capability under* $(\mathbf{e}, \mathbf{x}, \mathbf{y})$.[34] Notice that for all $(\mathbf{e}, \mathbf{x})$, common capabilities are non-empty sets. Given $\mathbf{e} = (\mathbf{a}, \mathbf{s}, C, f) \in E$ and $\mathbf{x} \in [0, \overline{x}]^n$, let

(5) $\mathcal{CC}(\mathbf{e}, \mathbf{x}) \equiv \{CC(\mathbf{e}, \mathbf{x}, \mathbf{y}) \mid \mathbf{y} \in Y(\mathbf{e}, \mathbf{x})\}$[35]

---

[34] Herrero, Iturbe-Ormaetxe, and Nieto (1998), Bossert, Fleurbaey, and Van de Gaer (1999), and Arlegi and Nieto (1999) also discussed, in the problem of ranking opportunity profiles, a "common opportunity" which is defined as the intersection of all individuals' opportunity sets.

[35] For the sake of notational convenience, we sometimes denote the feasible allocation by $(\mathbf{x}, \mathbf{y})$ instead of $\mathbf{z}$ when $\mathbf{z} = (\overline{\mathbf{x}} - \mathbf{x}, \mathbf{y}) \in Z(\mathbf{e})$.

be the set of common capabilities under $(\mathbf{e}, \mathbf{x})$. Moreover, let

(6) $\mathcal{CC}(\mathbf{e}) \equiv \underset{\mathbf{x}\in[0,\overline{x}]^n}{\cup} \mathcal{CC}(\mathbf{e}, \mathbf{x})$ and $\mathcal{CC} \equiv \underset{\mathbf{e}\in E}{\cup} \mathcal{CC}(\mathbf{e})$.

Complicated though it may look, the intuitive meaning of the common capability is in fact very simple, and it has some intuitive appeal to those who are interested in distributive fairness. Given $\mathbf{e} = (\mathbf{a}, \mathbf{s}, C, f) \in E$, when individuals decide to supply $\mathbf{x} \in [0, \overline{x}]^n$, they are minimally warranted of functioning vectors in the common capability, no matter how much they differ in their utilization abilities. Clearly, this warranted set of functioning vectors hinges squarely on the feasible distribution of the produced good, viz, $\mathbf{y} \in Y(\mathbf{e}, \mathbf{x})$. By choosing a distribution rule appropriately, we are interested in warranting individuals the "most fair" common capability. It is itself a problem to determine what is the "most fair" common capability, which is purely of social decision to choose one distribution rule from the admissible set of distribution rules so as to guarantee every individual a desirable common capability.

In this section, we assume that each and every individual judges the desirability of distribution rules through evaluating the common capabilities which the distribution rules guarantee to all individuals. Moreover, there is an aggregation procedure of all individuals' judgements about what is the "most fair" common capability, which just formulates the social decision process for choosing one distribution rule. Let every individual i's value judgement about common capabilities be represented by an ordering relation $J_i \subseteq \mathcal{CC} \times \mathcal{CC}$. Let $J_i(\mathbf{e}) \equiv J_i \cap [\mathcal{CC}(\mathbf{e})\times\mathcal{CC}(\mathbf{e})]$ and $J_i(\mathbf{e}, \mathbf{x}) \equiv J_i(\mathbf{e}) \cap [\mathcal{CC}(\mathbf{e}, \mathbf{x})\times \mathcal{CC}(\mathbf{e}, \mathbf{x})]$, and the asymmetric and symmetric parts of $J_i(\mathbf{e})$ (resp. $J_i(\mathbf{e}, \mathbf{x})$) will be denoted by $P(J_i(\mathbf{e}))$ (resp. $P(J_i(\mathbf{e}, \mathbf{x}))$) and $I(J_i(\mathbf{e}))$ (resp. $I(J_i(\mathbf{e}, \mathbf{x}))$), respectively. The universal class of value judgements will be denoted by $\mathcal{J}$. The social decision process for choosing one distribution rule is formulated as a social welfare function ψ which is defined as follows: for every value judgement profile $\mathbf{J} = (J_i)_{i\in N} \in \mathcal{J}^n$, $J = \psi(\mathbf{J})$ is an ordering on $\mathcal{CC}$. We assume that ψ meets the *Pareto Principle*: for all $\mathbf{J} = (J_i)_{i\in N}$, all $(\mathbf{e}, \mathbf{x})$, and all $\mathbf{y}, \mathbf{y}^* \in Y(\mathbf{e}, \mathbf{x})$, if $(CC(\mathbf{e}, \mathbf{x}, \mathbf{y}), CC(\mathbf{e}, \mathbf{x}, \mathbf{y}^*)) \in P(J_i(\mathbf{e}, \mathbf{x}))$ for all $i \in N$, then $(CC(\mathbf{e}, \mathbf{x}, \mathbf{y}), CC(\mathbf{e}, \mathbf{x}, \mathbf{y}^*)) \in P(J(\mathbf{e}, \mathbf{x}))$ where $J = \psi(\mathbf{J}) \in \mathcal{J}$.

Although each of the value judgements in $\mathcal{J}$ is interpreted as representing one possible idea as to what constitutes the "most fair" common capability, we are particularly interested in value judgements which satisfy the following two conditions:

Set-Inclusion Subrelations: *For all* $(\mathbf{e}, \mathbf{x})$ *and all* $\mathbf{y}, \mathbf{y}^* \in Y(\mathbf{e}, \mathbf{x})$,

(α) $CC(\mathbf{e}, \mathbf{x}, \mathbf{y}) \supseteq CC(\mathbf{e}, \mathbf{x}, \mathbf{y}^*) \Rightarrow (CC(\mathbf{e}, \mathbf{x}, \mathbf{y}), CC(\mathbf{e}, \mathbf{x}, \mathbf{y}^*)) \in J(\mathbf{e}, \mathbf{x})$; *and*

(β) $CC(\mathbf{e}, \mathbf{x}, \mathbf{y}) \supsetneq CC(\mathbf{e}, \mathbf{x}, \mathbf{y}^*) \Rightarrow (CC(\mathbf{e}, \mathbf{x}, \mathbf{y}), CC(\mathbf{e}, \mathbf{x}, \mathbf{y}^*)) \in P(J(\mathbf{e}, \mathbf{x}))$.

Anonymity: *For all* $\mathbf{e} \in E$, *all* $i, j \in N$ *such that* $a_i = a_j$ *and* $s_i = s_j$, *all* $\mathbf{x} \in [0, \overline{x}]^n$, *and all* $\mathbf{y}, \mathbf{y}^* \in Y(\mathbf{e}, \mathbf{x})$,

$(CC(\mathbf{e}, \mathbf{x}, \mathbf{y}), CC(\mathbf{e}, \mathbf{x}, \mathbf{y}^*)) \in$
$J(\mathbf{e}, \mathbf{x}) \Leftrightarrow (CC(\mathbf{e}, \rho_{ij}(\mathbf{x}, \mathbf{y})), CC(\mathbf{e}, \rho_{ij}(\mathbf{x}, \mathbf{y}^*))) \in J(\mathbf{e}, \rho_{ij}(\mathbf{x}))$

where $\rho_{ij}(\mathbf{x}, \mathbf{y}) = ((x_i^\rho, y_i^\rho), (x_j^\rho, y_j^\rho), (\mathbf{x}_{N\setminus\{i,j\}}, \mathbf{y}_{N\setminus\{i,j\}}))$, $x_i^\rho = x_j$, (*resp.* $y_i^\rho = y_j$) *and* $x_j^\rho = x_i$ (*resp.* $y_j^\rho = y_i$).

Let $\mathcal{J}_{SIA}$ be the class of value judgements which contain *set-inclusion subrelations* and satisfy **Anonymity**. The condition of **Set-Inclusion Subrelations** is to require the monotonicity of orderings over common capabilities in terms of set-inclusion. It is based upon the idea that the larger the minimally warranted capability for all individuals is, the more fair it will be. The condition of **Anonymity** implies that the ranking of common capabilities should not be influenced by replacement of the names of any two individuals who have the same objective characteristics.

B.4.2 The **J***-Based Capability Maximin Rule and its Social Choice Process*

Based upon the *social value judgement* $\psi(\mathbf{J})$ defined by ψ and $\mathbf{J}$, let us introduce a best element set by $B(\mathcal{CC}(\mathbf{e},\mathbf{x}),\psi(\mathbf{J})) \equiv \{CC(\mathbf{e},\mathbf{x},\mathbf{y}) \mid \forall CC(\mathbf{e},\mathbf{x},\mathbf{y}') \in \mathcal{CC}(\mathbf{e},\mathbf{x}) : (CC(\mathbf{e},\mathbf{x},\mathbf{y}),\ CC(\mathbf{e},\mathbf{x},\mathbf{y}')) \in \psi(\mathbf{J})\}$. Then, we can define a rational choice function φ as follows: for every $\mathbf{J} = (J_i)_{i\in N}$, $\varphi(\mathcal{CC}(\mathbf{e},\mathbf{x}),\psi(\mathbf{J})) \in B(\mathcal{CC}(\mathbf{e},\mathbf{x}),\psi(\mathbf{J}))$ for each $\mathbf{e} \in E$ and $\mathbf{x} \in [0,\overline{x}]^n$. Let $C^{\min}_{\varphi\cdot\psi(\mathbf{J})}(\mathbf{e},\mathbf{x}) \equiv \varphi(\mathcal{CC}(\mathbf{e},\mathbf{x}),\psi(\mathbf{J}))$. We refer to this $C^{\min}_{\varphi\cdot\psi(\mathbf{J})}(\mathbf{e},\mathbf{x})$ as a reference capability under $(\mathbf{e},\mathbf{x})$. Given the social welfare function ψ and the rational choice function φ, such a reference capability can vary, depending upon a profile of individuals' value judgements, $\mathbf{J}$. Thus, we call it $\mathbf{J}$-*based minimal capability under* $(\mathbf{e},\mathbf{x})$.

Given $\mathbf{x} = (x_g)_{g\in N} \in [0,\overline{x}]^n$ and $i \in N$, let $\mathbf{x}_{-i} \equiv (x_g)_{g\in N\setminus\{i\}} \in [0,\overline{x}]^{n-1}$. Given $\mathbf{x} = (x_g)_{g\in N} \in [0,\overline{x}]^n$ and $i, j \in N$, let $\rho_{ij}(\mathbf{x}) \equiv (x_i^\rho, x_j^\rho, \mathbf{x}_{N\setminus\{i,j\}})$ where $x_i^\rho = x_j$ and $x_j^\rho = x_i$. Given $\mathbf{x} = (x_g)_{g\in N} \in [0,\overline{x}]^n$ and $i, j \in N$, let $(\rho_{ij}(\mathbf{x}))_{-i} \equiv \mathbf{x}'_{-i}$ where $\mathbf{x}' = \rho_{ij}(\mathbf{x})$. Given $\mathbf{e} \in E$, $\mathbf{x}_{-i} \in [0,\overline{x}]^{n-1}$, and a distribution rule h, let $h_i(\mathbf{e},[0,\overline{x}],\mathbf{x}_{-i}) \equiv \{y \in \mathbb{R}_+ \mid \exists x \in [0,\overline{x}] : y = h_i(\mathbf{e},x_i,\mathbf{x}_{-i})\}$. Then, we can introduce an anonymity requirement for distribution rules in the following:

Equal Attainable Sets for Equal Handicaps (EAEH):[36] *For all* $\mathbf{e} = (\mathbf{a},\mathbf{s},C,f)$, *all* $i, j \in N$ *such that* $a_i = a_j$ *and* $s_i = s_j$, *and all* $\mathbf{x} \in [0,\overline{x}]^n$, $h_i(\mathbf{e},[0,\overline{x}],\mathbf{x}_{-i}) = h_j(\mathbf{e},[0,\overline{x}],(\rho_{ij}(\mathbf{x}))_{-j})$ *and* $h_i(\mathbf{e},[0,\overline{x}],(\rho_{ij}(\mathbf{x}))_{-i}) = h_j(\mathbf{e},[0,\overline{x}],\mathbf{x}_{-j})$.

The society can determine a desirable distribution rule by choosing a reference capability called $\mathbf{J}$-based minimal capability and by using an anonymous requirement in the sense of **EAEH**:

Definition 1 Given ψ, φ, and $\mathbf{J} \in \mathcal{J}^n$, the $\mathbf{J}$-based capability maximin rule ($\boldsymbol{CM}_{\mathbf{J}}^{\psi,\varphi}$) is a function $h^{\mathbf{CM}_{\mathbf{J}}^{\psi,\varphi}} : E \times [0,\overline{x}]^n \to \mathbb{R}^n_+$ satisfying **EAEH** such that for all $\mathbf{e} \in E$ and all $\mathbf{x} = (x_i)_{i\in N} \in [0,\overline{x}]^n$, $h^{\mathbf{CM}_{\mathbf{J}}^{\psi,\varphi}}(\mathbf{e},\mathbf{x}) = \mathbf{y} = (y_i)_{i\in N}$ satisfies:
(α) for all $i \in N$, $C(a_i, \overline{x} - x_i, y_i) \supseteq C^{\min}_{\varphi\cdot\psi(\mathbf{J})}(\mathbf{e},\mathbf{x})$,
(β) there is no other $\mathbf{y}^* \in Y(\mathbf{e},\mathbf{x})$ such that $CC(\mathbf{e},\mathbf{x},\mathbf{y}^*) \supsetneq C^{\min}_{\varphi\cdot\psi(\mathbf{J})}(\mathbf{e},\mathbf{x})$.

The implication of the $\mathbf{J}$-based capability maximin rule is that all individuals are always guaranteed a maximum of common capability under $(\mathbf{e},\mathbf{x})$, where the maximum is determined on the basis of all individuals' judgements over common capabilities, $\mathbf{J} \in \mathcal{J}^n$.

[36] A similar requirement was originally discussed by Fleurbaey (1995a, 1998).

Note that the **J**-based capability maximin rule is not always necessarily well-defined by the Paretian social welfare function ψ: First, if the social judgement $\psi(\mathbf{J})$ has no maximal element on $\mathcal{CC}(\mathbf{e}, \mathbf{x})$ for some $(\mathbf{e}, \mathbf{x})$, then the **J**-based capability maximin rule is not well-defined. Second, if the social judgement $\psi(\mathbf{J})$ does not contain the set-inclusion subrelation in $\mathcal{CC}(\mathbf{e}, \mathbf{x})$ for some $(\mathbf{e}, \mathbf{x})$, then this rule cannot be generated through ψ. So, the problem is to determine under what conditions this rule can be generated through the Paretian social welfare function.

As an auxiliary step to guarantee well-definedness of the **J**-based capability maximin rule, let us introduce an appropriate topology into the space of compact sets in $\mathbb{R}^m_+$ in terms of the Hausdorff metric.[37] Equipped with this topology and given $\mathbf{e} \in E$ and $\mathbf{x} \in [0, \overline{x}]^n$, let us say that the common capability $CC(\mathbf{e}, \mathbf{x}, \mathbf{y}) \in \mathcal{CC}(\mathbf{e}, \mathbf{x})$ is *undominated under* $(\mathbf{e}, \mathbf{x})$ if there is no $\mathbf{y}' \in Y(\mathbf{e}, \mathbf{x})$ such that $CC(\mathbf{e}, \mathbf{x}, \mathbf{y}') \supsetneq CC(\mathbf{e}, \mathbf{x}, \mathbf{y})$. Let $\mathcal{UC}(\mathbf{e}, \mathbf{x})$ denote the set of undominated common capabilities under $(\mathbf{e}, \mathbf{x})$. Moreover, given $\mathbf{e} \in E$, $CC(\mathbf{e}, \mathbf{z}) \in \mathcal{CC}(\mathbf{e}, \mathbf{x})$, and an ordering $J(\mathbf{e}, \mathbf{x})$ on $\mathcal{CC}(\mathbf{e}, \mathbf{x})$, let[38]

$$\mathcal{L}\,(CC(\mathbf{e}, \mathbf{z}), J(\mathbf{e}, \mathbf{x})) \equiv \{CC(\mathbf{e}, \mathbf{z}') \in \mathcal{CC}(\mathbf{e}, \mathbf{x}) \mid (CC(\mathbf{e}, \mathbf{z}),\ CC(\mathbf{e}, \mathbf{z}')) \in P(J(\mathbf{e}, \mathbf{x}))\}.$$

The ordering relation $J(\mathbf{e}, \mathbf{x})$ is *upper semi-continuous on* $\mathcal{UC}(\mathbf{e}, \mathbf{x})$ if for all $CC(\mathbf{e}, \mathbf{z}) \in \mathcal{UC}(\mathbf{e}, \mathbf{x})$, $\mathcal{L}\,(CC(\mathbf{e}, \mathbf{z}), J(\mathbf{e}, \mathbf{x})) \cap \mathcal{UC}(\mathbf{e}, \mathbf{x})$ is open in the Housdorff relative topology on $\mathcal{UC}(\mathbf{e}, \mathbf{x})$.

Let $N^{SIA} (\subseteq N)$ be the set of individuals whose proposed value judgements always belong to $\mathcal{J}_{SIA}$, and are always upper-semi continuous on $\mathcal{UC}(\mathbf{e}, \mathbf{x})$ for all $(\mathbf{e}, \mathbf{x}) \in E \times [0, \overline{x}]^n$.

Lemma 1 *Suppose that* $\#N^{SIA} \geq 1$. *Then, there exists a Paretian social welfare function* ψ *such that for each proposed* $\mathbf{J} \in \mathcal{J}^n$, $B(\mathcal{CC}(\mathbf{e}, \mathbf{x}), \psi(\mathbf{J})) \neq \varnothing$ *and* $B(\mathcal{CC}(\mathbf{e}, \mathbf{x}), \psi(\mathbf{J})) \subseteq \mathcal{UC}(\mathbf{e}, \mathbf{x})$ *for all* $(\mathbf{e}, \mathbf{x}) \in E \times [0, \overline{x}]^n$.

We are now ready to put forward the result on the possibility of social choice of the **J**-based capability maximin rule.

Theorem 1 *Suppose that* $\#N^{SIA} \geq 1$. *Then, there exists a Paretian social welfare function* ψ *and the corresponding rational choice function* φ *by which the* **J** *-based capability maximin rule* $h^{\mathbf{CM}_{\mathbf{J}}^{\psi,\varphi}}$ *is always generated. In addition, the* **J** *- based capability maximin rule is uniquely determined.*

Theorem 1 shows the existence of a Paretian social welfare function which never fails to generate the **J**-based capability maximin rule whenever there exists a person whose proposed value judgement, which is always upper semi-continuous, always

---

[37]For any compact sets $C,\ C' \subseteq \mathbb{R}^m$, the Hausdorff metric is defined by $d(C, C') \equiv \max\{\max\{\delta(\mathbf{b}, C) \mid \mathbf{b} \in C'\}, \max\{\delta(\mathbf{b}, C') \mid \mathbf{b} \in C\}\}$, where $\delta(\mathbf{b}, C) \equiv \min_{\mathbf{b}' \in C} \parallel \mathbf{b}, \mathbf{b}' \parallel$, and $\parallel \mathbf{b}, \mathbf{b}' \parallel$ denotes the Euclidean distance between $\mathbf{b}$ and $\mathbf{b}'$.

[38]For the sake of notational convenience, we sometimes denote the common capability by $CC(\mathbf{e}, \mathbf{z})$ instead of $CC(\mathbf{e}, \mathbf{x}, \mathbf{y})$ when $\mathbf{z} = (\overline{\mathbf{x}} - \mathbf{x}, \mathbf{y}) \in Z(\mathbf{e})$.

satisfies **Anonymity** and **Set-Inclusion Subrelation**. Let ψ be just such a function and φ its corresponding rational choice function, both of which are assumed to be fixed in the following discussion.

B.4.3 A Characterization of the Social Value Judgement

We now characterize the social value judgement $\psi(\mathbf{J})$ which rationalizes the $\mathbf{J}$-based capability maximin rule. First, we define a ranking of the feasible assignments of capabilities by an ordering relation $R^{\mathcal{FC}} \subseteq \mathcal{FC} \times \mathcal{FC}$ such that $(\mathbf{C}(\mathbf{e}, \mathbf{z}), \mathbf{C}(\mathbf{e}', \mathbf{z}')) \in R^{\mathcal{FC}}$, where $\mathbf{C}(\mathbf{e}, \mathbf{z}) \equiv (C(a_i, z_i))_{i \in N}$ and $\mathbf{C}(\mathbf{e}', \mathbf{z}') \equiv (C(a_i', z_i'))_{i \in N}$, which implies that the feasible assignment of capabilities $\mathbf{C}(\mathbf{e}, \mathbf{z})$ is at least as good as the feasible assignment of capabilities $\mathbf{C}(\mathbf{e}', \mathbf{z}')$. The asymmetric and symmetric parts of $R^{\mathcal{FC}}$ are denoted by $P(R^{\mathcal{FC}})$ and $I(R^{\mathcal{FC}})$ respectively. Given $\mathbf{e} \in E$ and $\mathbf{x} \in [0, \overline{x}]^n$, let $R^{\mathcal{FC}}(\mathbf{e}, \mathbf{x}) \equiv R^{\mathcal{FC}} \cap (\mathcal{FC}(\mathbf{e}, \mathbf{x}))^2$ and $B(\mathcal{FC}(\mathbf{e}, \mathbf{x}), R^{\mathcal{FC}}) \equiv \{\mathbf{C}(\mathbf{e}, \mathbf{z}) \in \mathcal{FC}(\mathbf{e}, \mathbf{x}) \mid \forall \mathbf{C}(\mathbf{e}, \mathbf{z}') \in \mathcal{FC}(\mathbf{e}, \mathbf{x}) : (\mathbf{C}(\mathbf{e}, \mathbf{z}), \mathbf{C}(\mathbf{e}, \mathbf{z}')) \in R^{\mathcal{FC}}\}$. Among various orderings on $\mathcal{FC}$, we are particularly interested in an ordering $R^{\mathcal{FC}}_{\psi(\mathbf{J})} \subseteq \mathcal{FC} \times \mathcal{FC}$ defined as follows: for all $\mathbf{e}, \mathbf{e}' \in E$, all $\mathbf{z} \in Z(\mathbf{e})$, and all $\mathbf{z}' \in Z(\mathbf{e}')$, $(\mathbf{C}(\mathbf{e}, \mathbf{z}), \mathbf{C}(\mathbf{e}', \mathbf{z}')) \in R^{\mathcal{FC}}_{\psi(\mathbf{J})}$ if and only if $(CC(\mathbf{e}, \mathbf{z}), CC(\mathbf{e}', \mathbf{z}')) \in \psi(\mathbf{J})$.

Second, we introduce axioms concerning the rankings of the feasible capability assignments as follows:

Pareto Inclusion in Capability Assignments (PICA): *For all* $\mathbf{e} \in E$, *all* $\mathbf{x} \in [0, \overline{x}]^n$, *and all* $\mathbf{y}, \mathbf{y}' \in Y(\mathbf{e}, \mathbf{x})$,
$[C(a_i, \overline{x} - x_i, y_i) \supseteq C(a_i, \overline{x} - x_i, y_i')$ $(\forall i \in N)$ and $C(a_j, \overline{x} - x_j, y_j) \supsetneq C(a_j, \overline{x} - x_j, y_j')$ $(\exists j \in N) \Rightarrow (\mathbf{C}(\mathbf{e}, \mathbf{z}), \mathbf{C}(\mathbf{e}, \mathbf{z}')) \in P(R^{\mathcal{FC}}(\mathbf{e}, \mathbf{x}))]$.

Anonymity in Capability Assignments (ACA): *For all* $\mathbf{e} \in E$, *all* $\mathbf{x} \in [0, \overline{x}]^n$, *all* $\mathbf{y}, \mathbf{y}' \in Y(\mathbf{e}, \mathbf{x})$, *and all* $i, j \in N$ *such that* $a_i = a_j$ *and* $s_i = s_j$, $[(\mathbf{C}(\mathbf{e}, \mathbf{x}, \mathbf{y}), \mathbf{C}(\mathbf{e}, \mathbf{x}, \mathbf{y}')) \in R^{\mathcal{FC}}(\mathbf{e}, \mathbf{x}) \Leftrightarrow (\mathbf{C}(\mathbf{e}, \rho_{ij}(\mathbf{x}, \mathbf{y})), \mathbf{C}(\mathbf{e}, \rho_{ij}(\mathbf{x}, \mathbf{y}'))) \in R^{\mathcal{FC}}(\mathbf{e}, \rho_{ij}(\mathbf{x}))]$.

Let us define a *relative advantage function* $\mu : \mathcal{FC} \times N \rightarrow \mathbb{R}_+$ such that for all $\mathbf{C}(\mathbf{e}, \mathbf{x}, \mathbf{y}) \in \mathcal{FC}$ and all $i \in N$:
(α) $[C(a_i, \mathbf{c}, \overline{x} - x_i, y_i) = CC(\mathbf{e}, \mathbf{x}, \mathbf{y}) \Rightarrow \mu(\mathbf{C}(\mathbf{e}, \mathbf{x}, \mathbf{y}), i) = 0]$,
(β) for all $j \in N$, $[C(a_i, \overline{x} - x_i, y_i) \supseteq C(a_j, \overline{x} - x_j, y_j) \Rightarrow \mu(\mathbf{C}(\mathbf{e}, \mathbf{x}, \mathbf{y}), i) \geq \mu(\mathbf{C}(\mathbf{e}, \mathbf{x}, \mathbf{y}), j)]$.

This function provides a measure that is intended to capture the extent of inequality in capability assignments: *the higher the real number of* $\max_{i \in N} \mu(\mathbf{C}(\mathbf{e}, \mathbf{x}, \mathbf{y}), i)$ *is, the higher the degree of inequality in capabilities will be*. Among possibly various relative advantage functions, we are particularly interested in the following one: $\mu^* : \mathcal{FC} \times N \rightarrow \mathbb{R}_+$ such that for all $\mathbf{C}(\mathbf{e}, \mathbf{x}, \mathbf{y}) \in \mathcal{FC}$ and all $i \in N$, $\mu^*(\mathbf{C}(\mathbf{e}, \mathbf{x}, \mathbf{y}), i) \equiv \min\{\eta - 1 \in \mathbb{R}_+ \mid \exists \mathbf{b} \in \partial C(a_i, \overline{x} - x_i, y_i) \text{ s.t. } \eta^{-1}\mathbf{b} \in \partial CC(\mathbf{e}, \mathbf{x}, \mathbf{y}))\}$. We can easily check that the function μ^* meets the two conditions (α) and (β) of relative advantage functions. By using this μ^*, we introduce the following:

μ^*-Equity in Capability Assignments (μ^*ECA): *For all* $\mathbf{e} \in E$ *and all* $\mathbf{x} \in [0, \overline{x}]^n$, *there exists* $\max_{i \in N} \mu^*(\mathbf{C}(\mathbf{e}, \mathbf{x}, \mathbf{y}^*), i) \equiv \min_{\mathbf{y} \in Y(\mathbf{e}, \mathbf{x})} \max_{i \in N} \mu^*(\mathbf{C}(\mathbf{e}, \mathbf{x}, \mathbf{y}), i)$ *such that* $\mathbf{C}(\mathbf{e}, \mathbf{x}, \mathbf{y}^*) \in B(\mathcal{FC}(\mathbf{e}, \mathbf{x}), R^{\mathcal{FC}})$.

The implication of μ^***ECA** will be explained as follows: Given $(\mathbf{e}, \mathbf{x}, \mathbf{y})$ and given $i \in N$, any functioning vectors $\mathbf{b}_i, \mathbf{b}'_i \in \partial C(a_i, \overline{x} - x_i, y_i)$ are incomparable from each other and maximal in $C(a_i, \overline{x} - x_i, y_i)$ with respect to vector inequalities. Note that for any $\mathbf{b}_i \in \partial C(a_i, \overline{x} - x_i, y_i)$, there is a functioning vector $\mathbf{b}(\mathbf{b}_i) \equiv \eta^{-1}\mathbf{b}_i$ in $\partial CC(\mathbf{e}, \mathbf{x}, \mathbf{y})$ where $\eta \in [1, +\infty)$ implies the degree of advantage of the functioning $\mathbf{b}_i$ over the minimally warranted functioning $\mathbf{b}(\mathbf{b}_i)$. Among such functioning vectors in $\partial C(a_i, \overline{x} - x_i, y_i)$, there is a functioning vector $\mathbf{b}^*_i$ such that its corresponding scalar η^* is the *minimum* value in $\partial C(a_i, \overline{x} - x_i, y_i)$, which implies that the advantage of $\mathbf{b}^*_i$ over $\mathbf{b}(\mathbf{b}^*_i)$ is less than the advantage of any vector in $\partial C(a_i, \overline{x} - x_i, y_i)$. In the function μ^*, individual i's relative advantage over other individuals in capability assignments under $(\mathbf{e}, \mathbf{x}, \mathbf{y})$ is measured by $\eta^* - 1$. The axiom μ^***ECA** says that the capability assignment under which the degree of inequality in capabilities in terms of μ^* is minimized should be most preferable.

Theorem 2 *Given* $\mathbf{J} \in \mathcal{J}^n$, *suppose that there exists at least one individual* $i \in N$ *such that* $J_i \in \mathcal{J}_{SIA}$ *and* $J_i(\mathbf{e}, \mathbf{x})$ *is upper-semi continuous on* $\mathcal{UC}(\mathbf{e}, \mathbf{x})$. *Then, the ordering* $R^{\mathcal{FC}}_{\psi(\mathbf{J})} \subseteq \mathcal{FC} \times \mathcal{FC}$ *satisfies PICA, ACA, and* μ^**ECA. Conversely, if the ordering* $R^{\mathcal{FC}} \subseteq \mathcal{FC} \times \mathcal{FC}$ *satisfies PICA, ACA, and* μ^**ECA , then* $R^{\mathcal{FC}} = R^{\mathcal{FC}}_{\psi(\mathbf{J})}$ *for some* $\mathbf{J} \in \mathcal{J}^n$.

We should mention the literature related to the characterization of the ordering $R^{\mathcal{FC}}_{\psi(\mathbf{J})}$. Herrero et al. (1998) and Bossert et al. (1999) respectively defined the ordering of opportunity profiles, which is similar to $R^{\mathcal{FC}}_{\psi(\mathbf{J})}$, in the abstract *rich* domains, and provided axiomatic characterizations under the assumption of *richness* in Herrero et al. (1998) and Bossert et al. (1999). Note that their characterization results cannot be directly applied to $R^{\mathcal{FC}}_{\psi(\mathbf{J})}$, since the domain of the ordering $R^{\mathcal{FC}}$, which is the Hausdorff space $\mathcal{FC}$, does not necessarily satisfy the *richness* condition. Thus, in contrast to their results, our axiomatic characterization on $R^{\mathcal{FC}}_{\psi(\mathbf{J})}$ is obtained independently of the *richness* condition. Moreover, it is obtained by adopting a specific equity axiom, μ^**ECA*, instead of the *Hammond's equity* axioms in Herrero et al. (1998) and Bossert et al. (1999).

B.5 Characterizations of the Class of J-Based Capability Maximin Rules

B.5.1 Axioms on Distribution Rules

In this subsection, we discuss the desirability of distribution rules from the viewpoints of fair opportunity to well-being. Here, individual opportunity to well-being is identified with individual capabilities attainable through the application of distribution rules. How can we define the fairness of opportunity to well-being in this context?

In support of these viewpoints, we consider the following axioms:

Minimal Equality of Capability (MEC): *For all* $\mathbf{e} = (\mathbf{a}, \mathbf{s}, C, f) \in E$ *and all* $\mathbf{x} = (x_i)_{i \in N} \in [0, \overline{x}]^n$,
$[\forall i, j \in N, a_i = a_j \text{ and } x_i = x_j] \Rightarrow [\forall i, j \in N, C(a_i, \overline{x} - x_i, h_i(\mathbf{e}, \mathbf{x})) = C(a_j, \overline{x} - x_j, h_j(\mathbf{e}, \mathbf{x}))]$.
Note that NP implies MEC, and CP also implies MEC whenever $s_i = s_j \Leftrightarrow a_i = a_j$ for all $i, j \in N$.

The next three axioms are related to *responsibility* and *compensation* discussed in Bossert (1995), Fleurbaey (1994, 1995a, 1995b, 1998), and Fleurbaey and Maniquet (1994, 1996), etc. The first axiom is motivated by the following discussion: if there is reason to compensate someone in their capabilities, then there should exist differences in individuals' utilization abilities. To formulate a similar argument in the context of compensating inequal utility distributions, Fleurbaey (1995a, 1998), etc., introduced the *equal resource for equal handicap* axiom and/or other similar ones. Since our distribution rules are game forms, the formulation of which differs from that of allocation rules by Fleurbaey (1995a, 1998), etc., we cannot directly apply the *equal resource for equal handicap* and/or other similar axioms to our context. However, the following axiom seems to be along the same line as the *equal resource for equal handicap* axioms:

No Domination of Resources among Equally Handicapped (NDEH): *For all* $\mathbf{e} = (\mathbf{a}, \mathbf{s}, C, f) \in E$, *all* $\mathbf{x} \in [0, \overline{x}]^n$, *and all* $i, j \in N$ *such that* $a_i = a_j$, $[x_i = x_j \Rightarrow h_i(\mathbf{e}, \mathbf{x}) = h_j(\mathbf{e}, \mathbf{x})]$ and $[x_i < x_j \Rightarrow h_i(\mathbf{e}, \mathbf{x}) < h_j(\mathbf{e}, \mathbf{x})]$.
It is easy to show that *NDEH* implies *MEC*. Note that *NDEH* and *EAEH* are logically independent of each other.

The following two axioms are relevant to "*principle of compensation in capabilities.*"

No Domination of Capabilities among Equal Efforts (NDEE): *For all* $\mathbf{e} = (\mathbf{a}, \mathbf{s}, C, f) \in E$, all $\mathbf{x} \in [0, \overline{x}]^n$, *and all* $i, j \in N$ *such that* $x_i = x_j$,
[neither $C(a_i, \overline{x} - x_i, h_i(\mathbf{e}, \mathbf{x})) \subsetneq C(a_j, \overline{x} - x_j, h_j(\mathbf{e}, \mathbf{x}))$
nor $C(a_i, \overline{x} - x_i, h_i(\mathbf{e}, \mathbf{x})) \supsetneq C(a_j, \overline{x} - x_j, h_j(\mathbf{e}, \mathbf{x}))$].

No Strict Domination of Capabilities among Equal Efforts (NSDEE): *For all* $\mathbf{e} = (\mathbf{a}, \mathbf{s}, C, f) \in E$, *all* $\mathbf{x} \in [0, \overline{x}]^n$, *and all* $i, j \in N$ *such that* $x_i = x_j$, [neither $C(a_i, \overline{x} - x_i, h_i(\mathbf{e}, \mathbf{x})) \subsetneq int\ C(a_j, \overline{x} - x_j, h_j(\mathbf{e}, \mathbf{x}))$
nor $int\ C(a_i, \overline{x} - x_i, h_i(\mathbf{e}, \mathbf{x})) \supsetneq C(a_j, \overline{x} - x_j, h_j(\mathbf{e}, \mathbf{x}))$].
These two axioms mean that, given that one chooses the same amount of labor time as another, then should the individual's utilization ability be worse than the other, this should not necessarily determine a worse situation in that person's capability. Note that it seems to be more appealing if the principle of compensation in capabilities requires equal capabilities for any two persons who respectively provide the same amount of labor time. However, such a requirement is generally empty. So, these kinds of "non-domination in terms of set-inclusion" are more appropriate in discussing compensation of capabilities. Note that *NSDEE* is implied by *NDEE*. Moreover, it is

easy to show that *NSDEE* implies *MEC*. However, *NSDEE* and *NP* are independent of each other.

The next two axioms concern "solidarity" conditions of distribution rules. The first axiom is relevant to the change in individuals' supplies of labor time. If, as a result of a change in their supplies of labor time, someone's capability is worse relative to another's, then the first one should be described as suffering the negative effect of the change more than the second. The axiom, *Solidarity in Rank of the Weakest Functioning Vectors*, defined below precludes any individual from falling into such a situation.

As an auxiliary step in introducing the above axiom, let us discuss the following: Given $\mathbf{e} = (\mathbf{a}, \mathbf{s}, C, f) \in E$, $\mathbf{z} \in Z(\mathbf{e})$, and $\mathbf{b}_i \in \partial C(a_i, z_i)$ *of* $i \in N$, let $N(i, \mathbf{b}_i, \mathbf{e}, \mathbf{z}) \equiv \{j \in N \mid \exists \lambda_j \geq 1, \text{s.t. } \lambda_j \mathbf{b}_i \in C(a_j, z_j)\}$.

Definition 2 Given $\mathbf{e} = (\mathbf{a}, \mathbf{s}, C, f) \in E$ and $\mathbf{z} \in Z(\mathbf{e})$, the functioning vector $\mathbf{b}_i \in \partial C(a_i, z_i)$ of $i \in N$ is the weakest vector for $i \in N$ if for any other $\mathbf{b}_i^* \in \partial C(a_i, z_i)$, $\#N(i, \mathbf{b}_i, \mathbf{e}, \mathbf{z}) \geq \#N(i, \mathbf{b}_i^*, \mathbf{e}, \mathbf{z})$.

Given $\mathbf{e} = (\mathbf{a}, \mathbf{s}, C, f) \in E$ and $\mathbf{z} \in Z(\mathbf{e})$, let us denote the set of the weakest functioning vectors for $i \in N$ by $B_i^w(\mathbf{e}, \mathbf{z})$, and denote an element of $B_i^w(\mathbf{e}, \mathbf{z})$ by $\mathbf{b}_i^w(\mathbf{e}, \mathbf{z})$.

Solidarity in Rank of the Weakest Functioning Vectors (SRWF): *For all* $\mathbf{e} = (\mathbf{a}, \mathbf{s}, C, f) \in E$ *and all* $\mathbf{x} = (x_i)_{i \in N} (\neq \mathbf{0}), \mathbf{x}' = (x_i')_{i \in N} (\neq \mathbf{0}) \in [0, \overline{x}]^n$ *such that for all* $i \neq j$, $x_i = x_i'$ *and* $x_j \leq x_j'$, *there is no* $i \in N$ *such that* $\#N(i, \mathbf{b}_i^w(\mathbf{e}, \mathbf{z}), \mathbf{e}, \mathbf{z}) > \#N(i, \mathbf{b}_i^w(\mathbf{e}, \mathbf{z}'), \mathbf{e}, \mathbf{z}')$ *where* $\mathbf{z} = (\overline{\mathbf{x}} - \mathbf{x}, h(\mathbf{e}, \mathbf{x}))$, $\mathbf{z}' = (\overline{\mathbf{x}} - \mathbf{x}', h(\mathbf{e}, \mathbf{x}'))$, *and* $\overline{\mathbf{x}} = (\overline{x}, \ldots, \overline{x}) \in \mathbb{R}_+^n$.

This axiom stipulates that no one's rank in the weakest functioning vector will shift up through additional labor time by an individual.

The next axiom is relevant to the change in individuals' ability endowments. Consider that someone suffers from a bad accident, and as a result, can no longer maintain her current capability. The following axiom requires compensating the unlucky person in such a situation for her loss of capability.

No Relative Advantage by Bad Accidents (NRABA): *For all* $\mathbf{e} = (\mathbf{a}, \mathbf{s}, C, f)$, $\mathbf{e}' = (\mathbf{a}', \mathbf{s}, C, f) \in E$ *such that for some* $j \in N$, $a_j \geq a_j'$ *and for any other* $i \neq j$, $a_i = a_i'$, *and all* $\mathbf{x} \in [0, \overline{x}]^n$, *there is no* $i \in N$ *such that* $\#N(i, \mathbf{b}_i^w(\mathbf{e}, \mathbf{z}), \mathbf{e}, \mathbf{z}) > \#N(i, \mathbf{b}_i^w(\mathbf{e}', \mathbf{z}'), \mathbf{e}', \mathbf{z}')$ *where* $\mathbf{z} = (\overline{\mathbf{x}} - \mathbf{x}, h(\mathbf{e}, \mathbf{x}))$ *and* $\mathbf{z}' = (\overline{\mathbf{x}} - \mathbf{x}, h(\mathbf{e}', \mathbf{x}))$.

This axiom requires precluding every individual from making her rank of the weakest vector shift up through another's unfortunate accident. This implies that all individuals are required to share the effect of someone's brute luck.

The following axiom is a requirement for *non-wastefulness* of resource allocations in the sense that it only requires distributing total outputs exhaustively.

Pareto Efficiency with respect to Capabilities (PEC): *For all* $\mathbf{e} = (\mathbf{a}, \mathbf{s}, C, f) \in E$, *all* $\mathbf{x} \in [0, \overline{x}]^n$, *and all* $\mathbf{y}' \in \mathbb{R}_+^n$, $[C(a_i, \overline{x} - x_i, y_i') \supsetneq C(a_i, \overline{x} - x_i, h_i(\mathbf{e}, \mathbf{x}))\ (\forall i \in N) \Rightarrow (\overline{x} - x_i, y_i')_{i \in N} \notin Z(\mathbf{e})]$.

Note that PEC and $NSDEE$ together imply NP.

B.5.2 Characterizations of the Class of J-Based Capability Maximin Rules

Note, that if the profile of individual value judgements changes from $\mathbf{J}$ to $\mathbf{J}^*$, then the distribution rule selected through ψ and φ would change from $h^{\mathbf{CM}_{\mathbf{J}}^{\psi,\varphi}}$ to $h^{\mathbf{CM}_{\mathbf{J}^*}^{\psi,\varphi}}$, where $h^{\mathbf{CM}_{\mathbf{J}}^{\psi,\varphi}} \neq h^{\mathbf{CM}_{\mathbf{J}^*}^{\psi,\varphi}}$. This implies that there are many $\mathbf{J}$-based capability maximin rules which are socially chosen according to the profile of individual value judgements $\mathbf{J} \in \mathcal{J}^n$. Based upon this property, we can introduce the *class of* $\mathbf{J}$ *-based capability maximin rules* which are socially chosen through individual value judgements, and denote this class by $UCM \equiv \{h^{\mathbf{CM}_{\mathbf{J}}^{\psi,\varphi}} \mid \mathbf{J} \in \mathcal{J}^n\}$. One of the properties of the set UCM deserves attention. The set UCM is defined independently of ψ and φ, whenever ψ satisfies the Pareto principle. To understand this point, let us take a distribution rule $h^{\mathbf{CM}_{\mathbf{J}}^{\psi,\varphi}}$ from UCM. By definition, this distribution rule is socially chosen through ψ and φ under the profile of individual value judgements $\mathbf{J} \in \mathcal{J}^n$. Then, corresponding to $h^{\mathbf{CM}_{\mathbf{J}}^{\psi,\varphi}}$, $C^{\min}_{\varphi\cdot\psi(\mathbf{J})}(\mathbf{e},\mathbf{x}) \in \mathcal{UC}(\mathbf{e},\mathbf{x})$ is defined for each and every $(\mathbf{e},\mathbf{x}) \in E \times [0,\overline{x}]^n$. Let us define another Paretian social welfare function ψ^* and the associated rational choice function φ^*. Let us also consider another profile of individual value judgements $\mathbf{J}^* \in \mathcal{J}^n$ such that for each and every $(\mathbf{e},\mathbf{x}) \in E \times [0,\overline{x}]^n$, $(C^{\min}_{\varphi\cdot\psi(\mathbf{J})}(\mathbf{e},\mathbf{x}), CC(\mathbf{e},\mathbf{x},\mathbf{y})) \in P(J_i^*(\mathbf{e},\mathbf{x}))$ for all $\mathbf{y} \in Y(\mathbf{e},\mathbf{x})$ and all $i \in N$. Then, we can definitely obtain $\varphi^*(\mathcal{CC}(\mathbf{e},\mathbf{x}), \psi^*(\mathbf{J}^*)) = C^{\min}_{\varphi\cdot\psi(\mathbf{J})}(\mathbf{e},\mathbf{x})$ for each and every $(\mathbf{e},\mathbf{x}) \in E \times [0,\overline{x}]^n$, since ψ^* satisfies the Pareto principle. This implies that the set UCM is determined, regardless of the Paretian social welfare functions and the rational choice functions.

To characterize the class of $\mathbf{J}$-based capability maximin rules by means of the axioms defined in the previous section, we first introduce the following concept concerning assignments of capabilities by distribution rules:

Definition 3 The distribution rule h meets undominated property if for all $\mathbf{e} = (\mathbf{a},\mathbf{s},C,f) \in E$ and all $\mathbf{x} \in [0,\overline{x}]^n$, there is no $i \in N$ such that for all $j \neq i$, int $C(a_i, \overline{x} - x_i, h_i(\mathbf{e},\mathbf{x})) \supsetneq \bigcap_{j\neq i} C(a_j, \overline{x} - x_j, h_j(\mathbf{e},\mathbf{x}))$.

Let us denote the class of undominated distribution rules by UD.

Lemma 3 $UCM = EAEH \cap UD \cap PEC$.

By using Lemma 3, we obtain the following characterizations of UCM*:*

Theorem 3 $UCM = EAEH \cap MEC \cap SRWF \cap NRABA \cap PEC$.

This characterization shows that UCM is the set of anonymous and non-wasteful distribution rules satisfying MEC and the two solidarity conditions. By this characterization, we may see that if we support *equality of capabilities* [Sen (1980)] as the answer to the problem on "equality of what," all rules in UCM would be egalitarian in the sense of Sen (1980).

We can show that the above five axioms in Theorem 3 are logically independent. To see this, consider the following examples:

Example 1 Let h be a distribution rule having the following property: there is $\mathbf{J} \in \mathcal{J}^n$ such that for all $\mathbf{e} \in E$ and all $\mathbf{x} \in [0, \overline{x}]^n$,

(1) if for all $i, j \in N$, $x_i = x_j \neq 0$, then $h(\mathbf{e}, \mathbf{x}) = h^{\mathbf{CM}_{\mathbf{J}}^{\psi,\varphi}}(\mathbf{e}, \mathbf{x})$,
(2) otherwise, $h(\mathbf{e}, \mathbf{x}) = \mathbf{0}$.
Then, h satisfies $EAEH$, MEC, $SRWF$, and $NRABA$, but not PEC.

Example 2 Let h be a distribution rule having the following property: there is $\mathbf{J} \in \mathcal{J}^n$ such that for all $\mathbf{e} \in E$ and all $\mathbf{x} \in [0, \overline{x}]^n$,

(1) if there exists $j \in N$ such that $x_j > 0$, and for any $i \neq j$, $x_i = 0$, then

$$h_j(\mathbf{e}, \mathbf{x}) = f(s_j x_j) \text{ and } h_i(\mathbf{e}, \mathbf{x}) = 0,$$

(2) otherwise, $h(\mathbf{e}, \mathbf{x}) = h^{\mathbf{CM}_{\mathbf{J}}^{\psi,\varphi}}(\mathbf{e}, \mathbf{x})$.
Then, h satisfies $EAEH$, MEC, PEC, and $NRABA$, but not $SRWF$.

Example 3 Let h be a distribution rule having the following property: there is $\mathbf{J} \in \mathcal{J}^n$ such that for all $\mathbf{e} \in E$ and all $\mathbf{x} \in [0, \overline{x}]^n$,

(1) if there exists a pair of individuals $\{i, j\} \subseteq N$ such that $a_i = a_j$, then $h(\mathbf{e}, \mathbf{x}) = h^{\mathbf{CM}_{\mathbf{J}}^{\psi,\varphi}}(\mathbf{e}, \mathbf{x})$,
(2) otherwise, h has the property that $f(\sum s_g x_g) = \sum h_g(\mathbf{e}, \mathbf{x})$, and there exists a partition of N, $\mathcal{N}(\mathbf{e}, \mathbf{x}) \equiv \{N^1(\mathbf{e}, \mathbf{x}), N^2(\mathbf{e}, \mathbf{x}), \cdots, N^T(\mathbf{e}, \mathbf{x})\}$ where $2 \leq T \leq n$, such that

(α) for all $N^t(\mathbf{e}, \mathbf{x}) \in \mathcal{N}(\mathbf{e}, \mathbf{x})$ and all $i, j \in N^t(\mathbf{e}, \mathbf{x})$,

$$\#N(i, \mathbf{b}_i^w(\mathbf{e}, (\mathbf{x}, h(\mathbf{e}, \mathbf{x})), \mathbf{e}, (\mathbf{x}, h(\mathbf{e}, \mathbf{x})) = \#N(j, \mathbf{b}_j^w(\mathbf{e}, (\mathbf{x}, h(\mathbf{e}, \mathbf{x})), \mathbf{e}, (\mathbf{x}, h(\mathbf{e}, \mathbf{x})),$$

(β) there exists $N^t(\mathbf{e}, \mathbf{x}) \in \mathcal{N}(\mathbf{e}, \mathbf{x})$ such that for all $i \in N^t(\mathbf{e}, \mathbf{x})$,

$$\#N(i, \mathbf{b}_i^w(\mathbf{e}, (\mathbf{x}, h(\mathbf{e}, \mathbf{x})), \mathbf{e}, (\mathbf{x}, h(\mathbf{e}, \mathbf{x})) < n, \text{ and}$$

(γ) for any other $\mathbf{x}' \in [0, \overline{x}]^n$, $\mathcal{N}(\mathbf{e}, \mathbf{x}') = \mathcal{N}(\mathbf{e}, \mathbf{x})$.
Then, h satisfies $EAEH$, MEC, PEC, and $SRWF$, but not $NRABA$.

Example 4 Let h be a distribution rule having the following property: there is $\mathbf{J} \in \mathcal{J}^n$ such that for all $\mathbf{e} = (\mathbf{a}, \mathbf{s}, C, f) \in E$ and all $\mathbf{x} \in [0, \overline{x}]^n$,

(1) if there exists a pair of individuals $\{i, j\} \subseteq N$ such that $s_i = s_j$, then $h(\mathbf{e}, \mathbf{x}) = h^{\mathbf{CM}_{\mathbf{J}}^{\psi,\varphi}}(\mathbf{e}, \mathbf{x})$,
(2) otherwise, h has the property that $f(\sum s_g x_g) = \sum h_g(\mathbf{e}, \mathbf{x})$, and

(α) if for all $i, j \in N$, $a_i = a_j$ and $x_i = x_j \neq 0$, then
$h_1(\mathbf{e}, \mathbf{x}) < h_2(\mathbf{e}, \mathbf{x}) < \cdots < h_n(\mathbf{e}, \mathbf{x})$,

(β) otherwise, $C(a_1, \overline{x} - x_1, h_1(\mathbf{e}, \mathbf{x})) \subsetneq C(a_2, \overline{x} - x_2, h_2(\mathbf{e}, \mathbf{x})) \subsetneq \cdots \subsetneq C(a_n, \overline{x} - x_n, h_n(\mathbf{e}, \mathbf{x}))$ whenever $\mathbf{x} \neq \mathbf{0}$, and $h(\mathbf{e}, \mathbf{x}) = \mathbf{0}$ if $\mathbf{x} = \mathbf{0}$.
Then, h satisfies $EAEH$, $SRWF$, $NRABA$, and PEC, but not MEC.

Example 5 Let h be a distribution rule having the following property:

(1) for all $\mathbf{e} \in E$ and all $\mathbf{x} \in [0, \overline{x}]^n$, there exists $\mathbf{J} \in \mathcal{J}^n$ such that $h(\mathbf{e}, \mathbf{x}) = h^{\mathbf{CM}_{\mathbf{J}}^{\psi,\varphi}}(\mathbf{e}, \mathbf{x})$,
(2) there is an economy $\mathbf{e}' = (\mathbf{a}', \mathbf{s}', C, f) \in E$ and a pair of individuals $\{i, j\} \subseteq N$ such that $a'_i = a'_j$ and $s'_i = s'_j$, but

$$h_i(\mathbf{e}', \mathbf{x}') \neq h_j(\mathbf{e}', \rho_{ij}(\mathbf{x}')) \text{ and } h_j(\mathbf{e}', \mathbf{x}') \neq h_i(\mathbf{e}', \rho_{ij}(\mathbf{x}'))$$

for some $\mathbf{x}' \in [0, \overline{x}]^n$ such that $x'_i \neq x'_j$.
Then, h satisfies MEC, $SRWF$, $NRABA$, and PEC, but not $EAEH$.

The following characterization shows that UCM is the unique class of anonymous and non-wasteful distribution rules satisfying the Needs Principle and the two solidarity conditions:

Theorem 4 $UCM = NP \cap EAEH \cap SRWF \cap NRABA \cap PEC$.[39]

Since the Needs Principle and the two solidarity conditions together may be important requirements in determining resource allocations from the viewpoints of social security, it might be plausible to adopt the distribution rules in UCM in order to implement social security.

We can check the independence of the five axioms in Theorem 4 if $\#N \geq 3$. The independence of PEC, $SRABA$, NP, and $EAEH$ is shown by the above **Examples 1**, **2**, **4**, and **5**, respectively. The independence of $NRABA$ is shown by the following example:
Example 3*: Let h be a distribution rule having the properties of **Example 3**-(1) and (2). Moreover, for all $\mathbf{e} \in E$ and all $\mathbf{x} \in [0, \overline{x}]^n$, there is no pair of individuals, $\{i, j\} \subsetneq N$, such that

$$int\ C(a_i, \overline{x} - x_i, h_i(\mathbf{e}, \mathbf{x})) \supsetneq C(a_j, \overline{x} - x_j, h_j(\mathbf{e}, \mathbf{x})).$$

Then, h satisfies $EAEH$, NP, PEC, and $SRWF$, but not $NRABA$.

Theorem 5 *There exists a distribution rule h such that* $h \in EAEH \cap NDEH \cap NDEE$.*Moreover, for some* $\mathbf{J} \in \mathcal{J}^n$, $h = h^{\mathbf{CM}_{\mathbf{J}}^{\psi,\varphi}}$.[40]

[39] If we assume two-person economies, Theorem 4 is reduced to the following:

$[\#N = 2] \Rightarrow [UCM = NP \cap EAEH \cap SRWF \cap PEC]$.

[40] We also obtain the following results similar to Theorem 5 : $UCM = NDEH \cap EAEH \cap SRWF \cap NRABA \cap PEC$, $UCM = NSDEE \cap EAEH \cap SRWF \cap NRABA \cap PEC$.

Among the above three characterizations on UCM, it is particularly worth noting regarding Theorem 5 that UCM contains a class of rules satisfying the axioms of responsibility and of compensation, when we evaluate individuals' well-being by Sen's capabilities. In contrast, previous works showed the incompatibility between the axioms of responsibility and of full compensation, when individual well-being is evaluated by the standard individual utility [Fleurbaey (1994, 1995a), etc.]. This difference between us and the previous works may come from the different evaluative basis of comparing individuals' well-being: The basis in the previous works is put on individuals' achieved satisfactions (utilities), while in ours it is on individuals' opportunities (capabilities) to achieve satisfactions. In fact, in our model, if we introduce individual utility functions and define the axiom which requires equal utility for any two individual with equal utility functions in the same way as *Equal Welfare for Equal Preference* (EWEP) in Fleurbaey (1994, 1995a), then it might lead to the incompatibility result similar to Fleurbaey (1994, 1995a). This implies that if only the objective states of individual well-being, like capability assignments, are the informational basis for evaluating individuals' outcomes in resource allocations, the conflict between the requirements of responsibility and of compensation is not so serious as the one when the subjective states of individual well-being are the informational basis.

B.5.3 Discussion

As was shown in the formulation of capabilities and in the proposal of **J**-based capability maximin rules, we focussed only on the relevant functionings of consumption aspects in human life and on the determination of the opportunity sets of such functionings through the application of distribution rules. So, in this paper, there is no discussion about determining, through the application of distribution rules, the opportunity sets of functionings of production aspects such as that of "being able to work as much as one wants." This is because of the simple, static setting of production economies and resource allocations where every individual is endowed with a fixed production skill and the same set of labor time, and engages in the same type of labor.[41] So, the application of distribution rules does not influence the sizes of the opportunity sets of labor. Although we believe that such a limited analysis can be drawn from the Rawlsian viewpoint of distributive justice, of course, there may well be an argument that the opportunity sets of some functionings of production aspects such as "being able to work as much as one wants" should be variable, depending upon the results of resource allocations. This would be true even if we assume only one type of labor. For example, the Marxian theory on *reproduction of labor-power*

[41] By taking skills of individuals fixed, we are in effect excluding the possibility of improving skills through education. Likewise, by assuming only one type of labor, we are in effect excluding the possibility of searching for alternative job opportunities.

seems to lead us to such a perspective on the opportunity sets of some functionings of production aspects.

The last argument may make us consider resource allocation schemes which fairly assign to every individual, opportunity sets of functionings not only for consumption activities, but also for production activities. We think that this problem can appropriately be treated in dynamic settings of resource allocation problems. In this case, the reproduction process of "labor-power" and/or the education and learning process for improving production skills are explicitly discussed, although this is far beyond the scope of this paper.

B.6 Concluding Remarks

In this paper, we formalize, in cooperative production economies, the distribution rules as game forms, and define Sen's capability set in the context of existence of interaction among individuals concerning assignment of capabilities. Moreover, we propose a class of distribution rules, the class of **J**-*based capability maximin rules*, and discuss axiomatic characterizations of these rules mainly from normative viewpoints. Strategic aspects of the **J**-based capability maximin rules are discussed by Gotoh and Yoshihara (1997).

Although this paper discusses the social decision procedure for selecting distribution rules, which chooses the **J**-based capability maximin rule in the primordial stage of rule selection, the object of this paper is not to formalize systematically the *two principles of justice* proposed by Rawls (1971). This formalization has been done by Gotoh, Suzumura, and Yoshihara (1999).

B.7 Proofs of Theorems

Proof of Lemma 1 Given $\mathbf{J} \in \mathcal{J}^n$, let $\bigcap_{i \in N^{SIA}} J_i$. Note that $\bigcap_{i \in N^{SIA}} J_i$ is a quasi-ordering, and $\bigcap_{i \in N^{SIA}} J_i(\mathbf{e}, \mathbf{x})$ is upper semi-continuous on $\mathcal{UC}(\mathbf{e}, \mathbf{x})$ for each $\mathbf{e} \in E$ and each $\mathbf{x} \in [0, \overline{x}]^n$. Let $J_{SIA}^{\mathcal{UC}}(\mathbf{e}, \mathbf{x}) \equiv \bigcap_{i \in N^{SIA}} J_i(\mathbf{e}, \mathbf{x}) \cap (\mathcal{UC}(\mathbf{e}, \mathbf{x}) \times \mathcal{CC}(\mathbf{e}, \mathbf{x}))$ and $J_{SIA}^{\mathcal{UC}} \equiv \bigcup_{(\mathbf{e}, \mathbf{x}) \in E \times [0, \overline{x}]^n} J_{SIA}^{\mathcal{UC}}(\mathbf{e}, \mathbf{x})$. Since $J_{SIA}^{\mathcal{UC}}$ is quasi-ordering, by Jaffray's (1975) theorem, there exists an ordering extension J^{SIA} of $J_{SIA}^{\mathcal{UC}}$ such that for each $\mathbf{e} \in E$ and each $\mathbf{x} \in [0, \overline{x}]^n$, $J^{SIA}(\mathbf{e}, \mathbf{x}) \cap (\mathcal{UC}(\mathbf{e}, \mathbf{x}))^2$ is upper semi-continuous on $\mathcal{UC}(\mathbf{e}, \mathbf{x})$.

Next, given $\mathbf{J} \in \mathcal{J}^n$, let $J_N \equiv \bigcap_{i \in N} J_i$. Then, since we can easily show that the relation $J^{SIA} \cup J_N$ is *consistent* in the sense of Suzumura (1983, Chap. 1),[42] there exists

[42] A binary relation R on a set X is *consistent* if there exists no finite subset $\{x^1, \cdots, x^t\}$ of X, where $2 \leq t < +\infty$, such that $(x^1, x^2) \in P(R)$, $(x^2, x^3) \in R$, $\cdots$, $(x^t, x^1) \in R$ hold. A binary relation R^* on X is called an *extension* of R if and only if $R \subseteq R^*$ and $P(R) \subseteq P(R^*)$ hold. It is

an ordering extension J of $J^{SIA} \cup J_N$ over $\mathcal{CC}$. Let $\psi(\mathbf{J}) \equiv J$. Since $\psi(\mathbf{J})$ contains J^{SIA}, and every individuals in N^{SIA} always proposes the value judgement containing the set-inclusion subrelation, $B(\mathcal{CC}(\mathbf{e}, \mathbf{x}), \psi(\mathbf{J})) \subseteq \mathcal{UC}(\mathbf{e}, \mathbf{x})$. Moreover, by the proof of Lemma 1 in Gotoh, Suzumura, and Yoshihara (1999), $\mathcal{UC}(\mathbf{e}, \mathbf{x})$ is shown to be non-empty and compact.[43] Thus, $B(\mathcal{CC}(\mathbf{e}, \mathbf{x}), \psi(\mathbf{J})) = B(\mathcal{UC}(\mathbf{e}, \mathbf{x}), \psi(\mathbf{J})) \neq \varnothing$. Finally, by the construction of $\psi(\mathbf{J})$, it is clear that ψ satisfies the Pareto principle. ■

Given $\mathbf{e} = (\mathbf{a}, \mathbf{s}, C, f) \in E$ and $\mathbf{x} = (x_i)_{i\in N} \in [0, \overline{x}]^n$, let $Y(\mathbf{e}, \mathbf{x}, \psi(\mathbf{J}), \varphi) \equiv \{\mathbf{y} = (y_i)_{i\in N} \in Y(\mathbf{e}, \mathbf{x}) \mid \text{ for all } i \in N,\ C(a_i, \overline{x} - x_i, y_i) \supseteq C^{\min}_{\varphi\cdot\psi(\mathbf{J})}(\mathbf{e}, \mathbf{x})\}$.

Lemma 2 *Suppose that the* $\mathbf{J}$*-based capability maximin rule* $h^{\mathbf{CM}_{\mathbf{J}}^{\psi,\varphi}}$ *is generated through the Paretian social welfare function* ψ*. Then, for all* $\mathbf{e} = (\mathbf{a}, \mathbf{s}, C, f) \in E$ *and all* $\mathbf{x} = (x_i)_{i\in N} \in [0, \overline{x}]^n$*, the* $\mathbf{J}$ *-based minimal capability* $C^{\min}_{\varphi\cdot\psi(\mathbf{J})}(\mathbf{e}, \mathbf{x})$*, which corresponds to* $h^{\mathbf{CM}_{\mathbf{J}}^{\psi,\varphi}}$*, has the following property: for all* $i \in N$ *, there exists* $b_i \in \partial C(a_i, \overline{x} - x_i, y_i)$ *such that* $b_i \in \partial C^{\min}_{\varphi\cdot\psi(\mathbf{J})}(\mathbf{e}, \mathbf{x})$ *where* $\mathbf{y} = (y_i)_{i\in N} \in Y(\mathbf{e}, \mathbf{x}, \psi(\mathbf{J}), \varphi)$*.*

Proof Let $\mathbf{e} = (\mathbf{a}, \mathbf{s}, C, f) \in E$ and $\mathbf{x} \in [0, \overline{x}]^n$. Suppose that for some $\mathbf{y} = (y_i)_{i\in N} \in Y(\mathbf{e}, \mathbf{x}, \psi(\mathbf{J}), \varphi)$, there exists $j \in N$ such that for all $b_j \in \partial C(a_j, \overline{x} - x_j, y_j)$, $b_j \notin C^{\min}_{\varphi\cdot\psi(\mathbf{J})}(\mathbf{e}, \mathbf{x})$. Let us denote the set of such individuals by $N(\mathbf{e}, \mathbf{x}, \psi(\mathbf{J}), \varphi, \mathbf{y})$. Then, we can consider another distribution as follows:

$$\mathbf{y}' \equiv \begin{cases} y_j' = y_j - \varepsilon_j > 0\ (\exists \varepsilon_j > 0) \text{ for } j \in N(\mathbf{e}, \mathbf{x}, \psi(\mathbf{J}), \varphi, \mathbf{y}) \\ y_i' = y_i + \dfrac{\sum\limits_{j\in N(\mathbf{e},\mathbf{x},\psi(\mathbf{J}),\varphi,\mathbf{y})} \varepsilon_j}{\#[N\backslash N(\mathbf{e}, \mathbf{x}, \psi(\mathbf{J}), \varphi, \mathbf{y})]} \text{ for } i \in N\backslash N(\mathbf{e}, \mathbf{x}, \psi(\mathbf{J}), \varphi, \mathbf{y}) \end{cases}$$

where $\bigcap_{i\in N\backslash N(\mathbf{e},\mathbf{x},\psi(\mathbf{J}),\varphi,\mathbf{y})} C(a_i, \overline{x} - x_i, y_i') \subseteq C(a_j, \overline{x} - x_j, y_j')$ for any $j \in N(\mathbf{e}, \mathbf{x}, \psi(\mathbf{J}), \varphi, \mathbf{y})$. The existence of such a distribution is guaranteed by (1)-(δ). By (1)-(β), $C(a_i, \overline{x} - x_i, y_i') \supsetneq C(a_i, \overline{x} - x_i, y_i)$. Then, since $\bigcap_{i\in N\backslash N(\mathbf{e},\mathbf{x},\psi(\mathbf{J}),\varphi,\mathbf{y})} C(a_i, \overline{x} - x_i, y_i') = \bigcap_{i\in N} C(a_i, \overline{x} - x_i, y_i')$,
$\bigcap_{i\in N} C(a_i, \overline{x} - x_i, y_i') \supsetneq C^{\min}_{\varphi\cdot\psi(\mathbf{J})}(\mathbf{e}, \mathbf{x})$. Since $\mathbf{y}' \in Y(\mathbf{e}, \mathbf{x})$,
$\bigcap_{i\in N} C(a_i, \overline{x} - x_i, y_i') = CC(\mathbf{e}, \mathbf{y}', \mathbf{x}) \in \mathcal{CC}(\mathbf{e}, \mathbf{x})$, that is a contradiction. ■

Proof of Theorem 1 Given $\mathbf{e} \in E$ and $\mathbf{x} \in [0, \overline{x}]^n$, let $i, j \in N$ be such that $a_i = a_j$ and $s_i = s_j$. Then, by the definition of $\mathcal{J}_{SIA}$, we obtain that $J^{\mathcal{UC}}_{SIA}(\mathbf{e}, \mathbf{x}) = J^{\mathcal{UC}}_{SIA}(\mathbf{e}, \rho_{ij}(\mathbf{x}))$, where the quasi-ordering $J^{\mathcal{UC}}_{SIA}(\mathbf{e}, \mathbf{x})$ is defined in the proof of Lemma 1. Thus, by way of the proof of Lemma 1, we can guarantee that there exists an upper semi-continuous ordering extension J^{SIA^*} of $J^{\mathcal{UC}}_{SIA}$ such that for all $\mathbf{e} \in E$, all $\mathbf{x} \in [0, \overline{x}]^n$, and all $i, j \in N$ such that $a_i = a_j$ and $s_i = s_j$, $J^{SIA^*}(\mathbf{e}, \mathbf{x}) =$

---

shown in Suzumura (1983, Theorem A(5)) that *there exists an ordering extension of* R *if and only if* R *is consistent*.

[43]To show that $\mathcal{UC}(\mathbf{e}, \mathbf{x})$ is non-empty and compact, the Hasudorff metric is used in Gotoh, Suzumura, and Yoshihara (1999).

$J^{SIA^*}(\mathbf{e}, \rho_{ij}(\mathbf{x}))$. Moreover, by the same way as in the proof of Lemma 1, there exists an ordering extension J^* of $J^{SIA^*} \cup J_N$ over $\mathcal{CC}$. Let $\psi(\mathbf{J}) \equiv J^*$. Then, by Lemma 1, ψ satisfies the Pareto principle, and $B(\mathcal{CC}(\mathbf{e}, \mathbf{x}), \psi(\mathbf{J})) \neq \varnothing$ and $B(\mathcal{CC}(\mathbf{e}, \mathbf{x}), \psi(\mathbf{J})) \subseteq \mathcal{UC}(\mathbf{e}, \mathbf{x})$ for each $\mathbf{e} \in E$ and $\mathbf{x} \in [0, \overline{x}]^n$.

Given $\mathbf{e} \in E$ and $\mathbf{x} \in [0, \overline{x}]^n$, let $i, j \in N$ be such that $a_i = a_j$ and $s_i = s_j$. We next show that $CC(\mathbf{e}, \mathbf{x}, \mathbf{y}) \in B(\mathcal{CC}(\mathbf{e}, \mathbf{x}), \psi(\mathbf{J}))$ if and only if $CC(\mathbf{e}, \rho_{ij}(\mathbf{x}, \mathbf{y})) \in B(\mathcal{CC}(\mathbf{e}, \rho_{ij}(\mathbf{x})), \psi(\mathbf{J}))$. First, note that $\mathcal{CC}(\mathbf{e}, \mathbf{x}) = \mathcal{CC}(\mathbf{e}, \rho_{ij}(\mathbf{x}))$. Second, by construction of $\psi(\mathbf{J})$, we obtain that

$$B(\mathcal{CC}(\mathbf{e}, \mathbf{x}), \psi(\mathbf{J})) = B(\mathcal{UC}(\mathbf{e}, \mathbf{x}), J^{SIA^*}(\mathbf{e}, \mathbf{x})) \text{ and}$$
$$B(\mathcal{CC}(\mathbf{e}, \rho_{ij}(\mathbf{x})), \psi(\mathbf{J})) = B(\mathcal{UC}(\mathbf{e}, \rho_{ij}(\mathbf{x})), J^{SIA^*}(\mathbf{e}, \rho_{ij}(\mathbf{x}))).$$

Since $J^{SIA^*}(\mathbf{e}, \mathbf{x}) = J^{SIA^*}(\mathbf{e}, \rho_{ij}(\mathbf{x}))$, we obtain that $B(\mathcal{UC}(\mathbf{e}, \mathbf{x}), J^{SIA^*}(\mathbf{e}, \mathbf{x})) = B(\mathcal{UC}(\mathbf{e}, \rho_{ij}(\mathbf{x})), J^{SIA^*}(\mathbf{e}, \rho_{ij}(\mathbf{x})))$. Thus, $CC(\mathbf{e}, \mathbf{x}, \mathbf{y}) \in B(\mathcal{CC}(\mathbf{e}, \mathbf{x}), \psi(\mathbf{J}))$ if and only if $CC(\mathbf{e}, \rho_{ij}(\mathbf{x}, \mathbf{y})) \in B(\mathcal{CC}(\mathbf{e}, \rho_{ij}(\mathbf{x})), \psi(\mathbf{J}))$.

Thus, let us define a rational choice function φ as follows: for all $\mathbf{e} \in E$, all $\mathbf{x} \in [0, \overline{x}]^n$, and all $i, j \in N$ such that $a_i = a_j$ and $s_i = s_j$, $\varphi(\mathcal{CC}(\mathbf{e}, \mathbf{x}), \psi(\mathbf{J})) \in B(\mathcal{CC}(\mathbf{e}, \mathbf{x}), \psi(\mathbf{J}))$ and $\varphi(\mathcal{CC}(\mathbf{e}, \rho_{ij}(\mathbf{x})), \psi(\mathbf{J})) = \varphi(\mathcal{CC}(\mathbf{e}, \mathbf{x}), \psi(\mathbf{J}))$. The former property of φ implies that for each $\mathbf{e} \in E$ and $\mathbf{x} \in [0, \overline{x}]^n$, $Y(\mathbf{e}, \mathbf{x}, \psi(\mathbf{J}), \varphi)$ is non-empty. Let us define a distribution rule $h : E \times [0, \overline{x}]^n \to \mathbb{R}^n_+$ such that for all $\mathbf{e} \in E$ and all $\mathbf{x} \in [0, \overline{x}]^n$, $h(\mathbf{e}, \mathbf{x}) \in Y(\mathbf{e}, \mathbf{x}, \psi(\mathbf{J}), \varphi)$. Then by the definition of $\varphi(\mathcal{CC}(\mathbf{e}, \mathbf{x}), \psi(\mathbf{J}))$, $CC(\mathbf{e}, \mathbf{x}, h(\mathbf{e}, \mathbf{x})) \in \mathcal{UC}(\mathbf{e}, \mathbf{x})$ for all $\mathbf{e} \in E$ and all $\mathbf{x} \in [0, \overline{x}]^n$. Moreover, the second property of φ implies that the distribution rule h satisfies the **EAEH**. Since $CC(\mathbf{e}, \mathbf{x}, h(\mathbf{e}, \mathbf{x})) = C^{\min}_{\varphi \cdot \psi(\mathbf{J})}(\mathbf{e}, \mathbf{x})$, this implies that h is a **J**-based capability maximin rule: $h^{\mathbf{CM}_\mathbf{J}^{\psi,\varphi}} \equiv h$.

Next, we show that given $\psi(\mathbf{J})$ and φ, the **J** -based capability maximin rule $h^{\mathbf{CM}_\mathbf{J}^{\psi,\varphi}}$ is uniquely determined: there is no other distribution rule h' such that for all $\mathbf{e} \in E$ and all $\mathbf{x} \in [0, \overline{x}]^n$, $h'(\mathbf{e}, \mathbf{x}) \in Y(\mathbf{e}, \mathbf{x}, \psi(\mathbf{J}), \varphi)$ and $CC(\mathbf{e}, \mathbf{x}, h'(\mathbf{e}, \mathbf{x})) \in \mathcal{UC}(\mathbf{e}, \mathbf{x})$, and for some $\mathbf{e} \in E$ and some $\mathbf{x} \in [0, \overline{x}]^n$, $h'(\mathbf{e}, \mathbf{x}) \neq h^{\mathbf{CM}_\mathbf{J}^{\psi,\varphi}}(\mathbf{e}, \mathbf{x})$. It is sufficient to show that for any $\mathbf{e} \in E$, any $\mathbf{x} \in [0, \overline{x}]^n$, any $\mathbf{J} \in \mathcal{J}^n$ and ψ, and any φ, $Y(\mathbf{e}, \mathbf{x}, \psi(\mathbf{J}), \varphi)$ is singleton. Given $\mathbf{e} \in E$, $\mathbf{x} \in [0, \overline{x}]^n$, $\psi(\mathbf{J})$, and φ, let $C^{\min}_{\varphi \cdot \psi(\mathbf{J})}(\mathbf{e}, \mathbf{x})$ be the **J**-based minimal capability under $(\mathbf{e}, \mathbf{x})$, and $\mathbf{y} \in Y(\mathbf{e}, \mathbf{x}, \psi(\mathbf{J}), \varphi)$. Suppose that there exists another distribution $\mathbf{y}' \in Y(\mathbf{e}, \mathbf{x}, \psi(\mathbf{J}), \varphi)$ such that $\mathbf{y}' \neq \mathbf{y}$. By strict monotonicity of c_k and lemma 2, $\mathbf{y}$ and $\mathbf{y}'$ in $Y(\mathbf{e}, \mathbf{x}, \psi(\mathbf{J}), \varphi)$ have the following property: $\sum y_i = \sum y'_i = f(\sum s_i x_i)$. This implies that there exist at least two individuals $i, j \in N$ such that $y'_i < y_i$ and $y'_j > y_j$. Then, by (1)-(β) of the correspondence C, $\partial C(a_i, \overline{x} - x_i, y'_i) \subsetneq int\, C(a_i, \overline{x} - x_i, y_i)$. By lemma 2, there exists $b_i \in \partial C(a_i, \overline{x} - x_i, y_i)$ such that $b_i \in \partial C^{\min}_{\varphi \cdot \psi(\mathbf{J})}(\mathbf{e}, \mathbf{x})$. Hence, $b_i \notin \partial C(a_i, \overline{x} - x_i, y'_i)$, so that $C(a_i, \overline{x} - x_i, y'_i) \not\supseteq C^{\min}_{\varphi \cdot \psi(\mathbf{J})}(\mathbf{e}, \mathbf{x})$. This is a contradiction. ■

Proof of Theorem 2 First, we show that the ordering $R^{\mathcal{FC}}_{\psi(\mathbf{J})} \subseteq \mathcal{FC} \times \mathcal{FC}$ satisfies *PICA*, *ACA*, and μ^**ECA*. By definition of $R^{\mathcal{FC}}_{\psi(\mathbf{J})}$, it satisfies *ACA*. For any two capability assignments $\mathbf{C}(\mathbf{e}, \mathbf{x}, \mathbf{y}), \mathbf{C}(\mathbf{e}, \mathbf{x}, \mathbf{y}') \in \mathcal{FC}(\mathbf{e}, \mathbf{x})$, if $C(a_i, \overline{x} - x_i, y_i) \supseteq C(a_i, \overline{x} - x_i, y'_i)$ for all $i \in N$ and $C(a_j, \overline{x} - x_j, y_j) \supsetneq C(a_j, \overline{x} - x_j, y'_j)$ for some $j \in N$, then this implies that $CC(\mathbf{e}, \mathbf{x}, \mathbf{y}) \supsetneq CC(\mathbf{e}, \mathbf{x}, \mathbf{y}')$. Since $\psi(\mathbf{J})$ contains the set-inclusion subrelation by Theorem 1, $(\mathbf{C}(\mathbf{e}, \mathbf{z}), \mathbf{C}(\mathbf{e}, \mathbf{z}')) \in P(R^{\mathcal{FC}}_{\psi(\mathbf{J})}(\mathbf{e}, \mathbf{x}))$. Thus, $R^{\mathcal{FC}}_{\psi(\mathbf{J})}$ satisfies *PICA*. Next, we show that $R^{\mathcal{FC}}_{\psi(\mathbf{J})}$ satisfies μ^*ECA. Suppose that given $\mathbf{e} \in E$ and $\mathbf{x} \in [0, \overline{x}]^n$, $\mathbf{C}(\mathbf{e}, \mathbf{x}, \mathbf{y}^*) \in B(\mathcal{FC}(\mathbf{e}, \mathbf{x}), R^{\mathcal{FC}}_{\psi(\mathbf{J})})$. This supposition is not empty, since there exists an undominated common capability $CC(\mathbf{e}, \mathbf{x}, \mathbf{y}^*) \equiv C^{\min}_{\varphi \cdot \psi(\mathbf{J})}(\mathbf{e}, \mathbf{x}) \in \mathcal{CC}(\mathbf{e}, \mathbf{x})$, and by the definition of $R^{\mathcal{FC}}_{\psi(\mathbf{J})}$ and Theorem 1, $(\mathbf{C}(\mathbf{e}, \mathbf{x}, \mathbf{y}^*), \mathbf{C}(\mathbf{e}, \mathbf{x}, \mathbf{y})) \in R^{\mathcal{FC}}_{\psi(\mathbf{J})}(\mathbf{e}, \mathbf{x})$ for all $\mathbf{y} \in Y(\mathbf{e}, \mathbf{x})$. Then, by definition of μ^*, $\max_{i \in N} \mu^*(\mathbf{C}(\mathbf{e}, \mathbf{x}, \mathbf{y}^*), i) = 0$. Since $\mu^*(\mathbf{C}(\mathbf{e}, \mathbf{x}, \mathbf{y}), i) \geq 0$ for all $i \in N$,

$$\max_{i \in N} \mu^*(\mathbf{C}(\mathbf{e}, \mathbf{x}, \mathbf{y}^*), i) = \min_{\mathbf{y} \in Y(\mathbf{e}, \mathbf{x})} \max_{i \in N} \mu^*(\mathbf{C}(\mathbf{e}, \mathbf{x}, \mathbf{y}), i).$$

Next, suppose that the ordering $R^{\mathcal{FC}} \subseteq \mathcal{FC} \times \mathcal{FC}$ satisfies PICA, ACA, and μ^*ECA. Note that for all $\mathbf{e} \in E$, all $\mathbf{x} \in [0, \overline{x}]^n$, and all $\mathbf{y} \in Y(\mathbf{e}, \mathbf{x})$, if $CC(\mathbf{e}, \mathbf{x}, \mathbf{y}) \in \mathcal{UC}(\mathbf{e}, \mathbf{x})$, then $\mu^*(\mathbf{C}(\mathbf{e}, \mathbf{x}, \mathbf{y}), i) = 1$ for all $i \in N$, while if $CC(\mathbf{e}, \mathbf{x}, \mathbf{y}) \in \mathcal{CC}(\mathbf{e}, \mathbf{x}) \setminus \mathcal{UC}(\mathbf{e}, \mathbf{x})$, then for some $i \in N$, $\mu^*(\mathbf{C}(\mathbf{e}, \mathbf{x}, \mathbf{y}), i) > 0$. This implies that $\max_{i \in N} \mu^*(\mathbf{C}(\mathbf{e}, \mathbf{x}, \mathbf{y}^*), i) = \min_{\mathbf{y} \in Y(\mathbf{e}, \mathbf{x})} \max_{i \in N} \mu^*(\mathbf{C}(\mathbf{e}, \mathbf{x}, \mathbf{y}), i)$ for all $CC(\mathbf{e}, \mathbf{x}, \mathbf{y}^*) \in \mathcal{UC}(\mathbf{e}, \mathbf{x})$. By the property of $R^{\mathcal{FC}}$ which satisifies the above three axioms, for all $\mathbf{e} \in E$, all $i, j \in N$ such that $a_i = a_j$ and $s_i = s_j$, and all $\mathbf{x} \in [0, \overline{x}]^n$, there exists $\mathbf{C}(\mathbf{e}, \mathbf{x}, \mathbf{y}^*) \in B(\mathcal{FC}(\mathbf{e}, \mathbf{x}), R^{\mathcal{FC}})$ such that

$$\max_{i \in N} \mu^*(\mathbf{C}(\mathbf{e}, \mathbf{x}, \mathbf{y}^*), i) = \min_{\mathbf{y} \in Y(\mathbf{e}, \mathbf{x})} \max_{i \in N} \mu^*(\mathbf{C}(\mathbf{e}, \mathbf{x}, \mathbf{y}), i),$$

$$CC(\mathbf{e}, \mathbf{x}, \mathbf{y}^*) \in \mathcal{UC}(\mathbf{e}, \mathbf{x}) \text{ , and } \mathbf{C}(\mathbf{e}, \rho_{ij}(\mathbf{x}, \mathbf{y}^*)) \in B(\mathcal{FC}(\mathbf{e}, \rho_{ij}(\mathbf{x})), R^{\mathcal{FC}}).$$

Let us consider a profile of individual value judgements $\mathbf{J}^* \in \mathcal{J}^n$ such that for all $i \in N$, $(CC(\mathbf{e}, \mathbf{x}, \mathbf{y}), CC(\mathbf{e}', \mathbf{x}', \mathbf{y}')) \in J_i^* \Leftrightarrow (\mathbf{C}(\mathbf{e}, \mathbf{x}, \mathbf{y}), \mathbf{C}(\mathbf{e}', \mathbf{x}', \mathbf{y}')) \in R^{\mathcal{FC}}$. This implies for all $i \in N$, $J_i^* \in \mathcal{J}_{SIA}$. Thus, by construction of ψ, $\psi(\mathbf{J}^*) = J_i^*$ for all $i \in N$. Then, for all $\mathbf{e} \in E$, all $\mathbf{x} \in [0, \overline{x}]^n$, and all $i, j \in N$ such that $a_i = a_j$ and $s_i = s_j$, $CC(\mathbf{e}, \mathbf{x}, \mathbf{y}^*) = C^{\min}_{\varphi \cdot \psi(\mathbf{J}^*)}(\mathbf{e}, \mathbf{x})$ and $CC(\mathbf{e}, \rho_{ij}(\mathbf{x}, \mathbf{y}^*)) = C^{\min}_{\varphi \cdot \psi(\mathbf{J}^*)}(\mathbf{e}, \rho_{ij}(\mathbf{x}))$. Since $\psi(\mathbf{J}^*)$ rationalizes the $\mathbf{J}^*$-capability maxmin rule $h^{\mathbf{CM}^{\psi, \varphi}_{\mathbf{J}^*}}$, $R^{\mathcal{FC}} = R^{\mathcal{FC}}_{\psi(\mathbf{J}^*)}$. ■

Proof of Lemma 3 By Lemma 2, it is easy to see that for any $\mathbf{J} \in \mathcal{J}^n$, $h^{\mathbf{CM}^{\psi, \varphi}_{\mathbf{J}}}$ meets the undominated property, and it also satisfies PEC. We show that for any $h \in EAEH \cap UD \cap PEC$, there exists $\mathbf{J} \in \mathcal{J}^n$ such that $h = h^{\mathbf{CM}^{\psi, \varphi}_{\mathbf{J}}}$.

First, we show that for any $h \in EAEH \cap UD \cap PEC$, all $\mathbf{e} = (\mathbf{a}, \mathbf{s}, C, f) \in E$, and all $\mathbf{x} \in [0, \overline{x}]^n$, there is no $\mathbf{y} \in Y(\mathbf{e}, \mathbf{x})$ such that $\mathbf{y} \neq h(\mathbf{e}, \mathbf{x})$ and $CC(\mathbf{e}, \mathbf{x}, \mathbf{y}) \supsetneq CC(\mathbf{e}, \mathbf{x}, h(\mathbf{e}, \mathbf{x}))$. Suppose that for some $\mathbf{y} \in Y(\mathbf{e}, \mathbf{x})$ such that $\mathbf{y} \neq h(\mathbf{e}, \mathbf{x})$, $CC(\mathbf{e}, \mathbf{x}, \mathbf{y}) \supsetneq CC(\mathbf{e}, \mathbf{x}, h(\mathbf{e}, \mathbf{x}))$. By UD, for all $i \in N$, there is $b_i \in \partial C(a_i, \overline{x} - x_i, h_i(\mathbf{e}, \mathbf{x}))$ such that $b_i \in \partial CC(\mathbf{e}, \mathbf{x}, h(\mathbf{e}, \mathbf{x}))$. Hence, $CC(\mathbf{e}, \mathbf{x}, \mathbf{y}) \supsetneq CC(\mathbf{e}, \mathbf{x}, h(\mathbf{e}, \mathbf{x}))$ implies that for some $j \in N$,

$$int\ C(a_j, \overline{x} - x_j, y_j) \supsetneq C(a_j, \overline{x} - x_j, h_j(\mathbf{e}, \mathbf{x}))$$

by (1)-(β) of the correspondence C. Thus, $y_j > h_j(\mathbf{e}, \mathbf{x})$ and for any other $i \neq j$, $y_i \geq h_i(\mathbf{e}, \mathbf{x})$. However, such a distribution is infeasible, because $h \in PEC$.

Second, let us show that if $h \in EAEH \cap UD \cap PEC$, then for some $\mathbf{J} \in \mathcal{J}^n$, for all $\mathbf{e} \in E$ and all $\mathbf{x} \in [0, \overline{x}]^n$, $CC(\mathbf{e}, \mathbf{x}, h(\mathbf{e}, \mathbf{x})) = C^{\min}_{\varphi \cdot \psi(\mathbf{J})}(\mathbf{e}, \mathbf{x})$. By the above argument, for each $\mathbf{e} \in E$ and $\mathbf{x} \in [0, \overline{x}]^n$, $CC(\mathbf{e}, \mathbf{x}, h(\mathbf{e}, \mathbf{x})) \in \mathcal{UC}(\mathbf{e}, \mathbf{x})$. Let $\mathbf{J}^* \in \mathcal{J}^n$ be such that for each $\mathbf{e} \in E$ and each $\mathbf{x} \in [0, \overline{x}]^n$, $(CC(\mathbf{e}, \mathbf{x}, h(\mathbf{e}, \mathbf{x})), CC(\mathbf{e}, \mathbf{x}, \mathbf{y})) \in P(J_i^*(\mathbf{e}, \mathbf{x}))$ for all $\mathbf{y} \in Y(\mathbf{e}, \mathbf{x}) \backslash \{h(\mathbf{e}, \mathbf{x})\}$ and all $i \in N$. Then, by the Pareto Principle of ψ, $CC(\mathbf{e}, \mathbf{x}, h(\mathbf{e}, \mathbf{x})) = C^{\min}_{\varphi \cdot \psi(\mathbf{J}^*)}(\mathbf{e}, \mathbf{x})$. This implies that $h = h^{\mathbf{CM}^{\psi,\varphi}_{\mathbf{J}^*}}$ for $\mathbf{J}^* \in \mathcal{J}^n$. ■

Proof of Theorem 3 Given $\mathbf{J} \in \mathcal{J}^n$, let $h^{\mathbf{CM}^{\psi,\varphi}_{\mathbf{J}}} \in UCM$. Then, by Lemma 3, $h^{\mathbf{CM}^{\psi,\varphi}_{\mathbf{J}}} \in EAEH \cap UD \cap PEC$. It is easy to show that $h^{\mathbf{CM}^{\psi,\varphi}_{\mathbf{J}}} \in MEC$. So, we show first $h^{\mathbf{CM}^{\psi,\varphi}_{\mathbf{J}}} \in SRWF$. Suppose that there exist $\mathbf{e} = (\mathbf{a}, \mathbf{s}, C, f) \in E$, $\mathbf{x} = (x_i)_{i \in N} \in [0, \overline{x}]^n$, and $\mathbf{x}' = (x'_i)_{i \in N} \in [0, \overline{x}]^n$ such that for all $g \neq j$, $x_g = x'_g$ and $x_j \leq x'_j$, and for some $i \in N$,

$$\begin{aligned} &\#N(i, b_i^w(\mathbf{e}, (\mathbf{x}, h^{\mathbf{CM}^{\psi,\varphi}_{\mathbf{J}}}(\mathbf{e}, \mathbf{x}))), \mathbf{e}, (\mathbf{x}, h^{\mathbf{CM}^{\psi,\varphi}_{\mathbf{J}}}(\mathbf{e}, \mathbf{x}))) \\ &> \#N(i, b_i^w(\mathbf{e}, (\mathbf{x}', h^{\mathbf{CM}^{\psi,\varphi}_{\mathbf{J}}}(\mathbf{e}, \mathbf{x}'))), \mathbf{e}, (\mathbf{x}', h^{\mathbf{CM}^{\psi,\varphi}_{\mathbf{J}}}(\mathbf{e}, \mathbf{x}'))). \end{aligned}$$

This implies that for all $b_i \in \partial C(a_i, \overline{x} - x_i, h_i^{\mathbf{CM}^{\psi,\varphi}_{\mathbf{J}}}(\mathbf{e}, \mathbf{x}'))$, there is $g \in N$ and $\lambda_g < 1$ such that $\lambda_g b_i \in \partial C(a_g, \overline{x} - x_g, h_g^{\mathbf{CM}^{\psi,\varphi}_{\mathbf{J}}}(\mathbf{e}, \mathbf{x}'))$, since $\#N(i, b_i^w(\mathbf{e}, (\mathbf{x}', h^{\mathbf{CM}^{\psi,\varphi}_{\mathbf{J}}}(\mathbf{e}, \mathbf{x}'))), \mathbf{e}, (\mathbf{x}', h^{\mathbf{CM}^{\psi,\varphi}_{\mathbf{J}}}(\mathbf{e}, \mathbf{x}'))) < n$. This also implies that *int* $C(a_i, \overline{x} - x_i, h_i^{\mathbf{CM}^{\psi,\varphi}_{\mathbf{J}}}(e, \mathbf{x}')) \supsetneq C^{\min}_{\varphi \cdot \psi(\mathbf{J})}(\mathbf{e}, \mathbf{x}')$. It is a contradiction by Lemma 2. By the same way, we can show that $h^{\mathbf{CM}^{\psi,\varphi}_{\mathbf{J}}} \in NRABA$.

Next, we show that for any $h \in EAEH \cap PEC$, if $h \in MEC \cap SRWF \cap NRABA$, then $h \in UD$. Let $\mathbf{e} = (\mathbf{a}, \mathbf{s}, C, f) \in E$ and $\mathbf{x} = (x_i)_{i \in N} \in [0, \overline{x}]^n$ be such that for all $i, j \in N$, $a_i = a_j$ and $x_i = x_j$. Then, $h \in MEC \cap PEC$ implies that

$$h_i(\mathbf{e}, \mathbf{x}) = \frac{f(\sum s_i x_i)}{n} \text{ for all } i \in N .$$

Since for all $i, j \in N$,

$$C(a_i, \overline{x} - x_i, h_i(\mathbf{e}, \mathbf{x})) = C(a_j, \overline{x} - x_j, h_j(\mathbf{e}, \mathbf{x})),$$

we obtain

$$\#N(i, b_i^w(\mathbf{e}, (\mathbf{x}, h(\mathbf{e}, \mathbf{x}))), \mathbf{e}, (\mathbf{x}, h(\mathbf{e}, \mathbf{x}))) = n \text{ for all } i \in N.$$

Let $\mathbf{e}' = (\mathbf{a}', \mathbf{s}, C, f) \in E$ and $\mathbf{x}' = (x'_i)_{i \in N} \in [0, \overline{x}]^n$ be given. Without loss of generality, we assume that $a'_1 \leq \cdots \leq a'_n$ and $x'_1 \leq \cdots \leq x'_n$. Let $\mathbf{e}'' = (\mathbf{a}'', \mathbf{s}, C, f) \in E$ such that $\mathbf{a}'' = (a'_n, \cdots, a'_n)$ and $\mathbf{x}'' = (x'_1, \cdots, x'_1) \in [0, \overline{x}]^n$. Then, by $h \in MEC$,

$$\#N(i, b_i^w(\mathbf{e}'', (\mathbf{x}'', h(\mathbf{e}'', \mathbf{x}''))), \mathbf{e}'', (\mathbf{x}'', h(\mathbf{e}'', \mathbf{x}''))) = n \text{ for all } i \in N.$$

By repeatedly applying the $SRWF$ and $NRABA$, we obtained

$$\#N(i, b_i^w(\mathbf{e}', (\mathbf{x}', h(\mathbf{e}', \mathbf{x}'))), \mathbf{e}', (\mathbf{x}', h(\mathbf{e}', \mathbf{x}'))) = n \text{ for all } i \in N.$$

This implies that $h \in UD$. By Lemma 3, for some $\mathbf{J} \in \mathcal{J}^n$, $h = h^{\mathbf{CM}_\mathbf{J}^{\psi,\varphi}} \in UCM$. ■

Proof of Theorem 4 Since NP implies MEC, from Theorem 3, it is sufficient to show that UCM implies NP. Let $\mathbf{e} = (\mathbf{a}, \mathbf{s}, C, f) \in E$, and $\mathbf{x} \in [0, \overline{x}]^n$ be such that for all $i, j \in N$, $x_i = x_j$. Then, $C^H(\mathbf{e}, \mathbf{x}) \in \mathcal{CC}(\mathbf{e}, \mathbf{x})$. If $\mathbf{a}$ is such that for all $i, j \in N$, $a_i = a_j$, then $C^H(\mathbf{e}, \mathbf{x}) = C^{\min}_{\varphi \cdot \psi(\mathbf{J})}(\mathbf{e}, \mathbf{x})$ for any $\mathbf{J} \in \mathcal{J}^n$. Otherwise, there exists an individual $i^* \in N$ such that for any other $j \neq i^*$, $a_{i^*} < a_j$, and that $C^H(\mathbf{e}, \mathbf{x}) = C(a_{i^*}, \overline{x} - x_{i^*}, y^H(\mathbf{e}, \mathbf{x}))$. Then, consider other distribution $\mathbf{y}^*$ such that for some $\varepsilon > 0$, for some $j \neq i^*$, $y_j^* = y^H(\mathbf{e}, \mathbf{x}) - \varepsilon$, for i^*, $y_{i^*}^* = y^H(\mathbf{e}, \mathbf{x}) + \varepsilon$, and for any other $g \neq i^*, j$, $y_g^* = y^H(\mathbf{e}, \mathbf{x})$. Then, by continuity and strict monotonicity of C, $CC(\mathbf{e}, \mathbf{x}, \mathbf{y}^*) = C(a_{i^*}, \overline{x} - x_{i^*}, y_{i^*}^*) \supseteq C^H(\mathbf{e}, \mathbf{x})$. This implies that for any $\mathbf{J} \in \mathcal{J}^n$, $C^{\min}_{\varphi \cdot \psi(\mathbf{J})}(\mathbf{e}, \mathbf{x}) \supseteq C^H(\mathbf{e}, \mathbf{x})$. Since $C(a_i, \overline{x} - x_i, h_i^{\mathbf{CM}_\mathbf{J}^{\psi,\varphi}}(\mathbf{e}, \mathbf{x})) \supseteq C^{\min}_{\varphi \cdot \psi(\mathbf{J})}(\mathbf{e}, \mathbf{x})$ for all $i \in N$, there is no $i \in N$ such that $C^H(\mathbf{e}, \mathbf{x}) \supsetneq C(a_i, \overline{x} - x_i, h_i^{\mathbf{CM}_\mathbf{J}^{\psi,\varphi}}(\mathbf{e}, \mathbf{x}))$. ■

Proof of Theorem 5 First, we show that UCM implies $NDEH$ and $NSDEE$. Given $\mathbf{J} \in \mathcal{J}^n$, let $h^{\mathbf{CM}_\mathbf{J}^{\psi,\varphi}} \in UCM$. Suppose that $h^{\mathbf{CM}_\mathbf{J}^{\psi,\varphi}}$ violates $NDEH$. Then, for some $(\mathbf{e}, \mathbf{x}) \in E \times [0, \overline{x}]^n$ and some $i, j \in N$ such that $a_i = a_j$, we obtain either (α) $x_i = x_j$ and $h_i^{\mathbf{CM}_\mathbf{J}^{\psi,\varphi}}(\mathbf{e}, \mathbf{x}) < h_j^{\mathbf{CM}_\mathbf{J}^{\psi,\varphi}}(\mathbf{e}, \mathbf{x})$ or (β) $x_i < x_j$ and $h_i^{\mathbf{CM}_\mathbf{J}^{\psi,\varphi}}(\mathbf{e}, \mathbf{x}) \geq h_j^{\mathbf{CM}_\mathbf{J}^{\psi,\varphi}}(\mathbf{e}, \mathbf{x})$. In case (α), $C(a_i, \overline{x} - x_i, h_i^{\mathbf{CM}_\mathbf{J}^{\psi,\varphi}}(\mathbf{e}, \mathbf{x})) \subsetneq int\ C(a_j, \overline{x} - x_j, h_j^{\mathbf{CM}_\mathbf{J}^{\psi,\varphi}}(\mathbf{e}, \mathbf{x}))$, and in case (β), $int\ C(a_i, \overline{x} - x_i, h_i^{\mathbf{CM}_\mathbf{J}^{\psi,\varphi}}(\mathbf{e}, \mathbf{x})) \supsetneq C(a_j, \overline{x} - x_j, h_j^{\mathbf{CM}_\mathbf{J}^{\psi,\varphi}}(\mathbf{e}, \mathbf{x}))$. The both cases imply that $h^{\mathbf{CM}_\mathbf{J}^{\psi,\varphi}} \notin UD$, which is a contradiction by Lemma 3. Suppose that $h^{\mathbf{CM}_\mathbf{J}^{\psi,\varphi}}$ violates $NSDEE$. Then, for some $(\mathbf{e}, \mathbf{x}) \in E \times [0, \overline{x}]^n$ and some $i, j \in N$ such that $x_i = x_j$, $int\ C(a_i, \overline{x} - x_i, h_i^{\mathbf{CM}_\mathbf{J}^{\psi,\varphi}}(\mathbf{e}, \mathbf{x})) \supsetneq C(a_j, \overline{x} - x_j, h_j^{\mathbf{CM}_\mathbf{J}^{\psi,\varphi}}(\mathbf{e}, \mathbf{x}))$. This implies that $int\ C(a_i, \overline{x} - x_i, h_i^{\mathbf{CM}_\mathbf{J}^{\psi,\varphi}}(\mathbf{e}, \mathbf{x})) \supsetneq \bigcap_{j \neq i} C(a_j, \overline{x} - x_j, h_j^{\mathbf{CM}_\mathbf{J}^{\psi,\varphi}}(\mathbf{e}, \mathbf{x}))$. Hence, $h^{\mathbf{CM}_\mathbf{J}^{\psi,\varphi}} \notin UD$, which is a contradiction by Lemma 3.

Next, based upon $h^{\mathbf{CM}_\mathbf{J}^{\psi,\varphi}} \in UCM$, we construct another distribution rule $h \in EAEH \cap PEC$ satisfying the undominated property as follows: for each $(\mathbf{e}, \mathbf{x}) \in E \times [0, \overline{x}]^n$,

(α) if there is $i^* \in N$ such that $C(a_{i^*}, \overline{x} - x_{i^*}, h_{i^*}^{\mathbf{CM}_\mathbf{J}^{\psi,\varphi}}(\mathbf{e}, \mathbf{x})) = C^{\min}_{\varphi \cdot \psi(\mathbf{J})}(\mathbf{e}, \mathbf{x})$ and there is a group $N(i^*) \subseteq N \setminus \{i^*\}$ such that for all $j^* \in N(i^*)$,

$$C(a_{i^*}, \overline{x} - x_{i^*}, h_{i^*}^{\mathbf{CM}_\mathbf{J}^{\psi,\varphi}}(\mathbf{e}, \mathbf{x})) \subsetneq C(a_{j^*}, \overline{x} - x_{j^*}, h_{j^*}^{\mathbf{CM}_\mathbf{J}^{\psi,\varphi}}(\mathbf{e}, \mathbf{x})),$$

then

$$h_{i^*}(\mathbf{e},\mathbf{x}) = h_{i^*}^{\mathbf{CM}_{\mathbf{J}}^{\psi,\varphi}}(\mathbf{e},\mathbf{x}) + \varepsilon \text{ for some } \varepsilon > 0,$$
$$h_{j^*}(\mathbf{e},\mathbf{x}) = h_{j^*}^{\mathbf{CM}_{\mathbf{J}}^{\psi,\varphi}}(\mathbf{e},\mathbf{x}) - \alpha_{j^*}\varepsilon \text{ for all } j^* \in N(i^*)$$

$$\text{where } \alpha_{j^*} \geq 0 \text{ and } \sum_{N(i^*)} \alpha_{j^*} = 1,$$

$$\text{and } h_g(\mathbf{e},\mathbf{x}) = h_g^{\mathbf{CM}_{\mathbf{J}}^{\psi,\varphi}}(\mathbf{e},\mathbf{x}) \text{ for all } g \in N \setminus (N(i^*) \cup \{i^*\})$$

such that there is no $i \in N$,

$$C(a_i, \overline{x} - x_i, h_i(\mathbf{e},\mathbf{x})) \supsetneq \bigcap_{j \neq i} C(a_j, \overline{x} - x_j, h_j(\mathbf{e},\mathbf{x})),$$

and moreover, if there exists a pair of individuals $\{i, j\} \subseteq N$ such that $a_i = a_j$ and $s_i = s_j$, then for $\mathbf{x}' = \rho_{ij}(\mathbf{x}) \in [0, \overline{x}]^n$,

$$h_i(\mathbf{e},\mathbf{x}') = h_j(\mathbf{e},\mathbf{x}), h_j(\mathbf{e},\mathbf{x}') = h_i(\mathbf{e},\mathbf{x}),$$
$$\text{and } h_g(\mathbf{e},\mathbf{x}') = h_g(\mathbf{e},\mathbf{x}) \text{ for all } g \in N \setminus \{i, j\},$$

(β) otherwise, $h(\mathbf{e},\mathbf{x}) = h^{\mathbf{CM}_{\mathbf{J}^*}^{\psi,\varphi}}(\mathbf{e},\mathbf{x})$.

The case (α) is possible by the continuity of the capability correspondence C. Then, by definition, $h \in EAEH \cap PEC \cap UD$. By Lemma 3, for some $\mathbf{J}^* \in \mathcal{J}^n$, $h = h^{\mathbf{CM}_{\mathbf{J}^*}^{\psi,\varphi}}$. Thus, by the above arguments, $h \in NDEH \cap NSDEE$. Moreover, the construction of h implies that $h \in NDEE$. ■

B.8 References

Arlegi, R., & Nieto, J. (1999). Equality of opportunities: cardinality-based criteria. In H. Swart (Ed.), *Logic, game theory and social choice* (pp. 458–481). Tilburg University Press: Tilbrug.

Arneson, R. (1989). Equality and equal opportunity for welfare. *Philosophical Studies, 56*, 77–93.

Atkinson, A. B. (1995). Capability and the supply of goods. In K. Basu, P. Pattanaik, & K. Suzumura (Eds.), *Choice, welfare, and development* A Festchrift in Honour of Amartya K. Sen (pp. 17–31). Oxford: Oxford Univ. Press.

Bossert, W. (1995). Redistribution mechanisms based on individual characteristics. *Mathematical Social Sciences, 29*, 1–17.

Bossert, W., & Fleurbaey, M. (1996) Redistribution and compensation. *Social Choice and Welfare, 13*, 343–356.

Bossert, W., Fleurbaey, M., & Van de gaer, D. (1999). Responsibility, talent, and compensation: A second-best analysis. *Review of Economic Design, 4*, 35–55.

Cohen, G. A. (1989). On the currency of Egalitarian justice. *Ethics 99*, 906–944.

Cohen, G. A. (1993). Equality of what ? On welfare, goods, and capabilities. In M. Nussbaum, & Sen A. (Eds.), *The quality of life* (pp. 9–29). Oxford: Oxford University Press.

Dworkin, R. (1981). What is equality? Part 2: Equality of resources. *Philosophy & Public Affairs, 10*, 283–345.

Fleurbaey, M. (1994). On fair compensation. *Theory and Decision, 36*, 277–307.
Fleurbaey, M. (1995a). Three solutions to the compensation problem. *Journal of Economic Theory, 65*, 505–521.
Fleurbaey, M. (1995b). Equal opportunity or equal social outcome. *Economics and Philosophy, 11*, 25–55.
Fleurbaey, M. (1998). Equality among responsible individuals. In J.-F. Laslier, M. Fleurbaey, N. Gravel, & Trannoy, A. (Eds.), *Freedom in economics* (pp. 25–55). New York: Routledge.
Fleurbaey, M., & Maniquet, F. (1994). Fair allocation with unequal production skills: The solidarity approach to compensation. *Social Choice and Welfare* (forthcoming).
Fleurbaey, M., & Maniquet, F. (1996). Fair allocation with unequal production skills: The no-envy approach to compensation. *Mathematical Social Sciences, 32*, 71–93.
Gartener, W., Pattanaik, P. K., & Suzumura, K. (1992). Individual rights revisited. *Economica, 59*, 161–177.
Gotoh, R., Suzumura, K., & Yoshihara, N. (1999). *On the existence of procedurally fair allocation rules in economic environments*. Mimeo.
Gotoh, R., & Yoshihara, N. (1997). A game form approach to theories of distributive justice: formalizing needs principle. Discussion Paper No. 407, The Institute of Social and Economic Research, Osaka University.
Herrero, C. (1996). Capabilities and utilities. *Economic Design, 2*, 69–88.
Herrero, C. (1997). Equitable opportunities: An extention. *Economics Letters, 55*, 91–95.
Herrero, C., Iturbe-Ormaetxe, I., & Nieto, J. (1998). Ranking opportunity profiles on the basis of the common opportunities. *Mathematical Social Sciences, 35*, 273–289.
Iturbe-Ormaetxe, I. (1997). Redistribution and individual characteristics. *Review of Economic Design, 3*, 45–56.
Iturbe-Ormaetxe, I., & Nieto, J. (1996). On fair allocations and monetary compensations. *Economic Theory, 7*, 125–138.
Jaffray, J.-Y. (1975). Semicontinuous extension of a partial order. *Journal of Mathematical Economics, 2*, 395–406.
Kranich, L. (1994). Equal division, efficiency, and the sovereign supply of labor. *American Economic Review, 84*, 178–189.
Kranich, L. (1996). Equitable opportunities: An axiomatic approach. *Journal of Economic Theory, 71*, 131–147.
Kranich, L. (1997). Equitable opportunities in economic environments. *Social Choice and Welfare, 14*, 57–64.
Kranich, L., & Ok, E. A. (1998) The measurement of opportunity inequality: A cardinality-based approach. *Social Choice and Welfare, 15*, 263–287.
Maniquet, F. (1998). An equal right solution to the compensation-responsibility Dilemma. *Mathematical Social Sciences, 35*, 185–202.
Moulin, H., & Shenker, S. (1994). Average cost pricing versus serial cost sharing: An axiomatic comparison. *Journal of Economic Theory, 64*, 178–201.
Rawls, J. (1971). *A theory of justice*. Cambridge, MA: Harvard University Press.
Rawls, J. (1993). *Political liberalism*. New York: Columbia University Press.
Roemer, J. E. (1993). A pragmatic theory of responsibility for the Egalitarian planner. *Philosophy & Public Affairs, 22*, 146–166.
Roemer, J. E. (1996). *Theories of distributive justice*. Cambridge, MA: Harvard University Press.
Sen, A. K. (1980). Equality of what? In S. McMurrin (Ed.), *Tanner lectures on human values* (Vol.1). Cambridge, MA: Cambridge University Press.
Sen, A. K. (1983). Poor, relatively speaking. *Oxford Economic Papers, 35*, 153–169.
Sen, A. K. (1985a). Well-being, agency and freedom: The Dewey lectures 1984. *The Journal of Philosophy, 82*, 169–224.
Sen, A. K. (1985b). *Commodities and capabilities*. Amsterdam: North-Holland.
Suzumura, K. (1983). *Rational choice, collective decisions and social welfare*. New York: Cambridge University Press.

Appendix C
Securing Basic Well-Being for All

Reiko Gotoh and Naoki Yoshihara

Abstract. The[44] purpose of this paper is to examine the possibility of a social choice rule to implement a social policy for " securing basic well-being for all." The paper introduces a new scheme of social choice, called a *social relation function* (**SRF**), which associates a reflexive and transitive binary relation over a set of social policies to each profile of *individual well-being appraisals* and each profile of *group evaluations*. As part of the domains of **SRF**s, the available class of group evaluations is constrained by three conditions. Furthermore, the *non-negative response* (**NR**) and the *weak Pareto condition* (**WP**) are introduced. **NR** demands giving priority to group evaluation, while treating the groups as formally equal relative to each other. **WP** requires treating impartially the well-being appraisals of all individuals. In conclusion, this paper shows that under some reasonable assumptions, there exists an **SRF** that satisfies **NR** and **WP**.

JEL Classification Number: D63
Keywords: Basic well-being; Individual well-being appraisals; Social relation functions

C.1 Introduction

Despite the United Nations' declaration of universal human rights in 1948, persons with disabilities have long been restricted in their effective exercise of these rights.

[44] We are extremely grateful to the editor in charge of the journals and the two referees for their helpful comments to improve the readability of the paper substantially. We also thank to Carmen Herrero, Laurence Kranich, Prasanta Pattanaik, Yongsheng Xu, Marc Fleurbaey, James Foster, Peter Hammond, and Yoshi Saijo for their fruitful discussions relevant to this paper. This Appendix was originally published in *Review of Social Economy*, Volume 76 (Taylor and Francis, 2018)

R. Gotoh, *The Ethics and Economics of the Capability Approach*, Hitotsubashi University IER Economic Research Series 46, https://doi.org/10.1007/978-981-15-5140-6

The Convention on the Rights of Persons with Disabilities, which was adopted by the United Nations in 2006, has brought about new insights on human rights as well as democracy. The convention is innovative in that it requires the effective exercise of human rights for persons with disabilities by, for example, removing discriminatory practices that have built up over time and implementing "reasonable accommodations" in public places.[45] Further, a remarkable aspect of drafting this convention is that, persons with disabilities have taken the initiative and offered their expertise in assessing alternative articles, going by the slogan " Nothing about us, without us."

The above example urges us to reconsider the appropriateness of the standard framework of social choice theory, as there is little discussion about the relationship between asymmetrical prior treatments of individual preferences and the different types of social choice problems they are admissible in. In addition, it indicates that the asymmetrical prior treatment of individual preferences could be appropriate when the given social choice problem is on the effective exercise of universal human rights with respect to the particularity of those individuals. The main purpose of this paper is to formulate a social choice procedure that permits prior treatments for disadvantaged groups not as exceptions but as a general rule under some reasonable and socially imposed conditions. More specifically, we focus on a specific type of social choice problem: selecting a public policy in terms of securing basic well-being for all and defining the concept of a " group" as a representation of particularity that requires a prior treatment in order to secure basic well-being for all.

The framework of this paper is as follows. First, the key concept of this paper, an individual's " well-being,"[46] is defined as a function of individuals' abilities and social policies (called *well-being transformations*). While no particular type of a well-being indicator is presumed, it is generically multi-dimensional in the space of plural attributes,[47] each of which is observable in public. For the sake of simplicity and without loss of generality, individuals' well-being transformations are assumed to be fixed and the profile of each individual well-being is identified corresponding to each alternative social policy. The paper also refers to " basic well-being," which represents a critical reference point of multi-dimensional well-beings that one can legitimately claim to have met by social policies, and each group can refer to it to identify the "injustice" of social policies.[48]

Second, a social choice rule to select a social policy for securing basic well-being for all is introduced and examined. This social choice rule, which we call a *social relation function* (**SRF**), is defined as having three elements as its informational basis: the individual appraisal of well-being contents, the group appraisal of well-

[45] See Convention on the Rights of Persons with Disabilities (Article 2).

[46] The concept of " functionings vector" or " capability" a la Amartya Sen are typical examples of the well-being indicator (Sen 1980, 1985).

[47] For a detailed discussion of evaluative attributes, see Pattanaik and Xu (2007, 2012). Also see Fleurbaey (2007) and Fleurbaey and Hammond (2004) for a discussion of well-being indicators.

[48] For instance, if the well-being indicator is specified by " capability," basic well-being implies " basic capability" (Sen 1980, p. 367).

being contents, and the group evaluation of social policies. The individual appraisal is formulated as a binary relation defined over the universal class of well-being contents; the group appraisal is formulated as the intersection of its members' appraisals; and the group evaluation is formulated as a binary relation defined over social policies, focusing on its least advantaged members who are identified on the basis of the group appraisal. By using the three elements of information, an **SRF** forms a social evaluation, which is a binary relation defined over social alternatives.

Some remarks on the **SRF** framework are necessary. First, the individual appraisal of well-being contents is based on her own conception of the good, while the group appraisal of well-being contents is based on the conception shared by the members. In contrast, the group evaluation of social policies is supposed to correspond to conceptions of justice shared in the society, which are embodied explicitly by the axioms and conditions and implicitly by public reasoning. Thus, throughout this paper, "better or worse" is used in the comparative evaluation of well-being contents, while "more or less just" or "less or more unjust" is used in the comparative evaluation of social policies.[49]

Second, because of the multiplicity of attributes for well-being, the types of disadvantages may be diversified, which could generate different types of " the least advantaged." Although they share the common feature that they lack access to basic well-being, as illustrated in Sect. C.2, the concrete contents (the lists, scales, and sizes) of basic well-being might differ from each other, depending upon the types of disadvantages and their corresponding conceptions of justice.[50] Therefore, in this paper, the concept of "group" is operationally defined as a maximum unit that can commonly share a concrete content of basic well-being and can identify "the least advantaged" within the group.

Third, due to the multi-dimensionality of well-being contents, the individual and group appraisals could be *incomplete*,[51] which implies that intra-personal full comparability of these appraisals cannot be generally presumed, while inter-personal comparability of these appraisals can be legitimately presumed to some extent at least in a group.

Due to the three-component structure of the informational basis, **SRF** s allow the appropriate asymmetric and prior treatment of specific groups of individuals relevant to the underlying social choice problem in question as well as the symmetric treatment of individual appraisals. To incorporate this idea formally, we introduce two basic axioms, the *non-negative response* (**NR**) and the *weak Pareto* (**WP**) axioms

---

[49]This usage is derived from the distinction of concepts of "the good" and of " justice" according to Rawls (Rawls 1971, pp. 396–397), while "less or more unjust" is derived from Sen, as mentioned in Sect. C.4.

[50]Our framework follows John Rawls' difference principle in that securing basic well-being of the least advantaged respective to each policy is necessary and sufficient for achieving the social goal of securing basic well-being for all. Yet, although Rawls' model assumes inter-personal level-comparability for society as a whole, our model starts from the possibility of different types of "the least advantaged" derived from different types of disadvantages.

[51]Note that the line of research on ranking opportunity sets initiated by Pattanaik and Xu (1990) also does not presume completeness of binary relations over opportunity sets.

for **SRF**s within this framework. **NR** requires that **SRF**s should give priority to a disadvantaged group's evaluation whenever any other groups' evaluations are not completely opposite to this group's, while **WP** requires that **SRF**s should treat every individual's appraisal symmetrically.

Given the possibility of a prior treatment of disadvantaged groups, we introduce domain conditions of group evaluations to restrict groups' " decisive powers" so as not to depart from the general societal goal. We name the domain conditions the *basic well-being condition*, the *restricted monotonicity*, and the *refrain condition*. These conditions together stipulate that any specific disadvantaged group should evaluate social state x as "more just" than social state y whenever (i) its least advantaged members' well-being contents under x (*resp.* y) are better or at least not worse (*resp.* not better or even worse) than under basic well-being; or (ii) its least advantaged members' well-being contents are better under x than under y, given that their respective well-being contents are worse under x and y respectively than under basic well-being. Moreover, this group should refrain from comparing x and y whenever its least advantaged members' well-being contents are better under x and y respectively than under basic well-being.

An interesting question is to examine the general existence of an **SRF** satisfying the three domain conditions as well as the two basic axioms. On the one hand, such an existence problem may have some similarity to the dominance and context-dependence paradox observed by Pattanaik and Xu (2007; 2012). As a typical example of this kind of paradox, recall the Pareto-liberal paradox initiated by Sen (1970), which points out the incompatibility of minimal liberty and the Pareto principle, where the former is formulated as the local decisiveness of some individuals, while the latter is formulated as the global decisiveness of all individuals. Incidentally, in our framework, the three conditions of group evaluations and **NR** together imply that a disadvantaged group is given locally decisive power, in a weak sense,[52] over the specific pairs of alternatives.

On the other hand, the existence issue of **SRF**s should not be argued analogical to the original Pareto-liberal paradox. For, firstly, the locally decisive power of a disadvantaged group is much weaker than the standard notion of local decisive power discussed in Arrow (1951/1963) and Sen (1970); secondly, the least advantaged members of each group may vary owing to the change of social policies, which makes it more complicated to identify each group evaluation; and finally, the domain of **SRF**s is not universal but restricted by the three conditions. Moreover, among other things, the key factor of this existence issue is the incompleteness of binary relations as the informational basis of **SRF**s.[53] In fact, our paper shows the extent to which the incompleteness of group appraisals is acceptable so as not to rule out the existence of **SRF**s that are compatible with **NR** and **WP**.

---

[52]The intention of "in a weak sense" here is that this group's 'local decisiveness' over such pairs is conditional on there being no resistance of any other groups.

[53]Incompleteness of binary relations as the informational basis is not assumed in the context of the Pareto-liberal paradox as well as other types of the dominance and context-dependence paradox discussed by Pattanaik and Xu (2012).

In the following discussion, Sect. C.2 provides remarks on the concept of "group" with regard to the aim of securing basic well-being for all. Section C.3 provides the basic **SRF** framework and sect. C.4 the three conditions for group evaluations and the relevant two axioms. Section C.5 discusses the existence problem of **SRF** s satisfying these properties. Section C.6 provides some philosophical implications of this paper, and Sect. C.7 concludes the paper.

C.2 Group Characteristics: Differences in " Basic Well-being" and the Corresponding Conceptions of Justice

As mentioned in Sect. C.1, basic well-being represents a critical reference point that one can legitimately claim to have met by social policies. Assuming three types of disadvantages, this section illustrates the differences in the contents of basic well-being and in their corresponding conceptions of justice.

The first type of disadvantage is closely related to what Aristotle called " corrective justice." It is based on recognizing the cause of the suffered disadvantage as an injustice that needs to be redressed. Examples are disadvantages that derive from historical injustices such as colonial exploitation and the ill-treatment of indigenous populations and victims of social diseases. The corresponding conception of justice in contemporary context is, for example, Robert Nozick's discussion on historical injustice (Nozick 1974).

The second type of disadvantage is related to the concept of " justice as compensation." This concept implies that individuals should be recognized as disadvantaged if their vulnerability is due to the failure of social institutions to protect them from " undeserved inequalities," such as persons with disabilities or certain diseases, or those discriminated on the basis of age, nationality, gender, or being a single parent. This concept is supported by the recent discussion on " compensation and responsibility."[54]

The third type of disadvantage relates to the concept of " justice as protection." This concept considers it unjust that some individuals have less than what is necessary for a minimum standard of living.[55] It focuses on individuals, unlike the first two concepts, whose specific causes of difficulties can be hard to identify. The corresponding conception of justice is the behind idea of Rawls's difference principle, which takes a form of outcome equality and requires bringing every individual up to a reference point (Rawls 1993).

Because of this diversity of disadvantages and of the forms of justice underlying them, the concrete conception of basic well-being becomes plural. Moreover, under a common concept of basic well-being, special needs must be addressed relative to the

[54] Refer to, for example, Fleurbaey (1994) and Fleurbaey and Maniquet (2011).

[55] For example, article 25 of the Japanese Constitution stipulates " the right to the minimum standards of wholesome and cultured living.".

different types of disadvantages. To demonstrate this, consider some examples of each disadvantage type. Individuals who have suffered historical injustice due to an atomic bomb, an event that completely changed their life-goals, are affected by the first type of disadvantage. Many have decided to live as witnesses of this social disaster in order to prevent it from ever happening again at any other place or time. In such cases, air tickets to fly to New York, which holds the "No more Hiroshima/Nagasaki Congress," or a grant for publishing their memoirs may be counted as a necessity for securing their basic well-being. Similarly, with respect to the second type of disadvantage, fundamental freedoms should be promoted, protected, and ensured for individuals with disabilities to function as active members of society. For example, for individuals using the wheelchair, one of the essential claims to secure basic well-being would be to remove environmental barriers such as inaccessible buses or staircases. Finally, for individuals affected by the third disadvantage type, such as the homeless, it is important to claim basic needs including food, closing, shelter, and health care to protect their right to the minimum standards of wholesome and cultured living as a means to secure basic well-being.

Lastly, it should be noted that an individual might actually suffer from all three types of disadvantages mentioned above and as a result will be included in each of the three groups. This implies that such an individual's basic well-being consists of three aspects that cannot be compared intra-personally, while each of the three aspects permits inter-personal comparison within each group. In this case, the individual can participate in the process of making an evaluation of each group, also deserving to take advantage of social policies addressing all three types of disadvantages, although the actual amount of provision might be reduced considering combination effects of the three policies.

C.3 The Basic Model

Consider a society with population $N = \{1, 2, ..., i, ..., n\}$, where $2 \leq n < +\infty$. Let us denote a *social state* by x, and the set of all possible social states by X, where $3 \leq \#X < +\infty$. Each $x \in X$ may be interpreted as representing an admissible social policy. Thus, we sometimes call each $x \in X$ a *social policy* x. Note that a social policy x does not necessarily represent a single policy. For instance, it may present a bundle of multiple social policies or a state of resource allocation realized by a certain bundle of social policies.

For each $i \in N$, let Z_i be a product of subsets of metric spaces, which represents the *set of conceivable well-being contents for* i. Let $Z \equiv \cup_{i \in N} Z_i$. For each $i \in N$, let i's *well-being transformation* be a mapping $C_i : X \to Z_i$ such that for each $x \in X$, $C_i(x)$ is a vector in Z_i.[56] C_i represents an individual's ability to transform each social policy to a content of well-being and $C_i(x)$ represents individual i's well-being

[56] Although C_i (x) is formulated as a vector in Z_i, this formulation may allow an interpretation that Z_i is a Hausdorff topological space whose elements are all non-empty, compact, and comprehensive subsets of $\mathbb{R}^m_+$, and each C_i $(x) \in Z_i$ represents i's *capability* (Sen, 1980; 1985) associated with

available under the social policy x. Let $\mathbf{C} \equiv (C_i)_{i \in N}$ be a profile of the well-being transformations.

Given Z, for each $i \in N$, let us define a binary relation $\succsim_i$ on Z, which is *reflexive* and *transitive*. We call this $\succsim_i$ a *well-being appraisal of i*. The interpretation of the well-being appraisal $\succsim_i$ is that, for any $C, C' \in Z$, $C \succsim_i C'$ if and only if C is at least as good as C' for i. Given $\succsim_i$ defined on Z, let $C \succ_i C'$ if and only if $C \succsim_i C'$ holds but $C' \succsim_i C$ does not hold; let $C \sim_i C'$ if and only if $C \succsim_i C'$ and $C' \succsim_i C$ hold. If Z is a partially ordered set endowed with a partial ordering $\geq$ on Z,[57] it may be assumed that for any $i \in N$ and any $C, C' \in Z$, if $C \geq C'$, then $C \succsim_i C'$, and if $C > C'$, then $C \succ_i C'$. The well-being appraisal $\succsim_i$ reflects a bundle of criteria for comparing i's well-being contents.

Next, let us define the concept of group. Given society N, there exists a set of characteristics T with generic element t such that (1) $0 < \#T \leqq \#N$; and (2) for each $t \in T$, there exists a unique subset N^t of N. Note that N^t may be empty for some $t \in T$, and N^t may be identical to N for some $t \in T$. Each group $t \in T$ is characterized by a type of conceivable disadvantage, t, and the set of group members, N^t contains all t-type disadvantaged individuals in society$N$.[58] Thus, $N \backslash \left(\cup_{t \in T} N^t\right)$ represents the set of non-disadvantaged individuals in society N.[59]

C.3.1 *Definition of Group Appraisals, Group Evaluations, and Social Relation Functions*

C.3.1.1 Group Appraisals

Again as argued in Sect. C.1, it is assumed that each group t is able to construct a criterion for comparing their well-being contents, which is shared by every member of this group, due to the commonality of disadvantages. Such a shared criterion for comparing well-being contents in group t is formulated by the intersection of all members' well-being appraisals, $\succsim_t \equiv \cap_{i \in N^t} \succsim_i$, which is called hereafter a *well-being appraisal of group t*. To represent a feature of the shared criterion of all of its

---

the social policy x, as Herrero (1996) and Gotoh and Yoshihara (2003) did. Basu and Lopez-Calva (2011) provide an illuminating survey on the formulation of functionings and capabilities.

[57]The precise definitions of $\geq$ and its asymmetric part $>$ depend on the mathematical structure of the space Z. For instance, if each C represents a vector on $Z \subseteq \mathbb{R}^m_+$, then $(\geq, >)$ represents the standard *vector inequality*. If each C represents a compact and comprehensive subset in $\mathbb{R}^m_+$, so that $Z \subseteq 2^{\mathbb{R}^m_+} \backslash \varnothing$, then $(\geq, >)$ represents the standard *set-inclusion* as $C \geq C'$ if and only if for any $z \in C'$, $z \in C$ holds; and $C > C'$ if and only if $C \geq C'$ and $C' \not\geq C$.

[58]As argued in Sect. C.1, each group is assumed to be a maximum unit that can share a concrete content of basic well-being and can identify the least advantaged among its members. In this sense, we can include as a member of this group a person who ethically accepts the criteria shared by other members, whether he/she actually has the same disadvantage or not.

[59]This formuation allows a possibility that there exist $t, t' \in T$ such that $N^t \cap N^{t'} \neq \varnothing$.

members, $\succsim_t$ is assumed to be non-empty for each $t \in T$.[60] Note that, since each $\succsim_i$ is reflexive and transitive, so is the well-being appraisal of each group. Finally, let $\succsim \equiv \left((\succsim_i)_{i \in N}, (\succsim_t)_{t \in T}\right)$ be a *profile of well-being appraisals*.[61] Denote the admissible set of profiles of well-being appraisals by $\mathcal{A}$.

C.3.1.2 The Least Advantaged in Each Group and the Basic Well-Being

With the well-being appraisal of the group, the least advantaged within the group can be defined as follows. Given society N and a profile of well-being appraisals $\succsim \in \mathcal{A}$, the *set of the least advantaged individuals of type t under social policy* $x \in X$ is defined by

$$L^t(x; \succsim_t) \equiv \left\{ i \in N^t \mid \nexists j \in N^t : C_i(x) \succ_t C_j(x) \right\}.$$

That is, the least advantaged under social policy x is defined as an individual whose well-being content never dominates the well-being contents of others. Note that $L^t(x; \succsim_t)$ is non-empty for each $x \in X$ and for each $t \in T$ with $N^t \neq \varnothing$. Moreover, it is not necessarily a singleton.

While the set of the least advantaged individuals $L^t(x; \succsim_t)$ specifies the relatively least position of individuals within the gruop, it does not refer to their absolute well-being conditions. To refer to this point, the concept of *basic well-being* $BC^t \in Z$, which is unique to each $t \in T$, is introduced. As argued in Sect. C.1, BC^t is a reference well-being content that one can legitimately claim to have met by social policies, and each group can refer to it to identify the "injustice" of social policies. In other words, the group should concern about its members' absolute well-being conditions in comarison with the basic well-being BC^t.

When making an appraisal of the well-being contents of the least advantaged members in comparison with the basic well-being, the group appraisal should respect such members' own appraisals of their own well-being contents in comparison with the basic well-being. That is, for any group t and any individual i of the least advantaged members within the group t at the social state x, this individual's appraisal $\succsim_i$ should be respected in the group appraisal $\succsim_t$ at least over the comparison of her well-being $C_i(x)$ under x with the basic well-being BC^t of the group. To ensure this property, the following assumption is imposed on group appraisals:
For each $x \in X$, each $t \in T$, and each $i \in L^t\left(x; \succsim_t\right)$, if $\left[BC^t \succsim_i C_i(x)\right]$ (resp. $\left[C_i(x) \succsim_i BC^t\right]$), then $\left[BC^t \succsim_t C_i(x)\right]$ (resp. $\left[C_i(x) \succsim_t BC^t\right]$) holds.

---

[60] The idea behind this formulation is that each individual of each group appraises the well-being contents of the members of the group, including her own, not in terms of a personal conception of the good but in terms of a shared conception of the good, on the basis of some commonality among members.

[61] In this case, as it is argued in footnote 14, it is possible that there exist $t, t' \in T$ such that there exists $i \in N^t \cap N^{t'}$ with $N^t \backslash N^{t'} \neq \varnothing$ and $N^{t'} \backslash N^t \neq \varnothing$. In this case, it is still possible that $\succsim_t \neq \succsim_{t'}$ (or even $\succsim_t \cap \succsim_{t'} = \varnothing$) while $\succsim_i \supseteq \succsim_t$ and $\succsim_i \supseteq \succsim_{t'}$.

This assumption, combined with the definition of $\succsim_t$, implies that the appraisal by the least advantaged individual of his/her own well-being condition in comparison with the basic well-being is approved by all other members of the same group, in that all of them do not reveal the opposite appraisal of this individual's well-being in comparison with the basic well-being.

C.3.1.3 Group Evaluations

While the group appraisal of each group is used to identify the least advantaged individuals among the group members, each group is also assumed to evaluate alternative social policies in order to improve the well-being of the least advantaged members. Such a scheme of evaluation is defined as a binary relation over the set of social policies X, which is formulated as follows. Given society N and a profile of well-being appraisals $\succsim \in \mathcal{A}$, for each $t \in T$, the *group evaluation* of type t is defined as a *reflexive* relation R^t on X, where let P^t be defined as the strict part of R^t. Likewise, let I^t be the indifferent part of R^t. Moreover, let NR^t denote the *non-comparable part* of R^t; that is, $xNR^t y$ if and only if neither $xR^t y$ nor $yR^t x$. The interpretation of R^t is that it represents an evaluation of alternative social policies, which is defined on the domain respective to this group, and which can be agreed upon by all individuals in this group, N^t. Given society N and a profile of well-being appraisals $\succsim \in \mathcal{A}$, let us denote the admissible class of such group evaluations of type t on X by $D^t(\succsim_t)$. Moreover, let $D(\succsim) \equiv \times_{t \in T} D^t(\succsim_t)$ and $R^T \equiv (R^t)_{t \in T}$.

C.3.1.4 Social Relation Functions

With this basic framework, we are ready to formally define our scheme of social choice rules as follows:

Definition 1 *Given a society N with a profile of well-being transformations* **C**, *the* social relation function (**SRF**) *is the mapping F, which associates each well-being appraisal $\succsim \in \mathcal{A}$ and each profile of group evaluations $R^T \in D(\succsim)$ to the reflexive and transitive relation R on X.*

R is called a *social evaluation over X* in a society.

By assuming that disadvantaged groups are given prior treatment in incorporating their information into a social policy, the two types of informational bases for disadvantaged groups, namely group appraisals and group evaluations, may play different functional roles. Group appraisals are necessary to identify the least advantaged members in each group on the basis of its own conception of the good. Each group evaluation is formed on the basis of its own group appraisal by focusing on the least advantaged members of this group. The policy maker can choose appropriate social policies based on the social evaluation derived from the **SRF**, into which she can incorporate each individual's appraisal as well as each disadvantaged group's evaluation.

C.4 Axioms for Group Evaluations and Social Relation Functions

In this section, we define several conditions assumed to be publicly imposed on **SRF**s.

C.4.1 Axioms for Group Evaluations

A part of such conditions is to restrict the available class of group evaluations. As argued in Sect. C.1, the group evaluation is introduced to evaluate alternative social policies in order to ensure that the well-being contents of the least advantaged members of the group is not worse than the basic well-being. We incorporate this idea as domain conditions of **SRF**s in this section.

Firstly, with the concept of *basic well-being* $BC^t \in Z$, for each $t \in T$, let the domain of group evaluations be classified for each $\succsim \in \mathcal{A}$, each $t \in T$ and each $x, y \in X$ as follows.

- Case α**-1).** $C_i(x) \succsim_t BC^t$ for all $i \in L^t\left(x; \succsim_t\right)$, and $BC_t^t \succsim_t C_j(y)$ for all $j \in L^t\left(y; \succsim_t\right)$;
- Case α**-2).** Case α**-1)** holds and moreover, $C_i(x) \succ_t BC^t$ for all $i \in L^t(x; \succsim_t)$ or $BC^t \succ_t C_j(y)$ for all $j \in L^t(y; \succsim_t)$;
- Case β). $C_i(x) \succsim_t BC^t$ for all $i \in L^t(x; \succsim_t)$, and *not* $\left[BC^t \succsim_t C_j(y)\right]$ & *not* $\left[C_j(y) \succsim_t BC^t\right]$ for some $j \in L^t\left(y; \succsim_t\right)$;
- Case γ). *not* $\left[BC^t \succsim_t C_i(x)\right]$ & *not* $\left[C_i(x) \succsim_t BC^t\right]$ for some $i \in L^t\left(x; \succsim_t\right)$, and $BC^t \succ_t C_j(y)$ for all $j \in L^t(y; \succsim_t)$;
- Case δ). $BC^t \succ_t C_i(x)$ for all $i \in L^t\left(x; \succsim_t\right)$, and $BC^t \succ_t C_j(y)$ for all $j \in L^t(y; \succsim_t)$;
- Case ϵ). $C_i(x) \succ_t BC^t$ for all $i \in L^t\left(x; \succsim_t\right)$, and $C_j(y) \succ_t BC^t$ for all $j \in L^t\left(y; \succsim_t\right)$;
- Case ε). Otherwise.

That is, Case α-1) refers to the domain where the least advantaged individuals' well-beings in policy x are all at least as good as basic well-being, while the least advantaged individuals' well-beings in policy y are all at least as bad as their basic well-being. Case α-2) refers to the domain where α-1) applies, and the least advantaged individuals' well-beings in policy x are all better than basic well-being, or the least advantaged individuals' well-beings in policy y are all worse than basic well-being. Case β) refers to the domain where the least advantaged individuals' well-beings in policy x are *either* all better than basic well-being *or* all indifferent to basic well-being , while at least one of the least advantaged individuals' well-beings in policy y is non-comparable with basic well-being. Case γ) refers to the domain where at least one of the least advantaged individuals' well-beings in policy x is non-comparable with their basic well-being, while the least advantaged individuals' well-beings in policy y are all worse than their basic well-being . Case δ) refers to the domain where the least advantaged individuals' well-beings are all worse than their basic well-being in both policies x and y. Case ϵ) refers to the domain where the least advantaged individuals' well-beings in both policies x and y are all better than their basic well-being.

Based on this classification, let us introduce three conditions imposed on group evaluations, which result in restricting the domain of the **SRF** F.

Basic Well-being Condition (BWC): For each $\succsim \in \mathcal{A}$, and each $t \in T$, and for each $x, y \in X$, $x R^t y$ (*resp.* $x P^t y$) holds if (x, y) corresponds to at least one of cases α**-1)** (*resp.* α-2), β), and γ).

Restricted Monotonicity (RM): For each $\succsim \in \mathcal{A}$, and each $t \in T$, and for each $x, y \in X$, $x R^t y$ (*resp.* $x P^t y$) holds if (x, y) corresponds to case δ), and $C_i(x) \succsim_t C_j(y)$ (*resp.* $C_i(x) \succ_t C_j(y)$) holds for all $i \in L^t(x; \succsim_t)$ and all $j \in L^t(y; \succsim_t)$.

Refrain Condition (RC): For each $\succsim \in \mathcal{A}$, and each $t \in T$, and for each $x, y \in X$ with $x \neq y$, $x N R^t y$ holds if (x, y) corresponds to either case ϵ) or case ε).

BWC requires each group to evaluate a social policy x, under which the well-being contents of the least advantaged are at least as good as their basic well-being, as being *more just* than another social policy y, under which the well-being contents of the least advantaged *either* fall beneath their basic well-being *or* cannot be compared with it. Furthermore, it requires each group to evaluate a social policy y, under which the well-being contents of the least advantaged fall beneath their basic well-being, as being *less just* than another social policy x in which the well-being contents of the least advantaged cannot be compared with their basic well-being.

RM requires each group to evaluate a social policy x as being *more just* than another social policy y whenever the corresponding profile of the least advantaged members' well-beings is better in x than y, given that all of their well-being contents derived from both policies fall beneath their basic well-being. **RM** represents a kind of monotonicity criterion,[62] although its applicability is constrained to a proper domain of alternatives.

Lastly, **RC** requires a group evaluation *not* to make pair-wise rankings of the social policies if the well-being contents of the least advantaged corresponding to these social policies are better than their basic well-being or they cannot be compared with their basic well-being.[63]

Thus, the three conditions together define the available class of group evaluations, which make their rankings over pairs of social policies deserve being called *more* or *less unjust*. The last comparative adjective is motivated from the " comparative approach to justice" proposed by Sen in place of a " transcendental approach to justice" (Sen 2009a, pp. 15–18, Sen 2009b, p. 46f.). According to Sen, the latter is a traditional approach in ethics, which focuses on the description of an ideal just

---

[62]The concept of dominance proposed by Pattanaik and Xu (2007, p. 361–362), which is closely related to Sen's idea of " dominance partial ordering" (Sen 1987, pp. 29–30) is a good example.

[63]This condition is similar to the "focus axiom" proposed by Sen (1981; p. 186), which requests that the difference between two social states, both of which bring about capabilities at least as good as basic capability, is not reflected in the social evaluation. We are grateful to James Foster and Prasanta Pattanaik for pointing this out. See Foster (1984; p. 217) and Sen (1997; p. 172).

state, while the former is a new approach in ethics, which ranks alternative social states in terms of justice but does not necessarily identify an ideal just state. The three conditions constitute an attempt to formulate a " comparative approach to justice," in that they together make the available group evaluations consistent with the common goal of securing basic well-being for all members of each group, on the one hand by identifying " unjust" policies as those fall short of basic well-being and comparing them with one another to make evaluations of them as "less unjust" or " more unjust," on the other hand by refraining from identifying any of the policies as ideal just when they warrant everyone's well-being beyond basic well-being.

We examine the mutual consistency of these three conditions.

Lemma 1 *Let the reflexive R^t satisfy **BWC**, **RM**, and **RC**. Then, it is transitive.*

Due to this lemma, each group can form its own evaluation based on the three conditions that are rational in terms of logical consistency.

C.4.2 Axioms for Social Relation Functions

The next task for us is to introduce two basic axioms regarding how to aggregate plural group evaluations as well as diverse individual well-being appraisals in order to form a consistent social evaluation. To explore this problem, let us introduce the following conditions.

Non-negative Response (NR): For each $\succsim \in \mathcal{A}$, each $R^T \in D(\succsim)$, and each $x, y \in X$, if there exists $t' \in T$ such that $x R^{t'} y$ (*resp.* $x P^{t'} y$) and there exists no $t'' \in T$ such that $y P^{t''} x$, then xRy (*resp.* xPy) holds, where $R = F(\succsim, R^T)$.

Weak Pareto (WP): For each $\succsim \in \mathcal{A}$, each $R^T \in D\left(\succsim\right)$, and each $x, y \in X$, if $C_i(x) \succ_i C_i(y)$ holds for all $i \in N$, then xPy holds, where $R = F(\succsim, R^T)$.

Recall that each $t \in T$ represents a particular type of disadvantage, so $N \setminus \left(\cup_{t \in T} N^t\right)$ is the set of non-disadvantaged individuals in society N. Hence, **NR** requires giving priority to the evaluations of disadvantaged groups over the evaluations of non-disadvantaged individuals in the aggregation procedure, while there is no priority rule in the treatments of evaluations among the different disadvantaged groups. That is, even if the well-being contents of all non-disadvantaged individuals become worse in y than in x, the social evaluation must be that y is at least as just as x whenever a group t evaluates y as being at least as just as x and no other group evaluates x as *more just* than y. Such a requirement seems quite reasonable whenever persons with a particular disadvantage can be considered as "experts" on that disadvantage and these persons are expected to provide a reasonable group evaluation. In this respect, **NR** together with the available class of group evaluations constrained by **BWC**, **RM**, and **RC** warrant the reasonableness of preferential treatments of specific types of groups in the aggregation procedure.

In contrast, **WP** requires no prior treatment of any particular individuals' appraisals. It simply states that, if the well-being contents of all individuals are better in x than in

y, then the social evaluation must be that x is more just than y. In terms of respecting the plurality of the conceptions of the good, **WP** also seems quite reasonable.

It is also worth mentioning that, although **WP** is a weaker condition of welfarism, the requirement of **NR** with the scheme of group evaluations makes **SRF**s *non-welfaristic*. To see this point, remember that the neutrality property of social choice rules is necessary for welfarism in the standard Arrovian framework.[64] In our framework, *neutrality* of **SRF**s is defined as follows: for every $x, y, z, w \in X$, and for any two profiles of well-being appraisals $\succsim, \succsim' \in \mathcal{A}$, if $[C_i(x) \succsim_i C_i(y)$ if and only if $C_i(z) \succsim_i' C_i(w)]$ holds for every $i \in N$, then $[xRy$ if and only if $zR'w]$ holds, where $R = F(\succsim, R^T)$ and $R' = F(\succsim', R'^T)$.

The following example shows that if **SRF**s satisfies **NR** with the scheme of group evaluations satisfying **BWC**, **RM**, and **RC**, then it does not satisfy neutrality.

Example 1 Let $N = \{1, 2, 3, 4\}$, $T = \{t^1, t^2, t^3\}$ with $N^{t^1} = \{1\}$, $N^{t^2} = \{2\}$, and $N^{t^3} = \{3\}$, and $X = \{x, y, z, w\}$. Let us define two profiles of well-being appraisals $\succsim, \succsim' \in \mathcal{A}$ as follows:

$$C_i(z) \succ_i C_i(x) \succ_i BC^{t^i} \succ_i C_i(w) \succ_i C_i(y) \text{ for } i \in \{1, 3\};$$
$$C_2(w) \succ_2 C_2(z) \succ_2 BC^{t^2} \succ_2 C_2(x) \succ_2 C_2(y);$$
$$C_4(x) \succ_4 C_4(y) \succ_4 C_4(w) \succ_4 C_4(z); \text{ and}$$

$\succsim_{t^i} = \succsim_i$ for $i \in \{1, 2, 3\}$, and

$$C_i(x) \succ_i' C_i(z) \succ_i' BC^{t^i} \succ_i' C_i(w) \succ_i' C_i(y) \text{ for } i \in \{1, 3\};$$
$$C_2(z) \succ_2' C_2(w) \succ_2' BC^{t^2} \succ_2' C_2(x) \succ_2' C_2(y);$$
$$C_4(z) \succ_4' C_4(y) \succ_4' C_4(w) \succ_4' C_4(x); \text{ and}$$

$\succsim_{t^i}' = \succsim_i'$ for $i \in \{1, 2, 3\}$. Given this structure, note that $[C_i(z) \succsim_i C_i(w)$ if and only if $C_i(x) \succsim_i' C_i(z)]$ holds for every $i \in N$. Therefore, if an **SRF** F satisfies neutrality, then $[zRw$ if and only if $xR'z]$ must hold, where $R = F(\succsim, R^T)$ and $R' = F(\succsim', R'^T)$. In contrast, by **BWC**, $C_1(z) \succ_{t^1} BC^{t^1} \succ_{t^1} C_1(w)$ implies $zP^{t^1}w$, and $C_3(z) \succ_{t^3} BC^{t^3} \succ_{t^3} C_3(w)$ implies $zP^{t^3}w$; while by **RC**, $C_2(w) \succ_2 C_2(z) \succ_2 BC^{t^2}$ implies $zNP^{t^2}w$. Similarly, by **BWC**, $C_2(z) \succ_2' BC^{t^2} \succ_2' C_2(x)$ implies $zP'^{t^2}x$; while by **RC**, $C_1(x) \succ_1' C_1(z) \succ_1' BC^{t^1}$ implies $zNP'^{t^1}x$, and $C_3(x) \succ_3' C_3(z) \succ_3' BC^{t^3}$ implies $zNP'^{t^3}x$. Therefore, zPw and $zP'x$, where $R = F(\succsim, R^T)$ and $R' = F(\succsim', R'^T)$, hold by **NR**. Thus, this F does not satisfy neutrality. ■

---

[64]The basic idea of neutrality can be summarized as follows: if the individual preferences over (x, y) in one case are "identical" to the individual preferences over (a, b) in another case, then the social preference in the latter would place a and b respectively where x and y figured in the former (Sen 2002; p. 333). See Fleurbaey and Mongin (2005; p. 386) for an excellent survey of studies on neutrality. As pointed out, Sen has examined the essential nature of neutrality in terms of " welfarism" (e.g., Sen 1970, Chs. 5 and 5*).

In summary, the group evaluations scheme constrained by **BWC**, **RM**, and **RC** and the axiom **NR** together imply non-welfarism.

C.5 On (Im)possibility of Social Relation Functions

The aim of this section is to verify the possibility of an **SRF** satisfying **NR** and **WP** under the constraints of **BWC**, **RM**, and **RC** on group evaluations. This is a legitimate and interesting question when a social choice problem is to select a public policy to secure basic well-being for all in a democratic way while admitting a prior treatment of disadvantaged individuals. Indeed, **NR** specifies under what conditions as well as to what extent some of disadvantaged individuals should be entitled to receive the prior treatments based on their group evaluations. In contrast, **WP** equally treats every individual's appraisal and, moreover, there is no constraint for the application of this principle. Therefore, **NR** and **WP** represent mutually different principles, though they are respectively weak as the claims for the local decisiveness of specific as well as of all individuals. Then, provided that the group evaluations satisfy **BWC**, **RM**, and **RC**, it is not obvious whether the compatibility of **WP** and **NR** is verified.

We examine, in the first step, whether or not there exists an **SRF** that satisfies **NR**. To do this, we introduce another axiom, the *Positive Response* (**PR**), which is even weaker than **NR**. Proposition 1 discussed below shows that there is no **SRF** that satisfies **PR**.

Therefore, in the second step, to avoid this negative result, we introduce an additional condition, *Full Comparability of Destitution* (**FCD**), which insures the full comparability of policies when the well-beings of all of the least advantaged members become worse than their basic well-being. Proposition 2 proves that under the presumption of **FCD**, there exists an **SRF** that satisfies **NR**.

However, in the third step, we show in Theorem 1 that it is impossible to guarantee the compatibility of **NR**and **WP** even under the presumption of **FCD**. Given these results, Theorem 2 clarifies what kind of further condition is required for the compatibility of these two axioms.

Assume, for the sake of simplicity, that the profile of the disadvantaged groups $\left(N^t\right)_{t\in T}$ is fixed independent of the types of **SRF**s. As our first step, let us introduce the following axiom for **SRF**s:

Positive Response (PR): For each $\succsim\in \mathcal{A}$, each $R^T \in D(\succsim)$, and each $x, y \in X$, if there exists $t' \in T$ such that $xP^{t'}y$ and there is no $t'' \in T$ such that $yP^{t''}x$, then xPyholds, where $R = F(\succsim, R^T)$.

PR is a weaker version of **NR**. This condition, as well as **NR**, seems quite reasonable, given that persons with a particular disadvantage can be considered as "experts" on that disadvantage.

Then,

Proposition 1 *There exists a profile of well-being appraisals $\succsim$ under which no **SRF** F satisfies **PR**.*

This impossibility holds whenever there are at least three different disadvantaged groups, $t^1, t^2, t^3 \in T$, and also at least three alternatives, $x, y, z \in X$. To focus on the simplest case, let there be no other group, $T = \{t^1, t^2, t^3\}$, and each of the three groups have only one member, $N^{t^i} = \{i\}$ for $i = 1, 2, 3$. Then, each individual $i = 1, 2, 3$ is also the least advantaged member of her group, and her appraisal is identical to her group's appraisal.

Given this setting, assume that the well-being contents of all the three individuals under any of the three alternatives are worse than their corresponding basic well-being contents: $BC^{t^i} \succ_{t^i} C_i(w)$ for any $w \in \{x, y, z\}$ and for each $i = 1, 2, 3$. Moreover, assume that, according to group t^1's appraisal, x is better than y, y and z are non-comparable, and z and x are non-comparable; according to group t^2's appraisal, y is better than z, z and x are non-comparable, and x and y are non-comparable; and according to group t^3's appraisal, z is better than x, x and y are non-comparable, and so are y and z. Then, **RM** implies that $xP^{t^1}y$, $yP^{t^2}z$, and $zP^{t^3}x$. Moreover, let $yNR^{t^1}z$ and $zNR^{t^1}x$; $zNR^{t^2}x$ and $xNR^{t^2}y$; and $xNR^{t^3}y$ and $yNR^{t^3}z$. Such group evaluations are available due to the assumptions of the three groups' appraisals. However, by **PR**, the corresponding social evaluation R should have xPy, yPz, and zPx, which implies that there is no **SRF** satisfying **PR**.

The above arguments indicate that the incompleteness of group appraisals is the key factor to generate such a cyclical social evaluation.[65] Given this impossibility, let us introduce an additional condition on well-being appraisals:

Full Comparability of Destitution (*FCD*): For each $t \in T$ and each $x, y \in X$, if case δ) applies, then for all $i \in L^t(x; \succsim_t)$ and all $j \in L^t(y; \succsim_t)$, $C_i(x) \succsim_t C_j(y)$ or $C_j(y) \succsim_t C_i(x)$.

Case δ) is the situation where in each policy, the well-being contents of the least advantaged are all worse than their basic well-being. ***FCD*** requires that the well-beings of the least advantaged are all comparable when they are in such "destitution". This condition seems reasonable, since the plurality of evaluations over social policies tends to be reduced under a situation of " destitution." Moreover, it would be desirable that relatively "less unjust" policies can be selected under the situation of " destitution," and ***FCD*** insures the feasibility of such a social choice.

The next proposition proves that if we introduce ***FCD*** into the group appraisal, we can warrant the existence of an **SRF** F, which satisfies **NR**, a strong version of **PR**.

Proposition 2 *Let **FCD** hold. Then, there exists an **SRF** F that satisfies **NR**.*

To show Proposition 2, let us define F_{NR} as follows: for each $\succsim \in \mathcal{A}$, each $R^T \in D(\succsim)$, and each $x, y \in X$, $xR^{NR}y$ holds if and only if there exists $t' \in T$ such that $xR^{t'}y$ and there is no $t'' \in T$ such that $yP^{t''}x$, where $R^{NR} = F_{NR}(\succsim, R^T)$. This R^{NR} is shown to be transitive.

---

[65] Indeed, in the three-group and three-alternative example, for each group, if at least one non-comparable pair is changed to be comparable, then the cyclical social evaluation is no longer generated.

As $\boldsymbol{FCD}$ seems to be a strong condition, it is not so surprising that under this condition, the existence of **SRF** satisfying **NR** is ensured. A more interesting question is whether there exists an **SRF** satisfying **NR** and **WP** or not. Surprisingly, even under the strong assumption of $\boldsymbol{FCD}$, there is no **SRF** satisfying **NR** and **WP**, as the following theorem shows.

Theorem 1 *Suppose* $\boldsymbol{FCD}$*. Then, there exists a profile of well-being appraisals* $\succsim$ *under which no* ***SRF*** *satisfies* ***PR*** *and* ***WP***.

The essential factor to generate this theorem is that at least two least advantaged members may exist within a group under a social policy, whose well-being positions relative to basic well-being are different, and at least one of such members is no longer the least advantaged under another social policy. To see this, let us suppose that i and j are the least advantaged members within a group t, where i's well-being is worse than BC^t and j's well-being is non-comparable with BC^t in policy x, according to the group appraisal $\succsim_t$. Moreover, let us suppose that all individuals' well-being contents are improved as a result of the change from policy x to policy y, and j's well-being becomes better than BC^t in y, although i's is still worse than BC^t. Moreover, let i be the unique least advantaged member of the group t under y, so that j is no longer the least advantaged of this group. This situation corresponds to case γ), so **BWC** applies and this group evaluates that x is more just than y. Then, if no other groups make any objection, **PR** requires that x is better than y. Yet, **WP** requires that y is better than x.

This argument suggests that, unlike the Pareto-liberal paradox, **PR** and **WP** can be incompatible even if the social evaluation R is not requested to be acyclic. Note also that the existence of only one disadvantaged group is sufficient to generate this incompatibility; in contrast, in the Pareto-liberal paradox, at least two agents must exercise their local decisive powers to generate a conflict with the Pareto principle.

For the purpose of our four steps, let us introduce an additional condition that requires even greater comparability of each group's well-being appraisal:

Dominance (*D*): For each $t \in T$, each $x \in X$, and each $i, j \in N^t$, if $i, j \in L^t(x; \succsim_t)$, then $C_i(x) \sim_t C_j(x)$.

$\boldsymbol{D}$ states that for any social state $x \in X$, if there are two individuals who are both deemed least advantaged under this state, then their well-being contents are indifferent. It has the following interesting implication: for each $t \in T$, each $x \in X$, and each $i, j \in N^t$ with $i \in L^t(x; \succsim_t)$, if $BC^t \succ_t C_i(x)$ and *not* $BC^t \succsim_t C_j(x)$, then $C_j(x) \succ_t C_i(x)$. That is, if one well-being content is appraised to be worse than BC^t, while another is not, a comparative judgment should be made between the two, in that the latter is better than the former. Thus, $\boldsymbol{D}$ makes it impossible that j is deemed least advantaged if j's well-being content is non-comparable with basic well-being and there is another least advantaged member i whose well-being content is worse than basic well-being.

As argued above, the essential factor to derive the incompatibility between **NR** and **WP** was the existence of at least two least advantaged members within a group under a social policy, whose well-being positions relative to basic well-being are different.

The assumption of $\boldsymbol{D}$ excludes such a situation, and so it seems indispensable for the existence of **SRF** satisfying both of **NR** and **WP** . Indeed, the following theorem guarantees the existence of such an **SRF** F under the assumption of $\boldsymbol{D}$ in addition to $\boldsymbol{FCD}$:

Theorem 2 *Let* $\boldsymbol{FCD}$ *and* $\boldsymbol{D}$ *hold. Then, there exists an* ***SRF*** F *that satisfies* ***NR*** *and* ***WP****.*

To show Theorem 2, let us define F_{WP} as follows: for each $\precsim \in \mathcal{A}$, each $R^T \in D(\precsim)$, and each $x, y \in X$, $xP^{WP}y$ holds if and only if $C_i(x) \succ_i C_i(y)$ holds for all $i \in N$, and $xI^{WP}y$ holds if and only if $x = y$, where $R^{WP} = F_{WP}(\precsim, R^T)$. Moreover, let us define F_* as follows: for each $R^T \in D(\precsim)$, $F_*(\precsim, R^T) = R^*$, where $R^* \equiv R^{NR} \cup R^{WP}$.

In the following discussion, we show that this R^* is transitive. Let $(x, y), (y, z) \in R^*$. Then, there are the following four possible cases:

(1) $(x, y), (y, z) \in R^{NR}$;
(2) $(x, y), (y, z) \in R^{WP}$;
(3) $(x, y) \in R^{NR}$ and $(y, z) \in R^{WP}$; and
(4) $(x, y) \in R^{WP}$ and $(y, z) \in R^{NR}$.

Proposition 2 shows that if case (1) applies, $(x, z) \in R^{NR}$ holds. Moreover, it is easy to see that if case (2) applies, then $(x, z) \in R^{WP}$ holds. Next, let us consider cases (3) and (4):

Lemma 2 *For each* $\precsim \in \mathcal{A}$, *and each* $R^T \in D(\precsim)$, *if* $(x, y) \in R^{NR}$ *and* $(y, z) \in P^{WP}$, *then* $(x, z) \in P^*$.

Lemma 3 *For each* $\precsim \in \mathcal{A}$ *and each* $R^T \in D(\precsim)$, *if* $(x, y) \in P^{WP}$ *and* $(y, z) \in R^{NR}$, *then* $(x, z) \in P^*$.

Proof of Theorem 2 By **Lemmas 2** and **3**, it holds. ■

Theorem 1 indicates that, given the incompleteness of the informational basis, the moderate prior treatments of disadvantaged groups are unable to ensure consistent and Paretian social decision-making for social policies. This impossibility, however, does not necessarily imply that there is an *intrinsic* conflict between the claim of the prior treatment of specific individuals and the equal treatment of all. Rather, it may originate from a lack of sufficient information on the part of a disadvantaged group to make a deliberate appraisal of their own states. Indeed, as condition **D** and Theorem 2 show, the main reason for the impossibility is the existence of the least disadvantaged member whose well-being content is deemed non-comparable to basic well-being despite the existence of another least advantaged whose well-being content is deemed worse than basic well-being. If such "tentative" non-comparability can be resolved via further scrutiny of this member's condition, consistent and Paretian social decision-making for desired polices can be compatible with the prior treatment of specific people.[66] In other words, the difficulty of constructing the desired

[66]The notions of "tentative incompleteness" and "assertive incompleteness" are introduced by Sen, where the former consists of " some pairs of alternatives that are not yet ranked (although all may

social choice due to " tentative" non-comparability within the same disadvantaged group could be resolved by technical progress at least in the future, which should be discriminated from the more intrinsic types of impossibility problems.

It is also worth noting that, while $\boldsymbol{FCD}$ and $\boldsymbol{D}$ make any pairs of social policies satisfying cases α), β), γ), δ) of group evaluations comparable, the remaining non-comparable parts in group evaluations is " assertive" rather than " tentative" , as warranted by **RC** for group evaluations. Interestingly, however, such "assertive" non-comparability is also indispensable for the existence of **SRF**s satisfying **NR** and **WP**. Indeed, regardless of whether $\boldsymbol{FCD}$ and $\boldsymbol{D}$ are imposed, allowing comparability for group evaluations even within the domains of any pairs satisfying cases ϵ) and ε) may restore the incompatibility of **NR** and **WP**, as the following example suggests.

Example 2 Let $N = \{h, i^1, j^1, i^2, j^2\}, T = \{t^1, t^2\}$ with $N^{t^1} = \{i^1, j^1\}$ and $N^{t^2} = \{i^2, j^2\}$, and $X = \{x, y, z\}$. Let $Z \equiv \mathbb{R}^2$ and

$$\begin{aligned}
&C_{i^1}(x) = (4, 4)\,;\; C_{i^1}(y) = (1, 3.3)\,;\; C_{i^1}(z) = (5, 3)\,;\\
&C_{j^1}(x) = (3.9, 2)\,;\; C_{j^1}(y) = (2, 3.6)\,;\; C_{j^1}(z) = (6, 3.5)\,;\\
&C_{i^2}(x) = (4, 0.5)\,;\; C_{i^2}(y) = (3, 3)\,;\; C_{i^2}(z) = (1, 1)\,;\\
&C_{j^2}(x) = (5, 2)\,;\; C_{j^2}(y) = (1.5, 1.5)\,;\; C_{j^2}(z) = (1.5, 4)\,;\\
&C_h(x) = (6, 6)\,;\; C_h(y) = (5, 5)\,;\; C_h(z) = (4, 4)\,.
\end{aligned}$$

For each $k \in \{h, i^1, j^2\}$, let $\succsim_k$ be given by $C_k(v) \succsim_k C_k(u)$ if and only if $C_k(v) \geq C_k(u)$; and $C_k(v) \succ_k C_k(u)$ if and only if $C_k(v) > C_k(u)$, where $\geq$ (*resp.* $>$) is the vector inequality (*resp.* the strict vector inequality). For each $l \in \{j^1, i^2\}$, let $\succsim_l$ be given by $C_l(v) \succsim_l C_l(u)$ if and only if $(C_l(v))_1 \geq (C_l(u))_1$; and $C_l(v) \succ_l C_l(u)$ if and only if $(C_l(v))_1 > (C_l(u))_1$, where $(C_l(v))_1$ represents the first component of the vector $C_l(v)$. Finally, let $\succsim_{t^1} \equiv \succsim_{i^1}$ and $\succsim_{t^2} \equiv \succsim_{j^2}$. Moreover, let $BC^{t^1} \equiv (0, 0.5)$ and $BC^{t^2} \equiv (0.5, 0)$.

Given these settings, it follows that

$$\begin{aligned}
&C_\ell(x) \succ_\ell C_\ell(y) \text{ for all } \ell \in N;\\
&L^{t^1}(x; \succsim_{t^1}) = \{j^1\}\,;\; L^{t^1}(y; \succsim_{t^1}) = \{i^1\}\,;\; L^{t^1}(z; \succsim_{t^1}) = \{i^1\}\,;\text{ and}\\
&L^{t^2}(x; \succsim_{t^2}) = \{i^2\}\,;\; L^{t^2}(y; \succsim_{t^2}) = \{j^2\}\,;\; L^{t^2}(z; \succsim_{t^2}) = \{i^2\}\,.
\end{aligned}$$

Then,

$$not\left[C_{j^1}(x) \succsim_{t^1} C_{i^1}(y)\right] \;\&\; not\left[C_{i^1}(y) \succsim_{t^1} C_{j^1}(x)\right]$$

by $C_{j^1}(x) \ngeq C_{i^1}(y)$ & $C_{j^1}(x) \nleq C_{i^1}(y)$;

$$not\left[C_{i^1}(y) \succsim_{t^1} C_{i^1}(z)\right] \;\&\; not\left[C_{i^1}(z) \succsim_{t^1} C_{i^1}(y)\right]$$

---

get ranked with more deliberation or information)," while the latter consists of " some pairs of alternatives that are asserted to be 'non-rankable'" (Sen 2002, p. 182).

by $C_{i^1}(y) \not\geq C_{i^1}(z)$ & $C_{i^1}(y) \not\leq C_{i^1}(z)$; and

$$C_{i^1}(z) \succ_{t^1} C_{j^1}(x) \text{ by } C_{i^1}(z) > C_{j^1}(x).$$

Similarly,

$$not\left[C_{i^2}(x) \succsim_{t^2} C_{j^2}(y)\right] \ \& \ not\left[C_{j^2}(y) \succsim_{t^2} C_{i^2}(x)\right]$$

by $C_{i^2}(x) \not\geq C_{j^2}(y)$ & $C_{i^2}(x) \not\leq C_{j^2}(y)$;

$$not\left[C_{i^2}(x) \succsim_{t^2} C_{i^2}(z)\right] \ \& \ not\left[C_{i^2}(z) \succsim_{t^2} C_{i^2}(x)\right]$$

by $C_{i^2}(z) \not\geq C_{i^2}(x)$ & $C_{i^2}(z) \not\leq C_{i^2}(x)$; and

$$C_{j^2}(y) \succ_{t^2} C_{i^2}(z) \text{ by } C_{j^2}(y) > C_{i^2}(z).$$

Now, let R^{t^1} and R^{t^2} do not satisfy **RC**, and so $zP^{t^1}x$ and $yP^{t^2}z$, while $xNR^{t^1}y$, $yNR^{t^1}z$, $xNR^{t^2}y$, and $zNR^{t^2}x$. Then, **NR** implies that zPx and yPz, while xPy follows from **WP**, where $R = F(\succsim, R^T)$. Thus, R violates transitivity. ■

The above example implies that, under the imposition of $\boldsymbol{FCD}$ and $\boldsymbol{D}$, a further increase of comparable parts in group evaluations via the elimination of **RC** results in the impossibility of **SRF**s satisfying **NR** and **WP**.

C.6 Discussion

Before concluding the paper, we first comment on another prominent feature of our **SRF** framework. In Arrovian social welfare functions, a social choice is made simply on the basis of the structure of preference profiles announced by individuals and thus is independent of information on the characteristics of individuals and alternatives. Note that this property of Arrovian social welfare functions derives from the three conditions imposed by Arrow, namely the universal domain, the Pareto principle, and the independence of irrelevant alternatives. It is known that these three conditions lead to *neutrality* or *welfarism,* that is, these conditions together require that individuals' ordinal rankings of alternatives are the sole relevant information to make a social choice. This structure of Arrovian models well represents the spirit of traditional liberalism, which gives priority to individual autonomy and prohibits arbitrarily unequal treatment.[67] In contrast, in our **SRF**s, a social choice is made on the basis of not only the preference profiles expressed by individuals but also the information of the characteristics of individuals and of alternatives. We have shown that this change is a clue to avoid *welfaristic* nature of social choice. Besides, this

[67] According to Arrow," The decision as to which preferences are relevant and which are not is itself a value judgement and cannot be settled on an a priori basis" (Arrow 1963, p. 18).

formulation allows us to explore another possibility of liberalism, that is, substantive equality of political freedom that allows the preferential treatment of ordinal rankings. The reasonableness of such preferential treatment is ensured by the introduction of an explicit device for public scrutiny, which is represented in this paper by the observability of well-being indicators and the three-component structure of the informational basis.

Second, let us clarify the basic ideas underlying this paper. The first idea is relevant to two kinds of " incomparability." In this paper, the least advantaged are identified as individuals whose well-being contents never dominate the well-beings of others in each social policy. Due to the multiplicity of attributes that define the notion of well-being, there could remain incomparability among the least advantaged even within a group. However, the meaning of incomparability within a group should be kept distinct from incomparability (also called " incommensurability") between groups. The reason is that the former is a technical or political problem and certain conditions of compromise can be introduced to deal with it, as we have done by introducing ***FDC*** and ***D*** in this paper. On the other hand, the latter is a kind of incomparability for which no compromise can be found as long as the plurality of disadvantages is taken seriously. This distinction between these two forms of incomparability corresponds to the distinction introduced by Sen (2002) between "tentative incompleteness" and " assertive incompleteness."

The second idea concerns two types of conflicts between groups—one arises from each group's need to achieve basic well-being, while the other derives from each group's desire to enjoy well-being beyond basic well-being. While the former type of conflict is avoidable if there are sufficient resources to secure basic well-being for all groups, the latter is not, if the desire towards better well-being is without limit. The former deserves consideration in terms of justice that this paper is concerned with, while the latter does not. This is the reason why in this paper, the application of the monotonicity condition is restricted to the domain below basic well-being through the application of **RM**, while in the domain above basic well-being, conflicts are avoided through the application of **RC** , which prohibits groups from making rankings.

C.7 Conclusion

This paper addressed and formulated a social choice problem for " securing basic well-being for all," where individual well-being was defined in the space of multi-dimensional attributes; the notion of basic well-being was introduced as a critical reference point of multi-dimensional well-beings in order to identify the "injustice" of social policies; and the mutually incommensurable types of disadvantages were allowed to exist. Given such an environment, a new scheme of social choice rule, a *social relation function* (**SRF**), was introduced with three elements of informational basis: individuals' appraisals of their respective well-being contents; each disadvantaged group's appraisal of its members' well-being contents to identify the least advantaged members on the basis of the members' shared conception of the good;

and each group's evaluation of alternative social policies, formed on the basis of its own appraisal by focusing on the least advantaged members. In the scheme of **SRF**, while individuals' appraisal is equally treated, group evaluations are allowed a prior treatment as experts on their own disadvantages. The former property is formulated as *weak Pareto condition* (**WP**) and the latter as *non-negative response* (**NR**) along with three constraints, *basic well-being condition* (**BWC**), *restricted monotonocity* (**RM**), and *refrain condition* (**RC**), on the admissible group evaluations. It was shown that **NR** together with **BWC**, **RM**, and **RC** makes an **SRF** *non-welfaristic*.

Then, the paper showed that the three constraints are compatible in that a group evaluation is transitive if it satisfies these constraints, while there exists an **SRF** that satisfies **NR** if full comparability among the disadvantaged individuals' well-being contents within a group is allowed under the situation of " destitution." It also showed that any **SRF** cannot simultaneously satisfy **WP** and **NR** together with **BWC** , **RM**, and **RC** if "tentative" non-comparability of the least advantaged's well-being contents within the same group remains, while there exists an **SRF** satisfying these axioms if the remaining non-comparability is " assertive," where the " assertive" property of the remaining non-comparability is insured by **RC**. Finally, it was shown that the existence of the "assertive" non-comparability is indispensable for the existence of such an **SRF**.

Essentially, this study presents the set of disadvantaged types, the profiles of individual and group appraisals, and group evaluations along with the concrete conceptions of basic well-being contents for the respective groups as parameters in the framework of **SRF**s. It would be interesting to develop an analytical framework to address the structure of interaction in the formation process of these profiles and lists, as the adoption of the Convention on the Rights of Persons with Disabilities and its ratification by each party suggest. This is thus a topic worth discussing in future research.

C.8 References

Arrow, K. J. (1951/1963). *Social choice and individual values* (2nd ed.). New York: Wiley.

Basu, K., & Lopez-Calva, L. F. (2011). Functionings and capabilities. In K. J. Arrow, A. Sen, & K. Suzumura (eds.), *Handbook of social choice and welfare* (Vol. 2, pp. 54–187). Amsterdam: North-Holland.

d'Aspremont, C., & Gevers, L. (2002). Social welfare functionals and interpersonal comparability. In K. J. Arrow, A. Sen, & K. Suzumura (eds.), *Handbook of social choice and welfare* (Vol. 1, pp. 459–541). Amsterdam: North-Holland.

Fleurbaey, M. (1994). On fair compensation. *Theory and Decision, 36*, 277–307.

Fleurbaey, M. (2007). Social choice and the indexing dilemma. *Social Choice and Welfare, 29*, 633–648.

Fleurbaey, M., & Hammond, P. J. (2004). Interpersonally comparable utility. In S. Barbera, P. J. Hammond, & C. Seidl (eds.), *Handbook of utility theory* (Vol. 2). Boston: Kluwer.
Fleurbaey, M., & Maniquet, F. (2011). Compensation and responsibility. *Handbook of Social Choice and Welfare, 2*, 508–604.
Fleurbaey, M., & Mongin, P. (2005). The news of the death of welfare economics is greatly exaggerated. *Social Choice and Welfare, 25*, 381–418.
Foster, J. (1984). On economic poverty: A survey of aggregate measures. *Advances in Econometrics, 3*, 215–251.
Gotoh, R., & Yoshihara, N. (2003). A class of fair distribution rules à la Rawls and Sen. *Economic Theory, 22*, 63–88.
Herrero, C. (1996). Capabilities and utilities. *Economic Design, 2*, 69–88.
Norzick, R. (1974). *Anarchy, state and utopia*. Oxford: Basil Blackwell.
Pattanaik, P. K., & Xu, Y. (1990). On ranking opportunity sets in terms of freedom of choice. *Recherches Economiques de Louvain, 56*, 383–390.
Pattanaik, P. K., & Xu, Y. (2007). Minimal relativism, dominance, and standard of living comparisons based on functionings. *Oxford Economic Papers, 59*, 354–374.
Pattanaik, P. K., & Xu, Y. (2012). On dominance and context-dependence in decisions involving multiple attributes. *Economics and Philosophy, 28*, 117–132.
Rawls, J. (1971). *A theory of justice*. Cambridge, MA: Harvard University Press.
Rawls, J. (1993). *Political liberalism*. New York: Columbia University Press.
Sen, A. K. (1970). *Collective choice and social welfare*. San Francisco: Holden-Day.
Sen, A. K. (1980). Equality of what? *The tanner lectures on human values* (Vol. I). University of Utah Press, Salt Lake City (reprinted in 1982, *Choice, welfare, and measurement* (pp. 353–369). Oxford: Blackwell).
Sen, A. K. (1981). *Poverty and famines: An essay on entitlement and deprivation*. Oxford: Oxford University Press.
Sen, A. K. (1984). The living standard. *Oxford Economic Papers, 36*, 198, 74–90.
Sen, A. K. (1985). *Commodities and capabilities*. Amsterdam: North-Holland.
Sen, A. K. (1997). *On economic inequality, expanded edition with a substantial annex* by J. E. Foster and A. K. Sen. Oxford: Clarendon Press.
Sen, A. K. (2002). *Rationality and freedom*. Cambridge, MA: Harvard University Press.
Sen, A. K. (2009a). *The idea of justice*. London: Allen Lane.
Sen, A. K. (2009b). *Economics, ethics and law*. In R. Gotoh & P. Dumouchel (eds.), *Against injustice: The new economics of Amartya Sen* (pp. 39–54). Cambridge, MA: Cambridge University Press.

C.9 Appendix

Proofs

Proof of Lemma 1 Let $x R^t y R^t z$. We will show $x R^t z$ holds. Note that $x R^t y$ is derived from imposing either **BWC** or **RM** upon the pair (x, y).
Case 1. Assume $x R^t y$ by **BWC**.

Then, $C_i(x) \succsim_t BC^t$ holds for all $i \in L^t(x; \succsim_t)$, or *not* $\left[BC^t \succsim_t C_i(x)\right]$ & *not* $\left[C_i(x) \succsim_t BC^t\right]$ holds for some $i \in L^t(x; \succsim_t)$.

Sub-case 1-1. $BC^t \sim_t C_j(y)$ for all $j \in L^t(y; \succsim_t)$.

Then, $x R^t y$ is derived by imposing **BWC** under the case α- 1) or α-2).

Suppose that case α-1) holds but case α-2) does not hold. Hence, $C_i(x) \sim_t BC^t$ holds for all $i \in L^t(x; \succsim_t)$, which implies that $y R^t x$ is also derived from **BWC** under case α)-1). Thus, $x I^t y$. Moreover, $y R^t z$ is only derived from **BWC** upon the pair (y, z). Therefore, the pair (x, z) satisfies case α-1) or α-2), so that $x R^t z$ holds by **BWC**. In particular, if $y P^t z$, then $x P^t z$ also holds, while if $y I^t z$, then $x I^t z$ also holds.

Suppose that case α-2) holds. Then, $C_i(x) \succ_t BC^t$ holds for all $i \in L^t(x; \succsim_t)$ and $x P^t y$. Again, $y R^t z$ is only derived from applying **BWC** to the pair (y, z). Therefore, the pair (x, z) satisfies case α-2), so that $x P^t z$ holds by **BWC**.

Sub-case 1-2. *not* $\left[C_j(y) \succsim_t BC^t\right]$ and *not* $\left[BC^t \succsim_t C_j(y)\right]$ for some $j \in L^t(y; \succsim_t)$.

Then, case β) holds for the pair (x, y), so that $x P^t y$ holds. Moreover, $y R^t z$ is only derived from **BWC** under case γ) upon the pair (y, z), where $BC^t \succ_t C_j(z)$ must hold for all $j \in L^t(z; \succsim_t)$, so that $y P^t z$ holds. Therefore, the pair of (x, z) satisfies case α-2), so that $x P^t z$ holds by **BWC**.

Sub-case 1-3. $BC^t \succ_t C_j(y)$ for all $j \in L^t(y; \succsim_t)$.

Then, the case α-2) or γ) holds for the pair (x, y), so that $x P^t y$ holds. Moreover, $y R^t z$ is then derived only from **RM** upon the pair (y, z), which implies that $C_i(y) \succsim_t C_j(z)$ holds for all $i \in L^t(y; \succsim_t)$ and all $j \in L^t(z; \succsim_t)$, so that $BC^t \succ_t C_j(z)$ holds for all $j \in L^t(z; \succsim_t)$ by the transitivity of $\succsim_t$. Thus, the pair of (x, z) corresponds to the case α-2) or γ), so that $x P^t z$ holds by **BWC**.

Case 2. Assume $x R^t y$ by **RM**.

Then, $y R^t z$ should also be derived from **RM** upon the pair (y, z). Hence, the pair (x, z) satisfies case δ). Moreover, $C_i(x) \succsim_t C_j(y) \succsim_t C_h(z)$ holds for all $i \in L^t(x; \succsim_t)$, all $j \in L^t(y; \succsim_t)$, and all $h \in L^t(z; \succsim_t)$. Then, by the transitivity of $\succsim_t$, $C_i(x) \succsim_t C_h(z)$ holds for all $i \in L^t(x; \succsim_t)$ and all $h \in L^t(z; \succsim_t)$. Thus, $x R^t z$ holds by **RM**. Moreover, if $x P^t y$ or $y P^t z$, then $x P^t z$ holds, while if $x I^t y$ and $y I^t z$, then $x I^t z$ holds by the transitivity of $\succsim_t$ and **RM**. ■

Proof of Proposition 1 Let a binary relation P^{PR} be defined as: for each $(R^t)_{t\in T} \in D(\succsim)$, and each $x, y \in X$,

$$x P^{PR} y \text{ holds if and only if}$$
$$\text{there exists } t' \in T \text{ such that } x P^{t'} y \text{ and there is no } t'' \in T \text{ such that } y P^{t''} x.$$

Note that any **SRF** F should associate a quasi-ordering $R = F\left(\succsim, (R^t)_{t\in T}\right)$ with each $\left(\succsim, (R^t)_{t\in T}\right)$ such that $P^{PR} \subseteq R$ if F satisfies **PR**. Therefore, it is sufficient for this proof to show that P^{PR} is not transitive.

Let $\{t^1, t^2, t^3\} = T$, and let us consider $\left(\succsim, (R^t)_{t\in T}\right)$ satisfying the following properties:

(1) Let $BC^{t^1} \succ_{t^1} C_i(x)$ for all $i \in L^{t^1}(x; \succsim_{t^1})$; $BC^{t^1} \succ_{t^1} C_j(y)$ for all $j \in L^{t^1}(y; \succsim_{t^1})$; and $BC^{t^1} \succ_{t^1} C_h(z)$ for all $h \in L^{t^1}(z; \succsim_{t^1})$. Moreover, let $C_i(x) \succ_{t^1} C_j(y)$ for all $i \in L^{t^1}(x; \succsim_{t^1})$ and all $j \in L^{t^1}(y; \succsim_{t^1})$; *not* $\left[C_i(x) \succsim_{t^1} C_h(z)\right]$ & *not* $\left[C_h(z) \succsim_{t^1} C_i(x)\right]$ for some $i \in L^{t^1}(x; \succsim_{t^1})$ and some $h \in L^{t^1}(z; \succsim_{t^1})$; and *not* $\left[C_j(y) \succsim_{t^1} C_h(z)\right]$ & *not* $\left[C_h(z) \succsim_{t^1} C_j(y)\right]$ for some $j \in L^{t^1}(y; \succsim_{t^1})$ and some $h \in L^{t^1}(z; \succsim_{t^1})$.

(2) Let $BC^{t^2} \succ_{t^2} C_i(x)$ for all $i \in L^{t^2}(x; \succsim_{t^2})$; $BC^{t^2} \succ_{t^2} C_j(y)$ for all $j \in L^{t^2}(y; \succsim_{t^2})$; and $BC^{t^2} \succ_{t^2} C_h(z)$ for all $h \in L^{t^2}(z; \succsim_{t^2})$. Moreover, let $C_i(y) \succ_{t^2} C_h(z)$ for all $i \in L^{t^2}(y; \succsim_{t^2})$ and all $h \in L^{t^2}(z; \succsim_{t^2})$; *not* $\left[C_i(x) \succsim_{t^2} C_j(y)\right]$ & *not* $\left[C_j(y) \succsim_{t^2} C_i(x)\right]$ for some $i \in L^{t^2}(x; \succsim_{t^2})$ and some $j \in L^{t^2}(y; \succsim_{t^2})$; and *not* $\left[C_i(x) \succsim_{t^2} C_h(z)\right]$ & *not* $\left[C_h(z) \succsim_{t^2} C_i(x)\right]$ for some $i \in L^{t^2}(y; \succsim_{t^2})$ and some $h \in L^{t^2}(z; \succsim_{t^2})$.

(3) Let $BC^{t^3} \succ_{t^3} C_i(x)$ for all $i \in L^{t^3}(x; \succsim_{t^3})$; $BC^{t^3} \succ_{t^3} C_j(y)$ for all $j \in L^{t^3}(y; \succsim_{t^3})$; and $BC^{t^3} \succ_{t^3} C_h(z)$ for all $h \in L^{t^3}(z; \succsim_{t^3})$. Moreover, let $C_h(z) \succ_{t^3} C_i(x)$ for all $h \in L^{t^3}(z; \succsim_{t^3})$ and all $i \in L^{t^3}(x; \succsim_{t^3})$; *not* $\left[C_j(y) \succsim_{t^3} C_h(z)\right]$ & *not* $\left[C_h(z) \succsim_{t^3} C_j(y)\right]$ for some $h \in L^{t^3}(z; \succsim_{t^3})$ and some $j \in L^{t3}(y; \succsim_{t^3})$; and *not* $\left[C_i(x) \succsim_{t^3} C_j(y)\right]$ & *not* $\left[C_j(y) \succsim_{t^3} C_i(x)\right]$ for some $i \in L^{t^3}(x; \succsim_{t^3})$ and some $j \in L^{t^3}(y; \succsim_{t^3})$.

Under (1), $x P^{t^1} y$ by **RM**, and $z N R^{t^1} x$ and $y N R^{t^1} z$ by **RC**. Under (2), $y P^{t^2} z$ by **RM**, and $z N R^{t^2} x$ and $x N R^{t^2} y$ by **RC**. Under (3), $z P^{t^3} x$ by **RM**, and $y N R^{t^3} z$ and $x N R^{t^3} y$ by **RC**. Therefore, by the definition of **PR**, $x P^{PR} y P^{PR} z P^{PR} x$ holds, which implies that P^{PR} is not transitive. ■

Proof of Proposition 2 Let $x R^{NR} y R^{NR} z$. This implies that there exists $t^1 \in T$ such that $x R^{t^1} y$ and *not* $y P^t x$ for any other $t \in T$, and there exists $t^2 \in T$ such that $y R^{t^2} z$ and *not* $z P^t y$ for any other $t \in T$. Moreover, $x R^{t^1} y$ (resp. $y R^{t^2} z$) is derived from **BWC** by applying either of the cases α), β), and γ); or it is derived from **RM** by applying case δ).

1. First of all, let us show that if $x R^{t^1} y$ and *not* $z P^{t^1} y$, then $x R^{t^1} z$.

Case 1: Let $x R^{t^1} y$ be derived from **BWC** by applying α-1).

Then, $BC^{t^1} \succsim_{t^1} C_j(y)$ for all $j \in L^{t^1}(y; \succsim_{t^1})$, and $C_i(x) \succsim_{t^1} BC^{t^1}$ for all $i \in L^{t^1}(x; \succsim_{t^1})$. Suppose $z P^{t^1} x$. Note that neither of the case α), β), γ) , δ) can derive

$zP^{t^1}x$, thus (z, x) satisfies ϵ) or ε), which leads to $xNR^{t^1}z$ by **RC** , a contradiction. Thus, $xNR^{t^1}z$ or $xR^{t^1}z$ holds. Suppose $xNR^{t^1}z$. This implies that (x, z) corresponds to ϵ), so that $C_i(z) \succ_{t^1} BC^{t^1}$ for all $i \in L^{t^1}(z; \succsim_{t^1})$. Then, $zP^{t^1}y$ from **BWC** by applying case α-2), which is a contradiction. Thus, $xR^{t^1}z$ holds.

Case 2: Let $xP^{t^1}y$ be derived from **BWC** by applying β).

Then, *not* $\left[C_j(y) \succsim_{t^1} BC^{t^1}\right]$ for some $j \in L^{t^1}(y; \succsim_{t^1})$, and $C_i(x) \succsim_{t^1} BC^{t^1}$ for all $i \in L^{t^1}(x; \succsim_{t^1})$. Suppose $zP^{t^1}x$. Note that neither of α), β), γ) , δ) can derive $zP^{t^1}x$, thus (z, x) corresponds to ϵ) or ε), which leads to $xNR^{t^1}z$ by **RC**, a contradiction. Thus, $xNR^{t^1}z$ or $xR^{t^1}z$ holds. Suppose $xNR^{t^1}z$. This implies that (x, z) satisfies property ϵ), so that $C_i(z) \succ_{t^1} BC^{t^1}$ for all $i \in L^{t^1}(z; \succsim_{t^1})$. Then, $zP^{t^1}y$ from **BWC** by applying case β), which is a contradiction from *not* $zP^{t^1}y$. Thus, $xR^{t^1}z$ holds. Finally, suppose that $zR^{t^1}x$. This is only available by applying case α-1), and $C_i(x) \sim_{t^1} BC^{t^1}$ for all $i \in L^{t^1}(x; \succsim_{t^1})$ and $C_i(z) \sim_{t^1} BC^{t^1}$ for all $i \in L^{t^1}(z; \succsim_{t^1})$. Then, $zP^{t^1}y$ from **BWC** by applying case β), which is a contradiction from *not* $zP^{t^1}y$. Thus, $zR^{t^1}x$ is impossible, so that $xP^{t^1}z$ holds.

Case 3: Let $xP^{t^1}y$ be derived from **BWC** by applying the case α-2) or γ).

Case 3-1: Suppose that $BC^{t^1} \sim_{t^1} C_i(y)$ for all $i \in L^{t^1}(y; \succsim_{t^1})$.

Then, $C_i(x) \succ_{t^1} BC^{t^1}$ for all $i \in L^{t^1}(x; \succsim_{t^1})$ so that $zR^{t^1}x$ is never possible. Moreover, if $zNR^{t^1}x$, then $C_i(z) \succ_{t^1} BC^{t^1}$ for all $i \in L^{t^1}(z; \succsim_{t^1})$ due to **RC** under case ϵ). Then, $zP^{t^1}y$ by **BWC** under case α-2), which is a contradiction from *not* $zP^{t^1}y$. Thus, $xP^{t^1}z$ is only possible.

Case 3-2: Suppose that $BC^{t^1} \succ_{t^1} C_i(y)$ for all $i \in L^{t^1}(y; \succsim_{t^1})$.

Case 3-2-1: Suppose $zR^{t^1}x$.

If *not* $\left[C_j(x) \succsim_{t^1} BC^{t^1}\right]$ for some $j \in L^{t^1}(x; \succsim_{t^1})$, then, in order to ensure $zR^{t^1}x$, $C_i(z) \succsim_{t^1} BC^{t^1}$ must hold for all $i \in L^{t^1}\left(z; \succsim_{t^1}\right)$. Thus, $zP^{t^1}y$ from **BWC** under case α-2), which is a contradiction from *not* $zP^{t^1}y$. If $C_j(x) \succsim_{t^1} BC^{t^1}$ for all $j \in L^{t^1}(x; \succsim_{t^1})$, then $zR^{t^1}x$ is possible only from **BWC** under case α). Then, it implies that $C_j(z) \succsim_{t^1} BC^{t^1}$ for all $j \in L^{t^1}(z; \succsim_{t^1})$, which again implies $zP^{t^1}y$ by **BWC** under case α-2), which is a contradiction from *not* $zP^{t^1}y$. In summary, $zR^{t^1}x$ is impossible.

Case 3-2-2: Suppose $zNR^{t^1}x$.

Note that $zNR^{t^1}x$ is derived from **RC** under case ϵ) or ε).

Case 3-2-2-1: Let case ϵ) hold.

Then $C_i(z) \succ_{t^1} BC^{t^1}$ holds for all $i \in L^{t^1}(z; \succsim_{t^1})$, so that $zP^{t^1}y$ from **BWC** by applying α-2), a contradiction.

Case 3-2-2-1: Let case ε) hold.

Then

$$\textit{not}\left[C_j(z) \succsim_{t^1} BC^{t^1}\right] \text{ for some } j \in L^{t^1}(z; \succsim_{t^1}); \text{ or}$$

$$\textit{not}\left[BC^{t^1} \succsim_{t^1} C_i(z)\right] \text{ for some } i \in L^{t^1}(z; \succsim_{t^1}).$$

Let both the former and the latter hold. Then, by the property of $L^{t^1}\left(z; \succsim_{t^1}\right)$, there is a common $i \in L^{t^1}(z; \succsim_{t^1})$ such that *not* $\left[C_i(z) \succsim_{t^1} BC^{t^1}\right]$ and *not* $\left[BC^{t^1} \succsim_{t^1} C_i(z)\right]$. Then, given that case ε) holds for $zNR^{t^1}x$, case γ) must hold for having $xP^{t^1}y$. Then, $zP^{t^1}y$ holds from **BWC** under case γ), a contradiction.

Hence, either the former does not hold or the latter does not hold. Let the former do not hold, so that $C_i(z) \succsim_{t^1} BC^{t^1}$ holds for all $i \in L^{t^1}(z; \succsim_{t^1})$. Then, $zP^{t^1}y$ from **BWC** under case α)-2), a contradiction. Let the latter do not hold, so that $BC^{t^1} \succsim_{t^1} C_i(z)$ for all $i \in L^{t^1}(z; \succsim_{t^1})$. Thus, *not* $zP^{t^1}y$ is derived from **RM** under case δ). Then, by ***FCD***, $yR^{t^1}z$ holds. Thus, by transitivity, $xP^{t^1}z$, which is a contradiction from $zNR^{t^1}x$. In summary, $zNR^{t^1}x$ is impossible. Thus, $xP^{t^1}z$ holds.

Case 4: Let $xR^{t^1}y$ be derived from **RM** under case δ).

Then, $BC^{t^1} \succ_{t^1} C_i(x)$ for all $i \in L^{t^1}(x; \succsim_{t^1})$; and also, $BC^{t^1} \succ_{t^1} C_i(y)$ for all $i \in L^{t^1}(y; \succsim_{t^1})$. Since *not* $zP^{t^1}y$, either $yR^{t^1}z$ or $yNR^{t^1}z$. Suppose $yNR^{t^1}z$. Since $BC^{t^1} \succ_{t^1} C_i(y)$ for all $i \in L^{t^1}(y; \succsim_{t^1})$, $yNR^{t^1}z$ implies that $BC^{t^1} \succ_{t^1} C_i(z)$ for all $i \in L^{t^1}(z; \succsim_{t^1})$. However, by ***FCD***, **RM** can be applied to evaluate (y, z), which implies *not* $yNR^{t^1}z$, a contradiction. Thus, $yR^{t^1}z$. Then, by transitivity of R^{t^1}, $xR^{t^1}z$ holds.

In summary, if $xR^{t^1}y$ and *not* $zP^{t^1}y$, then $xR^{t^1}z$.

2. Second, let us show that if $yR^{t^2}z$ and *not* $yP^{t^2}x$, then *not* $zP^{t^2}x$. Suppose $zP^{t^2}x$. Since $yR^{t^2}z$, it follows from transitivity of R^{t^2} that $(y, x) \in yP^{t^2}x$, which is a contradiction. Thus *not* $zP^{t^2}x$.

3. Third, let us show that for any $t \in T\setminus\left\{t^1\right\}$, if *not* yP^tx and *not* zP^ty, then *not* zP^tx. Suppose, in the contrary, zP^tx. Then, it is derived from **BWC** under either of the case α-2), β), or γ); or it is derived from **RM**-2) under case δ).

Let zP^tx be derived from **BWC**. Suppose that the case α- 2) or γ) is applied with $BC^t \succ_t C_i(x)$ for all $i \in L^t(x; \succsim_t)$. Thus, by ***FCD*** and **RM**, it is impossible that yNR^tx. Thus, xR^ty. Then, by transitivity, zP^ty, which is a contradiction.

Suppose that zP^tx is derived from **BWC** by applying property β). Then, *not* $\left[C_i(x) \succsim_{t^1} BC^t\right]$ and *not* $\left[BC^t \succsim_{t^1} C_i(x)\right]$ hold for some $i \in L^t(x; \succsim_{t^1})$. In this case, xR^ty or xNR^ty. Let xR^ty. This case is derived from **BWC** by applying γ), which implies that $BC^t \succ_t C_i(y)$ for all $i \in L^t(y; \succsim_t)$. Then, zP^ty holds by **BWC** with applying α-2). Thus, a contradiction. Next, let xNR^ty. This is derived from **RC** by applying case ε). To apply case ε) for (x, y), the case that *not* $\left[C_j(y) \succsim_t BC^t\right]$ and *not* $\left[BC^t \succsim_{t^1} C_j(y)\right]$ for some $j \in L^t(y; \succsim_t)$ must hold. Then, zP^ty is derived from **BWC** by applying case β), which is a contradiction.

Suppose that zP^tx is derived from **BWC** by applying case α-2) with $BC^t \sim_t C_i(x)$ for all $i \in L^t(x; \succsim_t)$. Then, yNR^tx is impossible. Thus, xR^ty. Then, by transitivity, zP^ty, which is a contradiction. In summary, zP^tx cannot be derived from **BWC**.

Let zP^tx be derived from **RM**-2) under case δ). Then, $BC^t \succ_t C_i(x)$ for all $i \in L^t(x; \succsim_t)$. Thus, by ***FCD*** and **RM**, it is impossible that yNR^tx. Thus, xR^ty.

Then, by transitivity, $zP^t y$, which is a contradiction. Thus, $zP^t x$ cannot be derived from **RM**-2).

In summary, for any $t \in T \setminus \{t^1\}$, if *not* $yP^t x$ and *not* $zP^t y$, then *not* $zP^t x$.

4. By the above arguments of **1.** and **3.**, we have $xR^{t^1}z$ and *not* $zP^t x$ for any $t \in T \setminus \{t^1\}$. Thus, $xR^{NR}z$ holds. ■

Proof of Theorem 1 Let $T = \{t^1\}$, $\{i, j, h, h'\} \subset N^{t1} = N$, $L^{t^1}(x; \succsim_{t^1}) = \{i, j, h\}$, $L^{t^1}(y; \succsim_{t^1}) = \{i, j, h\}$, and $L^{t1}(z; \succsim_{t^1}) = \{i, j, h, h'\}$. Suppose that:

$$
\begin{aligned}
BC^{t^1} &\succ_{t^1} C_i(x) \sim_{t^1} C_j(x) \sim_{t^1} C_h(x);\\
BC^{t^1} &\succ_{t^1} C_i(y) \sim_{t^1} C_j(y) \sim_{t^1} C_h(y);\\
BC^{t^1} &\succ_{t^1} C_i(z) \sim_{t^1} C_j(z) \sim_{t^1} C_h(z);\\
\textit{not}\ [BC^{t^1} &\succsim_{t^1} C_{h'}(z)\ \textit{or}\ C_{h'}(z) \succsim_{t^1} BC^{t^1}];\\
C_i(x) &\succ_i C_i(y) \succ_i C_i(z);\\
C_j(x) &\succ_j C_j(y) \succ_j C_j(z);\\
C_h(x) &\succ_h C_h(y) \succ_h C_h(z);\ \text{and}\\
C_{h'}(x) &\succ_{h'} C_{h'}(y) \succ_{h'} C_{h'}(z).
\end{aligned}
$$

Moreover, for any $k \in t^1 \setminus \{i, j, h, h'\}$, let $C_k(z) \succ_{t^1} C_{h'}(z)$, $C_k(x) \succ_{t^1} BC^{t^1}$, $C_k(y) \succ_{t^1} BC^{t^1}$, $C_k(z) \succ_{t^1} BC^{t^1}$, and $C_k(x) \succ_k C_k(y) \succ_k C_k(z)$.

Then, since $BC^{t^1} \succ_{t^1} C_i(x)$ for all $i \in L_{\mathbf{C}}^{t^1}(x; \succsim_{t^1})$, and *not* $BC^{t^1} \succsim_{t^1} C_{h'}(z)$ & *not* $C_{h'}(z) \succsim_{t^1} BC^{t^1}$ for $h' \in L^{t^1}(z; \succsim_{t^1})$, it follows that $zP^{t^1}x$ from **BWC** under case γ). Thus, since $T = \{t^1\}$ by **NR**, zPx holds, while by **WP**, xPz holds. Thus, a contradiction, which implies **NR** and **WP** are incompatible. ■

Proof of Lemma 2 **1.** Let $xR^{NR}y$ and $yP^{WP}z$. This implies that there exists $t^1 \in T$ such that $xR^{t^1}y$ and *not* $yP^t x$ for any other $t \in T$, and $C_i(y) \succ_i C_i(z)$ holds for all $i \in N$. Moreover, $xR^{t^1}y$ is derived from **BWC** by applying either of the case α), β), or γ); or it is derived from **RM** by applying case δ).

2. We show that for any $t \in T$, (i) *not* $yP^t x$, and (ii) $C_i(y) \succ_i C_i(z)$ holds for all $i \in N$ together imply that $xR^t z$ or $xNR^t z$. First of all, *not* $yP^t x$ if and only if $xR^t y$ or $xNR^t y$. If $xR^t y$, then it is derived from **BWC** by applying the case α), β), or γ), or from **RM** by applying property δ). If $xNR^t y$, then it is derived from **RC** by applying the case ϵ) or ε).

2-i). Suppose $xR^t y$ is derived from **BWC** by applying the case α), β), or γ). Then, *not* $\left[BC^t \succsim_t C_i(x)\right]$ for some $i \in L^t(x; \succsim_t)$. Note, since $C_i(y) \succ_i C_i(z)$ holds for all $i \in N^t$, *not* $\left[C_h(z) \succsim_t C_j(y)\right]$ holds for any $j \in L^t(y; \succsim_t)$ and any $h \in L^t(z; \succsim_t)$. To see this, let us suppose that $\left[C_h(z) \succsim_t C_j(y)\right]$ holds for some $j \in L^t(y; \succsim_t)$ and some $h \in L^t(z; \succsim_t)$. Then, it follows that $C_h(z) \succsim_t C_j(y) \succ_j C_j(z)$. If $j \in L^t(z; \succsim_t)$, then $C_j(z) \sim_t C_h(z)$ holds by ***D***, which implies $C_h(z) \succsim_j C_j(y) \succ_j C_j(z) \sim_j C_h(z)$ by the definition of $\succsim_t \equiv \cap_{i \in N^t} \succsim_i$. However, it is a contradiction, since $\succsim_j$ must be transitive. Therefore, $j \notin L^t(z; \succsim_t)$, which implies that there exists $k \in L^t(z; \succsim_t)$ such that $C_h(z) \succsim_t C_j(y) \succ_j C_j(z) \succ_t C_k(z)$. Then, since $C_k(z) \sim_t$

$C_h(z)$, it is also a contradiction by the definition of $\succsim_t$ and the transitivity of $\succsim_j$. Thus, *not* $\left[C_h(z) \succsim_t C_j(y)\right]$ holds for any $j \in L^t(y; \succsim_t)$ and any $h \in L^t(z; \succsim_t)$.

Suppose zP^tx. Then, if this relation is derived from **BWC**, it is due to the application of the case β) with *not* $\left[BC^t \succsim_t C_i(x)\right]$ and *not* $\left[C_i(x) \succsim_t BC^t\right]$ for some $i \in L^t(x; \succsim_t)$. This implies that $C_i(z) \succsim_t BC^t$ for any $i \in L^t(z; \succsim_t)$. In this case, xR^ty is derived from **BWC** by applying the case γ), so that $BC^t \succ_t C_i(y)$ for any $i \in L^t(y; \succsim_t)$. Thus, by the transitivity, $\left[C_h(z) \succ_t C_j(y)\right]$ holds for any $j \in L^t(y; \succsim_t)$ and any $h \in L^t(z; \succsim_t)$, which is a contradiction. Since there is no other situation to generate zP^tx together with xR^ty under **BWC** and the case α), β), or γ), the last result implies that zP^tx is impossible. Thus, xR^tz or xNR^tz.

2-ii). Suppose xNR^ty is derived from **RC** by applying the case ϵ) or ε). If ϵ) is applied for xNR^ty, then $\left[C_i(x) \succ_t BC^t\right]$ holds for any $i \in L^t(x; \succsim_t)$. Then, xR^tz or xNR^tz is derived by applying either of the case α), β), or ϵ).

If case ε) is applied for xNR^ty, then [*not* $\left[BC^t \succsim_t C_i(x)\right]$ for some $i \in L^t(x; \succsim_t)$ and *not* $\left[C_j(x) \succsim_t BC^t\right]$ for some $j \in L^t(x; \succsim_t)$] and [*not* $\left[BC^t \succsim_t C_i(y)\right]$ for some $i \in L^t(y; \succsim_t)$ and *not* $\left[C_j(y) \succsim_t BC^t\right]$ for some $j \in L^t(y; \succsim_t)$]. Note that in such a case, it does not follow that $\left[C_i(x) \succ_t BC^t\right]$ for some $i \in L^t(x; \succsim_t)$ and $\left[BC^t \succ_t C_j(x)\right]$ for some $j \in L^t(x; \succsim_t)$. Indeed, if so, the transitivity of $\succsim_t$ implies $C_i(x) \succ_t C_j(x)$ for some $i, j \in L^t(x; \succsim_t)$, which is a contradiction from the definition of $L^t(x; \succsim_t)$. Thus, if *not* $\left[BC^t \succsim_t C_i(x)\right]$ for some $i \in L^t(x; \succsim_t)$, then *not* $\left[C_i(x) \succsim_t BC^t\right]$ also holds. Similarly, *not* $\left[BC^t \succsim_t C_i(y)\right]$ and *not* $\left[C_i(y) \succsim_t BC^t\right]$ for some $i \in L^t(y; \succsim_t)$ also hold. Then, by either **RC** with case ε) or **BWC** with γ), xR^tz or xNR^tz is derived.

2-iii). Suppose xR^ty is derived from **RM** by applying case δ). Then, since $C_i(y) \succ_i C_i(z)$ holds for all $i \in N^t$, we have, by combining with **RM** with case δ), $C_i(x) \succsim_t C_j(y) \succ_j C_j(z)$ for any $i \in L^t(x; \succsim_t)$ and any $j \in L^t\left(y; \succsim_t\right)$. By definition of $L^t(z; \succsim_t)$, $\boldsymbol{FCD}$, and $\boldsymbol{D}$, $C_j(z) \succsim_t C_h(z)$ holds for any $h \in L^t(z; \succsim_t)$ and any $j \in L^t\left(y; \succsim_t\right)$. Indeed, unless $j \in L^t\left(z; \succsim_t\right)$, there is another $h \in L^t(z; \succsim_t)$ such that $C_j(z) \succ_t C_h(z)$. Then, since $C_h(z) \sim_t C_{h'}(z)$ holds for any $h' \in L^t(z; \succsim_t)$ by the definition of $L^t(z; \succsim_t)$, $\boldsymbol{FCD}$, and $\boldsymbol{D}$, the desired result holds. Then, it follows that $C_j(y) \succ_t C_h(z)$ for any $j \in L^t\left(y; \succsim_t\right)$ and any $h \in L^t(z; \succsim_t)$ from the definition of $L^t(z; \succsim_t)$. To see this, suppose $C_j(y) \precsim_t C_h(z)$ for some $j \in L^t\left(y; \succsim_t\right)$ and some $h \in L^t(z; \succsim_t)$. Then, by the definition of $\succsim_t$, $C_j(y) \succ_j C_j(z) \succsim_j C_h(z) \succsim_j C_j(y)$, which is a contradiction. Thus, $C_j(y) \succ_t C_h(z)$ for any $j \in L^t\left(y; \succsim_t\right)$ and any $h \in L^t(z; \succsim_t)$. Thus, $C_i(x) \succsim_t C_j(y) \succ_t C_h(z)$ for any $i \in L^t(x; \succsim_t)$, any $j \in L^t\left(y; \succsim_t\right)$, and any $h \in L^t(z; \succsim_t)$. By the transitivity of $\succsim_t$, $C_i(x) \succ_t C_h(z)$ for any $i \in L^t(x; \succsim_t)$ and any $h \in L^t(z; \succsim_t)$. Since xR^ty is derived from **RM** by applying case δ), the transitivity of $\succsim_t$ implies that $BC_t^t \succ_t C_h(z)$ for any $h \in L^t(z; \succsim_t)$, and so by **RM** with case δ), xP^tz holds.

3. Let $xR^{t^1}y$ be derived from **BWC** by applying either of the case α), β), or γ).

3-i): Let $xR^{t^1}y$ be derived from **BWC** by applying case α). Then, $BC^{t^1} \succsim_{t^1} C_j(y)$ for all $j \in L^{t^1}(y; \succsim_{t^1})$, and $C_i(x) \succsim_{t^1} BC^{t^1}$ for all $i \in L^{t^1}(x; \succsim_{t^1})$. Then, we can show that $C_i(x) \succsim_{t^1} BC^{t^1}$ holds for every $i \in N^{t^1}$. First, if $i \in N^{t^1}$ is $C_i(x) \succ_{t^1}$

$C_j(x)$ for some $j \in L^{t^1}(x; \succsim_{t^1})$, it is obvious. If $i \in N^{t^1}$ is *not* $\left[C_i(x) \succ_{t^1} C_j(x)\right]$ for any $j \in L^{t^1}(x; \succsim_{t^1})$, then $i \in L^{t^1}(x; \succsim_{t^1})$, so that $C_i(x) \succsim_{t^1} BC^{t^1}$ holds.

Let us consider $L^{t^1}(z; \succsim_{t^1})$. Since $C_i(y) \succ_i C_i(z)$ holds for all $i \in N$, we can show as in the step **2-i)** of this proof that *not* $\left[C_i(z) \succsim_{t^1} C_j(y)\right]$ holds for any $j \in L^{t^1}(y; \succsim_{t^1})$ and any $i \in L^{t^1}(z; \succsim_{t^1})$. Then, since $BC^{t^1} \succsim_{t^1} C_j(y) \succ_j C_j(z)$ for all $j \in L^{t^1}(y; \succsim_{t^1})$, *not* $\left[C_i(z) \succsim_{t^1} BC^{t^1}\right]$ holds for any $i \in L^{t^1}(z; \succsim_{t^1})$. In fact, if $\left[C_i(z) \succsim_{t^1} BC^{t^1}\right]$ holds for some $i \in L^{t^1}(z; \succsim_{t^1})$, it implies $C_i(z) \succsim_j BC^{t^1} \succsim_j C_j(y) \succ_j C_j(z) \succsim_j C_h(z) \sim_j C_i(z)$ for some $h \in L^{t^1}(z; \succsim_{t^1})$ as argued in the step **2-i)** of this proof, which is a contradiction. Therefore, *not* $\left[C_i(z) \succsim_{t^1} BC^{t^1}\right]$ holds for any $i \in L^{t^1}(z; \succsim_{t^1})$. Thus, $xP^{t^1}z$ is derived from **BWC** by applying the case α-2) or β). Note that in this case, it can be shown that *not* $zP^{WP}x$ holds.

3-ii): Let $xP^{t^1}y$ be derived from **BWC** by applying case β) but not applying case α). Then, *not* $\left[C_j(y) \succsim_{t^1} BC^{t^1}\right]$ and *not* $\left[C_j(y) \succsim_{t^1} BC^{t^1}\right]$ for any $j \in L^{t^1}(y; \succsim_{t^1})$ due to $\boldsymbol{D}$, and $C_i(x) \succsim_{t^1} BC^{t^1}$ for all $i \in L^{t^1}(x; \succsim_{t^1})$. Then, by the property of $\succsim_{t^1}$, *not* $\left[C_j(y) \succsim_j BC^{t^1}\right]$ and *not* $\left[C_j(y) \succsim_j BC^{t^1}\right]$. Note that as shown in the step **2)** of this proof, $xR^{t^1}z$ or $xNR^{t^1}z$ holds.

Suppose $xI^{t^1}z$. This is possible only when $C_i(x) \sim_{t^1} BC^{t^1}$ for all $i \in L^{t^1}(x; \succsim_{t^1})$ and $C_h(z) \sim_{t^1} BC^{t^1}$ for all $h \in L^{t^1}(z; \succsim_{t^1})$. Therefore, $C_h(y) \succ_h BC^{t^1} \sim_{t^1} C_h(z)$ for all $h \in L^{t^1}(z; \succsim_{t^1})$. Since $BC^{t^1} \sim_{t^1} C_h(z)$ for all $h \in L^{t^1}(z; \succsim_{t^1})$ implies $BC^{t^1} \sim_h C_h(z)$ for all $h \in L^{t^1}(z; \succsim_{t^1})$, $L^{t^1}(z; \succsim_{t^1}) \cap L^{t^1}(y; \succsim_{t^1}) = \varnothing$ follows from $C_i(y) \succ_i C_i(z)$ for all $i \in N$. Then, since $C_j(z) \succ_{t^1} BC^{t^1}$, $C_j(y) \succ_j C_j(z) \succ_j BC^{t^1}$ holds, which is a contradiction from *not* $\left[C_j(y) \succsim_j BC^{t^1}\right]$. Thus, $xI^{t^1}z$ is impossible.

Suppose $xNR^{t^1}z$. This implies that (x, z) corresponds to case ϵ), so that $C_i(z) \succ_{t^1} BC^{t^1}$ for all $i \in L^{t^1}(z; \succsim_{t^1})$. Again, in this case, $L^{t^1}(z; \succsim_{t^1}) \cap L^{t^1}(y; \succsim_{t^1}) = \varnothing$ follows from $j \notin L^{t^1}(z; \succsim_{t^1})$. If $j \in L^{t^1}(z; \succsim_{t^1})$, then $C_j(y) \succ_j C_j(z) \succ_j BC^{t^1}$ holds, which is a contradiction from *not* $\left[C_j(y) \succsim_j BC^{t^1}\right]$. However, $C_i(z) \succ_{t^1} BC^{t^1}$ for all $i \in L^{t^1}(z; \succsim_{t^1})$ implies that $C_i(z) \succ_i BC^{t^1}$ for all $i \in N^{t^1}$. Therefore, $C_j(y) \succ_j C_j(z) \succ_j BC^{t^1}$ holds, which is again a contradiction. Thus, $xNR^{t^1}z$ is impossible.

In conclusion, $xP^{t^1}z$ holds. Note that in this case, it can be shown that *not* $zP^{WP}x$ holds.

3-iii): Let $xP^{t^1}y$ be derived from **BWC** by applying the case α-2) or γ). This implies *not* $\left[BC^{t^1} \succsim_{t^1} C_i(x)\right]$ for some $i \in L^{t^1}(x; \succsim_{t^1})$, and $BC^{t^1} \succ_{t^1} C_j(y)$ for all $j \in L^{t^1}(y; \succsim_{t^1})$.

Suppose $zR^{t^1}x$. In order to ensure $zR^{t^1}x$, $C_i(z) \succsim_{t^1} BC^{t^1}$ holds for all $i \in L^{t^1}(z; \succsim_{t^1})$. However, since $BC^{t^1} \succ_{t^1} C_j(y) \succ_j C_j(z)$ for all $j \in L^{t^1}(y; \succsim_{t^1})$, we have $C_i(z) \succsim_{t^1} BC^{t^1} \succ_{t^1} C_j(y) \succ_j C_j(z)$ for all $j \in L^{t^1}(y; \succsim_{t^1})$ and all $i \in L^{t^1}(z; \succsim_{t^1})$. Therefore, $BC^{t^1} \succ_j C_j(z)$ for all $j \in L^{t^1}(y; \succsim_{t^1})$. However, $C_i(z) \succsim_{t^1} BC^{t^1}$ holds for all $i \in L^{t^1}(z; \succsim_{t^1})$ implies that $C_i(z) \succsim_{t^1} BC^{t^1}$ holds for all $i \in N^{t^1}$, and so $C_i(z) \succsim_i BC^{t^1}$ holds for all $i \in N^{t^1}$. Thus, we have a contradiction. Thus, $zR^{t^1}x$ is impossible.

Suppose $zNR^{t^1}x$. Note that $zNR^{t^1}x$ is derived from **RC** by applying the case ϵ) or ε). If case ϵ) is applied, then $C_i(z) \succ_{t^1} BC^{t^1}$ holds for all $i \in L^{t^1}(z; \succsim_{t^1})$. Then, as in the same argument as the case of supposing $zR^{t^1}x$, we have a contradiction. Thus, $zNR^{t^1}x$ is impossible to be derived from **RC** by applying the case ϵ).

If case ε) is applied, then

$$not\left[C_j(z) \succsim_{t^1} BC^{t^1}\right] \text{ for some } j \in L^{t^1}(z; \succsim_{t^1});$$
$$\text{or } not\left[BC^{t^1} \succsim_{t^1} C_i(z)\right] \text{ for some } i \in L^{t^1}(z; \succsim_{t^1}).$$

Let the former do not hold, so that $C_i(z) \succsim_{t^1} BC^{t^1}$ holds for all $i \in L^{t^1}\left(z; \succsim_{t^1}\right)$. Then, again, since $BC^{t^1} \succ_{t^1} C_j(y) \succ_j C_j(z)$ for all $j \in L^{t^1}(y; \succsim_{t^1})$, we have $BC^{t^1} \succ_{t^1} C_h(z)$ for all $h \in L^{t^1}\left(z; \succsim_{t^1}\right)$ by applying **D**, which is a contradiction. Let the latter do not hold, so that $BC^{t^1} \succsim_{t^1} C_i(z)$ for all $i \in L^{t^1}(z; \succsim_{t^1})$. Again, since $BC^{t^1} \succ_{t^1} C_j(y) \succ_j C_j(z)$ for all $j \in L^{t^1}(y; \succsim_{t^1})$, we have $BC^{t^1} \succ_{t^1} C_h(z)$ for all $h \in L^{t^1}\left(z; \succsim_{t^1}\right)$. Then, *not* $zP^{t^1}y$ is derived from **RM** by applying case δ). Then, by ***FCD***, $yR^{t^1}z$. Thus, by transitivity, $xP^{t^1}z$, which is a contradiction from $zNR^{t^1}x$. In summary, $zNR^{t^1}x$ does not hold.

In conclusion, $xP^{t^1}z$ holds. Note that in this case, it can be shown that *not* $zP^{WP}x$ holds.

4. Let $xR^{t^1}y$ be derived from **RM** by applying case δ). Then, $BC^{t^1} \succ_{t^1} C_i(x)$ for all $i \in L^{t^1}(x; \succsim_{t^1})$; and also, $BC^{t^1} \succ_{t^1} C_i(y)$ for all $i \in L^{t^1}_{\mathbf{C}}(y; \succsim_{t^1})$. Since $BC^{t^1} \succ_{t^1} C_j(y) \succ_j C_j(z)$ for all $j \in L^{t^1}_{\mathbf{C}}(y; \succsim_{t^1})$, ***D*** implies that $BC^{t^1} \succ_{t^1} C_h(z)$ for all $h \in L^{t^1}_{\mathbf{C}}(z; \succsim_{t^1})$. Thus, by ***FCD*** and **RM** with case δ), $yR^{t^1}z$ is derived. Hence, the pair (x, z) corresponds to case δ). Moreover, $C_i(x) \succsim_{t^1} C_j(y) \succ_{t^1} C_h(z)$ holds for all $i \in L^{t^1}(x; \succsim_{t^1})$, all $j \in L^{t^1}(y; \succsim_{t^1})$, and all $h \in L^{t^1}(z; \succsim_{t^1})$. Then, by the transitivity of $\succsim_{t^1}$, $C_i(x) \succ_{t^1} C_h(z)$ holds for all $i \in L^{t^1}(x; \succsim_{t^1})$ and all $h \in L^{t^1}(z; \succsim_{t^1})$. Thus, $xP^{t^1}z$ holds by **RM**. Note that in this case, it can be shown that *not* $zP^{WP}x$ holds.

5. In combining the above arguments, if $xR^{NR}y$ and $yP^{WP}z$, then $xP^{t^1}z$ or $xNR^{t^1}z$ holds and xR^tz or xNR^tz for any $t \in T\setminus\left\{t^1\right\}$, thus $xP^{NR}z$ or $xNR^{NR}z$. Moreover, *not* $zP^{WP}x$ holds. Therefore, by the transitive closure, xP^*z. ■

Proof of Lemma 3 Let $xP^{WP}y$ and $yR^{NR}z$. This implies that there exists $t^1 \in T$ such that $yR^{t^1}z$ and *not* zP^ty for any other $t \in T$, and $C_i(x) \succ_i C_i(y)$ holds for all $i \in N$.

1. We will show that, in this case, $xP^{t^1}z$ holds.

First, if $yP^{t^1}z$ is derived from **BWC** by applying either of the case α-2), β), or γ), then $xP^{t^1}z$ is derived from **BWC** by applying either of the case α-2), β), or γ).

Second, if $yI^{t^1}z$ is derived from **BWC** by applying case α-1), then $xR^{t^1}z$ is derived from **BWC** by case α). Moreover, since $C_i(x) \succ_{t^1} BC^{t^1}$ for all $i \in L^{t^1}(x; \succsim_{t^1})$, $xP^{t^1}z$ holds by **BWC** with case α-2).

Third, let $yR^{t^1}z$ be derived from **RM** by applying case δ). If $C_i(x) \prec_t BC^t$ for all $i \in L^t(x; \succsim_t)$, then $xP^{t^1}z$ is derived from **RM** and ***FCD***; otherwise, then $xP^{t^1}z$ is derived from **BWC** and ***FCD*** by applying the case α-2) or γ).

In summary, $xP^{t^1}z$ holds for $t^1 \in T$.

2. Next, we will show that *not* zP^tx for any $t \in T \setminus \{t^1\}$. Note that for any $t \in T \setminus \{t^1\}$, (i) *not* zP^ty, and (ii) $C_i(x) \succ_i C_i(y)$ holds for all $i \in N$ together imply that xR^tz or xNR^tz. First of all, *not* zP^ty if and only if yR^tz or yNR^tz.

If yR^tz, then it is derived from **BWC** by applying the case α), β), or γ), or from **RM** by applying case δ). Then, as shown in the case of **1.**, we can see that xP^tz holds for any $t \in T \setminus \{t^1\}$.

If yNR^tz, then it is derived from **RC** by applying the case ϵ) or ε). If case ϵ) is applied for yNR^tz, then xNR^tz also holds by **RC**. If case ε) is applied for yNR^tz, then [*not* $\left[BC^t \succsim_t C_i(y)\right]$ for some $i \in L^t(y; \succsim_t)$ and *not* $\left[C_j(y) \succsim_t BC^t\right]$ for some $j \in L^t(y; \succsim_t)$] and [*not* $\left[BC^t \succsim_t C_i(z)\right]$ for some $i \in L^t(z; \succsim_t)$ and *not* $\left[C_j(z) \succsim_t BC^t\right]$ for some $j \in L^t(z; \succsim_t)$]. Then, since $C_i(x) \succ_t C_i(y)$ holds for all $i \in N$, **RC** with case ε) is again applied for xNR^tz or **BWC** with case β) is applied for xR^tz.

Thus, in summary, for any $t \in T \setminus \{t^1\}$, xR^tz or xNR^tz holds.

3. From **1.** and **2.**, $xP^{NR}z$ holds. Finally, in any case, it is impossible to have $zR^{WP}x$. Therefore, by transitivity, xP^*z. ■

References

Agassi, J. (1975). Institutional individualism. *British Journal of Sociology, 26*, 144–155.
Alkire, S. (2002). *Valuing freedoms: Sen's capability approach and poverty reduction*. Oxford: Oxford University Press.
Alkire, S. (2016). The capability approach and well-being measurement for public policy. In M. D. Adler & M. Fleurbaey (Eds.), *The Oxford handbook of well-being and public policy* (pp. 615–644). Oxford: Oxford University Press.
Alkire, S., & Foster, J. (2011). Counting and multidimensional poverty measures. *Journal of Public Economics, 95*(7–8), 476–487.
Alkire, S., Foster, J. E., Seth, S., Santos, M. E., Roche, J., & Ballon, P. (2015). *Multidimensional poverty measurement and analysis*. New York: Oxford University Press.
Anand, P., & van Hees, M. (2006). Capabilities and achievement: An empirical study. *Journal of Socio-Economics, 35*, 268–284.
Anderson, E. (1993). *Value in ethics and economics*. Cambridge, MA: Harvard University Press.
Aristotle. (4th Century BC/1980). *The Nicomachean ethics* (D. Ross, English Trans. Oxford: Clarendon Press, 1980).
Arneson, R. (1989). Equality and equal opportunity for welfare. *Philosophical Studies, 56*, 77–93.
Arrow, K. J. (1950). A difficulty in the concept of social welfare. *Journal of Political Economy, 58*, 328–346.
Arrow, K. J. (1951a/1963). *Social choice and individual values* (2nd edn.). New York: Wiley.
Arrow, K. J. (1951b). An extension of the basic theorems of classical welfare economics. In J. Neyman (Ed.), *Proceedings of the second berkeley symposium on mathematical statistics and probability* (pp. 507–532). Berkeley: University of California Press; reprinted in Collected Papers of Kenneth J. Arrow, Vol. 2: *General equilibrium* (Cambridge, MA: Belknap Press of Harvard University Press, 1983).
Arrow, K. J. (1973). Some ordinalist-Utilitarian notes on Rawls's theory of justice. *Journal of Philosophy, 70*(9), 245–263.
Arrow, K. J. (1974). *The limits of organization*. New York: W. W. Norton.
Arrow, K. J. (1977). Extended sympathy and the possibility of social choice. *American Economic Review, 67*, 219–225.

R. Gotoh, *The Ethics and Economics of the Capability Approach*, Hitotsubashi University IER Economic Research Series 46, https://doi.org/10.1007/978-981-15-5140-6

Arrow, K. J. (1979). The trade-off between growth and equity. In H. I. Greenfield, A. M. Levenson, W. Hamovitch, & E. Rotwein (Eds.), *Theory for economic efficiency: Essays in Honor of Abba P. Lerner* (pp. 1–11) (Reprinted in Arrow (1983), 190–200).

Arrow, K. J. (1999). Amartya K. Sen's contributions to the study of social welfare. *Scandinavian Journal of Economics*, *101*(2), 163–72.

Arrow, K. J. (2006). Freedom and social choice: Notes in the margin. *Utilitas*, *18*(1), 52–60.

Arrow, K. J., & Debreu, G. (1954). Existence of an equilibrium for a competitive economy. *Econometrica*, *22*(3), 265–290.

Arrow, K. J., Sen, A. K., & Suzumura, K. (Eds.). (2002). *Handbook of social choice and welfare* (Vol. I). Amsterdam: North-Holland.

Arrow, K. J., Sen, A. K., & Suzumura, K. (Eds.). (2011). *Handbook of social choice and welfare (Vol. II)*. Amsterdam: Elsevier.

Atkinson, A. B. (1970). On the measurement of inequality. *Journal of Economic Theory*, *2*, 244–263.

Atkinson, A. B. (1995). Capabilities, exclusion, and the supply of goods. In K. Basu, P. Pattanaik, & K. Suzumura (Eds.) (pp. 17–31).

Atkinson, A. B. (1999). The contributions of Amartya Sen to welfare economics. *Scandinavian Journal of Economics*, *101*(2), 173–90.

Barberà S., Bossert, W., & Pattanaik, P. K. (2002). Ranking sets of objects. In S. Barberà, P. Hammond, & C. Seidl (Eds.), *The handbook of utility theory* (Vol. 2, pp. 893–977). Kluwer Academic Publishers.

Barclay, L. (2016). The importance of equal respect: What the capabilities approach can and should learn from human rights law. *Political Studies*, *64*(2), 385–400.

Basu, K. (1987). Achievements, capabilities, and the concept of well-being. *Social Choice and Welfare*, *4*, 69–76.

Basu, K., & Kanbur, R. (Eds.), *Arguments for a better world: Essays in honor of Amartya Sen* (Vols. I & II). Oxford: Clarendon Press.

Basu, K., & Lopez-Calva, L. F. (2011). Functionings and capabilities. In A. Sen, & K. Suzumura (Eds.) (pp. 153–186).

Basu, K., Pattanaik, P., & Suzumura, K. (Eds.). (1995). *Choice, welfare, and development: A festschrift in honour of Amartya K. Sen*. Oxford: Oxford University Press.

Becker, G. (1965). A theory of the allocation of time. *Economic Journal*, *75*, 493–517.

Becker, G. (1976). *The economic approach to human behavior*. Chicago: University of Chicago Press.

Becker, L. C. (1986). *Reciprocity*. London: Routledge & Kegan Paul.

Ben-Porath, Y. (1970). The production of human capital over time. *NBER*, 129–154.

Bossert, W., Pattanaik, P. K., & Xu, Y. (1994). Ranking opportunity sets: An axiomatic approach. *Journal of Economic Theory*, *63*, 326–345.

Brandolini, A. (2009). On applying synthetic indices of multidimensional well-being: Health and income inequalities in France, Germany, Italy, and the United Kingdom. In R. Gotoh & P. Dumouchel (Eds.), *Against injustice? The new economics of Amartya Sen*. Cambridge: Cambridge University Press.

Brighouse, H., & Robeyns, I. (Eds.). (2010). *Measuring justice: Primary goods and capabilities*. Cambridge: Cambridge University Press.

Brooks, T., & Nussbaum, M. C. (Eds.). (2015). *Rawls's political liberalism*. New York: Columbia University Press.

Broome, J. (1991). *Weighing goods*. Oxford: Blackwell.

Bruni, L., Comim, F., & Pugno, M. (Eds.). (2008). *Capabilities and happiness*. Oxford: Oxford University Press.

Chiappero-Martinetti, E. (1994). A new approach to evaluation of well-being and poverty by fuzzy set approach. *Giornale Degli Economisti e Annali di Economia*, *7*(9), 367–388.

Chiappero-Martinetti, E. (1996). Standard of living evaluation based on Sen's approach: Some methodological suggestions. *Notizie di Politeia*, *12*(43/44), 37–53.

Chiappero-Martinetti, E. (2000). A multidimensional assessment of well-being based on Sen's functioning approach. *Rivista Internazionale di Scienze Sociali, 58*, 207–39.

Chiappero-Martinetti, E. (Ed.). (2009). *Debating global society: Reach and limits of the capability approach*. Milan: Fondazione Feltrinelli.

Chiappero-Martinetti, E., & Roche, J. M. (2009). Operationalization of the capability approach, from theory to practice: A review of techniques and empirical applications. In E. Chiappero-Martinetti (Ed.), *Debating global society: Reach and limits of the capability approach* (pp. 157–203). Milan: Fondazione Feltrinelli.

Claassen, R. (2011). Making capability lists: Philosophy versus democracy. *Political Studies, 59*, 491–508.

Coast, J., Peters, T. J., Natarajan, L., Sproston, K., & Flynn, T. (2008). An assessment of the construct validity of the descriptive system for the ICECAP capability measure for older people. *Quality of Life Research, 17*, 967–976.

Coast, J., Smith, R., & Lorgelly, P. (2008a). Should the capability approach be applied in health economics? *Health Economics, 17*, 667–670.

Coast, J., Smith, R., & Lorgelly, P. (2008b). Welfarism, extra-welfarism and capability: The spread of ideas in health economics. *Social Science & Medicine, 67*, 1190–1198.

Cohen, G. A. (1993). Equality of what? On welfare, goods, and capabilities. In M. Nussbaum & A. K. Sen (Eds.) (pp. 9–29).

Comim, F., & Nussbaum, M. (Eds.). (2014). *Capabilities, gender, equality: Towards fundamental entitlements*. Cambridge: Cambridge University Press.

Comim, F., Qizilbash, M., & Alkire, S. (Eds.). (2008). *The capability approach: Concepts, measures and applications*. Cambridge: Cambridge University Press.

Coser, L. (1988). *Refugee scholars in America: Their impact and their experiences*. New Haven: Yale University Press.

d'Aspremont, C., & Gevers, L. (2002). Social welfare functionals and interpersonal comparability. In K. Arrow, A. K. Sen, & K. Suzumura (Eds.), *Handbook of social choice and welfare* (Vol. 1, pp. 459–541). Amsterdam: North-Holland.

d'Agata. (2007). Endogenizing Sen's capabilities: An adaptive dynamics analysis. *Journal of Socio-Economics, 36*, 177–190.

d'Aspremont, C., & Gevers, L. (1977). Equity and the informational basis of collective choice. *Review of Economic Studies, 46*, 199–210.

Davis, D. M. (1992). The case against the inclusion of socio-economic demands in a bill of rights except as directive principles. *South African Journal of Human Rights, 8*, 475–90.

Deneulin, S. (2002). Perfectionism, paternalism and liberalism in Sen and Nussbaum's capability approach. *Review of Political Economy, 14*(4), 497–518.

Deneulin, S., Nebel, M., & Sagovsky, N. (Eds.). (2006). *Transforming unjust structures: The capability approach*. Dordrecht: Springer.

Doyal, L., & Gough, I. (1991). *A theory of human need*. London: Macmillan.

Drèze, J., & Sen, A. K. (2013). *An uncertain glory: India and its contradictions*. Princeton, NJ: Princeton University Press.

Dworkin, R. (1977). *Taking rights seriously*. Cambridge, MA: Harvard University Press.

Dworkin, R. (1981a). What is equality? Part I: Equality of welfare. *Philosophy & Public Affairs, 10*(3), 185–246.

Dworkin, R. (1981b). What is equality? Part II: Equality of resources. *Philosophy & Public Affairs, 10*(3), 283–345.

Dworkin, R. (2000). *Sovereign virtue: The theory and practice of equality*. Cambridge, MA: Harvard University Press.

Elster, J. (1982). Sour grapes. In A. K. Sen & B. Williams (Eds.), *Utilitarianism and beyond*. Cambridge: Cambridge University Press.

EuroQol Group (1990-12-01). EuroQol–A new facility for the measurement of health-related quality of life. *Health Policy, 16*(3), 199–208.

Farina, F., Hahn, F. H., & Vannucci, S. (Eds.). (1996). *Ethics, rationality and economic behaviour*. Oxford: Clarendon Press.

Farrina, F., Peluso, E., & Savaglio, E. (2004). Ranking opportunity sets in the space of functionings. *Journal of Economic Inequality*, *2*, 105–16.

Fleurbaey, M. (1994). On fair compensation. *Theory and Decision*, *36*, 277–307.

Fleurbaey, M. (1995a). Three solutions to the compensation problem. *Journal of Economic Theory*, *65*, 505–521.

Fleurbaey, M. (1995b). Equal opportunity or equal social outcome? *Economics and Philosophy*, *11*, 25–55.

Fleurbaey, M. (2002). Development, capabilities, and freedom. *Studies in Comparative International Development*, *37*(2), 71–77.

Fleurbaey, M. (2006). Capabilities, functionings and refined functionings. *Journal of Human Development*, *7*, 299–310.

Fleurbaey, M. (2014). Capabilities or functionings? Anatomy of a debate. In F. Comim & M. Nussbaum (Eds.), *Capabilities, gender, equality* (pp. 155–174). Cambridge: Cambridge University Press.

Fleurbaey, M., & Blanchet, D. (2013). *Beyond GDP: Measuring welfare and assessing sustainability*. Oxford: Oxford University Press.

Fleurbaey, M., & Maniquet, F. (2011). Compensation and responsibility. In K. J. Arrow, A. K. Sen, & K. Suzumura (Eds.), *Handbook of Social choice and welfare* (Vol. II, pp. 508–604). Amsterdam: Elsevier.

Fleurbaey, M., & Mongin, P. (2005). The news of the death of welfare economics is greatly exaggerated. *Social Choice and Welfare*, *25*, 381–418.

Frankfurt, H. (1987). Equality as a moral ideal. *Ethics*, *98*(1), 21–43.

Frazer, L. M. (2014). Including the unaffected. *Journal of Political Philosophy*, *22*(4), 377–395.

Gaertner, W., Pattanaik, P. K., & Suzumura, K. (1992). Individual rights revisited. *Economica*, *59*, 161–177.

Garnham, N. (1999). Amartya Sen's capability approach to the evaluation of welfare: Its application to communications. In A. Calabrese & J. Burgelman (Eds.), *Communication, citizenship and social policy*. Lanham: Rowman & Littlefield Publisher.

Gasper, D. (1997). Sen's capability approach and Nussbaum's capability ethic. *Journal of International Development*, *9*, 281–302.

Gibbard, A. (1974). A Pareto-consistent libertarian claim. *Journal of Economic Theory*, *7*, 388–410.

Girard, R. (1961): *Mensonge romantique et Vérité romanesque*. Paris: Grasset. English translation (1966): *Deceit, desire and the novel: Self and other in literary structure*. Baltimore: Johns Hopkins University Press.

Goffman, E. (1963a). *Stigma: Notes on the management of spoiled identity*. Englewood Cliffs, NJ: Prentice-Hall.

Goffman, E. (1963b). *Behavior in public places: Notes on the social organization of gatherings*. Free Press.

Gotoh, R. (2001). The capability theory and welfare reform. *Pacific Economic Review*, *6*(2), 211–222.

Gotoh, R. (2004). Well-being freedom and the possibility of public-provision unit in global context. *Ethics and Economics*, *2*, 1–17.

Gotoh, R. (2009). Justice and public reciprocity. In R. Gotoh & P. Dumouchel (Eds.), *Against injustice? The new economics of Amartya Sen* (pp. 140–160). Cambridge: Cambridge University Press.

Gotoh, R. (2014). The equality of the differences: Sen's critique of Rawls's theory of justice and its implications for welfare economics. *Journal of History of Economic Ideas*, *22*(1), 133–155.

Gotoh, R. (2015a). Arrow, Rawls and Sen: The transformation of political economics and the idea of liberalism. In P. Dumouchel and Gotoh R. (Eds.), *Social bonds as freedom—Revisiting the dichotomy of the universal and the particular* (pp. 259–284). New York: Berghahn Books.

Gotoh, R. (2015b). What Japan has left behind in the course of establishing a welfare state. *Proto-Sociology, 32*, 106–122.

Gotoh, R. (2016a). A coherent goals-rights system in the light of political liberalism. *International Institute of Language and Cultural Studies, Ritsumeikan University, 28*(1), 171–182.

Gotoh, R. (2016b). Capability approach to the equality of differences and the problem of adaptive preference–Focusing on individual positionality and individuality. In K. Nakatogawa, L. De Tienda Palop, Y. Mitsuke, & Y. Fukuyama (Eds.), *Discussing capabilities, emotions and values: A cross-cultural perspective*. Sapporo: Simpleprint.

Gotoh, R. (2019). Arrow and Sen—forming of social choice theory and its critical extension. *Waseda Journal of Political Science and Economics, 394*, 30–40. (in Japanese).

Gotoh, R., & Dumouchel, P. (Eds.). (2009). *Against injustice: The new economics of Amartya Sen*. Cambridge: Cambridge University Press.

Gotoh, R., & Yoshihara, N. (2003). A class of fair distribution rules a la Rawls and Sen. *Economic Theory, 22*, 63–88.

Gotoh, R., & Yoshihara, N. (2018). Securing basic capability for all. *Review of Social Economy, 76*(4), 422–452.

Graham, J. W., & Green, C. A. (1984). Estimating the parameters of a household production function with joint products. *Review of Economics and Statistics, 66*(2), 277–282.

Gutmann, A., & Thompson, D. (1996). *Democracy and disagreement*. Cambridge, MA: The Belknap Press of Harvard University Press.

Hahn, F. H. (1971). Equilibrium with transaction costs. *Econometrica, 39*, 417–443.

Hammond, P. J. (1976). Equity, Arrow's Conditions and Rawls' difference principle. *Econometrica, 44*, 793–804.

Hammond, P. J. (1995). Social choice of individual and group rights. In W. A. Barnett, H. Moulin, M. Salles, & N. Schofield (Eds.), *Social choice, welfare and ethics* (pp. 55–77). Cambridge: Cambridge University Press.

Hare, R. M. (1952/1963). *The language of morals*. Oxford: Oxford University Press.

Harsanyi, J. C. (1955). Cardinal welfare, individualistic ethics, and interpersonal comparisons of utility. *Journal of Political Economy, 63*, 309–321.

Hayek, F. A. (1952/2018). *The sensory order-an inquiry into the foundation of theoretical psychology*. London: Routledge & Kegan Paul Limited.

Heckman, J. (1974). Shadow prices, market wages and labor supply. *Econometrica, 42*, 679–694.

Heckman, J. (1979). Sample selection Bias as a specification error. *Econometrica, 47*, 153–162.

Heckman, J., & Corbin, C. O. (2016). Capabilities and skills. *Journal of Human Development and Capabilities, 17*(3), 342–59.

Heisenberg, W. (1958). The representation of nature in contemporary physics. *Daedalus, 87*(3), 95–108.

Hénaff, M. (2009). Gift, market and social justice. In R. Gotoh & P. Dumouchel (Eds.), *Against injustice: The new economics of Amartya Sen*. Cambridge: Cambridge University Press.

Herrero, C. (1996). Capabilities and utilities. *Economic Design, 2*, 69–88.

Hodgson, G. M. (2007). Meanings of methodological individualism. *Journal of Economic Methodology, 14*(2), 211–226.

Ireland, T. D., & Spezia, C. H. (2014). *Adult education in retrospective: 60 years of CONFINTEA*. Brasilia: UNESCO.

Kambayashi, R., Gotoh, R., & Kobayashi, H. (2020). *An application of the capability approach to data about going-out/staying-home activities. In Research on going out of elderly persons and persons with disabilities in a city*. Mimeo: Hitotsubashi University.

Kamiya, M. (1989). *Utsuwa no uta*. Tokyo: Misuzu-shobo (in Japanese).

Kanbur, R. (1987). The standard of living: Uncertainty, inequality and opportunity. In G. Hawthorn (Ed.), *The standard of living* (pp. 59–69). Cambridge: Cambridge University Press.

Kanbur, R. (2016). Capability, opportunity, outcome-and equality. In H. Charles (Ed.), *Dyson School of Applied Economics and Management, WP2016-5*. Cornell University.

Kant, I. (1785). Grundlegung zur Metaphysik der Sitten (T. K. Abbott, English Trans.) (1985). *Fundamental principles of the metaphysics of ethics*. London: Longmans.

Kim, H. (2007). Rethinking social recovery in Schizophrenia: What a capabilities approach might offer. *Social Science & Medicine*, *65*(5), 868–879.

Kleine, D. (2010). ICT4WHAT?-Using the choice framework to operationalize the capability approach to development. *Journal of International Development*, *22*(5), 674–692.

Klemisch-Ahlert, M. (1993). Freedom of choice: A comparison of different rankings of opportunity sets. *Social Choice and Welfare*, *10*(3), 189–207.

Knight, F. H. (1921/1947). Ethics and economic reform. *Economica* (new series), 6 (February, August, November): 1–29, 296–321, 398–422. Reprinted in *Freedom & Reform; and Selected Essays*, (Vol. 2), 1947.

Knight, F. H. (1921/1957). *Risk, uncertainty and profit*. Dover Publications, Inc. Printed in United States of America by Sentry Press, New York.

Knight, F. H. (1931/1997). *The ethics of competition*. New Brunswick and London: Transaction Publishers (Originally published in 1931 by Harper and Brothers).

Kobayashi, H., Takemura, Y., & Kanda, K. (2011). Patient perception of nursing service quality: An applied model of Donabedian's structure-process-outcome approach theory. *Scandinavian Journal of Caring Sciences, Nordic College of Caring Science*, *25*(3), 419–425.

Kolm, S.-C. (1972). *Justice et Equité*, Paris: Editions du CNRS (H. F. See, Trans. *Justice and equity*). Cambridge, MA: MIT Press, 1998.

Kolm, S. (2004). *Macrojustice: The political economy of fairness*. New York: Cambridge University Press.

Kolm, S. (2010). On real economic freedom. *Social Choice and Welfare*, *35*(3), 351–375.

Kuklys, W. (2005). *Amartya Sen's capability approach: Theoretical insights and empirical application*. Berlin: Springer.

Lakatos, I. (1970/1985). Falsification and the methodology of scientific research programmes. In I. Lakatos & A. Musgrave (Eds.), *Criticism and the growth of knowledge*. Cambridge: Cambridge University Press.

Lancaster, K. J. (1966). A new approach to consumer theory. *Journal of Political Economy*, *74*, 132–57.

Lancaster, K. J. (1971). *Consumer demand: A new approach*. New York: Columbia University Press.

Levinas, E. (1961). *Totalité et infini: Essai sur l'extériorité. The Hague: Martinus Nijhoff* (p. 1979). Translated by AlphonsoLingis, Totality and infinity: An essay on exteriority. Springer Science & Business Media.

Levinas, E. (1997). In R. Burggraeve (Ed.), *Emmanuel Levinas et la socialité de l'argent*. Leuven: Peeters.

Lorenz, M. O. (1905). Methods of measuring the concentration of wealth. *Publication of American Statistical Association*, *9*(70), 209–219.

Manheim, K. (1936/2015). *Ideology and Utopia: An introduction to the sociology of knowledge* (L. Wirth & E. Shils, Trans.) Martino Fine Books.

Maniquet, F. (2004). On the equivalence between welfarism and equality of opportunity. *Social Choice and Welfare*, *23*, 127–147.

Marmot, M. (2015). *The health gap: The challenge of an unequal world*. London: Bloomsbury.

Marshall, A. (1890). *Principles of economics, 8th edition 1920*. London: Macmillan.

Marx, K. (1844/1959). *Economic and philosophic manuscripts of 1844*. Moscow: Foreign Languages Publishing House.

Marx, K. (1875/1962). *Critique of the Gotha Programme*. Moscow: Foreign Languages Publishing House.

Mas-Colell, A., Whinston, M. D., & Green, J. R. (1995). *Microeconomic theory*. Oxford University Press.

Maskin, E., Sen, A. K., Arrow, P., Dasgupta, P., Pattanaik, K., & Stiglitz, J. E. (2014). *The Arrow impossibility theorem*. New York: Columbia University Press.

Matsuyama, J., & Mori, K. (2011). Freedom and achievement of well-being and adaptive dynamics of capabilities. *Metroeconomica, 62*(3), 494–511.

Menger, C. (1871/1976). *Principles of economics* (J. Dingwall & B. Hoselitz, Trans.). Ludwig von Mises Institute.

Mill, J. S. (1859/1977): *On liberty*, London: Parker, originally published in 1859. In J. M. Robson (Ed.), *The Collected Works of John Stuart Mill*, Vol. 18, Toronto: University of Toronto Press, 1977.

Mill, J. S. (1869). *The subjection of women*. London: Longmans.

Mirrlees, J. (1971). An exploration in the theory of optimum income taxation. *Review of Economic Studies, 38*, 175–208.

Miyagishima, K. (2010). Ranking linear budget sets. *Social Choice and Welfare, 35*(1), 163–73.

Miyagishima, K. (2012). Ranking linear budget sets with different available goods: A note. *Mathematical Social Sciences, 63*, 234–8.

Nozick, R. (1974). *Anarchy, state, and utopia*. New York: Basic Books.

Nussbaum, M. C. (1988). Nature, function, and capability: Aristotle on political distribution. *Oxford Studies in Ancient Philosophy, 6*, 145–184.

Nussbaum, M. C. (1990). Aristotelian social democracy. In R. B. Douglass, G. R. Mara, & H. S. Richardson (Eds.), *Liberalism and the good* (pp. 203–252). New York: Routledge.

Nussbaum, M. C. (1992). Human functionings and social justice: In defense of Aristotelian essentialism. *Political Theory, 20*, 202–246.

Nussbaum, M. C. (1993). Non-relative virtues: An Aristotelian approach. In Nussbaum & Sen (Eds.), (pp. 242–269).

Nussbaum, M. C. (1995). Aristotle on human nature and the foundations of ethics. In J. E. G. Altham & R. Harrison (Eds.), *World, mind, and ethics: Essays on the philosophy of Bernard Williams* (pp. 86–131). Cambridge: Cambridge University Press.

Nussbaum, M. C. (1997). Capabilities and human rights. *Fordham Law Review, 66*(2), 273–300.

Nussbaum, M. C. (2000). *Women and human development: The capabilities approach*. New York: Cambridge University Press.

Nussbaum, M. C. (2003). Capabilities as fundamental entitlements: Sen and social justice. *Feminist Economics, 9*(2/3), 40–50.

Nussbaum, M. C. (2004). *Hiding from humanity: Disgust, shame and the law*. Princeton: Princeton University Press.

Nussbaum, M. C. (2006). *Frontiers of justice: Disability, nationality, species membership*. Cambridge, MA: The Belknap Press of Harvard University Press.

Nussbaum, M. C. (2011a). *Creating capabilities*. Cambridge, MA: The Belknap Press of Harvard University Press.

Nussbaum, M. C. (2011b). Adaptive preferences and women's options. *Economics and Philosophy, 17*, 67–88.

Nussbaum, M. C., & Glover, J. (Eds.). (1995). *Women, culture, and development*. Oxford: Clarendon Press.

Nussbaum, M. C., & Sen, A. K. (Eds.). (1993). *The quality of life*. Oxford: Clarendon Press.

Osmani, S. R. (2005). Poverty and human rights: Building on the capability approach. *Journal of Human Development, 6*(2), 205–220.

Parfit, D. (1984). *Reasons and persons*. Oxford: Oxford University Press.

Parfit, D. (1991): *Equality or priority?* The Lindley Lecture, University of Kansas, November 21, 1991, 1–42.

Pattanaik, P. K. (2005). Little and Bergson on Arrow's concept of social welfare. *Social Choice and Welfare, 25*, 369–379.

Pattanaik, P. K., & Xu, Y. (1990). On ranking opportunity sets in terms of freedom of choice. *Recherches Économiques de Louvain, 56*(3/4), 383–90.

Pattanaik, P. K., & Xu, Y. (2000). On ranking opportunity sets in economic environments. *Journal of Economic Theory, 93*(1), 48–71.

Pattanaik, P. K., & Xu, Y. (2014). The ethical bases of public policies: A conceptual framework. *Economics and Philosophy, 30*, 175–194.

Pattanaik, P. K., & Xu, Y. (2017). On a concept of freedom. In A. Mishra & Tridip (Eds.), *Markets, governance, and institutions in the process of economic development* (pp. 31–46). Oxford: Oxford University Press.

Pettit, P. (2001). Capability and freedom: A defense of Sen. *Economics and Philosophy, 17*, 1–20.

Pigou, A. C. (1920/2013). *The economics of welfare*. London: Palgrave Macmillan.

Pogge, T. (2002). Can the capability approach be justified? *Philosophical Topics, 30*, 167–228.

Pogge, T. (2010). A critique of the capability approach. In Brighouse & Robeyns (Eds.), *Measuring justice: Primary goods and capabilities* (pp. 17–60). Cambridge: Cambridge University Press.

Pollak, R. A., & Wachter, M. L. (1975). The relevance of the household production function and its implications for the allocation of time. *Journal of Political Economy, 83*(2), 255–278.

Popper, K. (1959). *The logic of scientific discovery*. New York: Basic Books.

Puppe, C. (1995). An axiomatic approach to "preferences for freedom of choice". *Journal of Economic Theory, 93*, 48–71.

Putnam, H. (2008). Capabilities and two ethical theories. *Journal of Human Development, 9*, 377–388.

Putnam, H., & Walsh, V. (Eds.). (2012). *The end of value-free economics*. New York: Routledge.

Qizilbash, M. (1996). Capabilities, well-being, and human development: A survey. *Journal of Development Studies, 33*, 143–162.

Qizilbash, M. (2006). Capability, happiness and adaptation in Sen and. *J. S. Mill. Utilitas, 18*(1), 20–32.

Qizilbash, M. (2007). Social choice and individual capabilities. *Politics, Philosophy and Economics, 6*, 169–192.

Qizilbash, M. (2011). Sugden's critique of the capability approach. *Utilitas, 23*(1), 25–51.

Rawls, J. (1955). Two concepts of rule. In Freeman, S. (Ed.), *Collected papers*, (pp. 190–224). Cambridge, MA: Harvard University Press, 1999b.

Rawls, J. (1962). Justice as fairness. In P. Laslett & W. G. Runciman (Eds.), *Philosophy, politics and society 2nd series* (pp. 132–157). Oxford: Basil Blackwell.

Rawls, J. (1971a). *A theory of justice*. Cambridge, MA: Harvard University Press, Original edition, 1971. Revised edition, 1999.

Rawls, J. (1971b). Justice as reciprocity. In S. Gorowitz (Ed.), *John Stuart Mill: Utilitarianism, with critical essays*, reprinted in *Collected papers* (1999b), pp. 190–224.

Rawls, J. (1974). Reply to Alexander and Musgrave. *Quarterly Journal of Economics, 88*(4), 633–655. (reprinted in Rawls (1999b), pp. 232–253).

Rawls, J. (1982). Social unity and primary goods. In A. K. Sen & B. Williams (Eds.), *Utilitarianism and beyond* (pp. 159–185). Cambridge: Cambridge University Press.

Rawls, J. (1993). *Political liberalism*. New York: Columbia University Press.

Rawls, J. (1999a). *The law of peoples*. Cambridge, MA: Harvard University Press.

Rawls, J. (1999b). Collected papers. In S. Freeman (Ed.), *Cambridge*. MA: Harvard University Press.

Rawls, J. (2000). Lectures on the history of moral philosophy. In B. Herman (Ed.), *Cambridge*. MA: Harvard University Press.

Richardson, H. S. (2014). Rawlsian social-contract theory and the severely disabled. In F. Comim & M. C. Nussbaum (Eds.), *Capabilities, gender, equality* (pp. 57–95). Cambridge: Cambridge University Press.

Robeyns, I. (2003). Sen's capability approach and gender inequality: Selecting relevant capabilities. *Feminist Economics, 9*, 61–92.

Robeyns, I. (2006). The capability approach in practice. *Journal of Political Philosophy, 14*(3), 351–76.

Robeyns, I. (2009a). Justice as fairness and the capability approach. In Basu & Kanbur (Eds.), *Arguments for a better world: Essays in honor of Amartya Sen* (Vols. I & II, pp. 397–413). Oxford: Clarendon Press.

Robeyns, I. (2009b). Capability approach. In Peil & van Staveren (Eds.), *Handbook of economics and ethics* (pp. 39–46). Cheltenham: Edward Elgar.

Robeyns, I. (2016). Capabilitarianism. *Journal of Human Development and Capabilities, 17*(3), 397–414.

Robeyns, I. (2017). *Wellbeing, freedom and social justice: The capability approach re-examined.* Cambridge: Open Book Publishers.

Robinson, J. (1962). *Economic philosophy*. London: C. A. Watts

Roemer, J. E. (1993). A pragmatic theory of responsibility for the Egalitarian planner. *Philosophy & Public Affairs, 22*(2), 146–166.

Roemer, J. E. (1996). *Theories of distributive justice*. Cambridge, MA: Harvard University Press.

Roemer, J. E. (1998). *Equality of opportunity*. Cambridge, MA: Harvard University Press.

Rosen, S. (1974). Hedonic prices and implicit markets: Product differentiation in pure competition. *Journal of Political Economy, 82*(1), 34–55.

Rousseau, J.-J. (1762). Du Contrat Social, (Q. Hoare, Trans.) (1994). *Of the social contract*. London: Penguin Books.

Ruger, J. P. (2010). *Health and social justice*. Oxford: Oxford University Press.

Saito, M. (2003). Amartya Sen's capability approach to education: A critical exploration. *Journal of Philosophy of Education, 37*(1), 17–33.

Sakamoto, N. (2017). *Characterizations of social choice correspondences based on equality of capabilities in a pure exchange economy*. RCNE Discussion Paper Series: Institute of Economic Research, Hitotsubashi University.

Samuelson, P. A. (1947/1983). *Foundations of economic analysis*. Cambridge, MA: Harvard University Press.

Samuelson, P. A. (1950). Evaluation of real national income. *Oxford Economic Papers, 2*, 1–29.

Samuelson, P. A. (1956). Social indifference curves. *Quarterly Journal of Economics, 70*, 1–22.

Scanlon, T. (1982). Contractualism and utilitarianism. In A. K. Sen & B. Williams (Eds.), *Utilitarianism and beyond*. Cambridge: Cambridge University Press.

Schmitt C. (1923/1988). *The crisis of parliamentary democracy*. E. Kennedy, Trans., Cambridge, MA: MIT Press.

Schokkaert, E. (2009). The capabilities approach. In P. Anand, P. K. Pattanaik, & C. Puppe (Eds.), *The handbook of rational and social choice* (pp. 542–566). Oxford: Oxford University Press.

Sen A. K. (1992b). Minimal liberty. *Economica (new series), 59*, 139–159 (reprinted in Sen, 2002a, pp. 463–483).

Sen, A. K. (1973/1997). *On economic inequality, with a new technical Annexe by James Foster and Amartya Sen*. London: Oxford University Press.

Sen, A. K. (1976a). Liberty, unanimity and rights. *Economica, 43*, 217–245 (reprinted in Sen, 1997a, pp. 291–326).

Sen, A. K. (1976b). Poverty: An ordinal approach to measurement. *Econometrica, 44*, 219–231 (reprinted in Sen, 1997b).

Sen, A. K. (1976c). Real national income. *Review of Economic Studies, 43*, 19–39 (reprinted in Sen, 1997a, pp. 388–415).

Sen, A. K. (1977a). On weights and measures: Informational constraints in social welfare analysis. *Econometrica, 45*, 1539–1572 (reprinted in Sen, 1997a, pp. 226–263).

Sen, A. K. (1977b). Rational fools: A critique of behavioral foundations of economic theory. *Philosophy & Public Affairs, 6*, 317–344 (reprinted in Sen, 1997a, pp. 84–106).

Sen, A. K. (1979a). Personal utilities and public judgements: Or what's wrong with welfare economics? *Economic Journal, 89*, 537–558 (reprinted in Sen, 1997a, 327–352).

Sen, A. K. (1979b). The welfare basis of real income comparisons. *Journal of Economic Literature, 17*, 1–45 (reprinted in Sen, 1997b).

Sen, A. K. (1980a). Equality of what? In S. McMurrin (ed.) *The Tanner lectures on human values* (Vol. 4, 2nd ed.) (pp. 195–220). Cambridge: Cambridge University Press (reprinted in Sen, 1997a, 353–369).

Sen, A. K. (1981b). Ethical issues in income distribution: National and international. In S. Grassman & E. Lundberg (Eds.), *The world economic order: Past and prospects* (pp. 464–494). London: Macmillan (reprinted in Sen, 1997b, 277–306).
Sen, A. K. (1983). Liberty and social choice. *Journal of Philosophy, 80*(1), 5–28 (reprinted in Sen, 2002a).
Sen, A. K. (1985c). Social choice and justice. *Journal of Economic Literature, 23*(4), 1764–1776 (reprinted in Sen, 2002a).
Sen, A. K. (1986). Information and invariance of normative choice. In W. P. Heller, R. Starr, & D. A. Starrett (Eds.), *Social choice and public decision making: Essays in Honor of Kenneth. J. Arrow* (Vol. I, pp. 29–55). Cambridge: Cambridge University Press.
Sen, A. K. (1987b). *The standard of living*, The Tanner Lectures, Clare Hall, Cambridge, 1985. In G. Hawthorn (Ed.), *The standard of living*, with contributions by J. Muellbauer, R. Kanbur, K. Hart, & B. Williams, Cambridge: Cambridge University Press.
Sen, A. K. (1993a). Capability and well-being. In Nussbaum & Sen (Eds.) (pp. 30–53).
Sen, A. K. (1993c). Markets and freedoms: Achievements and limitations of the market mechanism in promoting individual freedom. *Oxford Economic Papers, 45*, 519–541 (reprinted in Sen, 2002a, pp. 501–530).
Sen, A. K. (1995). Rationality and social choice. *American Economic Review, 85*, 1–24 (reprinted in Sen, 2002a, pp. 261–299).
Sen, A. K. (1996a). On the foundations of welfare economics: Utility, capability and practical reason. In Farina, Hahn and Vannucci (Eds.) (pp. 50—65).
Sen, A. K. (1997a). *Choice, welfare and measurement*. Oxford: Blackwell. (first edition in 1982, Cambridge, MA: Harvard University Press).
Sen, A. K. (1997b). *Resources, values and development*. Oxford: Blackwell (first edition in 1984, Cambridge, MA: Harvard University Press).
Sen, A. K. (1997c). Individual preference as the basis of social choice. In K. J. Arrow, A. K. Sen, & K. Suzumura (Eds.), *Social choice re-examined* (Vol. 1, pp. 15–37). London: Macmillan.
Sen, A. K. (2004b). Disability and inclusive development: Sharing, learning and building alliances. Keynote speech delivered at a conference organized by the World Bank, Washington, November 30–December 1, 2004.
Sen, A. K. (2008). The economics of happiness and capability. In L. Bruni, F. Comim, & M. Pugno (Eds.), *Capabilities and happiness* (pp. 16–27). New York: Oxford University Press.
Sen, A. K. (2009b). Economics, ethics and law. In P. Dumouchel & R. Gotoh (Eds.), *Against injustice-The new economics of Amartya Sen*. Cambridge: Cambridge University Press.
Sen, A. K. (2009c). Capability: Reach and limit. In E. Chiappero-Martinetti (Ed.), *Debating global society. Reach and limit of the capability approach* (pp. pp. 15–28). Milan: Feltrinelli.
Sen, A. K. (2010). The place of capability in a theory of justice. In H. Brighouse & I. Robeyns (Eds.), *Measuring justice: Primary goods and capabilities* (pp. 239–253).
Sen, A. K. (1970a, 1979, 2017). *Collective choice and social welfare*. San Francisco: Holden-Day (1970). Republished, Amsterdam: North-Holland, 1979 (Expanded ed., p. 2017). London: Penguin.
Sen, A. K. (1962). *Choice of techniques: An aspect of the theory of planned economic development*. Oxford: Blackwell.
Sen, A. K. (1966a). Hume's law and Hare's rule. *Philosophy, 41*, 75–8.
Sen, A. K. (1966b). Labour allocation in a cooperative enterprise. *Review of Economic Studies, 33*, 361–171.
Sen, A. K. (1967a). The nature and classes of prescriptive judgements. *Philosophical Quarterly, 17*, 46–62.
Sen, A. K. (1967b). Isolation, assurance and the social rate of discount. *Quarterly Journal of Economics, 81*(1), 112–124.
Sen, A. K. (1969). Quasi-transitivity, rational choice and collective decisions. *Review of Economic Studies, 36*(3), 381–393.

Sen, A. K. (1970b). The impossibility of a Paretian liberal. *Journal of Political Economy, 78*, 152–157.
Sen, A. K. (1980b). The welfare basis of real income comparisons: A reply. *Journal of Economic Literature, 18*(4), 1547–1552.
Sen, A. K. (1981a). *Poverty and famines: An essay on entitlement and deprivation*. Oxford: Clarendon Press.
Sen, A. K. (1985a). *Commodities and capabilities*. Amsterdam: North-Holland.
Sen, A. K. (1985b). Well-being, agency and freedom: The Dewey Lectures 1984. *Journal of Philosophy, 82*, 169–221.
Sen, A. K. (1987a). *On ethics and economics*. Oxford: Blackwell.
Sen, A. K. (1988). Freedom of choice: Concept and content. *European Economic Review, 32*(2–3), 269–294.
Sen, A. K. (1989). Development as capability expansion. *Journal of Development Planning, 19*, 41–58.
Sen, A. K. (1990a). Justice: Means versus freedoms. *Philosophy & Public Affairs, 19*, 111–121.
Sen, A. K. (1990b). Gender and cooperative conflicts. In I. Tinker (Ed.), *Persistent inequalities*. New York: Oxford University Press.
Sen, A. K. (1992a). *Inequality reexamined*. Oxford: Clarendon Press.
Sen, A. K. (1993b). Positional objectivity. *Philosophy & Public Affairs, 22*, 126–145.
Sen, A. K. (1996b). Legal rights and moral rights: Old questions and new problems. *Ratio Juris, 9*, 153–167.
Sen, A. K. (1997d). *"Rights and capabilities" included in resources values and development*. Oxford: Blackwell.
Sen, A. K. (1999a). *Development as freedom*. New York: Alfred A. Knopf.
Sen, A. K. (1999b). *Reason before identity, The Romanes Lecture for 1998*. Oxford: Oxford University Press.
Sen, A. K. (2000). Consequential evaluation and practical reason. *Journal of Philosophy, 97*(9), 477–503.
Sen, A. K. (2002a). *Rationality and freedom*. Cambridge, MA: Harvard University Press.
Sen, A. K. (2002b). Open and closed impartiality. *Journal of Philosophy, 99*(9), 445–469.
Sen, A. K. (2004a). Capabilities, lists and public reason: Continuing the conversation. *Feminist Economics, 10*(3), 77–80.
Sen, A. K. (2004c). Elements of a theory of human rights. *Philosophy & Public Affairs, 32*(4), 315–56.
Sen, A. K. (2005). Human rights and capabilities. *Journal of Human Development, 6*(2), 151–66.
Sen, A. K. (2006a). Reason, freedom and well-being. *Utilitas, 18*(1), 80–96.
Sen, A. K. (2006b). *Identity and violence: The illusion of destiny*. New York: W.W. Norton.
Sen, A. K. (2009a). *The idea of justice*. Allen Lane: Penguin Books.
Sen, A. K., & Williams, B. (Eds.). (1982). *Utilitarianism and beyond*. Cambridge: Cambridge University Press.
Shionoya, Y. (2009). *Principles of economic philosophy: A hermeneutics approach*. Tokyo: University of Tokyo Press. (in Japanese).
Smith, A. (1759). *The theory of moral sentiments*. Printed for A. Millar, in the Strand and A. Kincaid and J. Bell, in Edinburgh, republished London: Penguin in 2009, with an introduction by A. K. Sen.
Smith, A. (1776). *An inquiry into the nature and causes of the wealth of nations*. London: W. Strahan and T. Cadell, republished, R. H. Campbell & A. S. Skinner, eds., Oxford: Clarendon Press, 1976.
Srinivasan, T. N. (1994). Human development: A new paradigm or reinvention of the wheel? *American Economic Review, 84*(2), 238–43.
Stewart, F. (2005). Groups and capabilities. *Journal of Human Development, 6*, 185–204.
Stiglitz, J. E. (1982). Self-selection and pareto efficient taxation. *Journal of Public Economics, 17*(2), 213–240.

Stiglitz, J. E., Sen, A. K., & Fitoussi, J.-P. (2010). *Mismeasuring our lives: Why GDP doesn't add up*. New York: The New Press.
Sugden, R. (1993). Welfare, resources, and capabilities: A review of inequality reexamined. *Journal of Economic Literature, 31*, 1947–1962.
Sugden, R. (1998). The metric of opportunity. *Economics and Philosophy, 14*, 307–37.
Sugden, R. (2006). What we desire, what we have reason to desire, whatever we might desire: Mill and Sen on the value of opportunity. *Utilitas, 18*(1), 33–51.
Sumner, L. W. (2006). Utility and capability. *Utilitas, 18*(1), 1–19.
Suppes, P. (1966). Some formal models of grading principles. *Synthese, 16*(3/4), 284–306.
Suzumura, K. (1978). On the consistency of libertarian claims. *Review of Economic Studies, 45*, 329–342.
Suzumura, K. (1979). On the consistency of libertarian claims: A correction. *Review of Economic Studies, 46*, 743.
Suzumura, K. (2011). Welfarism, individual rights, and procedural fairness. In K. J. Arrow, A. K. Sen, & K. Suzumura (Eds.), (pp. 605–685).
Suzumura, K. (2016a). Welfare economics beyond Welfarist-consequentialism. *Japanese Economic Review, 51*, 1–32. An abbreviated version reprinted in Suzumura, 731–753.
Suzumura, K. (2016b). Equitable allocation of maximal overall freedom: Sen's capability approach revisited. Presented at a plenary session of the 2016 HDCA conference in Tokyo.
Suzumura, K. (2016c). *Choice, preferences, and procedures: A rational choice theoretic approach*. Cambridge, MA: Harvard University Press.
Suzumura, K., & Xu, Y. (2001). Characterizations of consequentialism and non-consequentialism. *Journal of Economic Theory, 101*, 423–436, reprinted in Suzumura (2016a), pp. 505–519.
Suzumura, K., & Xu, Y. (2003). Consequences, opportunities, and generalized consequentialism and non-consequentialism. *Journal of Economic Theory, 111*, 293–304, reprinted in Suzumura (2016a), pp. 521–535.
Tadenuma, K., & Xu, Y. (2012). Extensions of the fundamental welfare theorems in a Non-welfaristic framework. *Hitotsubashi Journal of Economics, 53*, 107–120.
Tadenuma, K., & Xu, Y. (2017). Distributions of the budget sets: An axiomatic analysis. *Social Choice and Welfare, 48*, 221–237.
Tarski, A. (1944). The semantic conception of truth and the foundations of semantics. *Philosophy and Phenomenological Research, 4*(3), 341–376.
Terzi, L. (2005). Beyond the dilemma of difference: The capability approach to disability and special educational needs. *Journal of Philosophy of Education, 39*(3), 443–459.
Teubner, G. (trans.). (2008). *Nach Jacques Derrida und Niklas Luhmann: Zur (Un-) Moglichkeit einer Gesellschaftstheorie der Gerechtigkeit*. Stuttgart: Lucius & Lucius.
Townsend, P. (1985). A sociological approach to the measurement of poverty-A rejoinder to professor Amartya Sen. *Oxford Economic Papers (new series), 37*(4), 659–668.
Trani, J.-F., Bakhshi, P., Ballard, E., Gall, F., Eaton, J., & Vasquez-Escallon, J. (2016). *Home based intervention disability program impact evaluation study, preliminary results*. Presented at the 16th HDCA Conference in Tokyo, September 2016.
UNDP (1990-2020). Human development reports. Oxford: Oxford University Press.
UNICEF (1994). Gender equality and empowerment of women and girls: A policy review. E/ICEF/1994/L, S with Addendum.
Unterhalter, E. (2003). Crossing disciplinary boundaries: The potential of Sen's capability approach for sociologists of education. *British Journal of Sociology of Education, 24*(5), 665–669.
Van Hees, M. (1998). On the analysis of negative freedom. *Theory and Decision, 45*, 175–97.
Van Parijs, P. (1995). *Real freedom for all: What (if anything) is wrong with capitalism?*. Oxford: Clarendon Press.
Varian, H. R. (1980). Redistributive taxation as social insurance. *Journal of Public Economics, 14*, 49–68.
Varian, H. R. (1984). *Microeconomic analysis* (2nd ed.). New York: W. W. Norton.

Venkatapuram, S. (2011). *Health justice: An argument from the capabilities approach*. London: Polity Press.
Verkerk, M. A., Busschbach, J. J. V., & Karssing, E. D. (2001). Health-related quality of life research and the capability approach of Amartya Sen. *Quality of Life Research*, *10*(1), 49–55.
Vizard, P. (2006). *Poverty and human rights: Sen's 'capability perspective' explored*. Oxford: Oxford University Press.
Walsh, V. (2003). Sen after Putnam. *Review of Political Economy*, *15*(3), 315–394.
Weber, M. (1917/2011). *The meaning of 'ethical neutrality' in sociology and economics in the methodology of the social sciences*. New York: Routledge.
Weber, M. (1921–22/1978). *Economy and society* (2 Vols.). In G. Roth & C. Wittich (Eds.), Berkeley: University of California Press.
Williams, B. (1973). A critique of utilitarianism. In J. J. C. Smart & B. Williams (Eds.), *Utilitarianism: For and against*. Cambridge: Cambridge University Press.
Wittgenstein, L./G. E. M. Anscombe trans. (1953/1958/1967): *Philosophical investigations*. Oxford: Blackwell.
Wolff, J., & De-Shalit, A. (2007). *Disadvantage*. Oxford: Oxford University Press.
Xu, Y. (2002). Functioning, capability and the standard of living: An axiomatic approach. *Economic Theory*, *20*, 387–399.
Xu, Y. (2003). On ranking compact and comprehensive opportunity sets. *Mathematical Social Sciences*, *45*(2), 109–119.
Xu, Y. (2004). On ranking linear budget sets in terms of freedom of choice. *Social Choice and Welfare*, *22*(1), 281–289.
Yamamori, T. (2017). The concept of need in Adam Smith. *Cambridge Journal of Economics*, *41*(2), 327–347.
Zimmermann, B. (2006). Pragmatism and the capability approach: Challenges in social theory and empirical research. *European Journal of Social Theory*, *9*(4), 467–484.

Index

R. Gotoh, *The Ethics and Economics of the Capability Approach*, Hitotsubashi University IER Economic Research Series 46, https://doi.org/10.1007/978-981-15-5140-6

The manufacturer's authorised representative in the EU is Springer Nature Customer Service Centre GmbH, Europaplatz 3, 69115 Heidelberg, Germany. If you have any concerns regarding our products, please contact ProductSafety@springernature.com

Printed and bound by CPI Group (UK) Ltd, Croydon, CR0 4YY
06/10/2026
02225252-0007